SCRIBES AND SCHOLARS

A Guide to the Transmission of Greek and Latin Literature

BY

L. D. REYNOLDS

Fellow and Tutor of Brasenose College, Oxford

AND

N. G. WILSON

Fellow and Tutor of Lincoln College, Oxford

THIRD EDITION

CLARENDON PRESS · OXFORD

Oxford University Press, Walton Street, Oxford OX2 6DP
Oxford New York
Athens Auckland Bangkok Bombay
Calcutta Cape Town Dar es Salaam Delhi
Florence Hong Kong Istanbul Karachi
Kuala Lumpur Madras Madrid Melbourne
Mexico City Nairobi Paris Singapore
Taipei Tokyo Toronto
and associated companies in
Berlin Ibadan

Oxford is a trade mark of Oxford University Press

Published in the United States by
Oxford University Press Inc., New York

British Library Cataloguing in Publication Data
Data available

Library of Congress Cataloging in Publication Data
Scribes and scholars: a guide to the transmission of Greek and
Latin literature / by L. D. Reynolds and N. G. Wilson.—3rd ed.
Includes bibliographical references and index.
1. Classical literature—Criticism, Textual.   2. Classical
literature—Manuscripts.   3. Learning and scholarship—History.
4. Manuscripts, Renaissance.   5. Manuscripts, Medieval.
6. Transmission of texts.   7. Scriptoria.   I. Wilson, Nigel Guy.
II. Title.   PA47.R4 1991   001.2—dc20   90–41300
ISBN 0–19–872146–3

5 7 9 8 6 4

Printed in the United States of America
on acid-free paper

PREFACE

As we said in the preface to the first edition, this book is designed as a simple introduction for beginners to a field of classical studies which generally remains little known or understood despite its importance and intrinsic interest. In schools and universities students read Greek and Latin authors in editions equipped with an apparatus criticus, but they are too often unacquainted with the historical facts which make such an apparatus necessary, and are at a loss to evaluate the information that it gives. There are few works in English to which they can be referred, and a short guide is needed, especially one which can be read by those whose linguistic and historical knowledge is limited.

We have attempted to outline the processes by which Greek and Latin literature have been preserved, describing the dangers to which texts were exposed in the age of the manuscript book, and showing to what extent ancient and medieval readers or scholars were concerned to preserve or transmit classical texts. The history of texts cannot be separated from the history of education and scholarship, which also bulk large in these pages. On the other hand, matters of pure palaeography receive attention only if they are of direct importance for transmission.

The book is intended in the first place for students of Greek and Latin, but the theme handled is so inextricably connected with the cultural history of the Middle Ages and Renaissance that we think our account may be useful to anyone concerned with these periods. We also hope that students of biblical scholarship may find something of interest.

Whereas the first edition took the story no further than the Renaissance and lacked notes, the second was enlarged in both these respects. In order not to encumber a readable text with a heavy apparatus we put the notes at the end of the book and made them largely bibliographical. The new chapter had to be even more selective than the others, but it seemed worth the effort to complete the historical perspective.

Despite a widely held opinion to the contrary, classical studies make rapid advances, and after an interval of fifteen years there are many points at which our second edition no longer represents the current state of knowledge. We have tried to make the necessary adjustments, and some small additions, without in any way changing the character and purpose of the book.

Over the years we have profited a great deal from the kindness of friends, reviewers, and the translators who have rendered our work into Italian, Greek, French, and Spanish. We should like to record once again our gratitude for their contributions.

L.D.R.
N.G.W.

January 1990

CONTENTS

I

ANTIQUITY

I. ANCIENT BOOKS

A description of the processes by which classical literature has been transmitted from the ancient world to the present day may conveniently begin with a brief outline of the origin and growth of trade in books. In archaic Greece literature preceded literacy. The nucleus of the Homeric poems was handed down through several centuries during which the use of writing appears to have been completely lost; and in the second half of the eighth century, when the Phoenician alphabet was adapted for the writing of Greek, the tradition of oral literary composition was still strong, with the result that it may not have been thought necessary to commit the Homeric poems to writing at once. According to a tradition frequently repeated in antiquity the first written text of the epics was prepared at Athens in the middle of the sixth century by order of Pisistratus. This account is not above suspicion, and even if true would not prove that copies of the text of Homer began to circulate in any considerable numbers, for Pisistratus' object was in all probability to ensure the existence of an official copy of the poems to be recited at the festival of the Panathenaea. The habit of reading epic poetry instead of hearing it recited can hardly have been created overnight, and books remained something of a rarity until well into the fifth century. On the other hand the growth of forms of literature which do not depend on oral composition ensured that from the seventh century onwards there was a need for authors to put their works in writing, even if only one copy was made for the purpose of reference; thus Heraclitus is said to have deposited his famous treatise in a temple and perhaps for this reason it survived to be read by Aristotle in the middle of the fourth century (Diog. Laert. 9.6). The multiplication and circulation of copies was probably extremely limited, and it may be conjectured that the first works to reach even a modest public were either the writings of the Ionian philosophers and historians or those of the sophists. There must also have been a certain demand for copies of the poetic texts that formed the basis of school education. It is not until the middle of the fifth century or a little later that a book trade can be said to have existed in Greece: we find references to a part of the Athenian market where books can be bought (Eupolis fr. 327 K.–A.), and Socrates is represented by Plato as saying in his *Apology* (26D) that anyone can buy Anaxagoras' works for a drachma in the orchestra. All details of the trade, however, remain unknown.

Of the appearance of the books that were produced in classical Greece not much can be said with certainty. The number of books or fragments surviving from the fourth century is so tiny that it would not be reasonable to regard them as a representative sample. The general statements that follow are therefore based primarily on Hellenistic material, but it may be inferred with some plausibility that they are true also for the classical period. An attempt will be made to show how the physical differences between ancient and modern books affected the ancient reader in his relation to literary texts.

The form of the book was a roll, on one side of which the text was written in a series of columns. The reader would unroll it gradually, using one hand to hold the part that he had already seen, which was rolled up; but the result of this process was to reverse the coil, so that the whole book had to be unrolled again before the next reader could use it. The inconvenience of this book-form is obvious, especially when it is remembered that some rolls were more than ten metres long. Another disadvantage was that the material of which it was composed was by no means strong, and damage easily ensued. It is not difficult to imagine that an ancient reader faced with the need to verify a quotation or check a reference would rely if possible on his memory of the passage rather than go to the trouble of unwinding the roll and perhaps thereby accelerating the process of wear and tear. This would certainly account for the fact that when one ancient author quotes another there is so often a substantial difference between the two versions.

The standard writing material was papyrus (Plate I), prepared by cutting thin strips from the fibrous pith of a reed that grew freely in the Nile delta; in the first century A.D. there were also minor centres of production in Syria and near Babylon. Two layers of these strips, one laid at right angles over the other, were pressed together to form sheets (Pliny, *N.H.* 13.68ff.). The sheets could then be glued together in a long row to make a roll. Many sizes of sheet were made, but the average book allowed a column of text between eight and ten inches high, containing between twenty-five and forty-five lines. As there was only one large source of supply the book trade was presumably exposed to fluctuations arising from war or a desire by the producers to exploit their virtual monopoly. Some such difficulty is implied by Herodotus' remark (5.58) that when writing material was in short supply the Ionians had used sheep and goats' skins as a substitute. In resorting to this expedient they seem to have followed the practice of their Oriental neighbours. But leather as a writing material compared unfavourably with papyrus, and was no doubt used only in emergency. In the Hellenistic period, if Varro can be trusted (cf. Pliny, *N.H.* 13.70), the Egyptian government placed an embargo on the export of papyrus, which seems to have stimulated the search for an acceptable alternative. At Pergamum a process was devised for treating animal skins to give a better writing surface than leather, the result being what is now called parchment (otherwise known as vellum); the word owes part of its etymology to the name Pergamum, and the derivation can be seen more clearly from the Italian form *pergamena*. But if this tradition is true the experiment was at first short-lived; one must assume that the Egyptian embargo was soon removed, for it is not until the early centuries of the Christian era that parchment comes into common use for books; an early example is the fragment of Euripides' *Cretans* (P. Berol. 13217).

To what extent the supply and price of papyrus hindered or encouraged its use in Greece is impossible to say. But when employed for the production of a book it was almost invariably covered with writing on one side only. The form of the book made this necessary, since a text written on the back of a roll would have been very easily rubbed away, and perhaps the surface of the papyrus contributed to the formation of this convention, since

scribes always preferred to use first the side on which the fibres ran
horizontally. On rare occasions we hear of rolls written on both
sides (Juvenal 1.6, Pliny, *Epist.* 3.5.17), but such books were exceptional. A shortage of writing material did, however, sometimes
cause a literary text to be written on the reverse across the fibres: a
famous example is the manuscript of Euripides' *Hypsipyle* (P. Oxy.
852). It is important to note in this connection that the quantity of
text carried by an ancient book was very small: the maximum
capacity was a substantial dialogue of Plato or a book of Thucydides, and Books I and XVII of the late Hellenistic historian Diodorus
Siculus, which occupy 167 and 177 pages in a modern printed
edition, had to be subdivided.

Finally it should be emphasized that the text as arranged on the
papyrus was much harder for the reader to interpret than in any
modern book. Punctuation was usually rudimentary at best. Texts
were written without word-division, and it was not until the middle
ages that a real effort was made to alter this convention in Greek or
Latin texts (in a few Latin texts of the classical period a point is
placed after each word). The system of accentuation, which might
have compensated for this difficulty in Greek, was not invented
until the Hellenistic period, and for a long time after its invention it
was not universally used; here again it is not until the early middle
ages that the writing of accents becomes normal practice. In
dramatic texts throughout antiquity changes of speaker were not
indicated with the precision now thought necessary; it was enough
to write a horizontal stroke at the beginning of a line, or two points
one above the other, like the modern English colon, for changes
elsewhere; the names of the characters were frequently omitted.
The inaccuracy of this method, and the state of confusion to which
texts were soon reduced by it, may be seen from the condition of
the papyri containing Menanders' *Dyscolus* (P. Bodmer 4) and
Sicyonius (P. Sorbonne 72, 2272, 2273). Another and perhaps even
stranger feature of books in the pre-Hellenistic period is that lyric
verse was written as if it were prose; the fourth-century papyrus of
Timotheus (P. Berol. 9875) is an instance, and even without this
valuable document the fact could have been inferred from the tradition that Aristophanes of Byzantium (c. 257–180 B.C.) devised the

colometry which makes clear the metrical units of the poetry (Dion. Hal., *de comp. verb.* 156, 221). It is to be noted that the difficulties facing the reader of an ancient book were equally troublesome to the man who wished to transcribe his own copy. The risk of mis-interpretation and consequent corruption of the text in this period is not to be underestimated. It is certain that a high proportion of the most serious corruptions in classical texts go back to this period and were already widely current in the books that eventually entered the library of the Museum at Alexandria.

II. THE LIBRARY OF THE MUSEUM AND HELLENISTIC SCHOLARSHIP

The increase of the book trade made it possible for private individuals to form libraries. Even if the tradition that sixth-century tyrants such as Pisistratus and Polycrates of Samos possessed large collections of books is discounted (Athenaeus 1.3A), it is clear that by the end of the fifth century private libraries existed; Aristophanes pokes fun at Euripides for drawing heavily on literary sources in composing his tragedies (*Frogs* 943), and his own work, being full of parody and allusion, must have depended to some extent on a personal book collection.

There is no trace of any general library maintained at the public expense at Athens, but it is likely that official copies of plays performed at the leading festivals such as the Dionysia were kept at the theatre or in the public record office. Pseudo-Plutarch (*Lives of the ten orators* 841F) ascribes to the orator Lycurgus (c. 390–324 B.C.) a proposal to keep official copies in this way, but the need would probably have arisen earlier. We know that after the original performance plays were revived from time to time. New copies of the text must have been needed for the actors, and if they had been obliged to obtain these by a process of transcription from private copies it would be surprising that an almost complete range of plays survived into the Hellenistic age.

The advance of education and science in the fourth century made it only a matter of time before academic institutions with their own

libraries were founded. It is not surprising to find Strabo reporting
(13.1.54) that Aristotle built up a large collection of books, no doubt
representing the wide diversity of interests in the Lyceum. This
collection and that of the Academy were taken as a pattern soon
afterwards by the king of Egypt when establishing the famous
library at Alexandria (Diog. Laert. 4.1, 5.51). The main interests of
the Lyceum were scientific and philosophical, but literary studies
were not neglected. Aristotle himself wrote on problems of interpretation in Homer besides his well-known *Poetics* and *Rhetoric*; and
in connection with the latter there is some evidence that he and his
successors were interested in the study of Demosthenes' speeches.

Of much greater significance were the literary studies undertaken
at the Museum in Alexandria. This was formally, as the name
implies, a temple in honour of the Muses presided over by a priest.
It was in fact the centre of a literary and scientific community, and it
is essential not to underestimate this last aspect of it; the librarian
Eratosthenes (c. 295–c. 214 B.C.), though a literary man, was also a
scientist who achieved fame for his attempts to measure the
circumference of the earth, and it is probable that other distinguished Alexandrian scientists were members. The Museum was
maintained at the expense of the king, and the members of it had
study rooms and a hall in which they dined together. They also
received a stipend from the royal purse. It has been observed that
there is a superficial resemblance between this institution and an
Oxford or Cambridge college, but the analogy breaks down in one
important respect: there is no evidence that the scholars of the
Museum gave regular instruction to students. The community was
probably set up by Ptolemy Philadelphus c. 280 B.C., and it soon won
a reputation, perhaps arousing jealousy through the lavishness of its
arrangements, for we find the satirist Timon of Phlius writing of it c.
230 B.C. 'in populous Egypt they fatten up many bookish pedants
who quarrel unceasingly in the Muses' bird-cage' (Athenaeus
1.22D).

An essential part of this foundation, housed in the same complex
of buildings or in the near neighbourhood, was the famous library. It
seems that some steps had been taken already in the previous reign
by the first Ptolemy to set up a library, by inviting Demetrius of

Phalerum, the eminent pupil of Theophrastus, to come to Alexandria for the purpose c. 295 B.C. The library grew rapidly. The number of volumes is variously estimated by the ancient sources, but owing to the inaccuracy with which all large figures given by classical authors are transmitted it is difficult to calculate the true figure. If we accept as true the tradition that in the third century the library contained 200,000 or 490,000 volumes (Eusebius, *Praep. Evang.* 350B, Tzetzes, *Prolegomena de comoedia*), allowance must be made for the small capacity of each roll of papyrus. There is also no means of knowing to what extent the libraries made it their policy to stock duplicate copies. But despite this uncertainty it is beyond doubt that great efforts were made to form a complete collection of Greek literature, and there are anecdotes which throw light on the spirit in which the business of the library was conducted. The king is said to have been determined to obtain an accurate text of Attic tragedy, and persuaded the Athenians to lend him the official copy from the public record office. The Athenians asked for a deposit of fifteen talents as security for the return of the texts, but having once obtained these the Egyptian authorities decided to keep them and forfeit their deposit (Galen 17(1).607). We also learn from Galen that in their anxiety to complete their collection the librarians were frequently deceived into purchasing forgeries of rare texts (15.105).

The task of the librarians in reducing to order the mass of books flowing into the Museum was enormous. The principle of arrangement in the library is not known, but one indication of the vast labours involved is that Callimachus, who was not himself chief librarian, compiled a kind of bibliographical guide to all branches of Greek literature, which occupied one hundred and twenty books (the *Pinakes*, frr. 429–53). Owing to the conditions of ancient book production the librarians faced certain problems that do not trouble their modern counterparts. Texts copied by hand are quickly liable to corruption; to make an accurate copy of even a short text is a much harder task than is realized by those who have not had to do it. In addition to this pre-Hellenistic books gave no help to the reader in any difficulty. Consequently there must have been numerous passages where the author's meaning could no longer be discerned, and many others in which various copies of texts reaching the Museum showed serious discrepancies. The incentive that this gave to the librarians to put the text in order led to a great advance in learning and scholarly methods. It is no coincidence that five of the first six librarians (Zenodotus, Apollonius Rhodius, Eratosthenes, Aristophanes, and Aristarchus) were among the most famous literary men of their day, and it is in no small measure due to the success of their methods that classical Greek texts have come down to us in a state that is reasonably free from corruption.

In one case we can see clearly the influence which the scholars of the Museum exercised on the state of texts in common circulation. Of the many fragments of ancient copies of Homer a modest proportion are as early as the third century B.C. The text in these papyri is rather different from that now generally printed, and there are numerous lines added or omitted. But within a short time this type of text disappeared from circulation. This suggests that the scholars had not merely determined what the text of Homer should be, but succeeded in imposing this text as standard, either allowing it to be transcribed from a master copy placed at the disposal of the public, or perhaps employing a number of professional scribes to prepare copies for the book market. Discrepancies in the text of authors other than Homer were probably less serious, but not enough early papyri are preserved for us to generalize with much confidence; it is a reasonable assumption that the Alexandrians did what was necessary to prepare a standard text of all authors commonly read by the educated public.

After the standardization of texts the next feature of Alexandrian scholarship that merits attention is the development of a number of aids to the reader. The first step was to ensure that fifth-century books coming from Attica, some of which must have been written in the old alphabet, were all transliterated into the normal Greek spelling of the Ionic alphabet. Until 403 B.C. Athens had officially used the older alphabet in which the letter epsilon represented the vowels epsilon, epsilon-iota and eta; similarly omicron was used for omicron, omicron-upsilon and omega. The old alphabet also lacked the compound letters xi and psi. The drawbacks of this script need no comment, and already before the end of the fifth century the more accurate Ionic alphabet was being used for some Athenian inscriptions on stone: probably the same was true of Athenian books. Nevertheless it looks as if some texts reaching the Alexandrian library were in the old script, for we find Aristarchus explaining a difficulty in Pindar as due to misinterpretation of the old alphabet; he tells us that at *Nemeans* 1.24 an adjective which appears to be in the nominative singular (ἐϲλόϲ) is incorrect for metrical reasons and must be understood as the accusative plural (ἐϲλούϲ) (cf. schol. ad loc.). Another point at which the critics showed their awareness of the old alphabet was Aristophanes, *Birds* 66. It is important to note that the adoption of the Ionic alphabet for early Attic texts has been recognized as the norm since the Alexandrian period. In contrast to the procedure used for editing texts in all other literatures there has never been an attempt to restore the original orthography of the authors in its entirety.

A second aid for readers was an improvement in the method of punctuation and the invention of the system of accentuation, both commonly ascribed to Aristophanes of Byzantium. In a text lacking word-division the addition of a few accents gave the reader a substantial help, and it is rather strange that they did not immediately come to be regarded as indispensable to a written text. But though they were sometimes written over words that would otherwise have been difficult or ambiguous, in general it is hard to see what principle determines their use in ancient books, and they were not regularly added until the beginning of the tenth century.

Although these improvements in the outward appearance of literary texts had significant and lasting results, they were of far less importance than the advances in scholarly method made by members of the Museum. The need to establish the text of Homer and the other classical authors inspired scholars to define and apply the principles of literary scholarship more systematically than had been attempted before. Discussion of difficult passages led not merely to the production of a reliable text of the authors in question, but to commentaries in which the problems were discussed and interpretations offered. There had previously been some isolated works devoted to Homer; Aristotle had written on problems in the text, and much earlier Theagenes of Rhegium (c. 525 B.C.), perhaps spurred by Xenophanes' attacks on the

immorality of the Homeric gods, had attempted to tone down this
feature of the poems, an embarrassment to any teacher expounding
them to a class, by resorting to allegorical interpretation. But now a
mass of critical literature was produced for the first time. Some of it
was highly specialized; for instance Zenodotus apparently wrote a
life of Homer and a treatise on the length of time required for the
action of the *Iliad*. Aristophanes wrote on grammatical regularity
(περὶ ἀναλογίαc) and compiled corrections and supplements to the
bibliographical guide to Greek literature that Callimachus had
composed. Work of this character was not confined to Homer; we
hear of monographs on the characters of comedy by Hypsicrates
and on the myths of tragedy by Thersagoras (P. Oxy. 2192). These
explanatory works were normally written as separate texts independent of the work that they illustrated; apart from brief and
rudimentary notes commentary on an author was not at this date
added to the margin of a text, but occupied another book. In the
case of Homer especially, and less frequently in lyric poetry, drama,
Demosthenes, and Plato, a number of conventional signs were put
into the margin of the text to indicate that the passage was interesting in some way, for instance corrupt or spurious, and that the
reader would find comment on the point in the explanatory monograph. Although very little survives from this class of literature in its
original form, there is one famous example in the papyrus of part of
a work by the later scholar Didymus (1st cent. B.C.) on Demosthenes
(P. Berol. 9780). But in general our knowledge of these works
comes from fragments of them that have been incorporated into
the later form of commentary known as scholia; these are regularly
transmitted in the margins of medieval manuscripts, and more will
be said of their history below.

We come now to a brief discussion of the critical signs and the
commentaries. The first and most important sign was the *obelos*, a
horizontal stroke placed in the margin just to the left of a verse. It
was used already by Zenodotus, and indicated that the verse was
spurious. Some other signs of less importance and frequency seem
to have been devised by Aristophanes. The final development of the
system as applied to Homer was made by Aristarchus, who
produced complete editions of both *Iliad* and *Odyssey*. He used six

signs: apart from the *obelos* we find the *diplē* >, which indicated any
noteworthy point of language or content; the dotted *diplē*
(περιεςτιγμένη) > referred to a verse where Aristarchus differed in
his text from Zenodotus; the *asteriskos* ※ marked a verse incorrectly
repeated in another passage; the *asteriskos* in conjunction with the
obelos marked the interpolation of verses from another passage; and
finally the *antisigma* Ɔ marked passages in which the order of the
lines had been disturbed (Plates I and II).

It is natural that a complicated system of this kind, which had the
drawback that the reader wishing to discover a scholar's reasons for
placing a sign at any given point had to consult another book,
commended itself to scholarly readers only. No more than a tiny
proportion of the surviving papyri, about fifteen of more than six
hundred, display them. In the medieval manuscripts of the tenth
century and later they are usually omitted; but there is one famous
and important exception to this rule, the tenth-century Venetian
manuscript of the *Iliad* (Marc. gr. 454), which preserves a vast
collection of marginal scholia. As the commentary on an author was
written in the margins by this date, and not in a separate book,
there was less incentive to transcribe the signs; but fortunately the
scribe of the Venice manuscript was determined to copy what he
found in his exemplar without omission. Consequently the book
shows a great number of the conventional signs, and it is by far the
most complete and reliable source of our knowledge of this feature
of the work carried out by the Alexandrians. It does not, however,
always agree exactly in the use of the signs at the points where it
can be compared with a papyrus, and there are signs which are not
linked with a corresponding note in the scholia.

Though the Homer commentaries of Aristarchus and his colleagues are lost, enough of them can be reconstructed from the
extant scholia, which are more copious than those on any other
Greek author, to allow us to form a good judgement of the scholarly
methods of the time. It is clear that many copies of the Homeric
text reached the Museum from widely different sources; the scholia
refer to texts coming from such places as Massilia, Sinope, and
Argos. These were sifted and evaluated by the scholars, but it is not
clear which text, if any, was taken to be the most authoritative. The

procedure which made the Alexandrians notorious was their
readiness to condemn lines as spurious (ἀθετεῖν, ἀθέτηcιc). Their
reasons for doing so, though possessing a certain specious logic,
generally fail to convince the modern reader. One ground
frequently alleged was undignified language or conduct (ἀπρέπεια).
The first passage of the *Iliad* which was condemned in this way will
serve as an example. At the opening of book I (29–31) Agamemnon,
when refusing to release Chryseis, says to her father the priest: 'I
will not set her free; no, sooner shall old age overtake her in my
palace at Argos, far from her home, where she shall work the loom
and serve my bed'. The lines are obelized in the Venice manuscript,
and the ancient commentary on them reads as follows: 'the lines are
athetized because they weaken the force of the meaning and the
threatening tone ... it is also improper for Agamemnon to make
such remarks'. Another typical instance occurs at *Iliad* 3.423–6,
where Zenodotus rejected the lines on the ground that it is unbecoming for the goddess Aphrodite to carry a seat for Helen. And
naturally all passages that tended to show the gods in an unflatter-
ing light were an easy target for critics of this frame of mind; hence
there were some who athetized the affair between Ares and
Aphrodite in *Odyssey* VIII.

Scholars capable of treating a text so drastically, especially in
their willingness to condemn lines as spurious for inadequate
reasons, might have done great damage to the text. But fortunately
for subsequent generations of readers the Alexandrians avoided the
temptation to incorporate all their proposed alterations into the
text itself and were content to note proposals in their commentaries; but for this restraint our text of Homer would have been
seriously disfigured. It is interesting to note that most of their
proposals did not commend themselves sufficiently to the ancient
reader to become part of the ordinary text in circulation; this of
course is not necessarily to be taken as evidence of the superior
judgement of the reading public in antiquity, which may scarcely
have given any thought to such matters. A count of the emendations made by the Alexandrians has shown that of the 413
alterations proposed by Zenodotus only 6 are found as readings in
all our papyri and manuscripts, and only a further 34 in a majority of

them, whereas 240 are never so found. Of the 83 emendations that can be ascribed to Aristophanes only one found universal approval, and 6 others appear in a majority of witnesses to the text, while 42 are never found in the text. Aristarchus was more influential, but even his suggestions were not readily accepted; out of 874 readings 80 are universally found, 160 occur in the majority of texts, and 132 in the scholia only.

It would be wrong to end this account of the Alexandrians without mentioning some more favourable specimens of their criticism. Certain parts of their work were of a high enough standard to be of permanent value. Their attempts to identify verses or passages of dubious authenticity were not always based on weak reasoning. They were suspicious of *Iliad* X, the story of Dolon, and had doubtless recognized that it was different in style from the rest of the *Iliad* and loosely attached to the narrative. In Odysseus' descent to the underworld in *Odyssey* XI Aristarchus noticed that lines 568–626 did not belong to the main thread of the story. Perhaps most interesting was the observation by Aristarchus and Aristophanes that the *Odyssey* ought to end at 23.296. Modern scholars might prefer to avoid condemning these passages as spurious and to regard them instead as products of a later stage of composition than the main body of the text; but this does not detract from the merit of the critics' observations.

Another matter for which the ancients, especially Aristarchus, deserve praise is the development of the critical principle that the best guide to an author's usage is the corpus of his own writings, and therefore difficulties ought to be explained wherever possible by reference to other passages in the same author (῞Ομηρον ἐξ Ὁμήρου caφηνίζειν). This notion underlies many notes in the scholia which state that a given word or expression is more typically Homeric than the alternative possible reading. The principle was naturally liable to abuse if employed by a critic of mediocre intelligence, as happened all too often; for it might be taken to imply that if a literary text contains an expression which is both unique and difficult it must be modified in order to agree with the author's general practice. Such an extreme interpretation of the rule could have led to disastrous results, and it is greatly to the credit of

Aristarchus or one of his pupils that he appears to have devised a complementary principle, that there are many words or expressions in Homer which occur only once but should be accepted as genuine and left standing in the text (cf. schol. A on *Iliad* 3.54). Problems which require the correct application of these principles still cause great difficulty to critics of the present day.

Finally it should be made clear that though the critics concerned themselves mainly with notes of a linguistic or antiquarian character, they were not blind to the literary merits of the poetry, and occasionally offer an apt comment on a fine passage. An example may be taken from the famous episode in *Iliad* VI, where Hector takes his leave of Andromache and Astyanax, and the poet describes how the child is frightened at the sight of the plume on his father's helmet. The critics commented: 'these verses are so full of descriptive power that the reader does not simply hear the sound of them but sees the scene before him; the poet took this scene from everyday life and copied it with supreme success'. Shortly afterwards comes the comment: 'while representing everyday life with such success the poet does not in the least destroy the stately tone appropriate to epic' (cf. schol. T on *Iliad* 6.467, 474, from MS. Burney 86 in the British Library).

Most of this account of Alexandrian scholarship has been concerned with the text of Homer because of the copious evidence available. But it is certain that Alexandrian work on other authors was of great importance, and a few facts may be briefly enumerated. The text of tragedy was established, probably by reference to the Athenian official copy, as was mentioned above. The colometry of the lyric passages, no longer written out as if they were prose, is usually attributed to Aristophanes of Byzantium; but an early papyrus of Stesichorus' *Thebaid* (P. Lille 76a + 73) is a serious obstacle to this view. A number of treatises on various aspects of the plays were written, and Aristophanes is credited with the authorship of the arguments outlining the plot prefixed to the plays; it is generally held, however, that the arguments now surviving are either not his work or have been considerably altered in the course of time. Marginal signs to guide the reader were much more sparingly used than in editions of Homer. The commonest was probably the letter chi, which indicated a point of interest in much the same way as the *diplē* in the Homeric text; this sign is mentioned in the scholia and occasionally is found in a medieval manuscript. Since critical work on both epic and tragedy began in Alexandria, it is very odd to find these different signs used for the same purpose. A specially interesting feature of Alexandrian work on tragedy is the detection of lines altered or added by actors, most frequently in the plays of Euripides, who was more popular than the other dramatists. These interpolations are probably quite numerous, but it is not always easy to prove that the line or lines in question are not original; and if they are clearly late, it may be uncertain whether they should be attributed to Hellenistic actors (or more strictly producers) or to later interpolators. The scholia, however, which depend ultimately on Hellenistic work, do designate some lines as actors' interpolations. At *Medea* 85–8 the scholiast accuses the actors of misunderstanding the proper punctuation of 85 and altering the text in consequence; he adds rightly that 87 is superfluous, and its origin is not far to seek. At *Orestes* 1366–8 the chorus announce that one of the Phrygians is about to come out onto the stage through the front door of the palace, whereas in 1369–71 the Phrygian says that he jumped down off the roof. According to the scholia the original stage direction required the actor to make the jump, but this was regarded as dangerous, and so the actor descended by the back of the scenery and came out through the front door; in an effort to disguise this change 1366–8 were composed. Though these lines are needed in order to give a proper introduction to the new character and are linguistically blameless, something is wrong with the passage, and perhaps the best solution is to suppose that 1366 is interpolated.

Other Alexandrian works that should not go without mention are the editions of comedy, Pindar and the lyric poets. Here too the colometry had to be determined, and at one point we can see how Aristophanes rightly used it to show that a phrase which did not correspond metrically with the antistrophe should be deleted from the text (schol. on Pindar, *Olympians* 2.48). The task of editing comedy was undertaken in the same way as that of tragedy. We do not know what copies of the text were taken as the basis of the edition, but the rich collection of material contained in the surviving scholia to Aristophanes shows that his plays were studied with energy and enthusiasm, even though there is no sign that they were still performed on the stage.

III. OTHER HELLENISTIC WORK

The great age of Alexandrian work occurred in the third and second centuries; in the early part of the period the Museum was unrivalled. After a time, however, the rulers of Pergamum decided to challenge this position by founding a library of their own. The scheme is primarily associated with the name of king Eumenes II (197–159 B.C.): vast buildings were erected, and excavation by German archaeologists in the last century brought to light some sections of the library. Much less is known of the Pergamene library than of the Alexandrian. The librarians clearly undertook bibliographical studies on a large scale, and literary men found it useful to consult their work along with that of the Alexandrians (Athenaeus 8.336D, Dion. Hal., *de Dinarcho* 1). But the Pergamene scholars are not credited with editions of the classical authors and appear to have confined themselves to short monographs on specific points, sometimes directly in controversy with the Alexandrians. Their interests were not exclusively literary; Polemon (c. 220–160 B.C.), though he collected examples of parody, was first and foremost a student of topography and inscriptions; these important topics of historical scholarship had both remained outside the usual range of studies undertaken in the Museum. The most famous name linked with Pergamum is that of Crates (c. 200–c. 140 B.C.). He is known to have worked on Homer; some of his proposals for emending the text are preserved in the scholia, and he paid special attention to geography in Homer, attempting to reconcile it with Stoic views on the subject. He was also the first Greek to give lectures on literary subjects in Rome (see p. 20).

The Stoics gave a good deal of attention to literature. To them an important part of interpreting Homer was the application of allegorical explanations, and one of their treatises on this, attributed to an otherwise unknown Heraclitus, has survived. Apart from Homeric studies they dealt with grammar and linguistics, elaborating a fuller terminology than had previously existed. But the first formal Greek grammar was by Dionysius Thrax (c. 170–c. 90 B.C.); he appears to have been just old enough to have been a pupil of Aristarchus, but is not to be counted as an Alexandrian in the full sense, since his teaching was done largely in Rhodes. His grammar begins with a definition of the parts of the subject, the last of which, described by the author as the noblest of all, is the criticism of poetry. He then goes on to deal with parts of speech, declensions and conjugations, but matters of syntax and style are not discussed. This brief guide enjoyed a lasting vogue, as is attested by the volume of commentary upon it written by later grammarians. It was the basis of Greek grammars until comparatively modern times, and had the distinction of being translated into Syriac and Armenian in late antiquity.

The best Alexandrian work had now been completed; the decline of the school was brought about by the action of Ptolemy Euergetes II, who instituted a persecution of Greek literary men (c. 145–4 B.C.); among others Dionysius Thrax, who had begun his career in Alexandria, went into exile. The only eminent figure in the remaining part of the Hellenistic age is Didymus (1st cent. B.C.). He achieved notoriety in the ancient world through the bulk of his writings (but the story that 4,000 books came from his pen must be an exaggeration, even if it is assumed that many of these may not have been any longer than modern pamphlets). His name is mentioned frequently in scholia, and it is clear that his work extended over the whole range of classical poetry. As far as can be judged from the fragmentary nature of the evidence his activity was not so much composition of original commentaries as compilation from the already huge mass of critical work, and he is important because his compilations were evidently one of the main sources of material used by the later scholars who drew up the scholia in their present form. One book of his whose influence can be traced in extant works is his collection of rare or difficult words from tragedy (τραγικαὶ λέξεις); from this source derive a number of entries in the later dictionaries such as Hesychius. Didymus is also important for his work on prose authors; he commented on Thucydides and the orators, and the only substantial passage from his writings that is still preserved is part of a monograph on Demosthenes (P. Berol. 9780). This book when complete contained notes on speeches IX–XI and XIII. It confirms the usual view of Didymus as a compiler without any great originality or independence of mind; there are many quotations from sources otherwise lost, such as Philochorus and Theopompus, whereas Didymus' own contribution is very small. He goes so far as to record without comment a report that speech XI is a compilation of Demosthenic topics put together by Anaximenes of Lampsacus; yet this view, whether correct or not, demands discussion from any commentator. Not all interesting passages are discussed, but this kind of monograph was often less comprehensive in scope than its modern counterpart would be. On the other hand it is a welcome surprise to find that the commentary, instead of being confined to matters of linguistic interest or of value only to teachers of rhetoric, deals with chronological problems and historical interpretation.

The finds of carbonized papyri at Herculaneum, which have added a great deal to our knowledge of Epicurean philosophy, especially now that modern technology makes the texts much more legible, have brought to light another aspect of Alexandrian scholarship. The writings of Epicurus were studied very closely by his later disciples, and corrupt copies posed many problems. One surviving work, an essay by Demetrius Lacon perhaps written c. 100 B.C. (P. Herc. 1012), displays considerable sophistication in dealing with these questions: it several times refers to faulty copies; it considers variation between copies; in one passage there is talk of damage caused by book-worms and the subsequent attempt of a reader to put right a defective text. The critical methods of Alexandria were not simply a tool to be used by students of literature.

IV. BOOKS AND SCHOLARSHIP IN THE ROMAN REPUBLIC

Although written records may have existed from very early times, Latin literature did not begin until the third century B.C. Inspired by

Greek example, it was probably committed from its first beginnings to the form of book which had long been standard in the Greek world, the papyrus roll. By the middle of the second century Rome had a considerable body of literature of her own, poetry and plays and prose, and the growth of such a sophisticated literary and philosophical coterie as the Scipionic circle implies that books circulated freely within a limited class of Roman society. A century later, when Cicero and Varro were at their peak, the world of books had become very much a part of the world of the educated Roman. The acceptance of writing as a serious occupation of the leisured class and the very nature of Latin literature itself, with its emphasis on *doctrina*, gave books a special place in Roman cultural life.

Little is known about the ways in which Latin literature was handed down during the first two hundred years of its life. In the days when there was no organized machinery for the multiplication and circulation of books, no established libraries to preserve them, and before scholarship had begun to take a critical interest in their contents, the channels of transmission must have been casual and hazardous. Some works fared better than others. The national epics of Naevius and Ennius enjoyed a special status and received some scholarly attention at a comparatively early date. Prose was probably less fortunate. The one work of Cato which has been transmitted to us directly, his *De agri cultura*, appears to have been mangled and modernized through frequent and uncontrolled copying. There seems to have been no corpus of his speeches available in Cicero's day; Cicero protests against the neglect into which they have fallen (*Brutus* 65 f.) and says that he had managed to gather together more than 150 of them. Dramatic texts had their own particular hazards, as we can see clearly in the case of Plautus. His plays were written for performance, bought by the magistrate or his agent, and transmitted initially as stage copies. We know from the prologue to the *Casina* that the plays were revived from time to time, and a subsequent restaging would mean that the script was cut, padded out, recast, or modernized to suit the taste of the producer or the audience. There are still traces of this early tampering with the text in our manuscripts; the different versions of the last scene of the *Poenulus* are an obvious example. Plautus'

popularity was so great that he readily attracted spurious accretions
and we are told (Gellius 3.3.11) that at one time no less than 130
plays were circulating under his name. Terence's plays enjoyed a
more sheltered transmission, but some manuscripts preserve an
alternative ending of the *Andria* which may go back to an early
date.

This period of fluid transmission may account for many of the
corruptions in these texts. In one place Varro has preserved for us
(*L.L.* 7.81) the authentic description of the shifty Ballio sidling
through the door (*Pseudolus* 955):

> ut transvorsus, non provorsus cedit, quasi cancer solet.

An attempt to get rid of the archaic *provorsus* produced the flat
version of the line presented by both the surviving recensions of the
text, the Ambrosian palimpsest (A) and the remaining manuscripts (P):

> non prorsus, verum ex transverso cedit, quasi cancer solet.

But in the *Miles Gloriosus* (24) A preserves the Plautine *epityra estur
insanum bene* ('his cheese and olive spread is madly good eating')
while both P and Varro (*L.L.* 7.86) read *insane*. In general the text of
Plautus seems to have suffered surprisingly little since the days of
Varro. The survival of what we have of early Latin literature is
largely due, in the first instance, to the renewed interest which was
taken in these writers during the last century of the Republic; and
the comparative soundness of their texts we must owe in part to the
work of the early Roman grammarians.

According to Suetonius (*Gram.* 2), the study of grammar was first
introduced into Rome by the Homeric scholar Crates of Mallos.
Crates came to Rome on a diplomatic mission, probably in 168 B.C.,
broke his leg in a sewer and turned his enforced convalescence to
good use by giving lectures on poetry. The gradual infiltration of
Hellenistic culture was of course governed by more complex factors
than the breaking of a bone, but we must be grateful to Suetonius
for turning his colourful spotlight onto a point in time when the
Romans, who by the death of Ennius had built up a well-established
literary tradition of their own, were ready to take an academic

interest in their literature and language. He names two grammarians of this early period, C. Octavius Lampadio and Q. Vargunteius. Lampadio worked on the *Punic War* of Naevius, which he divided into seven books, and may possibly have been interested in Ennius too, even if the evidence is suspect: a copy of the *Annals* thought to have been corrected by Lampadio himself was still extant in the second century A.D. (Gellius 18.5.11). Vargunteius is reported to have occupied himself with Ennius and to have recited the *Annals* to large audiences. Outside professional circles, a strong preoccupation with literary and linguistic matters is apparent in the poetry of Accius and Lucilius.

But the first of the great Roman grammarians was L. Aelius Stilo, of whom our ancient authorities speak with the highest respect. A firm and perhaps significant date in his life is the year 100 B.C., when he followed Metellus Numidicus into exile at Rhodes. It has been plausibly conjectured that he may have acquired his knowledge of Alexandrian scholarship there, from Aristarchus' own pupil Dionysius Thrax. At all events, Aelius is the first scholar who is recorded as having employed at Rome the conventional critical signs of the Alexandrians. The evidence for this is found in a remarkable document known as the *Anecdoton Parisinum*. This tract, preserved in a manuscript written at Montecassino towards the end of the eighth century (Paris lat. 7530), describes the critical signs used by Aristarchus and his successors. An important sentence reads (when some of the names have been conjecturally restored):

His solis [*sc.* notis] in adnotationibus Ennii Lucilii et historicorum [= writers of comedy?] usi sunt Varro Servius Aelius aeque et postremo Probus, qui illas in Vergilio et Horatio et Lucretio apposuit, ut Homero Aristarchus.

The name Aelius is not in doubt, and his interest in Plautus and the elucidation of archaic texts would naturally involve him in scholarship of the Alexandrian type. Although Plautus is a far cry from Homer, the nature of his text and the circumstances of its transmission presented problems similar to those that had exercised Hellenistic scholars and for which their critical methods had an obvious relevance. Plautus' text needed to be standardized: there was a mass of spurious plays, and the genuine ones contained

later accretions and interpolations and varied considerably from
copy to copy. The production of a list of the genuine plays had
already exercised Accius; Stilo occupied himself with the problem,
as did others, and pronounced twenty-five to be genuine. His son-
in-law Servius Claudius was certainly interested in detecting interpolations, for Cicero speaks of his skill in saying 'hic versus Plauti
non est, hic est' (*Fam.* 9.16.4). Aelius had a great influence on his
pupil Varro (116–27 B.C.). Varro was a polymath, with a special
interest in literary history, drama, and linguistics. He seems to have
played a decisive part in selecting which plays of Plautus should be
passed on to posterity as genuine. Although he accepted others as
authentic, Varro singled out twenty-one plays as being unquestion-
ably Plautine and this canon, known as the *fabulae Varronianae*, must
coincide with the twenty-one plays which have come down to us.
The establishment of the text of these early writers involved other
aspects of textual criticism besides authenticity, and Varro's awareness of textual corruption is clear from his definition of *emendatio* as
recorrectio errorum qui per scripturam dictionemve fiunt (fr. 236F), and
from his revealing remark *Plauti aut librarii mendum est* (*L.L.* 9.106).

Another scholarly pursuit for which there was ample scope was
the interpretation of obsolete or difficult words. Evidence for this
activity abounds in Varro and in what poor remains we have of the
first Latin lexicon, the important and influential *De verborum significatu* of the Augustan grammarian Verrius Flaccus. This survives,
partly in the abbreviated version made by Pompeius Festus, partly
in the still more jejune epitome of Festus made by Paul the Deacon
in the eighth century, with scattered references elsewhere. For
instance, the *Nervolaria* of Plautus contained a trenchant description of decrepit prostitutes:

> scrattae, scruppedae (?), strittabillae, sordidae.

These ladies were already encrusted with learning by Varro's
time: he quotes (*L.L.* 7.65) the views of three different writers on
the second word. Since the interpretations of these difficult words
were often written between the lines of one's copy (as Varro himself
testifies, *L.L.* 7.107), they could easily win a place in the text or give
rise to doublets. For instance, at *Epidicus* 620 the P recension offers

the reading *gravastellus* ('little old man'), while A has *ravistellus* ('little man with grey hair'); both variants were known to Festus and so go back at least to Augustan times. At *Miles Gloriosus* 1180 we have three variants, all ancient: the authentic reading is *exfafillato bracchio* ('uncovered'), preserved by P and attested by ancient authorities; but *expapillato* ('bared to the breast') can be traced back to antiquity; and A appears to offer a third variant (*expalliolato*), which must be at least as old as A itself (5th cent.).

The expansion of literature and scholarship in the late Republic was accompanied by important developments of a practical nature, and it is not surprising that during this period we first hear of plans for a public library at Rome and of the existence of more organized facilities for publishing books. There were already large private libraries. Greek books in particular had flowed in as part of the *praeda belli*, and Lucullus' library, open to those who wished to use it, continued to be a resource after his death; when Cicero dropped in to consult some books, he claims to have found Cato already installed (*Fin.* 3.2.7–8). Cicero took enormous trouble to build up a fine collection of books of his own; he received much help and advice from his friend Atticus and was fortunate to inherit the library of the scholar Servius Claudius. But it was Caesar who first planned a large public library. He commissioned Varro (among whose many works was one entitled *De bibliothecis*) to collect books for it, but the plan was not realized: the first public library at Rome was founded in the Atrium Libertatis by C. Asinius Pollio in 39 B.C.

We hear nothing of a book trade at Rome before the time of Cicero. Then the booksellers and copyists (both initially called *librarii*) carried on an active trade, but do not seem to have met the high standards of a discriminating author, for Cicero complains of the poor quality of their work (*Q.f.* 3.4.5, 5.6). Most readers depended on borrowing books from friends and having their own copies made from them, but this too demanded skilled copyists. It was perhaps for such reasons that Atticus, who had lived for a long time in Greece and there had some experience of a well-established book trade, put his staff of trained *librarii* at the service of his friends. It is not easy to see whether Atticus is at any given moment obliging Cicero as a friend or in a more professional capacity, but it is clear that Cicero could depend on him to provide all the services of a high-class publisher. Atticus would carefully revise a work for him, criticize points of style or content, discuss the advisability of publication or the suitability of a title, hold private readings of the new book, send out complimentary copies, organize its distribution. His standards of execution were of the highest and his name a guarantee of quality.

From the exchange of letters between Cicero and Atticus we can get a good idea of the casual and fluid nature of publication in the ancient world. There was no copyright or royalty (hence the importance of literary patronage) and private circulation could easily pass by degrees into full-scale publication; an author was able to incorporate changes into a text he had already published by asking his friends to alter their copies, but other copies would remain unaltered. Cicero drastically reshaped his *Academica* when Atticus was in the process of having copies made and consoled him for the effort wasted with the promise of a superior version. But copies of the first draft were in existence; both 'editions' survived, and we have a more substantial part of the first than of the second. Cicero also protests that his *Oratio in Clodium et Curionem*, of which fragments have survived in some scholia, was published without his consent. In the *Orator* (29) he had incorrectly attributed some lines of Aristophanes to Eupolis and asked Atticus to rectify the mistake quickly in all copies (*Att.* 12.6a.1). In this case he succeeded in correcting the tradition that has come down to us, but he was not so lucky when in the *Republic* (2.8) he wished to alter *Phliuntii* (as he had wrongly called the inhabitants of Phlius) to *Phliasii*; the sole manuscript of the work that has survived still has *Phliuntii*, and it is the modern editor who makes the change that Cicero requested.

V. DEVELOPMENTS UNDER THE EARLY EMPIRE

By the end of the Roman Republic the institutions and processes that govern and guard the transmission of the written word were already in existence, and under Augustus and his successors they were refined and consolidated. The book trade became more important, and we soon hear of the names of established book-sellers: Horace speaks of the Sosii, later Quintilian and Martial tell of Tryphon, Atrectus, and others. By the time of the Younger Seneca book collecting was derided as a form of extravagant ostentation. Augustus founded two public libraries, one in 28 B.C. in the Temple of Apollo on the Palatine, the other, not long after-wards, in the Porticus Octaviae. Thereafter libraries were a common form of both private and imperial munificence, in Rome and the provinces. Pliny founded a library in his native Comum and provided money for its upkeep; the best-preserved (and restored) ancient library is that built at Ephesus in memory of Titus Julius Celsus, proconsul of Asia A.D. 106–7; one of the most famous was the Bibliotheca Ulpia founded by Trajan, which long survived the disasters of fire and strife and was still standing in the fifth century. Given an enlightened emperor, patronage could foster scholarship as well as literature: under Augustus Hyginus was appointed Palatine librarian and Verrius Flaccus was made tutor to the imperial children. It was during this period that school education too took the form which it was to keep for centuries and, with the state taking an increasing interest in education, it became stand-ardized throughout the Roman world.

Secondary education at Rome was provided by the *grammaticus* and this largely consisted of the careful reading and detailed inter-pretation of poetry. Prose was more the concern of the *rhetor*, but their provinces to a certain extent overlapped. Sometime after 26 B.C. Q. Caecilius Epirota, a freedman of Atticus, instituted in the school he had opened the practice of studying Vergil and other modern writers (Suet., *Gram.* 16.2–3). Caecilius' school seems to have been more in the nature of a specialized seminar and his practice may have had little effect on the normal school curriculum; but such a change would be a natural outcome of Augustan pride in its own literary achievement and it was not long before modern writers were studied in the classroom. Vergil's entry into the school curriculum may have been at the expense of Ennius. From now on a successful poet, a Horace or an Ovid, saw his works passing into the syllabus before he was decently dead and this continued until the archaizing reaction that began at the end of the first century interrupted the process and froze the canon of classical authors. Although poets like Horace and Lucan continued to be read in the schools, two poets were studied above all others, Vergil and, more surprisingly perhaps, Terence, though he has been a popular school text at other times; in prose Cicero and Sallust occupied a similarly pre-eminent position.

The intense and minute study that was devoted to commonly read authors by expert and inexpert alike could affect their text for both good and ill. The large demand for popular works and those in the school curriculum might be expected to have flooded the market with poor copies and, while the close attention of scholars and grammarians would tend to safeguard the purity of the text, it is true that scholars at all periods and with the best intentions have the power to deprave as well as to emend a text which passes through their hands. Hence the fear of banalization on the one hand and pedantic interference on the other. Our evidence for the history of Latin texts in antiquity is so scrappy and so difficult to interpret with confidence that it is hard to picture the sort of text one might have encountered at any given period in the schoolroom or market-place, or to generalize about the quality of manuscripts that scholars and discerning readers would have at their disposal. On the whole, neither the ill effects of popularization nor the scholarly work which grew around the main classical authors appears to have affected our texts as much as we might have expected. Our textual traditions appear to have sprung in the main from books which had enjoyed a sheltered life in public or private libraries. There was also in antiquity a natural divide between scholarship and transmission, since texts and commentaries were normally in separate volumes. Ancient critics put their observations in their commentaries and marked the texts they studied with critical signs rather than alter them to suit their taste. But there is interesting evidence of some early corruption in standard authors. As early as the sixties Seneca (*Epist.* 94.28) quotes one of the unfinished lines of the *Aeneid*, *audentis fortuna iuvat* (10.284), with the supplement *piger ipse sibi obstat.* The gnomic quality of the half-line and the inviting vacuum it left to be filled might so easily have generated a proverb that it may be going too far to assume that

Seneca actually used an interpolated copy of Vergil; but we know from Servius and Donatus that the urge to complete unfinished lines of the *Aeneid* began soon after Vergil's death and some spurious supplements have found their way into our earliest manuscripts. Livy offers a clearer case. Quintilian, writing about thirty years after Seneca, tells us (9.4.74) that the preface to Livy's history began with the dactylic opening *facturusne operae pretium sim*, and that this should be preferred to the corrupt version current in his day. We owe the epic flourish of Livy's opening words to Quintilian, for all the manuscripts of the Nicomachean family, on which we depend at this point, read *facturusne sim operae pretium*. In the next century Gellius complains (20.6.14) that Sallust's *maiores vestrum* (*Cat.* 33.2) had been corrupted to *maiores vestri*, and the surviving manuscripts show that his complaint was justified. In the case of such authors it was never too soon for the textual critic to ply his trade.

The great Augustan scholar Verrius Flaccus still devoted his attention to the early writers, but his contemporary Julius Hyginus, a man of wide learning, turned his attention to more recent authors and wrote a work on Vergil which included observations on the text. Scholarship on Vergil was thus inaugurated by a younger contemporary of the poet himself. Two of his observations, preserved by later writers, have given rise to continuing debate. At *Georgics* 2.247 he wished to read *sensus... amaror* for *sensu... amaro*, on the authority of a manuscript *ex domo atque ex familia Vergilii* (Gellius 1.21.2). This reading has not commended itself to many, but most welcome his contribution to our text of Vergil at *Aeneid* 12.120: here he held that Vergil had written not *velati lino*, which could well be a banalization of the text, but *velati limo* (*limus* being a sacrificial apron). Remmius Palaemon, an influential grammarian, continued to put the emphasis on modern authors, and Asconius, who stands out amongst ancient commentators for his good sense and integrity, wrote on Cicero, Vergil, and Sallust. But of the scholars of the first century the most famous in his own day and in later ages was M. Valerius Probus of Beirut. His dates fall somewhere between A.D. 20–105 and his period of scholarly activity probably belongs to the closing decades of the century. He is a controversial figure, for our

information about him is scanty and easily exaggerated. Such facts
as we have about his life come from Suetonius (*Gram.* 24). He tells
us that Probus, disappointed in his hopes of military promotion,
turned to the study of the old authors whom he had learned to
admire at school in the provinces and who were now out of fashion
at Rome. He gathered together a large number of texts and went
through them in accordance with Alexandrian methods, correcting
errors of transcription, punctuating the text, and adding critical
signs in the margin: *multaque exemplaria contracta emendare ac dis-
tinguere et adnotare curavit.* He did not set himself up as a teacher, but
had a few followers with whom he would very occasionally read
texts; he published only a few short pieces, but left behind a fair-
sized *silva observationum sermonis antiqui.* His use of the tools of Alexandrian criticism is attested by the *Anecdoton Parisinum*: he is
credited with the use of certain *notae* (the *asteriscus, asteriscus cum
obelo, diplē*) and his employment of others is stated or implied in
later commentaries; he is said to have worked on Vergil, Horace,
and Lucretius. For specific examples of his activity we are dependent on reports in Gellius and the later commentators, Donatus
and Servius; here we find ample evidence for his work on Vergil
and Terence, and isolated references to an interest in Plautus and
Sallust. A Life of Persius which claims to have been taken *de com-
mentario Probi Valeri* is probably spurious.

An exaggerated view which credited Probus with authoritative
editions of a number of authors has now given way to more sober
judgement, but much about him remains unclear. Opinion is
divided on whether he wrote extended commentaries, of which
there is no mention in Suetonius, or whether his legacy was limited
to his *non mediocris silva observationum*, those of his views that
survived in the oral tradition long enough to be recorded by Gellius
and others, and the manuscripts he had corrected, punctuated, and
marked with his critical *notae*. Both his opinions and the actual
notae he used excited the interest of subsequent generations of
scholars and contributed to his considerable reputation. Such an
ambiguous term as *Probus legit* does not in itself make it clear
whether he is suggesting an emendation or recommending a
variant reading in his or another manuscript, and the extent to

which he collated texts is thus open to dispute. He certainly claims that his knowledge of Vergil's use of *i* and *e* in such accusatives as *urbes/urbis* and *turrem/turrim* was based on a manuscript corrected by Vergil's own hand (Gellius 13.21.1-8). An appeal to an authoritative text, even if not as authoritative as he thought it was, implies recourse to manuscript evidence and this seems likely in other cases too.

We have enough examples of his textual criticism to form an opinion of his methods and judgement. For instance, he put a sign against *Aen.* 1.21-2, which he considered otiose in the context; at 1.44 he seems to have preferred *tempore* to *pectore*; at 8.406 he found the expression *coniugis infusus gremio* unbecoming and would read *infusum*; at 10.173 he put a comma after *trecentos*; at 10.444 he was rightly puzzled by *aequore iusso*; at 10.539 he recommended *albis* for *armis*, at 12.605 *floros* for *flavos*; in Terence's *Adelphi* he assigned the words *quid festinas, mi Geta* (323) to Sostrata; in Sallust's *Catiline* (5.4 *satis eloquentiae, sapientiae parum*) he wished to foist upon Sallust the word *loquentia*. Some of his interventions, as at 10.539, have put our text of Vergil back on track, others still excite lively debate, some, if his views have been correctly reported, cast doubt on his judgement. Despite his prestige, there is little trace of his activity in the manuscripts of Vergil that survive from antiquity.

VI. ARCHAISM IN THE SECOND CENTURY

The marked decline in creative literature that set in during the second century was accompanied by a widespread academic interest in the writers of the past. In particular, there was a resurgence of enthusiasm for the early writers of Rome. The beginnings of this archaistic revival have been detected in Probus; it was encouraged by Hadrian, and its influence can be traced in the works of Fronto, Gellius, and Apuleius. This cult of the archaic, besides producing extremely baroque effects in the prose of the period, ensured that the writers of the early Republic—Ennius, Plautus, Cato, and lesser figures as well—were taken down from the shelves and studied with passionate interest. To this revival we owe much of our knowledge of these early writers. Their chances of ultimate survival were slim; their language was too archaic and obscure for them to survive the narrowing interests and declining literacy of the ages to come, and, with some notable exceptions, they lived on only in the fragments and gossip preserved by Gellius or one of the later collectors of words and facts.

We can glean from the pages of the *Attic Nights* of Aulus Gellius a remarkable picture of the antiquarian book trade in the second century A.D. He tells us that he saw on sale in a bookshop at Rome an ancient Latin version of the *Annals* of Fabius Pictor (5.4.1), and relates how one of his teachers, in order to look up a word, procured at immense pains and expense an old manuscript of Ennius' *Annals* 'almost certainly corrected by Lampadio himself' (18.5.11). Valuable finds could still be made in the libraries of Rome and the provinces: at Rome he found a rare work by Aelius Stilo (16.8.2), at Patras a venerable copy of Livius Andronicus (18.9.5), at Tibur a manuscript of the Sullan historian Claudius Quadrigarius (9.14.3). One of his friends had a Vergil *mirandae vetustatis, emptum in Sigillariis xx aureis* (2.3.5), quite a find to make, if the story be true, at a Christmas fair. Fronto corroborates this antiquarian's paradise when he speaks of the high price and prestige attached in his day to manuscripts of Cato, Ennius, Cicero, and other Republican writers, if they claimed to have been written by such men as Lampadio and Aelius Stilo, edited by Tiro, or copied by Atticus or Nepos (*Ad M. Caes.* 1.7.4). The venerability and authenticity of many of these books is difficult to credit, and may well have been exaggerated by commercial guile or the enthusiasm of the collector. Gellius in particular is fond of a good story. At the same time one should perhaps not be too sceptical about the survival of early texts. Evidence which the Elder Pliny and Quintilian provide for the previous century is less suspect in that it predates the change in literary fashion and therefore the motive for forgery on a large scale. Pliny claims (*N.H.* 13.83) to have seen documents—letters perhaps—written by the Gracchi, adding that autographs of Cicero, Vergil, and Augustus were common; Quintilian too (1.7.20) speaks of texts written in the hand of Cicero and Vergil. Claims to have consulted authoritative manuscripts were made, as we have seen, by scholars from Hyginus to Probus. There is a world of difference between Hyginus, head of the Palatine library under Augustus, and the book-hunters we meet in the *Attic Nights* of Gellius: various degrees of scepticism are called for, and some allowance must be made for good faith. At all events, even if many of the details are suspect, the general picture created by these tales should be given some weight, the continued availability of Republican writers, the value attached to old authors and old manuscripts, and the keenness of scholars to hunt these out in the hope of recovering an authentic reading. Manuscripts that did not have as venerable or illustrious a pedigree as they were thought to have might still have been old, or good, or at least right in places where one's own text was corrupt.

The practice of consulting other manuscripts to check or improve one's own copy is a natural act that must have happened to some extent at all times, and increasingly so with the growth of scholarship and antiquarianism and an understandable concern for the accuracy of texts on which time might well have left its mark. The earliest evidence for anything on the scale of a recension goes back to this period and concerns the activity of Statilius Maximus, a scholar of the second century who is known to have been interested in Cicero and Cato. In a manuscript of Cicero's speeches discovered in 1417 (see p. 138), Poggio added between the first and second speech *De lege agraria* a note that he found in the archetype and which had been handed down with the text to which it had been appended so many centuries earlier: *Statilius Maximus rursum emendavi ad Tironem et Laecanianum et Domitium et alios veteres III. oratio eximia.* The general sense is clear: Statilius corrected the text with reference to six manuscripts, including one that claimed descent from Cicero's secretary Tiro. It may be significant that this subscription, the earliest to have survived, accompanies a text with a strong legal content.

VII. THE COMPENDIUM AND THE COMMENTARY

The intellectual decline which had begun in the second century was accelerated by the economic breakdown and political chaos of the

third, and no major literary figures—Christian writers apart—
emerged until the age of Claudian. Indeed the virtual eclipse of
profane culture in the middle of the third century, between the
death of Alexander Severus in 235 and the accession of Diocletian
in 284, may have had a serious effect on the continuity of classical
culture. The absence of works of literature and a decline in the
monumental and epigraphic remains of the period is ominous, for it
would be curious if this lack of creative energy and the general
cultural disruption did not entail a corresponding apathy towards
the reading and copying of the literature of the past. The story that
the emperor Tacitus (275–6) ordered that the works of his name-
sake be copied ten times a year, *ne lectorum incuria deperiret* (*H.A.*
27.10.3), is almost certainly a fabrication of the late fourth century,
but the situation that it implies may not be far from the truth.

But many of the works produced in these centuries, though they
may be uninspiring in themselves and cut a poor figure when compared with some of the Christian writings of the period, have a
significant secondary role. Some are important because they
ensured the continuance of the classical tradition in ages when
great works of literature were not available or provided too rich a
diet for the taste or capacity of the time; others are valuable because
their sources have been lost or mutilated. Among these is the compendium. Florus had written an abridgement of Roman history in
the reign of Hadrian and an epitomized Livy was known before
that. These were followed in the third century by Justinus' epitome
of the Augustan writer Pompeius Trogus, and in the fourth by the
abbreviated histories of Eutropius, Aurelius Victor, and others
unnamed. Some of these were widely read in periods when Livy and
Tacitus were too long or too sophisticated or simply not generally
available. In other fields we have Festus' epitome of Verrius Flaccus
and Solinus' *Collectanea rerum memorabilium*, a summary of geographical facts almost entirely derived without acknowledgement
from the Elder Pliny and Pomponius Mela.

The period that produced so many potted handbooks was also
the great age of the commentator and scholiast, of whom the best
known are Acro and Porphyrio on Horace and the two great
scholars of the fourth century, Aelius Donatus and Servius; Donatus

wrote on Terence and Vergil, Servius contributed to the great Vergilian commentary that bears his name. Donatus was also the author of two grammars, the *Ars Minor* and *Maior*, which, together with the *Institutiones grammaticae* of Priscian (6th cent.), provided the Middle Ages with their main textbooks on grammar.

Two other compilations should be mentioned here in view of their significance for a later age, the *De compendiosa doctrina* of Nonius Marcellus, of uncertain date, and the *De nuptiis Mercurii et Philologiae* of Martianus Capella, written in the first part of the fifth century. The first is a dictionary, still valuable in that it contains many quotations from works now lost; the author appears to have excerpted two tragedies of Ennius himself. The *De nuptiis* is an allegorical treatise on the seven liberal arts, which appear as brides-maids at the wedding of Mercury and Philology. By the late first century the liberal arts had been standardized as grammar, rhetoric, dialectic, arithmetic, music, geometry, and astronomy. The canon-ical seven were handed on to the Middle Ages and became, in theory, the basis of medieval education. In time they split into two groups, the *trivium* (grammar, rhetoric, dialectic) and the *quad-rivium* (arithmetic, music, geometry, astronomy), thus forming an elementary and a more advanced course.

Classical scholars owe a great debt to these abridgements and commentaries, grammars and handbooks, for they have preserved, even if at second-hand or in fragmentary form, a very considerable amount of literature and learning that would otherwise have perished. They also enable us to correct passages in extant authors where the text has been corrupted in the direct manuscript tradi-tion. Moreover, they handed a life-line to following centuries by furnishing them with the tools for maintaining a basically classical education. Together with what could be gleaned from patristic authors, the grammarians often provided medieval readers with what was at times the sum of their knowledge of ancient literature. This enabled them to give their writings a veneer of learning which is often disconcertingly at variance with the narrowness of their actual reading, but at the same time it kept alive a genuine respect for classical literature and provided a familiar framework into which missing pieces of antiquity could be fitted as they became available.

VIII. FROM ROLL TO CODEX

Between the second and fourth centuries a development took place
which is of the utmost significance for the history of the book and
therefore for the transmission of classical texts in general. This was
the gradual disappearance of the roll in favour of the codex, that is
to say the adoption of a book with essentially the same appearance
as the one we use today.

Down to the second century A.D. the standard vehicle for all literary texts had been the papyrus roll, but from the earliest times an
alternative medium had existed in the writing tablet, which consisted of a number of wax-coated boards fastened together with a
thong or clasp. These were used throughout antiquity for letters,
school-exercises, rough notes, and other casual purposes. The
Romans extended their scope by using them for legal documents
and took the important step of replacing the wooden tablets with
parchment leaves. These parchment notebooks (*membranae*) were
in use by the end of the Republic, but it took a long time for them to
achieve the status of books.

The first mention of literary works being published in parchment
codices is found in Martial, in a number of poems written during the
years 84–6. He emphasizes their compactness, their handiness for
the traveller, and tells the reader the name of the shop where such
novelties can be bought (1.2.7–8). Although there is one surviving
fragment of a parchment codex in Latin written about A.D. 100 (the
anonymous *De Bellis Macedonicis*, P. Lit. Lond. 121), the pocket
editions that Martial was at pains to advertise were not a success.
The codex did not come into use for pagan literature until the
second century; but it rapidly gained ground in the third, and
triumphed in the fourth. It could be made of either papyrus or
parchment, but it was the parchment codex that eventually won the
day. Although papyrus is tougher than most people think and a roll
might last as long as 300 years (Galen 18(2).630), the average life
would be shorter, and parchment was a much more durable
material; in time its toughness was to prove a vital factor in the
survival of classical literature. The impulse to change the format of

the book must have come from the early Christians; for while the pagan codex was a rarity in the second century, the codex form was already universal for biblical texts.

The advantages of the codex over the roll were many: it was handier, more capacious, easier to consult, and it may have cost rather less to produce. Reference was made still easier by numbering the pages, and the addition of a list of contents guarded against forged interpolations and other interference with the text. These were important considerations in the days when much of life revolved around the authoritative texts of the Scriptures and the Code. The importance of the codex for religion and law is obvious. It had a relevance for literary texts too: a book which could hold the contents of several rolls meant that a corpus of related texts, or what was considered the best of an author's work, could be put under one cover, and this was attractive to an age which was inclined to trim its intellectual heritage to a manageable form.

The change from roll to codex involved the gradual but wholesale transference of ancient literature from one form to another. This was the first major bottle-neck through which classical literature had to pass. It must have been somewhat reduced in the process, but the losses are not easily specified or assessed. There was the danger that little-read works would not be transferred to codex form, and in time their rolls would perish. A voluminous author, if some of his rolls were not available at a critical moment, might never recover his missing books.

Since some of the earliest surviving books of antiquity are parchment codices of the fourth century, it may be appropriate to mention at this point the separate question of the main scripts used in Roman times for the production of books. These were Square Capitals, Rustic Capitals, Uncial, Half-uncial. The only manuscripts written throughout in Square Capitals are a few imposing manuscripts of Vergil; this script, modelled on the monumental style of inscriptions, seems to have been introduced as a deliberate refinement for *de luxe* copies of Rome's national poet. It is therefore somewhat unfortunate that the standard and elegant capital bookhand of antiquity, because of its comparatively less formal lines when set beside this monumental script, should traditionally be called 'Rustic Capital' (Plate IX), and this charming but rather misleading name is now giving way to 'Canonized' or 'Classic Capital' or plain 'Capital' script. The earliest specimens we can date are the Gallus papyrus (Cairo, P. Qaṣr Ibrîm, c. 50–20 B.C.) and the fragment of a poem on the battle of Actium (Naples, P. Herc. 817), written between the event it describes (31 B.C.) and the destruction of Herculaneum (A.D. 79), where it was found. This hand continued in much the same form down to the early sixth century; famous manuscripts in this script are the codex Bembinus of Terence (Vat. lat. 3226) and the great codices of Vergil, the Mediceus, Palatinus, and Romanus. The other bookhands of the Roman period came into being as the cursive forms of everyday writing were refined and standardized by reference to the calligraphic bookhands. Whether the dominant parent in the creation of Uncial was Rustic Capital, as some think, or Cursive, this handsome rounded script emerged as a fully developed hand in the fourth century and lasted until the ninth. An early example is the Vatican palimpsest of the *De republica* (Vat. lat. 5757 of the late 4th or early 5th cent., Plate X); one of the finest is the fifth-century Puteanus of Livy's third decade (Paris lat. 5730, Plate XI). Further development from cursive, and in particular from the later, minuscule cursive, led to the creation of the first minuscule bookhand, Half-uncial. There are a number of classical texts written in this script, mainly papyri, but it was predominantly used for Christian books.

IX. PAGANISM AND CHRISTIANITY IN THE FOURTH CENTURY IN THE WESTERN EMPIRE

The fourth century witnessed the final clash between Christianity and paganism. In 312 the first Christian emperor Constantine dramatically reversed the policy of his predecessor Diocletian by allowing the Christians freedom of worship, and within the space of a few decades they had taken the war into the pagan camp. The climax of the struggle found expression in the dignified debate that took place in 384 between Ambrose, then bishop of Milan and coming to the height of his power, and Q. Aurelius Symmachus, the pagan writer and administrator, who made a moving plea for the restitution of the Altar of Victory which had been removed from the Curia. In 394 the leader of the last pagan resistance, Virius Nicomachus Flavianus, was defeated by Theodosius and committed suicide in the old tradition. At the centre of the pagan opposition in the West were the Roman senators, who recaptured for a time the spirit of their ancestors and rallied to the defence of their traditions and heritage.

A vivid and sympathetic memorial to this movement is still extant in Macrobius' *Saturnalia*. The relevance of this learned symposium lies in the setting and *dramatis personae*. In the year 384, on the occasion of the Saturnalia, a number of cultivated upper-class Romans meet on successive days in the houses of Vettius Agorius Praetextatus, Virius Nicomachus Flavianus, and Symmachus, and have much learned talk about religion, history, philology, and in particular their great pagan poet Vergil. Among those present are other known opponents of Christianity. Servius is there as a representative of professional scholarship, a little over-awed by the company. We know that Praetextatus had died in 384, Flavianus in 394; Macrobius has nostalgically recreated the great pagan society of the past as a framework for his learned compilation and we see its members, before their world had crumbled around them, discussing the minutiae of Roman life and literature with the sophisticated learning of the great Romans of the Republic.

Fortunately the triumph of Christianity did not remove the need for readable texts of the pagan authors. Christians who were hostile to pagan literature found themselves in an acute dilemma. It was clearly ill suited to be the basic stuff of Christian education. The poets were polytheistic and the tales they told about their gods, and particularly about the father of them all, were usually devoid of edification or downright immoral; Roman rhetoric, though it could be useful if employed in the right cause, encouraged glibness in speech and argument out of keeping with simple piety; even the philosophers, who had so much to offer to the Christian thinker, also contained much that was inimical to religious faith and the Christian way of life; the magnitude of the pagan achievement in all spheres of human activity, of which its written as well as its material remains were a constant reminder, might tend to sap confidence in new values and institutions. On the other hand, the enormous debt which Christians owed to the classical heritage and the extent to which they could still benefit from it was obvious even at times when the tension between the two cultures was at its highest. Just as Ambrose in his *De officiis ministrorum* was able to produce an influential manual of Christian ethics by reworking the basically Stoic content of Cicero's *De officiis*, so Augustine, writing at a time when he was least sympathetic to secular letters, in his *De doctrina Christiana* successfully adapted classical Roman rhetoric and in particular the theory of the three styles as elaborated by Cicero in the *Orator* to the needs of the Christian preacher. The agony of the dilemma which faced the orthodox Christian nurtured in the pagan schools is in human terms most dramatically reflected in Jerome as he runs through the gamut of conscience and renunciation, temptation and compromise. The last was inevitable. In general it was recognized that pagan literature could be plundered with profit provided that due caution was observed and the end justified the means. Jerome uses the analogy of the captive woman in Deuteronomy (21: 10–13) who may be taken to wife and made a true Israelite when she has had her head shaved and her nails pared (*Epist.* 70.2). Augustine sanctions the use of secular learning by likening it to the despoiling of the Egyptians (*De doctrina* 2.60). Although the Christian attitude to pagan learning remained complex and fluid and generalization is dangerous, these two simple parables, quoted again and again through the ages, provided a convenient justification for those who wished to have the best of both worlds. In practice the division between pagan and Christian appears to have been bridged at the cultural level more easily than one might have expected; for the pagan aristocracy had quickly abandoned a cause that had been largely founded on sentiment and tradition and happily pursued their shared cultural interests as members of the new Christian élite. As far as the schools were concerned, there was no immediate alternative to the old Roman system of education. Christian writings were not suitable for the school syllabus, the basic textbooks were all pagan, and in any case the ordinary cultivated Roman had few qualms about the traditional education;

the obligations of polite society and his own highly developed sense of style made it difficult for him to turn over to the less sophisticated diet of Christian literature. The Roman educational system, authors and gods and all, continued until the monastic and episcopal schools were able to replace it with an education which, however much it owed to the traditional system, was essentially Christian in direction and purpose.

X. THE SUBSCRIPTIONS

The subscriptions provide a series of fascinating testimonies to the interest late antiquity appears to have taken in classical texts and their conservation. These are brief statements, formulaic in expression, which were appended at the end of a work or the books of a work to indicate that the text had been duly revised and corrected. The only certain autograph subscription in a classical text is that of Caecilius in the palimpsest codex of Fronto's *Letters* (Vat. Pal. lat. 24). Whether the subscription in the Medicean Vergil (Laur. 39.1, Plate IX) is the actual autograph of Asterius is uncertain, though it has been added to the finished manuscript in the usual way. In it Asterius, consul in 494, records that he had punctuated and corrected the text. But in most cases the subscription has to be recovered from manuscripts much later in date; these have transmitted it along with the text to which it was appended. The ninth-century archetype of Pomponius Mela (Vat. lat. 4929) mirrors its antique exemplar so faithfully in places that one can see the subscription as it was, inserted between the explicit of one work and the incipit of the next. Many subscriptions will have been lost, because no descendants of the subscribed manuscript survive or because the subscription itself was not copied: the work that Praetextatus did on the correction of texts is recorded in his epitaph (Dessau, *ILS* 1259, 8–12), but there is no trace of it in any surviving manuscripts. The fact that some 27 subscriptions or sets of subscriptions have survived in secular works alone is some indication of the extent of the activity. It is a common practice too in legal and ecclesiastical texts.

The earliest extant subscription, that of Statilius Maximus in Cicero's *De lege agraria*, has already been mentioned. The rest, which are couched in similar terms, begin towards the end of the fourth century and continue into the sixth. They vary from the simple *Julius Celsus Constantinus v.c. legi* (in Caesar's *Gallic War*) to more elaborate statements giving the date, place, and circumstances of the revision. Among the earliest is one appended to Book IX of Apuleius' *Golden Ass*:

> Ego Sallustius legi et emendavi Romae felix Olibrio et Probino v.c. conss. in foro Martis controversiam declamans oratori Endelechio. Rursus Constantinopoli recognovi Caesario et Attico conss.

The years in question are 395 and 397, and the Sallustius who carried out the revision is a member of a known family connected with Symmachus. The work was carried out under the supervision of Severus Sanctus Endelechius in the forum of Augustus, which, with the neighbouring forum of Trajan, accommodated schools of rhetoric and grammar and survived as a sort of university campus down to the end of the ancient world. One of the three families of Martial manuscripts goes back to an ancient recension which was corrected in the same forum by Torquatus Gennadius in 401.

A celebrated series of subscriptions is found in various books of Livy's first decade:

> Emendavi Nicomachus Flavianus v.c. ter praef. urbis apud Hennam.

> Nicomachus Dexter v.c. emendavi ad exemplum parentis mei Clementiani.

> Victorianus v.c. emendabam domnis Symmachis.

The Nicomachean recension of Livy's first decade was a collaborative effort on the part of the related families of the Nicomachi and Symmachi, who had conceived the ambitious project of correcting the whole of Livy. Nicomachus Flavianus is the son of the pagan leader, Nicomachus Dexter is his grandson; Tascius Victorianus, who is here helping the Symmachi, edited one of the works of Flavianus. Part of the work of revising Livy was carried out at the villa of the Nicomachi at Enna in Sicily.

The continuance of the family tradition can be seen in the subscription to Macrobius' commentary on Cicero's *Somnium Scipionis*:

Aurelius Memmius Symmachus v.c. emendabam uel distinguebam meum
(*sc.* exemplar) Ravennae cum Macrobio Plotino Eudoxio v.c.

Here the great grandson of the Symmachus who appears in the
Saturnalia is seen correcting another work by Macrobius, and helping him is the grandson of the author himself, who may of course
have had access to an authoritative text. Thus the chain of subscriptions extends to the very threshold of the Middle Ages, for this
Symmachus, consul in 485, was the father-in-law of Boethius. When
book production passed into the hands of the Church, the scriptoria
attached to monasteries and cathedrals replaced such private enterprise with their own system for supervising the writing and revising
of manuscripts.

These interesting documents have given rise to much debate.
The sudden reappearance of subscriptions in secular texts during
the last years of the fourth century encouraged the view that this
apparent intensification of interest was initially connected with the
pagan opposition and a desire on the part of the senatorial aristocracy to put together and refurbish a canon of secular scriptures.
Some of the persons and families involved reflect the society
pictured in the *Saturnalia* and have obvious links with the pagan
cause; and some of the authors they worked on, Vergil and Livy,
monuments to the greatness of the Roman past, or Apuleius, full of
unedifying adventures and an apostle of an exotic cult, would fit
such a view. While it cannot be denied that the Symmachi and
Nicomachi might take a particular satisfaction in editing Livy, the
continuity of the tradition, extending on the evidence we have from
the second to the sixth century, the fact that pagan literature was
much more of a neutral ground than is often supposed, and the
active participation of Christians in the process, deny any significant part in it to the short-lived pagan opposition. Endelechius,
who was taking part in the correcting of Apuleius as early as 395,
was a Christian. In the next century the Asterius who corrected
Vergil was also responsible for the publication of Sedulius' *Carmen
Paschale*, and Vettius Agorius Basilius Mavortius, a descendant of
the great pagan family, worked both on Horace and an early manuscript of Prudentius (Paris lat. 8084). Felix, the professor of rhetoric

who helped Mavortius with Horace, happily corrected Martianus Capella, for all that author's pagan mysticism, *Christo adiuvante*. A more probable hypothesis is that the process had been given special point and impetus by the transference of literature from roll to codex, as works were brought together and put into a new and more permanent form. But subscriptions continued even when that process was complete and must, whatever the original motivation, have become a traditional practice.

The philological as well as the historical significance of the activity that the subscriptions record is similarly disputed. Generalization is clearly impossible. Some texts were corrected by students as part of their training. Others appear to amount to nothing more than the correcting of one's own copy for personal use. Persius was revised twice by a young officer, Flavius Julius Tryphonianus Sabinus, while he was on military service in Barcelona and Toulouse; he worked *sine antigrapho*, as he disarmingly tells us, and *prout potui sine magistro*. Such protestations inspire little confidence in the quality of the product, but may nevertheless suggest that correction against an exemplar and the help of a professional was what one might reasonably expect. Other projects were much more serious: Symmachus himself, two Nicomachi, and Victorianus were all involved in correcting Livy's text, and Valerianus was taking an interest in the project (Symmachus, *Epist.* 9.13); Praetextatus' work on the correction of texts was thought worthy of record in his epitaph. In legal documents the accurate reproduction of an original was of paramount importance, and the careful copying and revising of ecclesiastical texts was often enjoined with fearful adjurations: this suggests that similar affidavits in literary texts might on occasion testify to a more serious purpose. Whether the practice did anything to promote significantly the survival of classical literature is doubtful, and the value of these subscriptions for us may lie more in their historical interest. They provide a fixed point in time or place for textual traditions which would otherwise emerge from the blue, and they show us the cultured classes of late antiquity, aristocrats and scholars, pagan and Christian alike, taking an active interest in the accuracy and readability of the books in circulation. The predominantly high status of the men recorded in surviving subscriptions strongly suggests that it was upon their stately shelves that many of our texts had resided before finding their way into the monasteries and cathedrals that ensured their survival.

THE GREEK EAST

1. SCHOLARSHIP AND LITERATURE UNDER THE ROMAN EMPIRE

In the early centuries of the Roman empire intellectual life in Greece and the Hellenized provinces of the Eastern Mediterranean was in a state of decline. Despite the existence of institutions of higher education such as the schools of philosophy and oratory at Athens, Rhodes, and elsewhere, there were few outstanding achievements in literature or scholarship. The Museum at Alexandria still existed; although the end of independent government in Egypt brought to a close the royal patronage of scholarship, the situation was soon restored, for we find Strabo reporting (17.1.8) that the Roman emperor now supported the Museum, and there are explicit references to scholars entitled to its privileges. But notable works of scholarship do not seem to have been produced. Only the library continued to render service as a leading collection of material for the scholarly public; the tradition that Caesar was accidentally responsible for its destruction during his visit to Egypt (48–47 B.C.) has been widely accepted, but the sources are not entirely in agreement as to the extent of the damage, and it seems likely that no more than a section of the library was burnt, or that the deficiencies were made good by Antony, who was said to have transferred the Pergamene library to Alexandria (Plutarch, *Antony* 58); total destruction is also difficult to reconcile with the evidence that Strabo apparently did his geographical research in Alexandria. Literary work is harder to trace. In the Augustan age Aristonicus did further selection of the Homeric commentaries, and Tryphon studied and classified figures of speech (the treatise which now passes under his name has been revised by later redactors). During the reign of Tiberius there are again signs of some activity. Theon commented on various poetic texts, especially Hellenistic, such as Theocritus, Apollonius Rhodius, and Callimachus; a scrap of his notes on Pindar's *Pythians* has recently come to light (P. Oxy. 2536). Apion prepared a glossary to Homer that is quoted by Hesychius and Eustathius (a little of it survives in P. Rylands 26). Heliodorus wrote a commentary on the metres of Aristophanes, parts of which are found in the extant scholia. But as far as we can see none of these works was outstanding as an advance in scholarly method or critical principles. Much the same is true of the second and third centuries, except that the grammarians Apollonius Dyscolus and his son Herodian were important in their own field, and some of their works survive independently of the scholia. Apollonius was the first grammarian to write on syntax in something approaching the modern sense of the term; the name Dyscolus is said to have been given to him owing to the difficulty of his subject-matter. Among other things he characterized the Greek perfect tense as a description of a present state; also he showed clearly for the first time the difference implied by the use of present and aorist in moods other than the indicative. In both these matters he made an advance on the Stoic theorists, who had already managed to develop a useful terminology for the tenses.

The decline of scholarship and criticism should not be seen as part of a general decline; in fact the first half of the second century is often thought to have been the period of Rome's greatest prosperity. There was another more tangible influence at work. Though school education included the reading of Homer and the other poets, especially tragedy and comedy, there was increasing emphasis on the study of rhetoric. As a result a large number of handbooks on oratory were written, and the Attic orators, in particular Demosthenes, received more attention than before. Interest was to some extent diverted from the poets. A more fundamental change in education may have been connected with the poverty of Greece and her evident inferiority to Rome in all spheres. It was easy to feel a nostalgic admiration for the achievements of the classical period; if men could no longer perform acts worthy of the great days of old, they might at least attempt to rival them in literary style. The growth of this feeling can be traced as early as the reign of Augustus, and it became especially prominent in the second century A.D. By this time the Greek language had undergone considerable changes, as can be seen from a comparison of the classical language with that of the New Testament or the letters and documents among the papyri. A desire to write in classical style at once created a need for manuals of instruction, and the energy of men with literary tastes was diverted to the writing of these textbooks. Dictionaries composed by Aelius Dionysius and Pausanias under Hadrian (117–38) have survived in fragments; we have also complete works by Pollux and Phrynichus dating from the reigns of Marcus Aurelius (161–80) and Commodus (180–92). These books all gave guidance to the would-be writer of classical Attic prose; in general they listed words or constructions current in everyday use which a writer might be tempted to employ, and then added the correct classical idiom. Any cultured person who interlarded his prose with modern expressions not found in the great Athenian writers was considered to have spoiled his style seriously and to have made a shameful display of ignorance and bad taste; this emerges quite clearly from the dedicatory letter which Phrynichus prefixed to his *Ecloge* and in the heading to the work. These experts in classical Attic did not always agree in their recommendations, nor were they equally strict in the construction of the rules they propounded. Some, such as Phrynichus, failed to appreciate the distinction between poetic and prose diction, and recommended usages which are found only in Greek tragedy; this made them unreliable guides for the school or university student. A certain degree of controversy arose among them. One issue was whether a single occurrence of a word in a classical author justified its usage, and three times in the *Ecloge* (206, 258, 400) we find Phrynichus stating that he is not satisfied to recommend words in this category, since he wishes to follow the well-established and common usage of Attic authors. Controversy also arose when incorrect instructions were given by a purist; there is a work by the so-called 'Anti-Atticist' showing that a number of prohibited expressions could be traced in Athenian texts earlier than c. 200 B.C.

Although the fashion was artificial in the extreme and had undesirable effects on literary compositions of every kind, the practice of Atticism lasted a very long time; it was the governing principle for all writers who aimed at a good style not merely under the Roman empire but right to the end of the Byzantine period. The Byzantines may as a rule have been less successful in their imitation of ancient models than the writers of the Second Sophistic age such as Lucian and Aristides, but there is no doubt that their aims were identical, since lexica of Attic diction were composed by later scholars, for example Photius in the ninth century and Thomas Magister in the fourteenth; and as late as the fifteenth century we find the historian Critobulus writing an account of the fall of Constantinople to the Turks in 1453 in a style which is clearly intended as an imitation of the classics; Thucydides and Arrian are the most prominent sources of his language. Stylistic archaism on this scale has no parallel except perhaps in China, where it was possible for Mao Tse-tung to think it worth writing lyrics in the style of eighth-century poets like Li Po.

Atticism had another important and less unfortunate consequence. The requirement to use only Attic diction of the best period ensured that in schools the classics of Athenian literature continued to be read as part of the regular curriculum, and this in turn meant that new copies of the text of major works were being steadily produced in sufficient numbers to guarantee the survival of most of them; only Menander was an exception. Even when the Eastern empire was at its lowest ebb the tradition of reading classical literature in the schools was never quite obliterated.

Close linguistic study of Attic texts led to other results. The occurrence of non-Attic words in a text supposed to come from the classical period might rouse suspicions as to its authenticity; and in fact we find Phrynichus remarking that the speech *Against Neaera* in the Demosthenic corpus is to be regarded as spurious partly on account of its impure language (*Ecloge* 203). But the minute linguistic observations of the schools were not entirely beneficial. They had the effect of instilling the forms and inflections of the Attic dialect so deeply that, when an educated man was transcribing a text, he tended to replace forms drawn from other dialects by the Attic forms which he knew so well. This is clear in works which contain Doric dialect, such as the lyrics of tragedy or

Theocritus' *Idylls*; in many parts of the text original Doric forms have been eliminated by successive generations of copyists. The text of Xenophon has suffered in the same way. Phrynichus tells us (*Ecloge* 71) that Xenophon departed from his native Attic dialect by writing the word for 'smell' as *odmē* instead of *osmē*; similarly Photius in his *Lexicon* says that Xenophon used the poetic form of the word for 'dawn', *eōs*, instead of the Attic *hēōs*; but in both these cases the surviving manuscripts of Xenophon regularly show the normal Attic forms. Here too the influence of the scribes is clear.

II. THE CHRISTIAN CHURCH AND CLASSICAL STUDIES

The effects of the growth of the Christian Church upon education and literary studies must now be considered. In earlier antiquity religious toleration had been the rule rather than the exception, and adherents of many different faiths had lived peacefully side by side, but the animosity with which Christians and pagans regarded each other brought about a substantial and permanent change. Many influential clergy disliked equally the unbelievers and the classical Greek literature which they studied with enthusiasm, and so the members of Christian communities were advised not to read such books. If this attitude had been adopted by all the clergy it would in due course, as the new religion became universal by the fifth century, have imposed an effective censorship on classical literature; as it is there can be little doubt that one of the major reasons for the loss of classical texts is that most Christians were not interested in reading them, and hence not enough new copies of the texts were made to ensure their survival in an age of war and destruction. But the literary merit of the classical authors was sufficient to tempt some Christians to read them, particularly as there were, at least in the early period, comparatively few Christian literary classics which could be recommended as an acceptable substitute for the traditional texts studied at school. Allegorical interpretation might be used to make certain passages inoffensive to Christian taste. Another important consideration was the need to make Christianity appeal to the well-educated pagan, and one

means to this end was the demonstration that some of the important concepts of the new faith could be discussed in terms borrowed
from the classical philosophers, especially the Stoics and Plato. The
fusion of Greek and Christian thought in Justin and Clement
exemplifies this attitude.

Early church fathers of the highest authority were content that
Christians should read some pagan texts during their education.
When Saint Gregory Thaumaturgus attended Origen's school at
Caesarea in 233–8 he found his master encouraging pupils to read
classical literature, and especially the philosophers; only those
authors who denied the existence of a deity or a divine providence
were to be avoided (Migne, *PG* 10.1088A, 1093A). It should be noted
that Origen's willingness to learn from pagan culture extended to
the realm of textual criticism. The interpretation of the Old
Testament had become a matter of controversy, since the Septuagint was at variance with some other early Greek versions, and difficulty arose if precise interpretation of a passage was required.
Origen adapted the system of marginal signs used by the Alexandrian critics to the Old Testament; an obelus marked a passage
found in the Greek but not in the Hebrew, and an asterisk passages
in which the Hebrew agreed with translations other than the
Septuagint. In his *Hexapla* Origen went further and devised a
method of presenting the Hebrew text and the translations in
parallel columns. The successive columns were the original
Hebrew, the Hebrew in Greek letters, the Greek translations of
Aquila, Symmachus, the Septuagint, and Theodotion. The resulting
book, a cumbrous anticipation of a modern apparatus criticus, must
have been enormous, and no doubt partly for that reason it has not
come down to us in its original form, except that fragments of a five-
column version omitting the text in Hebrew characters survive as
the lower script in a Milan palimpsest (Ambros. S.P. 11.251, *olim* O.
39 sup.).

The outlook of the fathers of the fourth century was no less
liberal. Saint Basil wrote a short treatise advising the young on the
best method of profiting from Greek literature, and Saint Gregory
of Nazianzus criticized the majority of Christians for their complete
rejection of pagan works, some of which he believed to be useful

(*PG* 36.508B). There was in general no attempt to alter the school curriculum by banishing the classical authors. For a brief period Julian's persecution of the Christians in 362 tempted Apollinaris (c. 310–90) to construct a totally Christian curriculum, for which he and his father composed a long poem in Homeric style on the antiquities of the Jews and a paraphrase of the Psalms, also in hexameters. He also recast the Gospels and Epistles in the form of Platonic dialogues (Sozomen, *Hist. eccl.* 5.18, Socrates, *Hist. eccl.* 3.16). But the persecution soon ended, and pagan and Christian continued to use the same educational system without serious polemic or controversy. Some professors of rhetoric were Christians, but they did not exclude pagans from their classes: in the fourth century at Athens the Christian Prohaeresius won the admiration of his staunchly pagan student Eunapius. Similarly at Gaza in the early sixth century the leading figures Procopius and Choricius pursued classical and Christian studies together.

The major classical texts, which had a firm position in the curriculum, were read by believer and unbeliever alike; but the survival of other texts was immediately put in danger when the new religion became universal, since the mass of the public, after the completion of their education, had no further interest in reading pagan books. It is sometimes asserted that the Church formally imposed a censorship and burnt pagan books as a matter of policy. The policy, if it ever existed as such, took a long time to have its intended effect; in the seventh century the poems of Sappho were still being read in Egypt (P. Berol. 5006). Occasionally there is a report of the burning of pagan books; Jovian in 363–4 is said to have burnt a library assembled at Antioch by his predecessor Julian (*Suda*, s.v. Iobianos). But this was an isolated case of vindictiveness: such destructive fervour was usually reserved for the works of fellow Christians who had deviated into heresy, and several ceremonial bonfires of unorthodox books are recorded in the fourth and fifth centuries.

The attitude of the church remained substantially unaltered throughout the Byzantine age. Classical authors maintained their place in the schools. Eminent members of the higher clergy figure among the most competent students of classical Greek at all times.

There is no reliable evidence for censorship. A famous statement by the humanist Petrus Alcyonius (1486–1527), to the effect that the ecclesiastical authorities caused the texts of pagan poets to be burnt, is not supported by any other evidence; it derives from a remark by the Byzantine refugee Demetrius Chalcondyles (1423–1511), and there is no reason to think that he had special sources of information. The numerous authors mentioned had probably been lost through other causes by the end of the Dark Ages. The Byzantine church was only concerned to destroy books by heretics; for instance in 1117, when the metropolitan Eustratius of Nicaea was examining arguments against the views of the Armenian church, he discovered works by Saint Cyril that appeared to contain heretical tendencies, and when copies of these works by Cyril began to circulate he brought the matter before the authorities, who ordered that all copies should be sent within forty days to Santa Sophia to be destroyed. Again in 1140 it came to the ear of the patriarch that a monk's heretical works were being circulated; after a search three copies were found and burnt. On the other hand no case has yet come to light in which the Church took such drastic measures against a classical text; even the works of the detested apostate Julian survived. The nearest approach to censorship occurred at the end of the eleventh century, when the philosopher John Italos lectured so enthusiastically about Plato that the church authorities issued a ruling which required that all orthodox persons should limit their interest in Plato to stylistic matters and not concern themselves with the philosophical content of the dialogues.

III. THE EARLY BYZANTINE PERIOD

While the general condition of the ancient world declined rapidly higher education in the Eastern part of the empire was more flourishing than ever before. Schools can be traced at Alexandria, Antioch, Athens, Beirut, Constantinople, and Gaza; they were in effect the universities of the ancient world. They varied in character and importance: at Alexandria Aristotle was one of the main topics of study; the chief subject at Beirut was law. The need for such institutions was created by a vast increase in the Roman civil service in the fourth century. The government required administrators of liberal education and good prose style, as the emperor Constantius stated explicitly in 360 in an edict preserved in the Theodosian code (14.1.1). The study of classical poetry and oratory continued in the schools as before; special attention was given to cultivating Attic prose style, and for this purpose a number of rhetorical tricks of style had to be mastered. The works of the early Atticist writers of the second century A.D. such as Lucian and Aristides were regarded as models no less deserving of imitation than the classics of ancient Athens; this equal valuation of Attic and Atticist lasted right through the Byzantine period. Literary education seems to have held its own for some time against the claims of more practical disciplines; but at the end of the fourth century we find Libanius, the head of a famous literary school, complaining that students are being attracted to the study of law and Latin, which were also of obvious benefit to potential civil servants (*Autobiography* 214 and 234). One by one the schools declined or closed, until by the middle of the sixth century only Constantinople and Alexandria remained: Justinian himself had closed the philosophical school at Athens in 529, and the other cities had been much reduced by war or natural disasters.

The emphasis on rhetoric and Atticism did not encourage much scholarship in the modern sense of the term. One achievement, however, which may belong to this period, is the conversion of ancient commentaries into the form of scholia, now placed in the margins of a text instead of occupying a separate book (Plates II and III). In particular there is reason to believe that work on Demosthenes and the other orators was carried out in the school at Gaza. The task was essentially one of compilation and selection, requiring intelligence in the choice of material selected from previous exegetical works; but in practice the scholia to all authors are marred by stupid or irrelevant notes. The date of this activity is usually placed in the fourth or fifth centuries, but it remains uncertain, since the identity of the compilers cannot be established. The idea of entering copious scholia in the margins of a text may have arisen at any time after the codex became the normal form of book; yet copious marginal scholia are not commonly found until the ninth century.

In t!iis connection it should perhaps be mentioned that Procopius of Gaza (c. 460–c. 530) is supposed to have invented a form of literature that bears some resemblance to scholia, namely the catena, a running commentary on a book of the Bible which puts together the opinions of several previous interpreters, normally with verbatim quotations of their arguments. This invention marked a new stage of biblical studies; but whether the catena is to be regarded as a forerunner of classical scholia or as an imitation of them is a question that has not yet been answered.

The last feature of this period which merits discussion is the progressive narrowing of the range of literature normally read. After the third century it becomes more and more uncommon to find any educated man showing knowledge of the texts that have not come down to the modern world. To explain this fact Wilamowitz formulated the theory that in the second or third century a school syllabus was selected by a prominent schoolmaster, and this became so influential that all schools adopted it. With the general decline of culture and impoverishment of the empire no texts outside this range were read and copied often enough to be guaranteed survival. To take an example: seven plays by Aeschylus and seven by Sophocles were selected, and because of this no others have come down to us; nine or ten plays of Euripides were chosen for reading in school, but in this case a lucky chance led to the survival of a single manuscript containing a number of other plays. Though the theory has much attraction there is reason to think that it presents too schematic a view of the history of texts. An initial objection is that there is no positive evidence as to the identity of the schoolmaster in question. One possible candidate would be Eugenius, who in the fifth century wrote on the colometry of fifteen plays. If this figure is correct it hints already at a selection of nine plays from Euripides and three from each of the other dramatists; but the reduction of the set books to the number of three is more probably a feature of the revised curriculum of late Byzantine schools. However, when so much remains unknown, it would be wrong to lay emphasis on our ignorance of the origin of the selection. More important is the reading of texts outside the syllabus in late antiquity; there are fifth-century fragments of Euripides' *Phaethon* (Paris gr. 107B) and *Melanippe Desmotis* (P. Berol. 5514), and still later fragments of Sappho (P. Berol. 9722) and Callimachus (P. Oxy. 2258), and three of the four documents in question come from the country districts of Egypt, where a taste for reading the less common pagan texts might have been expected to die out at a rather earlier date. By contrast Menander was still being read in the school at Gaza in the sixth century, but did not survive into the Middle Ages. Last and most important, it is clear that not all the losses of ancient literature took place so early. In the ninth century Photius was able to read a large number of prose texts that have subsequently disappeared and are known to us from no source except his own account of them. For these reasons it is perhaps best to abandon the idea that a conscious act of selection by an individual was a primary factor in determining the survival of texts.

By the latter part of the sixth century the decline of learning and culture was serious. The imperial university at Constantinople, refounded by Theodosius II c. 425, and a new clerical academy under the direction of the patriarchate, were the only major educational institutions in the main part of the empire; the school at Alexandria continued, but rather in isolation. The exhausted condition of the empire did nothing to encourage learning, and before any recovery could take place matters were made worse by the religious controversy over icon-worship. For some three centuries there is little record of education and the study of the classics. The iconoclasts were not finally defeated until 843, when a Church council formally restored the traditional practices of image worship. Very few manuscripts of any kind remain from this period, and there is little external evidence about classical studies. The only works of the epoch which deserve mention are those of Choeroboscus, a deacon who may have been a lecturer in grammar at the seminary in Constantinople, and the *Canons* of Theognostus, a lengthy work on orthography from the early ninth century; owing to the change in the pronunciation of Greek, spelling was as much an obstacle to schoolchildren as it is in Britain today.

IV. GREEK TEXTS IN THE ORIENT

Here a brief digression is needed in order to mention a rather
neglected chapter in the history of transmission, the significance of
translations of Greek texts into Oriental languages. At some point
during late antiquity Greek texts began to be translated into Syriac,
activity being centred in the towns of Nisibis and Edessa. The lands
of the eastern Mediterranean are commonly believed to have been
bilingual under the Roman empire. But this view is exaggerated,
and the mass of the population probably spoke little or no Greek.
When the authoress of the *Peregrinatio Egeriae*, a very early account
of pilgrimage, visited the Holy Land about 400, she noted that at
church services the officiating priest conducted the liturgy in
Greek, and an assistant immediately gave the Syriac version of what
he had just said (ch. 47). The Church could only achieve its
purposes by use of the vernacular.

Probably the first text to be translated was the New Testament,
followed shortly by a range of patristic works. The earliest manuscripts of these versions go back to the fourth and fifth centuries,
and it is well known that they are of value to theologians. It comes
as a surprise, however, to find that other forms of Greek literature
were translated. The schools of Nisibis and Edessa are known to
have prepared versions of Aristotle, and a section of Theophrastus'
Meteorology survives in Syriac alone. Philosophy and science were
not the only concerns of the Syrians. They translated some Lucian
and the grammar of Dionysius Thrax, as if attempting to give their
pupils the benefits of a Greek literary education in translation.
These latter translations are not of any great value to the modern
scholar interested in establishing the correct form of the Greek
text; it sometimes happens that the Syriac, instead of helping to
correct the Greek, has to be corrected from it.

Arabic versions of classical texts are perhaps more numerous
than their Syriac counterparts and certainly better known; this may
be due to the accident of survival. The stimulus to make these
translations seems to have come purely from a desire to use the best
handbooks of science and philosophy available, and it is unlikely

that a translation of the Bible preceded that of classical texts. As a rule the translations were made from an existing Syriac version, and so allowance must be made for two stages at which the inaccuracy of a translator could mar the expression of the original. When an Arabic version exists side by side with the Greek tradition one cannot assume as a matter of course that it will substantially help in determining the Greek text. Yet a famous example will show that utter pessimism is unjustified. In Aristotle's *Poetics* the Arabic text, though exceptionally difficult to understand, offers a few readings which the editor must accept and several more which he must consider seriously, a reasonable harvest if the brevity of the treatise is borne in mind. That the *Poetics* should have been translated is a cause of some surprise at first sight; but the explanation of both the Syriac and Arabic renderings may be simply that all the writings of 'the master of those who know' were held to be important enough to justify translation. For the most part, however, it was science and philosophy that interested the Arabs. Plato, Aristotle, and Theophrastus were much studied. The mathematicians received special attention. The version of Apollonius of Perga *On conic sections* is important because several books of it have been lost in the Greek; the same is true of Philo of Byzantium's *Mechanics* and works by Archimedes and Hero of Alexandria. The most recent significant addition to our knowledge in this field is the recovery of the missing portion of the treatise on algebra by Diophantus, found in a manuscript in Meshed. The medical writings of Hippocrates, Galen, and Dioscorides were closely investigated. Research on the Arabic versions of Galen has produced valuable results lately: a missing passage of a known text has been recovered, and in another essay an incomprehensible passage has been restored thanks to the discovery that two pages of the Greek archetype were accidentally reversed when a leaf fell out and was replaced incorrectly. By no means all the versions that are attested have yet been found in Arabic manuscripts; we know of many of them only from references to them in medieval Arabic encyclopedias. But since the study of Arabic manuscripts still has much progress to make there is hope that more versions will be recovered.

What has been said above about the general quality of the translations needs to be qualified in one respect. It is clear that in the ninth century there was one translator whose scholarly attainments were at least equal to those of his contemporaries in Byzantium. Hunain ibn Ishaq (809-73) was competent in Arabic, Persian, Greek, and Syriac, the last apparently being his mother tongue. He began his work as a translator at the age of seventeen, and if his command of languages was already good at that age it seems that he must have grown up in a multilingual community. He appears to have lived in Baghdad, where he founded a school of translators, and he refers to meetings in that city at which Christians gathered to read their ancient literature. Though he does not make it clear whether this reading was of originals or Syriac versions, he does say that Greek communities, perhaps using monasteries as focal points, preserved the use of the language, and that it was possible to find Greek manuscripts all over the Islamic world. He himself searched for them in Mesopotamia, Syria, Palestine, and Egypt. In a letter to a friend who had asked for a detailed list with indications of content of all Greek medical works known to him Hunain gives a long account of his method of work. He writes at length about Galen, and considers particularly which texts have been translated into Syriac only and which into Arabic also, who the translator was, to whom the work was dedicated, and where Greek manuscripts might be found of works not yet translated. His comments on his precedessors are revealing. He frequently claims that they were incompetent in linguistic knowledge, or were certainly working from damaged or illegible manuscripts, a hindrance which Hunain himself had to face from time to time. In such cases he collates the faulty existing version against as many Greek manuscripts as he can find and produces a revised rendering. The quantity of Greek books that he had access to and their damaged condition are emphasized more than once. It is possible that the scrupulous consideration and comparison of divergent texts was a technique that he learnt at least in part from Galen, who employs much the same methods in handling the difficult text of the Hippocratic corpus. Such merit as Arabic versions possess may well be due to the scholarship of Hunain and his associates.

One other language should be mentioned. Translation into

Armenian probably began for the purposes of the Church as it did
in Syria. The Armenian version of the Bible is one of the most
celebrated. In the field of patristic literature some works by Philo
have come down to us in Armenian alone, and the same is true of
part of Eusebius' *Chronicon*. As to classical texts, the translations of
Plato and Dionysius Thrax are mentioned in another context. An
intriguing and tantalizing report suggests that other Greek books of
purely literary and secular character were translated; apart from a
number of historians there is mention of unnamed works by Callimachus. An account of the plot of Euripides' *Peliades* comes from
an Armenian source.

V. THE RENAISSANCE OF THE NINTH CENTURY

The first real achievements of Byzantine scholarship belong to the
middle of the ninth century. There were men of outstanding ability
who were able to exercise their powers to the best advantage in the
more peaceful condition of the empire. The assistant emperor
Bardas revived the imperial university, which had disappeared in
the turmoil of the preceding centuries, by founding a school in the
capital c. 860 under the direction of Leo, a philosopher and
mathematician of distinction; other professors appointed at the
same time were Theodore the geometrician, Theodegius the
astronomer, and Cometas the literary scholar; the last of these may
have specialized in rhetoric and Atticism, but he also prepared a
recension of Homer. Leo's scholarly temperament can be seen from
an episode during his residence on the island of Andros. He met a
learned man who gave him some tuition in rhetoric, philosophy,
and arithmetic; this made him wish to pursue the subjects further
and he crossed over to the mainland in order to search for books in
monastic libraries. His motive is characteristic of the changed
atmosphere in Byzantium; during the Iconoclastic era emperors like
Leo the Armenian had hunted for books merely in order to find
texts which could lend them support in theological controversy.

  The revival of learning coincided with, and was perhaps assisted
by, certain changes in the appearance and production of manu-

scripts. Hitherto books had normally been written in the script known as uncial or biblical majuscule, which had reached its fully developed form as early as the fourth century, and had changed surprisingly little in the course of centuries. Despite its impressive appearance it had the serious disadvantage that it was slow to write and so large that the quantity of text on each page was strictly limited. When the cheaper writing material of the ancient world ceased to be readily available, as the papyrus plantations were either exhausted or used mainly by the Arabs after their conquest of Egypt in 641, the demand for parchment must have increased sharply; even in an age which was not much interested in literature, theological and liturgical texts were required and the needs of the civil service had to be satisfied. To meet this difficulty it appears that the expedient was devised of adapting for use in books the script that had been current for some time in official circles for letters, documents, accounts, and the like; the modern technical term for the revised script is minuscule. It occupied far less space on the page and could be written at high speed by a practised scribe. The first dated example belongs to the year 835, and is known as the Uspensky Gospels (Leningrad gr. 219). As the script of this book is by no means immature or primitive, the adoption of this style should probably be dated at least half a century earlier. The place of its origin is not known for certain, but there are some grounds for thinking that it was popularized by members of the important Stoudios monastery in the capital, which was a well-known centre of book production at a later date. Gradually the uncial hand was abandoned, and by the end of the tenth century it was no longer used except for a few special liturgical books. The new script facilitated the copying of texts by making more economical use of parchment, and not long afterwards the situation was improved by another invention. In 751 the Arabs had taken some Chinese prisoners of war at Samarkand and learnt from them the process of paper-making. Soon Arab production in the East and in Spain reached substantial proportions, and in due course it was exported to Byzantium. Hostilities between the two empires may have had an unfavourable effect on the trade, but there is no doubt that paper came to be widely used in Byzantium, and it seems to have been used in the imperial archives from the middle of the eleventh century.

The transliteration of old uncial books into the new script was energetically undertaken by the scholars of the ninth century. It is largely owing to their activity that Greek literature can still be read, for the text of almost all authors depends ultimately on one or more books written in minuscule script at this date or shortly after, from which all later copies are derived; the quantity of literature that is available to us from the papyri and the uncial manuscripts is only a small proportion of the whole. In the process of transliteration mistakes were sometimes made, especially by misreading letters that were similar in the uncial script and therefore easily confused. At many points in Greek texts there are errors common to all the extant manuscripts which appear to derive from the same source, and this source is usually taken to be a ninth-century copy. A further assumption generally made is that one minuscule copy was made from one uncial copy. The uncial book was then discarded, and the minuscule book became the source of all further copies. The theory has a certain a priori justification on two grounds, since the task of transliteration from a script that was becoming less and less familiar would not be willingly undertaken more often than was absolutely necessary, and there is at least some likelihood that after the destruction of the previous centuries many texts survived in one copy only. But these arguments do not amount to proof, and there are cases which can only be explained by more complicated hypotheses. In the tradition of Plato one manuscript (Vienna, supp. gr. 39) differs greatly from all others in its errors, and it is difficult to believe it derived from the same ninth-century exemplar; it may derive from the transliteration of a different uncial book, so that at least two old books would seem to have survived the Dark Ages. A confirmation of this is that when a Greek text has been translated into an Oriental language at an early date, perhaps the fifth century, the readings which are characteristic of the Oriental translation may occur also in a small group of the Greek manuscripts. This is true of the Armenian version of some of Plato's dialogues, the Arabic version of Aristotle's *Poetics*, and the Syriac translation of Saint Gregory of Nyssa's *De virginitate*. Another argument pointing in the same direction can be drawn from the difficulty which arises in the study of the manuscripts of some texts that were very frequently read during the Middle Ages, such as the Euripidean plays included in the school curriculum. Here the relation of the manuscripts cannot be established precisely by the usual method, since they do not fall into clearly defined groups that coincide regularly in error. This situation presupposes that medieval scholars and schoolmasters frequently compared their own copy of the text with others and made alterations or added variant readings above the line; this process is known as contamination or horizontal transmission. In such cases it may be that more than one copy survived the Dark Ages to be transcribed, so that two or more transliterations took place; alternatively, only one transliteration was made but this copy was deposited in some central place where it was consulted by interested readers and received as marginal additions the variant readings that had been found in other copies. It is easy to imagine, though there is no external evidence for the assumption, that such deposits of semi-official copies took place in the library of the academy set up by Bardas. It is also possible that similar copies existed in the patriarchal academy, for there is a manuscript of Plato's *Laws* (Vat. gr. 1) written in the early tenth century with marginal variants added in the next century by a scholar who refers to these additional readings as coming from 'the patriarch's book'; unfortunately we cannot be sure whether this was a private copy or part of the library in the seminary.

The Bardas school was founded under favourable conditions, and was probably the centre of a lively group of scholars concerned to recover and disseminate classical texts of many different kinds. Yet it does not seem to have had the influence that might have been expected, for there is very little reference to it at later dates. Its professors are completely overshadowed by their contemporary Photius (c. 810–c. 893), a man of remarkable attainments who is perhaps as important for his position in the Church and the affairs of the government as for his devoted encouragement of learning. Twice he held the patriarchal throne of Constantinople (858–67, 877–86), and in these years some of the negotiations which led to schism between the Eastern and Roman churches took place; it is

only one of the consequences of this schism that efforts to obtain
assistance for the weakened empire of the fourteenth and fifteenth
centuries were seriously impeded by the estrangement of the two
churches. For our purpose, however, the most interesting phase of
Photius' life is the time before his sudden and rapid elevation to the
patriarchate (he was still a layman until a week before the appointment). As a young man he had always been a keen student of a wide
range of subjects, and from an early age succeeded in leading two
different careers simultaneously. Jealousy and spite gave rise to a
tradition that, rather like Faust, he achieved his knowledge by
making a bargain with a Jewish magician, giving up his Christian
faith in return for success, learning, and riches. He was much in
favour at the court, and occupied positions of trust in the circle of
the emperor; but apart from this he conducted a kind of private
literary club. One of his duties was to take part in a diplomatic
mission—the date is uncertain, but it may have been 855—with the
task of negotiating an exchange of prisoners of war with the Arab
government. Before going on the long and dangerous journey
Photius wrote, as an offering and consolation to his brother
Tarasius, a summary of books that he had read over a long period of
time, omitting some standard texts that Tarasius might have been
expected to know. The resulting work, known as the *Bibliotheca*
(this title is not due to its author), is a fascinating production, in
which Photius shows himself the inventor of the book-review. In
280 sections which vary in length from a single sentence to many
pages Photius summarizes and comments on a wide selection of
pagan and Christian texts (the proportions are nearly equal, and
122 sections deal with secular texts). He claims to have compiled it
from memory, but it is generally regarded as a revised version of the
notes he had made in the course of his reading in the last twenty
years. It is not arranged according to any plan. Photius claims that
the order of the authors reviewed is that in which they occurred to
him, and he had not the time to be more systematic. The text
exhibits lacunae and duplications. Its oddly unfinished state makes
one wonder if the embassy did not actually take place, so that
Photius never bothered to finish his work once the original reason
for composing it had disappeared. Its value to the modern scholar is

that Photius summarizes many books that are now lost: that applies for example to some twenty of the thirty-three historians he discusses. Much can be learnt of the interests of a prominent Byzantine figure of the time: in the secular texts historians are most numerous, but among others there are orators, novelists, and compilers of Atticist dictionaries. The latter are significant, for they show the author's concern with stylistic considerations, which is also shown by his frequent brief characterizations of the style of an author; the desire to write and appreciate a good Attic style was never far from the thoughts of Byzantine literati. The breadth of Photius' interests is enormous. That a pious man and future patriarch should bother to read the Greek novelists is surprising; he enjoyed them linguistically, but could not bring himself to be favourable to their contents. It is also notable that he read heretics and anti-Christian writers; this is incidentally a strong argument against the notion that the ecclesiastical authorities attempted to impose a censorship. Philosophy is not well represented in the *Bibliotheca*, but there is evidence of his knowledge in this field elsewhere in his works. The most serious limitation of taste shown in the book is the almost complete absence of poetry. One wonders whether in this respect it is a true record of Photius' own reading. We know from his letters that he had read Aristophanes, *Plutus* and Aeschylus, *Prometheus Vinctus*; these and other school texts he might well omit because they were set books already known to his brother. But it looks as if other poetry did not interest him much, and perhaps it had little appeal to intellectuals of his generation.

Another work deserving mention here is his *Lexicon*, the first complete copy of which was discovered in 1959 in a remote monastery in Macedonia. It is a typical work of its class, valuable for its brief quotations of classical texts not now available. The purpose was to amalgamate and revise various existing books of the same kind; in the *Bibliotheca* Photius remarks how useful such a book would be. In his Atticism he was moderate and willingly admitted words from poetic sources if they seemed the most expressive means of conveying a notion. These quotations from the poets do not imply a reading of the full text, but were probably drawn as such from his sources. Besides this lexicon he was partly responsible for

the compilation of a supplement to another, and he further shows
his stylistic pedantry by correcting the usage of friends' letters.

Photius' interest in textual criticism can be demonstrated from a
discussion of difficult passages in the Bible. He notes that the difference of a single letter or a wrongly placed punctuation mark is sufficient to give rise to heresy, and he cites examples, adding that
similar considerations apply to classical texts (*Amphilochia* 1, *PG*
101.84ff.)

The sudden appearance of so distinguished a person after the
obscurity that had previously reigned is remarkable; it is all the
more strange that nothing is known of the identity of his tutors, nor
of the sources from which he was able to acquire knowledge of so
many rare texts. From this time onwards, as a result of the activity
in Photius' salon and in various schools, there is a practically con-
tinuous tradition of classical studies in Byzantium. Literary texts
were copied regularly and more technical works, especially
mathematical and medical, were much studied, not least because
they were still in general the best textbooks available. The first
major result of these new stimuli to scholarship can be seen in
Arethas (c. 860–c. 935), who became archbishop of Caesarea in Cappadocia; again it is a churchman who shows great interest in
learning.

Whereas Photius' own books do not survive, or at least have not
been identified, several volumes from the library of Arethas still
exist, and copies derived from other lost volumes are known, so that
a good picture of his collection can be obtained. The preserved
volumes are masterpieces of calligraphy on fine quality parchment,
and it happens that the prices of some of them were recorded by
the original owner. For his Euclid (D'Orville 301, A.D. 888) he paid
14 gold pieces; the cost of his Plato, a thicker volume of larger
format (E. D. Clarke 39, A.D. 895, Plate III), was 21 pieces. In relation
to contemporary incomes such prices are an indication of the high
cost of a book; civil service salaries started at 72 gold pieces per
annum, and might rise in exceptional circumstances to 3,500. Book
collecting was not a hobby for men of modest means.

Arethas commissioned books from professional scribes, in the
main monks of monasteries which accepted regular orders on

a commercial basis, and he then wrote a large amount of commentary in the margins in his own hand (Plate III). Though he was not a critic of great power or originality these marginal commentaries are valuable because they were drawn from good sources; the notes in his copies of Plato and Lucian are examples of this. Surviving volumes of his library include Plato, Euclid, Aristotle's *Organon*, Aristides, Lucian, and some Christian writers. Others that can be inferred from various evidence are Pausanias, Dio Chrysostom, and Marcus Aurelius; the last of these was probably the exemplar which ensured the further survival of this text. Once again there is an absence of interest in poetry, while Atticist writers are well represented; but Arethas evidently differs from Photius by showing no taste for historical writing.

The sources of Arethas' collection are unknown. The copies of Plato and Euclid were acquired while he was a deacon. At this date he was probably living in the capital, where copies of most authors must have been readily available for some time. For rarer texts it may have been necessary to look further afield, but we do not possess any information about the book trade that throws light on Arethas' acquisitions. However, since a historian of c. 800, George Syncellus, refers to old and valuable books coming from Caesarea in Cappadocia, one may speculate that when Arethas visited his archbishopric he made some discoveries there.

VI. THE LATER BYZANTINE PERIOD

With the death of Arethas some time in the thirties of the tenth century a new period begins, in which eminent scholars and bibliophiles are much more difficult to identify. Some stimulus to learning was given by the activity of the erudite emperor Constantine VII Porphyrogenitus (913–59). During a long period of enforced semi-retirement he compiled various manuals of statecraft which survive partially. These took the form of encyclopedic compilations based on a very wide range of historical sources, and as such are of some importance to classical scholars, since many of the texts do not survive elsewhere. This great activity of Constantine was doubtless not carried out by him single-handed, but nothing is known of the collaborators. Shortly afterwards, perhaps in the reign of John Tzimisces (969–76), the collaboration of scholars resulted in a work which is of value for much the same reason as the works of Constantine; this is the *Suda*, less correctly known as Suidas (as if it were a proper name), which might be best described as a combination of dictionary and elementary encyclopedia. It has articles on a great number of classical personages and topics, and despite a certain amount of dubious or erroneous material transmits much useful information. Some of its sources can be traced; among those most frequently used are the text and scholia to Aristophanes, for which the *Suda* is in effect a fairly important witness. However, it is the lost sources, some not now easily identifiable, which give it its value. Though the intelligence of the authors cannot be rated very highly, their work does mark some advance, in so far as it is considerably more than a lexicon of Attic diction and is one of the earliest books with a claim to the title of encyclopedia, and perhaps the earliest encyclopedia to have alphabetical arrangement.

It should not be assumed that because individual scholars of this date remain unknown, the impetus given to literary studies by Photius had entirely ceased to have effect. Extant manuscripts of classical texts make it clear that even in the early tenth century poets other than Homer and the dramatists were being read; the earliest copies of Theognis (Paris supp. gr. 388) and Musaeus (Barocci 50) almost certainly belong to this date. Other poetic texts were being read by the middle of the century or a little later, and in fact some of the most valuable of all surviving manuscripts are the result of this activity; one may give as instances the text of the Greek Anthology, sometimes known as the *Palatine Anthology*, which serves to distinguish it from the anthology later composed by Planudes (Heidelberg gr. 23 + Paris supp. gr. 384); the Venice *Iliad* (Marc. gr. 454, Plate II), the importance of which is even greater for the scholia than for the text; the Ravenna Aristophanes, which is the only medieval manuscript to contain all eleven plays (Ravenna gr. 429); Laur. 32.9, which besides being the only medieval copy of all seven plays of Aeschylus is also of fundamental importance for the texts of Sophocles and Apollonius Rhodius. Prose authors were not neglected, and we can instance the leading manuscript of Polybius, written by the monk Ephraem, probably in 947 (Vat. gr. 124), and two copies of Demosthenes (Paris gr. 2935 and Laur. 59.9). These three codices were written by scribes whose hands can be identified elsewhere, and thus we can form some impression of the range of books written by a single scribe, even if they were often commissioned works and hence not representative of the scribes' own interests. Ephraem can be identified as the scribe of three other books: Venice, Marc. gr. 201, Aristotle's *Organon*, A.D. 954; Athos, Lavra 184, *Acts* and *Epistles*, undated; Athos, Vatopedi 747, Gospels, A.D. 948. The Paris Demosthenes was mainly written by the scribe of the Plato mentioned earlier (Vat. gr. 1), while the other Demosthenes is probably in the same hand as the Ravenna MS. of Aristophanes. Many manuscripts of classical authors written at various dates in the Byzantine period can be connected in this way by identification of the scribe's hand. Though the surviving books may not be more than a small proportion of those copied, the number of possible identifications does suggest that the copying of ancient texts was in the hands of quite a small group of scholars, schoolmasters, and professional scribes.

Classical learning and education continued in the eleventh century much as before. The major change of this epoch consisted of a reorganization of the imperial university; whether this was provoked by a decline in the institution in the form that Bardas had given it is unknown, but the new arrangement included the setting up of a faculty of law and another of philosophy. The changes were made under the aegis of the emperor Constantine IX Monomachus, perhaps in 1047. The law school does not concern us here, except to note that its foundation antedates by some years that of the famous faculty at Bologna, from which modern law faculties ultimately derive their origin. The philosophical school, which also gave instruction in grammar, rhetoric and literary subjects, was under the direction of Michael Psellus (1018–78), much the most versatile man of his generation, who distinguished himself as civil servant, senior adviser to several emperors, historian, and academic philosopher. His literary output attests his wide reading of the classics, but his intellectual interests were rather more in philosophy, and his eminence as a lecturer and teacher led to a renewed interest in Plato and to a lesser extent Aristotle. The fortunes of the school were not entirely favourable. For reasons which may have been as much political as intellectual Psellus fell into disfavour at the court, and had to retire to a monastery for a time; but he returned to important positions in due course, and it is likely that the school continued its work.

Although most of Psellus' literary output falls outside the scope of the present book, there are about half a dozen essays, all except one very brief, which show him as a man of letters with a strong interest in both pagan and patristic literature, and are probably more revealing than other statements by Byzantine writers about themselves. Like Photius he was interested in the Greek novel and gave a not unintelligent comparison of Heliodorus and Achilles Tatius. In an analysis of the style of his own writings he acknowledges a debt to several classical models that he had studied, mentioning the stylistic qualities that struck him most in Demosthenes, Isocrates, Aristides, Thucydides, Plutarch, and Lysias; the only patristic author mentioned in this company is Gregory of Nazianzus. His characterizations of the styles of the Cappadocian Fathers and John Chrysostom are not outstanding as literary criticism, but they contain one revealing description of the sensitivity of a cultivated Byzantine reader to the sound of formal prose. Psellus confesses that in reading Gregory of Nazianzus 'every time I read him, and I turn to his work frequently, mainly for its Christian teaching but also for its literary charm, I am filled by an indescribable beauty and grace; and I often abandon my purpose and, forgetting the theological meaning, luxuriate in the rose-gardens of his diction, being carried away by my sensations; and knowing that I have been carried away I adore and venerate the writer who has carried me off'. We may suspect that in this capacity to savour the rhetoric of formal prose Psellus was typical of the literary élite. Whether he or any other Byzantines could gain much from classical poetry must remain doubtful in the extreme. One of the shortest of the essays is a perfectly serious consideration of the question put to him whether Euripides is superior as a writer of verse to George of Pisidia, who in the seventh century had written iambic verses on the classical pattern to celebrate the exploits of the emperor Heraclius and on some theological themes. Although the text of the essay is not easy to interpret it seems clear that Psellus fails to consider the difference between dramatic and narrative verse and to indicate the derivative mediocrity of the Byzantine writer.

A further revival of philosophy, this time with Aristotle as the main author for study, can perhaps be traced to the early twelfth century. Anna Comnena, the princess who was forced to live in the seclusion of a monastery and composed a famous *History*, was connected with two scholars who wrote commentaries on Aristotle, Eustratius of Nicaea and Michael of Ephesus. The most interesting fact about this activity is that their treatises are devoted not only to the *Politics* and *Ethics* but also to the zoological works; these latter texts had not yet been supplied with commentaries, despite the enormous amount of study of Aristotle that had taken place in the ancient world and early Byzantine period. It rather looks as if Anna may have noticed this gap and decided to commission the necessary commentaries. She may also be ultimately responsible for the composition of two commentaries on the *Rhetoric*.

From the twelfth century onwards the story can be carried forward once more by reference to outstanding individuals. Undoubtedly the most eminent figure in the scholarship of this age was Eustathius (c. 1115–c. 1195), who after being the professor of rhetoric in the patriarch's seminary in the capital was appointed to the archbishopric of Thessalonica c. 1175. During his teaching career in the capital he must be assumed to have accomplished most of his scholarly work. The libraries of Constantinople almost certainly still held treasures not yet exploited by men of learning, or at any rate not read by anyone since Photius; and one may suspect that Eustathius did not entirely relish the promotion which removed him to another city; though important, Thessalonica does not seem to have been at that date a centre of intellectual life. His interest in classics did not prevent him from taking his clerical duties seriously, and we still possess a treatise by him on the reform of the monastic life; among other things it shows that most monks had no interest in books or learning and were unworthy of their

vows, and the bibliophile in Eustathius comes out in an anecdote he
tells of an abbot who sold a beautiful calligraphic copy of Saint
Gregory of Nazianzus because his monastery had no use for it. This
section of the tract serves to remind us that the tradition of learning
was alien to the spirit of many members of the Church, however
much high prelates set an example by their display of deep learning.
Eustathius himself knew a number of texts that have since been lost
and would be useful to us if still preserved. This is apparent from his
use of otherwise unknown sources in his commentaries. There is a
famous passage in which he quotes a few lines of Sophocles'
Antigone, referring to 'good copies' (ἀκριβῆ ἀντίγραφα) which give
the full text of lines 1165–8, whereas all the manuscripts of
Sophocles now reduce the passage to incoherence by omitting one
of the lines. Eustathius had evidently noted the unsatisfactory state
of the text and gives us the impression that he had compared other
copies until he found one with the right text. However, the complete text of the Sophoclean passage is also given by Athenaeus, an
author known to Eustathius, and close study of minor variants in
the quotations now makes it seem likely that Eustathius derived his
knowledge entirely from Athenaeus. His awareness of the difficulty
nevertheless proves his high level of scholarly ability. It seems quite
likely, to judge from a remark in his introduction to Pindar, that he
read more of the *Epinicia* than we possess today.

His major works were his commentaries on classical authors.
What he wrote on Pindar does not survive except for the introduction, and of his notes to Aristophanes no more is known than
minute fragments preserved in late manuscripts. But we have his
notes to Dionysius Periegetes, a late poet of little merit who wrote
an account of geography in about 1,000 hexameters; these verses
have come down to us in so many manuscripts that they must be
presumed to have served as the textbook of geography in Byzantine
schools. More important and much more voluminous are his commentaries on Homer; that on the *Iliad* fills about 1,400 large pages
of print in the Leipzig edition of 1827–30. Both these commentaries
are essentially compilations, with very little that has been contributed by Eustathius himself. The scale of the commentaries, especially that on Homer, is enormous; the discussion of the first line of

the *Iliad* runs to 10 pages, and if even a modest proportion of this was ever used by a teacher in the Byzantine classroom, the result must have been to confuse the pupil by a mass of learning of dubious relevance and at the same time to prevent him reading through the text at a pace sufficient to yield some enjoyment. Eustathius is fond of allegorical interpretations, and criticizes Aristarchus for not adopting them. The work is useful to the modern scholar occasionally, but only because of those qualities which made it unduly cumbersome for the author's contemporaries; as far as relevance is concerned it is no advance on the average standard of commentary produced in the ancient world.

Two of Eustathius' lesser contemporaries deserve mention. John Tzetzes (c. 1110–80) was not in holy orders but appears to have run a school in Constantinople. Apart from some letters which reveal a good deal about his personality and day-to-day life his writings include commentaries on three plays of Aristophanes, Hesiod, and part of Homer. He is inferior to Eustathius in knowledge and intelligence, and is quite unjustifiably conceited about his own attainments: it is not easy to respect the man who in the middle of a note on Aristophanes (*Plutus* 677) states that he would not lengthen his explanation but for the fact that there is a good deal of space left on the present page of his book. Nevertheless the allusions in his letters show his wide reading, and we know that he attended meetings at which interpretations of classical texts were discussed; more information about this philological club would be very welcome. Like Eustathius he too had read some books that we no longer have, including some Callimachus and Hipponax. The same is true of Michael Choniates (less correctly known as Acominatus), a somewhat younger man who corresponded with Eustathius and like him was elevated to a bishopric at some distance from the capital, in this case Athens. In his letters he bemoans his fate; to have the use of the undamaged Parthenon as his cathedral was no compensation for the loss of educated society, and his congregations of ignorant peasants were incapable of appreciating the beauties of his high-flown Atticist sermons. But he was the proud owner of one very rare book no longer extant, the *Hecale* of Callimachus, and delighted in quoting from it in his letters. He and

Tzetzes are the latest Byzantines of whom we can say with certainty that they could read more classical poetry than we can.

The reason for this lies in an event of the utmost importance which Michael Choniates lived to see, the capture and sack of Constantinople by the Fourth Crusade in 1204. Great damage was done, and there is little doubt that libraries suffered severely. For the historian of literature this sack of the city was a greater disaster than the more famous one of 1453. In 1204 the rare texts mentioned in the previous paragraph were destroyed; at any rate there is no trace of them when the seat of government was restored to Constantinople in 1261 after the fall of the Latin kingdom. If the events of 1204 had not taken place these texts might well have found their way to the West through the agency of the numerous Italian visitors and book collectors who went to Greece and brought back manuscripts. By the time that the city fell into the hands of the Turks little remained to be discovered by the collectors; the only substantial and well-attested loss is recorded in the statement of Constantine Lascaris that a complete copy of the *Universal History* by Diodorus Siculus was destroyed by the Turks.

While the capital was occupied by the Franks and most of Greece was parcelled out among Western barons, the Byzantine administration dragged out a precarious existence at Nicaea, preserving the empire's possessions in Asia Minor. Despite the drastic reduction in the wealth and power of the empire this period of exile in Nicaea was by no means one of the worst for literary studies. The emperors John Vatatzes and Theodore Ducas Lascaris were concerned to promote schools and libraries and eventually built up quite a tradition of secondary education. Little is known in detail, since very few manuscripts can be identified as having been written in the Nicaean empire, but it seems clear that poets and orators were studied, and some of Theodore's own letters display cultivated and scholarly attitudes. Other scholarly work was done by the monk Nicephorus Blemmydes (c. 1197–c. 1272), who wrote on many topics, including logic, physics, and geography, and made a journey to parts of the old empire now under Latin control in search of books that could not be found in Asia Minor. This is one of the few short periods in which literary studies flourished outside the capital. It is also

possible that the thirteenth century was an age of considerable
culture in the outlying Byzantine province in the heel of Italy; Sicily
and the extreme south of Italy were largely Greek in speech during
the Middle Ages, and a good deal is known about the history of the
numerous Greek monasteries there from the tenth century
onwards. The part of this territory most closely in contact with
Constantinople was the district of Otranto, where there was a
famous monastery of Saint Nicholas that maintained a school and a
large library. A number of books written there and in the neighbouring towns of Nardò and Gallipoli do suggest a reasonably flourishing state of school education; there are copies of Homer, Hesiod,
and Aristotle safely attributable to these centres, and a number of
other books, including some lexica, may have been written there.
But there is no trace of any advanced scholarship or any attempt to
write commentaries on classical authors.

The Latin kingdoms in Constantinople and Greece were brought
to an end in 1261, and the Greek emperors reigned once again from
their traditional capital; but their empire was reduced in size and
power, being gradually whittled away by the invasions of the Turks
on the eastern side and the encroachment of Italian trading states
such as Genoa and Venice, which established settlements in the
capital and elsewhere; mercenaries hired to assist the empire often
did more harm than good, as for instance a band of Catalans who
did an immense amount of damage before setting up a small independent state in Athens. Nevertheless the late thirteenth and
early fourteenth centuries saw some of the best Byzantine work on
classical texts. Though little is known in detail of how education
was organized, there appear to have been several schools in Constantinople and Thessalonica, presided over by men of learning. In
an account of this brevity there is not room to describe more than
two of them. The first is the monk Maximus Planudes (c. 1255–c.
1305), who worked in the capital and achieved much in a rather
short life. Besides running a school for a time he was sent on a
diplomatic mission to Venice, and either before or during this
acquired a good working knowledge of Latin, an exceptionally rare
attainment in Byzantium (otherwise it appears to have been confined to a few lawyers and interpreters). He read widely in Latin,

evidently with considerable interest, for he prepared a large number of translations, among which figure Augustine, Boethius, Macrobius and very remarkably Ovid's *Heroides, Metamorphoses,* and amatory works. Not all these translations have yet been printed, but it has been plausibly suggested that those of the theological works might yet prove useful as an introduction for Greek theologians to the Latin fathers; the conservatism of the Greek literary language is such that Planudes' versions might still be understood without much difficulty. This first attempt by a Byzantine scholar to make contact with the West for purposes other than trade agreements or religious disputation had no immediate result; but in the next century the monk Demetrius Cydones continued the task of translation with some works of Aquinas, and a traffic of ideas moving in the opposite direction was continued by the Italians who came to Constantinople to learn Greek (one or two Italians had made the journey as early as the twelfth century). Of more practical and immediate importance was Planudes' study of Greek texts. He is generally thought to have been responsible for the production of a large volume (preserved in Florence as Laur. 32.16) containing a collection of classical poetry, which includes several school authors and the much more recherché *Dionysiaca* of Nonnus. His interests were far from being confined to the usual range of school texts; we find him conducting a successful search for Plutarch's works, of which he compiled a catalogue, and he drew up a revised version of the Greek Anthology which includes quite a number of epigrams that do not occur in the Palatine manuscript; of this latter work his autograph is now in Venice (Marc. gr. 481). His method of dealing with texts is open to two criticisms. He bowdlerized Ovid, altering words such as *amor* or *Venus* with results which are laughable or worse; and he also omitted from the anthology of epigrams poems which he thought unsuitable. His other shortcoming is seen in his dealings with the didactic poem on astronomy by Aratus (c. 315– c. 240 B.C.), which was probably used as a textbook on astronomy if the subject was taught in school. His autograph copy has now been identified (Edinburgh, Advocates' Library 18.7.15). Planudes could not resist the temptation to revise some parts of the text which were factually inaccurate. Instead of simply recording in a commentary the advances in knowledge, he replaced lines 481–96, 501–6, and 515–24 by passages of his own composition (Plate VI). Further information about his interests can be gleaned from his letters. He mentions manuscripts of the abstruse mathematical writer Diophantus, and we know that he was interested in other scientific authors such as Ptolemy and Euclid (he may have been responsible for reconstructing the maps in Ptolemy's *Geography*); he also wrote a pamphlet about the introduction of Arabic numerals (in general the Greeks still used the cumbrous alphabetic system of numerals). Another feature of his letters worthy of mention is that he frequently requests one of his correspondents who lives in Asia Minor to obtain for him some parchment, and is irritated when his friend can do no better than find him some asses' skins. The shortage of writing material experienced by one working in or near the capital is very surprising. It may be worth noting in passing that though he had been employed by the emperor on an embassy and was clearly a scholar of distinction, there is no sign that he ever obtained imperial patronage or support for his scholarly work, and this is generally true of Byzantine scholars with the partial exception of those working under the kingdom of Nicaea.

The width of Planudes' interests makes it tempting to suppose that he knew something of each of the seven liberal arts, which in turn provokes the question whether the Byzantines accepted a theory of education corresponding to the *trivium* and *quadrivium* of Western Europe. Although there are sporadic references in Byzantine authors of various dates to the *quadrivium* (τετρακτύς), the evidence is not sufficient to allow a clear answer to the question.

Rather less catholic in his tastes but no less important as a scholar than Planudes was Demetrius Triclinius, a schoolmaster who is known to have lived in Thessalonica c. 1305–20. His work on the standard poetic texts of the curriculum can be traced partly through autographs that survive and partly in the numerous later books which contain commentaries headed by his name (Plate VII). His claim to a place of honour in the history of scholarship is that he was the first Byzantine both to have a grasp of the metres of classical poetry and to exploit his knowledge. All his predecessors had either virtually ignored metrical questions or had failed to

appreciate the potential utility of the subject for a student of
classical poetry. But Triclinius came across a copy of the ancient
metrical treatise by Hephaestion and grasped the essentials of it
with a view to correcting the many passages in classical texts
which were suspect or undoubtedly corrupt. It seems likely that
he or his elder contemporaries were the first to emend texts
systematically, and in the case of Triclinius enough documents
survive to allow us a view of him at work. Though his knowledge
of metre was by no means perfect he could correct iambics; sometimes he achieved a result that has won the general approval of
modern critics, but often he resorted to facile measures such as
the insertion of stopgap words to heal a metrical fault, and it is
evident that he was not sensitive to questions of linguistic style in
classical poetry. In more complicated metres than iambics he was
less sure of his ground, but had one vital weapon: he knew that
the lyrics of the chorus in tragedy and comedy were intended to
have exact metrical responsion, and the text of Euripides which
contains his autograph corrections (Laur. 32.2) shows him willing
to use Procrustean violence in order to achieve the desired result
(see p. 232). Despite his many mistakes in the use of his knowledge it remains the most important step forward in the treatment
of poetic texts at this date. Textual criticism was thus raised again
to the level which it had reached in the ancient world, but the
task awaiting the critic had increased, since the practice of
copying by hand for a millennium and more had necessarily introduced many new errors into the texts.

Triclinius' other main work was a redrafting of the scholia on
various authors. He sifted the material of the old scholia and
selected what he believed to be most useful for school instruction.
The resulting new commentary contained a certain number of additional glosses or other elementary notes added by himself, and it
tended to omit or reduce parts of the scholia which are most valuable for modern scholars; ancient learning was not always directly
relevant to the text and Triclinius did not have the modern
scholar's reasons for wishing to preserve it. Being conscious of the
importance of his metrical knowledge he composed a separate
metrical commentary on many plays; in the case of Aristophanes he

had some guidance from the ancient metrical commentary by Heliodorus which survived in the old scholia. In his autograph copies he arranged in separate columns the metrical commentary of his own composition and the old scholia which he had revised.

By his work on text and scholia, which was on the whole more thorough and competent than that of his colleagues, Triclinius deserves to be counted as the forerunner of modern editors. Like other scholars he hunted for fresh manuscripts in the hope of improving the texts. In his notes he refers to the different readings that he had found, sometimes remarking that they came from old copies. On one occasion his searches appear to have been rewarded by a dramatic discovery: he came across a text of nine plays of Euripides that were otherwise almost unknown in Byzantium; the copies of this book that he had prepared by his pupils or in a local scriptorium, to which he added a good many alterations in his own hand, are our only source for the text of these plays. We therefore owe largely to Triclinius our knowledge of about half the surviving work of Euripides.

Planudes and Triclinius may be selected as the most important representatives of their age, and the latest Byzantines whose activities had any lasting effect on classical texts. Though they were not followed by men of comparable ability, they were not without colleagues and rivals in their own day, and the work of the latter can be seen in much the same way from surviving manuscripts. Some manuscripts of this comparatively late date are important for the constitution of texts. They contain good readings which are either due to the acumen of contemporary scholars or represent branches of tradition that cannot be traced earlier; the latter explanation is now thought to be more likely, because many obvious faults were left uncorrected even by the best scholars. Classical studies enjoyed great popularity; not only the literature was being read, but technical and scientific works written in antiquity were still sufficiently up to date to demand and reward attention. With some justification the period is referred to as the Palaeologan Renaissance, the name being drawn from that of the ruling house of the time. Secondary education seems to have increased substantially although the general condition of the empire was anything but satisfactory. Schoolmasters devoted themselves to the elucidation or correction of texts that can scarcely have formed part of the regular school curriculum; we have seen for instance how Planudes worked on Nonnus and scientific texts, while Triclinius' study of the newly found Euripidean plays apparently had no bearing on the school programme, for there is no evidence that any of them was added to the normal syllabus. This consisted of Attic or Atticist prose writers, textbooks of the art of rhetoric, especially Hermogenes and Aphthonios, and the poets, primarily Homer (Plate IV) and the selected plays of tragedy and comedy. By the late thirteenth century it had become the custom to read three plays of each tragedian and Aristophanes, sometimes known as the 'triad'; the habit may go back to the twelfth century or earlier, for Tzetzes composed a full commentary on only the three Aristophanic comedies that later were standard reading. Most manuscripts of these four authors contain only the triad; some of the later manuscripts have only one or two plays, which may well be an indication that the curriculum had been still further reduced. The plays outside the triad might easily have been lost through neglect, but fortunately they were preserved just long enough to be rescued by the Italian visitors and collectors of the Renaissance; all the most important manuscripts of these texts reached Italy during the Renaissance and many are still to be found there. The dramatic texts are only one instance of a general process. The chief merit of the Byzantines was that they took an interest in a wide range of classical texts and thus preserved them until scholars of another nation were in a position to use and appreciate them. The tradition of scholarship was taken up by the Italian humanists, who resembled their Byzantine colleagues in many ways. A vast number of manuscripts were brought back from the Byzantine empire in the last century of its history, and the collectors were active long after, so that today the libraries of the Greek East are virtually denuded of classical texts. This process was undoubtedly necessary in order to ensure the survival of Greek literature.

3

THE LATIN WEST

1. THE DARK AGES

The sixth century saw the final collapse of what remained of the
Roman empire in the West. In Italy the relatively enlightened rule
of Theodoric (493–526) was given distinction by the two most
notable figures of the transition period from the ancient to the
medieval world, Boethius and Cassiodorus; but it was followed by
the destruction of the Ostrogothic kingdom by the Byzantines and
a spectacular cultural decline. The provinces were to fare little
better. North Africa, now in Vandal hands, was soon to pass beyond
the pale of Western culture; some of its literary achievement, such
as the *Latin Anthology*, was transmitted in time to Europe and so to
posterity. Spain, prey to external attack and internal strife, was to
see a revival of Visigothic culture in the later sixth and early seventh
centuries, reaching a modest peak in Isidore of Seville, but it too
was to succumb in the early eighth century to the Moslem invaders.
Though traces of the older Roman culture lingered on among the
upper classes in Gaul, the Frankish Merovingian dynasty founded
by Clovis (481–511) was grotesquely ill-suited to foster any cultural
continuity.

The ravages of conquest and barbarism made the prospects for
cultural life extremely bleak, and within the narrowing world of
culture the place allotted to classical Latin literature was insecure.
Education and the care of books were rapidly passing into the
hands of the Church, and the Christians of this period had little
time for pagan literature. Decimated by the continued destruction
of war, faced by hostility or neglect at the hands of the new intellectuals, the Latin classics seemed to have a slim chance of survival.

But the fundamental condition for their survival obtained: there
were still books. We do not know how much survived of the

Monastic and other centres of Western Europe

twenty-eight public libraries of which Rome could boast in the fourth century; but there were remnants at least of the great private libraries of the age of the Symmachi, there were important collections in such ecclesiastical centres as Rome and Ravenna and Verona, and books were beginning to find a refuge in the monasteries. The luxury copies of Vergil show that the book trade had flourished down to the end of the fifth century, and the beautiful monastic productions that survive from sixth-century Italy demonstrate that nothing had been lost in the art of producing books when it passed into the hands of the Church. The cultural and intellectual surge that extended from the late fourth to the early sixth century had consolidated such a firm infrastructure of books and learning that, battered though it was by the political upheavals that transformed the Roman world and the years of neglect that followed, as the traditional Roman aristocracy was replaced by a new class with different tastes in reading, there was still a substantial inheritance to be rescued and reconstituted when the next renaissance came. Many of the capital and uncial manuscripts of this period have survived, some of them very splendid; in most cases we have only fragments of these books, but their contents include Plautus and Terence, Vergil, Ovid, Lucan, Persius, and Juvenal, a varied selection of Cicero's works, Sallust, Livy, the Elder and Younger Pliny, tragedies and prose works of Seneca, Fronto. Much of early Latin literature had probably been lost, but it is clear from the surviving books and the evidence of the writers and grammarians of the age that it was still possible in the year 500, at least in Italy, to obtain copies of most Latin authors; and other parts of the Roman world may have not lagged far behind. As late as the sixth century Johannes Lydus at Constantinople had more complete texts than we have of Seneca's *Natural Questions* and Suetonius' *Lives of the Caesars*; in Africa Fulgentius was able to cite passages of Petronius that have not come down to us; and in what is now Portugal, Martin, bishop of Braga, was able to plagiarize a lost work of Seneca that could barely have survived him.

The bulk of Latin literature was still extant; moreover, the machinery for its transmission to later ages was already being set up in the shape of the monastic library and scriptorium. It was the monastic centres that were destined, often in spite of themselves, to play the major part in both preserving and transmitting what remained of pagan antiquity; a more slender, but at times vital, line of descent can be traced through the schools and libraries which became associated with the great cathedrals.

An early and conspicuous example of the monastic tradition was the monastery of Vivarium which Cassiodorus founded some time after 540 on his estates at Squillace in the extreme south of Italy. It owed much of its conception and character to the urgencies of the times, when the devastation of war and conquest was threatening to destroy cultural centres and even the books on which learning and literacy depended. Cassiodorus endowed his foundation with a good working library and put a strong emphasis on education and the copying of manuscripts. His educational program is set out in the two books of his *Institutiones divinarum et saecularium litterarum*, composed c. 562. Although endowed with no exceptional intellectual gifts, Cassiodorus appears in retrospect as a man of vision who foresaw the role which monasteries were to play in succeeding centuries, who grasped the crucial fact that with the disintegration of political life these retreats provided the main hope for intellectual continuity. But he also had a practical bent and an eye for detail in keeping with a long and successful career in the Ostrogothic civil service. He realized the need for Latin translations of the Greek authorities on exegesis, philosophy, and science, and he was influential in both augmenting and disseminating the increasing body of Greek learning available in Latin dress. He appreciated the convenience of the omnibus volume and had related texts bound together whenever possible; one of his composite volumes contained Cicero's *De inventione*, Quintilian, and the *Ars rhetorica* of Fortunatianus, a book for which Lupus of Ferrières understandably searched far and wide in the ninth century. He insisted on the importance of the meticulous copying of books, paid great attention to orthography and presentation, and with moving eloquence conferred a new dignity upon the scribe: 'felix intentio, laudanda sedulitas, manu hominibus praedicare, digitis linguas aperire, salutem mortalibus tacitum dare, et contra diaboli subreptiones illicitas calamo atramentoque pugnare' (*Inst.* 1.30.1).

Cassiodorus' services to the classical tradition could easily be exaggerated; indeed, one of his main preoccupations had been to erode the secular monopoly of higher education. The pagan authors found a place in both his library and his educational program, but they were reduced to the rank of teaching books and manuals. The only classical works that to our certain knowledge he put on his shelves were Cicero's *De inventione*, Seneca's *De forma mundi* (now lost), Columella, Quintilian, pseudo-Apuleius' *De interpretatione*, some Aristotle, and a number of technical works; of the poets, whom he quotes and on whom he had been brought up, apparently nothing. The library of Symmachus, for example, the great grandson of the orator, who had a much more positive attitude to pagan culture, would probably have had a very different flavour. Nor does Vivarium appear to have played any direct part in the transmission of classical texts. The monastery seems to have died with its founder, and the theory that its books passed in time to the great monastery of Bobbio, founded in northern Italy in 614, and so to the Middle Ages, collapsed long ago: such of its books as can be traced appear to have found their way in the main to Rome, possibly to the Lateran Library, and from there to have been dispersed by the generosity of successive popes. A few manuscripts have been identified which were either written at Vivarium or had ancestors that originated in Cassiodorus' library, among them the famous codex Amiatinus of the Vulgate (see p. 261), but these do not include any classical texts. Cassiodorus is important for many reasons and not least because he provides us with our only example of a sixth-century library; but there must have been other—and from the classical point of view better—collections of which we know nothing.

More limited in aim, but immeasurably greater in effect, was the founding of Montecassino c. 529 by Benedict of Nursia, who, by the promulgation of his rule, laid the foundation on which monastic life in the West was based for centuries to come. Apart from setting aside a period each day for reading—a spiritual rather than intellectual operation—the Benedictine Rule had nothing to say about intellectual pursuits, and the copying of books had no explicit part in the monastic ideal; but, in saying nothing, it left the way open for liberal influences when the time was ripe, and reading could in any case not be carried on without books.

While Italy had enjoyed its late Renaissance in the first half of the sixth century, the blossoming of Visigothic culture in Spain did not come until the late sixth and early seventh centuries. This revival largely owes its place in the history of classical culture to the achievement of its greatest writer, Isidore of Seville (c. 570–636). Owing to the phenomenally rapid spread of his works throughout Europe, an amazing accomplishment for the pre-Carolingian period, Isidore was quickly established as one of the most influential agents in the transmission and elucidation of ancient learning. His *Etymologies* was at the same time the last product of the Roman encyclopedic tradition and the starting-point for most medieval compilations; its most frequently copied section, the first three books covering the subjects of the *trivium* and *quadrivium*, must have contributed enormously to the consolidation of the medieval educational system. This systematically arranged encyclopedia, packed with information and misinformation on every topic from angels to the parts of a saddle, descends so often into false etymologizing and the uncritical parade of absurd bric-à-brac that it cannot be read without a smile. But Isidore wins one's respect, and even affection, by his obvious appreciation of knowledge for its own sake. Hostility to pagan literature is explicit in some of his public pronouncements, and he was more at home in the neutral pages of the scholiast and compiler than in the classical authors themselves, whom with a few exceptions he quotes at second-hand; but his curiosity knew no barriers and he took for granted the independent value of profane culture. When he culls from the fathers of the Church the scraps of classical poetry and pagan learning that they contain and re-allocates them to their proper place in the traditional system of knowledge, this bishop is paradoxically recreating in a resecularized form the basic structure of ancient learning.

However, the process that has preserved Latin literature for us could not begin until there was a more sympathetic and more positive attitude to classical authors than generally obtained on the continent in the Dark Ages. Christians still lived in the shadow of pagan literature; its achievement dwarfed their own, and its threat to morals and doctrine was a real one. This was to change when Latin culture was transplanted to a distant soil, where those eager to learn the language of the Church could turn to antiquity without any sense of inferiority or fear, since rivalry was out of the question and men at large were protected from the dangers of ancient paganism by simple ignorance of the Latin language. But this spirit did not percolate on any scale to the continent of Europe until the Carolingian Revival in the late eighth century, and in the meantime much of classical literature perished.

Although few ages are so dark that they are not penetrated by a few shafts of light, the period from roughly 550 to 750 was one of almost unrelieved gloom for the Latin classics on the continent; they virtually ceased being copied. Among the mass of patristic, biblical, and liturgical manuscripts that survive from this period there are precious few texts of classical authors: from the sixth century we have scraps of two Juvenal manuscripts, remnants of one of the Elder and one of the Younger Pliny, but at least two of these belong to the early part of the century; from the seventh century we have a fragment of Lucan; from the early eighth century nothing.

The fate that often overtook the handsome books of antiquity is dismally illustrated by the surviving palimpsests—manuscripts in which the original texts have been washed off to make way for works which at the time were in greater demand. Many texts that had escaped destruction in the crumbling empire of the West perished within the walls of the monastery; some of them may have been too tattered when they arrived to be of practical use, and there was no respect for rags, however venerable. The peak period for this operation was the seventh and early eighth centuries, and although palimpsests survive from many centres, the bulk of them have come from the Irish foundations of Luxeuil and Bobbio. Texts perished, not because pagan authors were under attack, but because no one was interested in reading them, and parchment was too precious to carry an obsolete text; Christian works, heretical or superfluous, also went to the wall, while the ancient grammarians, of particular interest to the Irish, often have the upper hand. But the toll of classical authors was very heavy: amongst those palimpsested we find Plautus and Terence, Cicero and Livy, the Elder and Younger Pliny, Sallust and Seneca, Vergil and Ovid, Lucan, Juvenal and Persius, Gellius and Fronto. Fronto survives in three palimpsests, fated always to be the underdog. Among the texts that have survived solely in this mutilated form are some of outstanding interest, such as the *De republica* of Cicero (Vat. lat. 5757, Plate X) written in uncials of the fourth or fifth century and covered at Bobbio in the seventh with Augustine on the Psalms, a fifth-century copy of the *De amicitia* and *De vita patris* of Seneca (Vat. Pal. lat. 24) which succumbed in the late sixth or early seventh century to the Old Testament, and a fifth-century codex of Sallust's *Histories* (Orléans 192 + Vat. Reg. lat. 1283B + Berlin lat. 4° 364) which, in France and probably at Fleury, was supplanted at the turn of the seventh century by Jerome. Other important palimpsests are the Ambrosian Plautus (Ambros. S.P. 9/13–20, *olim* G. 82 sup.) and the Verona Livy (Verona XL (38)), both of the fifth century.

II. IRELAND AND ENGLAND

A new intellectual movement which was to put a higher value on classical texts than the price of their parchment had already begun in a remote outpost of Christianity. This was Ireland, possessed of a Latin culture as early as the late fifth century and destined to play a vital part in the civilization of Europe. The amount of actual classical literature known in Ireland in pre-Carolingian times is much debated and appears to have been small indeed; the close acquaintance with Latin poetry revealed by their major literary figure, Columbanus (c. 543–615), relates to the continental phase of his life and may belong more to the context of late antique culture than that of the monasteries of Ireland. The important feature of their culture was therefore not its classical content but the intensive and uninhibited way in which they read what books they possessed, their enthusiasm and aptitude for learning, however peculiar and bogus that learning sometimes was, and the industry that produced in the course of the seventh and eighth centuries a remarkable amount of grammatical and exegetical work. The Irish also had remarkable artistic talents: from the half-uncial manuscripts which they had acquired from Gaul in the fifth and sixth centuries they developed a beautiful half-uncial of their own, seen in its finest form in the Book of Kells (Dublin, Trinity College 58), and a more practical and equally individual minuscule script. Their importance for the transmission of classical texts begins when they leave Ireland, impelled by a missionary zeal of far-reaching consequence. The establishment of Iona as the centre of Celtic Christianity outside Ireland by Columba c. 563 marked the effective beginning of the conversion of Scotland and led on in time to the foundation of such important monasteries as Lindisfarne in Northumbria and Malmesbury in the south-west. Even more spectacular was the continental mission of Columbanus, who blazed a trail across Europe marked out by such important monastic foundations as those of Luxeuil in Burgundy (590), from which Corbie was founded a century later, Bobbio in northern Italy (614), and Saint Gall, which developed from a hermitage which his pupil Gallus established in Switzerland c. 613. The *Scotti peregrini* became a colourful feature of the continental scene in the eighth and ninth centuries and had a large contribution to make, as such men as Virgil of Salzburg, Dungal, Sedulius Scottus, John Scottus Eriugena serve to demonstrate. However much these scholars became part of the Carolingian revival, their learning tended to retain its strong Irish accent. Some of them must have taken, or subsequently procured, books from their homeland, and there are a few extant manuscripts containing grammatical and computistical texts which appear to have reached the continent from Ireland itself.

While the Latin culture of Ireland was percolating through northern England, a more direct link with Rome and its past was re-established in the south when, in 597, Gregory the Great sent Augustine to England with a mission to convert the Anglo-Saxons to Christianity. Canterbury became the centre of Roman Christianity and Augustine its first archbishop. More significant, because more effective, was the second mission of 668, headed by Theodore of Tarsus and Hadrian of Niridanum, which succeeded in establishing the Roman Church throughout the country. Theodore was a Greek, Hadrian an African by birth; both were men of wide

learning. An important feature of the renewed contact with Rome
was the inflow of books. To Augustine Gregory had sent the
necessary vestments and vessels for carrying on divine service *nec
non et codices plurimos* (Bede, *Hist. eccl.* 1.29). These would be bibles,
service-books, and the like, but most of them were doubtless
written in uncials, and it was these books that led to the development in England of a fine uncial script which enjoyed a couple of
centuries of glory before giving way in the eighth century to the
minuscule introduced into Northumbria by the Irish. Theodore and
Hadrian came with an educational and literary program; they must
have brought with them a large number of books, Latin and Greek,
probably pagan and Christian, but we have no details. The Anglo-
Latin culture that grew out of the converging influences of Ireland
and Rome created a need for books of all kinds; some came from
France and Spain, but the main source was Italy, Rome, and the
South. Wilfrid (c. 634–709), bishop of York and abbot of Ripon,
made several journeys to Rome and will not have come back
empty-handed, and the same applies to Aldhelm; but the great
traveller of the age was Benedict Biscop, the founder of the twin
monasteries of Wearmouth and Jarrow (674 and 682), who made no
less than six trips to Italy. The fifth may be the most significant:
innumerabilem librorum omnis generis copiam adportavit (Bede, *Hist.
abbatum* 6). A distinguished place in English history is owed to
Benedict Biscop and his protégé abbot Ceolfrid; they made it
possible for a local boy who had apparently never set foot outside
Northumbria, Bede, to acquire a breadth of scholarship unrivalled
in the Europe of his day and to leap the seemingly unbridgeable gulf
that separated his world from that of the later Roman empire. We
know of further importations of books in the eighth century, and
the result can be seen in the rich libraries that grew up at Canterbury and York.

   We know something of the breadth of reading of the English
scholars of the seventh and eighth centuries from the writings of
Aldhelm (c. 639–709) and Bede (673–735), the one a product of
Wessex and Kent, the other of Northumbria. Their range of reference was doubtless exceptional, but it is evidence of the books available to scholars in England. The impressive roll of classical authors

named or quoted shows a healthy respect for the classical tradition rather than first-hand knowledge, for much of it is derived from Macrobius and Isidore and the grammarians. Further reductions of the list may be necessary, but Aldhelm appears to have known Vergil and Lucan, Persius and Juvenal, the Elder Pliny, some Cicero, possibly Ovid, while Bede had first-hand knowledge of a large number of grammarians, Vergil, some books of the Elder Pliny, Macrobius, Eutropius, and Vegetius, more dubiously Ovid and Lucan. This is impressive, and it is corroborated by evidence of a slightly later date which we owe to the fortunate chance that Alcuin (c. 735–804), in the poem which he composed in praise of York, gives us a glimpse of the contents of that great library. When it comes to cataloguing, a poem is a far cry from a card-index: some authors and titles are excluded by metrical exigencies, so that the list is vague and incomplete. However, among a rich collection of theological names, we have a number of *auctores*: Vergil, Statius, Lucan, Cicero, Pliny, and Pompeius. Cicero, given the epithet *rhetor*, will mean the *De inventione*, and Pompeius will be Justinus' epitome of Pompeius Trogus. Such hints as we have reveal in England a broader and more systematic knowledge of both Christian and pagan literature than could be paralleled elsewhere at this period.

III. THE ANGLO-SAXON MISSIONARIES

The rich and vigorous culture which blossomed in Anglo-Saxon England soon spread to the continent. The Irish had passed on their missionary impulse, and the most famous of the successors of Columbanus were Willibrord (658–739), a native of Northumbria, and Boniface (c. 675–754), a product of Wessex. Willibrord set out on his mission to the Frisian people in 690 and so inaugurated a period of Anglo-Saxon influence on the continent which was to last into the ninth century; his consecration as archbishop of the Frisians by the Pope and at the suggestion of Pippin II marked the first step in cooperation between the Carolingian house and the Papacy. Boniface eventually settled on central Germany as his sphere of activity; but his missionary venture, forwarded by the active help of successive Carolingian patrons, particularly Charles Martel, by papal encouragement, and not least by his own tremendous capacity for ecclesiastical organization, so snowballed that it led to the reform of the whole Frankish Church and the establishment of Germany as a province of the Church of Rome.

One result of this alliance of missionary enthusiasm and temporal interest was the rise of important episcopal centres, like Mainz and Würzburg, and a new wave of monastic foundations, both needing libraries and scriptoria. Among the monasteries were Fulda, founded in 744 by Boniface's pupil Sturmi, and the closely allied Hersfeld, established c. 770 by his helper, the Anglo-Saxon Lullus. But two other important monasteries, Reichenau on Lake Constance (724) and its daughter-house of Murbach (727), were founded by Pirmin, a man of obscure origin, thought to have fled from Visigothic Spain with the coming of the Arabs in 711.

With them the Anglo-Saxons brought a script, books, a liberal intellectual outlook, and the recognition that a well-stocked and well-balanced library was the basis of ecclesiastical education. Books must have been imported on some scale, and not only from England; the letters of Boniface and Lullus are full of requests for books. The Anglo-Saxon script became established in centres under insular influence and was often practised alongside continental hands in the same scriptorium. Pockets of insular writing flourished until the middle of the ninth century, and some of its features, particularly abbreviation signs, were incorporated into the tradition of continental script.

IV. INSULAR INFLUENCE ON CLASSICAL TEXTS

The impact of Anglo-Latin culture on the intellectual rebirth of the continent, which finally culminated in the person of Alcuin, together with the practical provision of books, scriptoria, and scribes, must have had an immeasurable effect on the revival—and hence the survival—of Latin literature. But it is not easy to demonstrate this in detail, as the evidence is fragmentary and disparate.

Three classical manuscripts have survived from the eighth century to show that the textual tradition of the authors they contain actually passed at this stage through England. The first contains parts of Books II-VI of Pliny's *Natural History* (Voss. Lat. F. 4, Plate XII), written in Northumbria. The second, in all probability written in Northumbria too, is a manuscript of Justinus now reduced to just two leaves (Weinheim, MS. Fischer s.n. and British Library, Harley 5915, f. 10). Both these authors were, as we have seen, listed among the books said to be in the library at York. The manuscript of Justinus was probably carried to the continent by one of the Anglo-Saxon missionaries who were so active in this period. The third, a fragment containing excerpts of Servius' commentary on the *Aeneid* (Spangenberg, Pfarrbibliothek s.n.), appears to have been written in the first half of the century in south-west England; it is later associated with Fulda and it has been conjectured that it may have been taken to Germany by Boniface or one of his circle. Three commentaries on Donatus, all apparently written in England in the eighth century, were put under one cover somewhere on the continent before the year 800 (St. Paul in Carinthia 2.1), another token of the large insular contribution to the grammatical tradition.

For some other authors we have manuscripts which were written in insular script on the continent (paradoxically known as 'continental insular'), and the text of these authors is clearly indebted to the missionary activity of the English and the Irish. Texts which survive in manuscripts known to have been written or housed in insular monastic and episcopal centres on the continent are equally beneficiaries of the movement, though their script may show no trace of it. The same applies to those texts that show 'insular symptoms', i.e. errors that are best explained as originating in the faulty transcription of letters or abbreviations peculiar to English or Irish hands. These indicate that the text went through an insular tradition at an earlier stage in its history than that represented by the extant manuscripts. But such hypotheses have to be treated with caution: symptoms, especially when few in number, can be wrongly diagnosed, and insular ancestry has been more often claimed than substantiated. Authors and works which go back with at least a high degree of probability to an insular parent include

Ammianus Marcellinus, the *Tusculan disputations* and *De senectute* of Cicero, Macrobius' *Commentary on the Somnium Scipionis*, the epic poetry of Statius and Valerius Flaccus, the *De architectura* of Vitruvius, and claims can be made for others. The great centres of insular activity were Hersfeld and Fulda, which played a dominant part in the preservation of some texts. But their contribution belongs more to the story of the Carolingian revival, and will be appropriately described in that context.

V. THE CAROLINGIAN REVIVAL

The classical revival of the late eighth and early ninth centuries, without doubt the most momentous and critical stage in the transmission of the legacy of Rome, was played out against the background of a reconstituted empire which stretched from the Elbe to the Ebro, from Calais to Rome, welded together for a time into a political and spiritual whole by the commanding personality of an emperor who added to his military and material resources the blessing of Rome. Although the political achievement of Charlemagne (768–814) crumbled in the hands of his successors, the cultural movement which it fostered retained its impetus in the ninth century and survived into the tenth.

The secular and ecclesiastical administration of a vast empire called for a large number of trained priests and functionaries. As the only common denominator in a heterogeneous realm and as the repository of both the classical and the Christian heritage of an earlier age, the Church was the obvious means of implementing the educational program necessary to produce a trained executive. But under the Merovingians the Church had fallen on evil days; some of the priests were so ignorant of Latin that Boniface heard one carrying out a baptism of dubious efficacy *in nomine patria et filia et spiritus sancti* (*Epist.* 68), and knowledge of antiquity had worn so thin that the author of one sermon was under the unfortunate impression that Venus was a man. Reform had begun under Pippin the Short; but now the need was greater, and Charlemagne felt a strong personal responsibility to raise the intellectual and cultural level of the clergy, and through them of his subjects:

igitur quia curae nobis est ut nostrarum ecclesiarum ad meliora proficiat status, oblitteratam paene maiorum nostrorum desidia reparare vigilanti studio litterarum satagimus officinam, et ad pernoscenda studia liberalium artium nostro etiam quos possumus invitamus exemplo (*Epist. gen.*, *MGH*, *Legum sectio II*, *Capit. Regum Francorum I* (1883), p. 80).

When it came to creating an educated class out of next to nothing, the Anglo-Saxons were past masters, and it was a shrewd move on the part of Charles to turn to York, at this time the educational centre of England and indeed of Europe, and in 782 to invite Alcuin, the head of its school, to take charge of his palace school and be his adviser on educational matters.

Alcuin was above all an efficient teacher. There was nothing ambitious about the educational system which he transplanted to the continent and there refined: elementary and utilitarian, it aimed at literacy rather than literature, and the classical content, cut and dried, was entirely subsidiary to the Christian purpose. The Carolingian educational program waned before it could become widely established, but the setting up by imperial edict of schools attached to both the monasteries and the cathedrals guaranteed that a basic standard of literacy would be maintained at least here and there in the Europe of the future, to blossom into something greater when circumstances were favourable. But Carolingian culture was not chained to the schoolroom. Alcuin could rise to greater heights when he wished, and the court became the point of fruitful interaction between poets and scholars attracted to it from the whole of Europe, including men of imagination and elegance and learning, such as Peter of Pisa and Paul the Deacon from Italy, the Irish scholar Dungal, the poet Theodulfus from Spain. From this circle there emanated a higher and more secular cultural stream; men were found who rose above the rather constipated limits of much Carolingian thought and literature and approached the ancient classics with genuine intellectual curiosity and honest aesthetic appreciation. An important result of a rapidly developing and highly organized educational program, spreading from the court to the monasteries and cathedrals, was the need for books; these were produced on an unprecedented scale, in a flurry of activity which salvaged for us the greater part of Latin literature.

VI. THE DEVELOPMENT OF CAROLINE MINUSCULE

In keeping with the thoroughness and uniformity of the new order was the universal adoption of a new script, Caroline minuscule (Plate XIII), which, though it developed too early for Charlemagne or Alcuin to have had a hand in it, doubtless owed its acceptance and refinement to their encouragement. The late seventh and eighth centuries had been a period of universal experimentation in the art of writing, inspired by the need for a more economical and up-to-date script. While the Irish and the English had been developing a minuscule script out of half-uncial, other minuscule hands had come into being on the continent. These had a more humble origin, developing not from the uncial book-hands, though in places these influenced their evolution, but from Roman cursive, which had continued to be the script of business and officialdom. Out of this unpromising script was forged a calligraphic book-hand which evolved along its own lines in different regions and produced the 'national hands' of Spain, southern Italy, and Gaul—Visigothic, Beneventan, and Merovingian.

The Visigothic script, which flourished in Spain from the early eighth to the twelfth century, concerns us least, for there are few extant classical manuscripts written in this hand and very little evidence that it played a significant part in the transmission of classical texts. Beneventan, so called because it was conterminous with the old duchy of Benevento, has a marked similarity to Visigothic and became the normal script of Italy south of Rome and parts of the Dalmatian coast (Plate XIV). This fine hand, built up entirely from cursive elements, came into being in the eighth century, reached its peak in the eleventh, and lingered on into the sixteenth, though in the thirteenth it gave way to the standard minuscule of the period as the vehicle for literary texts. The great centre was Montecassino. There are a large number of classical manuscripts, some of them of the highest importance, written in this highly wrought and on first acquaintance rather difficult script.

The early minuscule scripts of Gaul and adjacent areas do not loom large in the transmission of classical texts, though a few manuscripts in pre-Caroline minuscule do survive and some other texts show signs of having passed through such a stage. But the various Merovingian hands are important as the forerunners of Caroline minuscule. For it was from these scripts, more fluid than those of Italy and Spain, that the calligraphic urge of the craftsman evolved, after trial and error, a minuscule that was destined to become the normal script of Western Europe. The first calligraphic minuscule of France was produced at Luxeuil and bears the name of that great Irish foundation; it reached its peak about 700. In the eighth century the palm passed to Corbie, where in the second half of the century no less than three scripts can be distinguished, all in use at the same time—known technically as the en script, the ab script, and the Maurdramn type. In the biblical books produced at Corbie under abbot Maurdramn (772–80) we see emerging from these pre-Caroline scripts the first example of a developed Caroline minuscule. The essential element in the process appears to be a return to half-uncial. The cursive elements are eliminated, the letters are rounded, separate, and regular, and the result is an unsurpassed grace and lucidity, which must have had a tremendous effect on the survival of classical literature by casting it in a form that all could read with both ease and pleasure. It became universal throughout the Carolingian empire in the course of a few decades, crossed to England in the tenth century, and by the end of the twelfth had swept its rivals from the field.

VII. CAROLINGIAN LIBRARIES AND THE LATIN CLASSICS

Recent research has enabled us to see to the heart of the Carolingian classical revival by demonstrating that a list of authors preserved in a manuscript at Berlin (Diez. B Sant. 66), and remarkable for the richness and rarity of its content, can be nothing less than a partial catalogue of books in the court library of Charlemagne about the year 790. The list includes Lucan, Statius' *Thebaid*, Terence, Juvenal, Tibullus, Horace's *Ars poetica*, Claudian, Martial, some of Cicero's speeches (the *Verrines*, *Catilinarians*, *Pro rege Deiotaro*), and a collection of orations excerpted from the *Bella* and *Historiae* of Sallust. Some of the works in this impressive list may have been ancient codices in capitals or uncials. The presence of other books in the library may reasonably be inferred from other evidence. Such rare works as Grattius' *Cynegetica* and Statius' *Silvae* are quoted in the court poetry of the period, and Alcuin implies in a letter to Charlemagne that a copy of the Elder Pliny would be to hand. Paul the Deacon made his abridgement of Festus expressly as a gift for Charlemagne's library, and we know that the *Liber medicinalis* of Quintus Serenus was copied by imperial command. Some of the books known to have been produced in the palace scriptorium are remarkable both for the quality of their texts and for their superb execution. Our best manuscripts of Lucretius and Vitruvius (Leiden, Voss. Lat. F. 30; London, Harley 2767) were written there about the year 800.

It is clear from the evidence that abbots and bishops who had the right connections could enrich their libraries with copies taken from the books in the palace library; and after Charlemagne's death, although the details of the way in which this library was dispersed are unknown, many of the books found their way to monastic libraries. There is a remarkable correlation between the items in the palace list and the works known to have been copied at Corbie about the middle of the century: the unique Corbie manuscript which contains the well-known collection of speeches and letters taken from Sallust (Vat. lat. 3864) is the most striking example. Another tell-tale item is the group of three Ciceronian speeches which reappear in the important codex Holkhamicus, now in the British Museum (Add. 47678): this was written at Tours in the early years of the ninth century—Alcuin was abbot of Saint Martin's at Tours from 796 to 804—and it can hardly be doubted that its parent had been the copy in the palace library. Again, one of the most famous manuscripts of Livy is the codex Puteanus of the third decade (Paris lat. 5730, Plate XI), written in the fifth century in Italy and the source of all the later manuscripts: this was copied at Tours about the year 800 (its copy is Vat. Reg. lat. 762, Plate XIII) and again at Corbie about the middle of the ninth century (Laur. 63.20), a pattern which strongly suggests that the home of the Puteanus was to be found in the palace. The importance of the palace scriptorium seems to have continued under Charles' successor Louis the Pious (814–40), for the manuscripts which have been attributed to it during the period of his rule include such outstanding books as the Bamberg manuscripts of Seneca's *Letters* (Class. 46) and Pliny's *Natural History* (Class. 42).

Books are naturally attracted to centres of power and influence, like wealth and works of art and all that goes with a prosperous cultural life. Some arrive as the perquisites of conquest, or as the gifts that pour in unasked when the powerful have made their wishes plain, some in response to the magnetic pull of an active and dynamic cultural movement. Others were actively sought out by those promoting the educational and cultural aims of the revival. There was such a break in the copying of the classics in the Dark Ages that many of the books that provided the exemplars from which the Carolingian copies were made must have been ancient codices, and this immediately raises a fundamental question: where did all the books that have salvaged so much of what we have of Latin literature come from? As far as we can tell from the evidence available, the total contribution of Ireland and England, Spain and Gaul, was small in comparison with what came from Italy itself, from Rome and Campania and particularly, it would seem, from Ravenna after its capture by the forces of Charlemagne. Nor did the wholesale transference of classical texts to northern Europe exhaust the deposits in Italy, for Italy continued, down to the end of the Renaissance and beyond, to produce from time to time texts which, as far as we can tell, had been unknown north of the Alps.

Gathering impetus with each decade, the copying of books went on apace through the length and breadth of Charlemagne's empire. Such ancient classical manuscripts as could be found, with their imposing majuscule scripts, were transformed, often at speed, into minuscule copies, and these in time begot further copies, branching out into those complex patterns to which the theory of stemmatics has reduced this fascinating process. The routes by which texts travelled as they progressed from place to place were naturally governed in part by geographical factors, as they moved along the valleys of the Loire or Rhine, but even more by the complex relationships that existed between institutions and the men who moved between them. There are so many gaps in our knowledge, and so many of the pieces in this puzzle have been irrevocably lost, that we can never hope to build up a convincing distribution map for the movements of texts in this period. But certain patterns are discernible, and the drift of texts south and west through the Low Countries and northern France, and down the Rhine to the shores of Lake Constance, appears to point to a fertile core in the area of Aachen, and this would confirm the crucial importance of the palace as a centre and a catalyst for the dissemination of classical texts.

Some idea of the scale, perhaps exceptional, on which classical books were copied may be derived from a block of manuscripts written at Corbie during a short period after the middle of the century. The exemplars from which they were copied came in part from the palace, and the credit for the burst of activity that produced them probably belongs to the Corbie librarian, Hadoard: they include a large collection of Cicero's philosophical works, the first and third decades of Livy, Sallust, Columella, the Elder Seneca, the Younger Pliny, Caesar's *Gallic War*, the *Ad Herennium*, Macrobius' commentary on the *Somnium Scipionis*, Statius' *Thebaid*, Martial, Ovid's *Heroïdes* and *Amores*, Terence, Vitruvius, and Vegetius. It is clear from extant catalogues of Carolingian libraries and from other evidence that comparable collections existed, or were being built up, at such centres as Tours, Fleury, Ferrières, Auxerre, Lorsch, Reichenau, and Saint Gall.

Though a recent foundation (764), the monastery of Lorsch, in Hesse, enjoyed the special patronage of Charlemagne and rapidly built up one of the richest Carolingian libraries. The famous codex Pithoeanus of Juvenal and Persius (Montpellier 125) was written at Lorsch, and it possessed copies of Cicero's *Letters*, which were a rarity at the time. Among the manuscripts it appears to have acquired in the Carolingian period are some very remarkable books. These include a fifth-century codex which is our only source for the fifth decade of Livy (Vienna lat. 15) and which had earlier been circulating in the Low Countries; the main manuscript of Seneca's *De beneficiis* and *De clementia* (Vat. Pal. lat. 1547), written in northern Italy about the year 800; the codex Palatinus of Vergil (Vat. Pal. lat. 1631), written in rustic capitals of the late fifth or early sixth century; a famous palimpsest from Italy (Vat. Pal. lat. 24), which had been made up from scraps of some of the oldest surviving books of antiquity, including codices of Seneca, Lucan, Fronto, and Gellius.

The importance of the insular foundations of Fulda and Hersfeld has already been mentioned. From these come the two manuscripts of Ammianus Marcellinus from which the rest derive, and we owe the survival of the *Opera minora* of Tacitus and the *De grammaticis* of Suetonius to a manuscript written at either Hersfeld or Fulda and preserved at the former (Iesi, Bibl. Balleani 8). Besides contributing important manuscripts to the textual tradition of some authors, such as the Younger Pliny, Aulus Gellius, Eutropius, and Nonius Marcellus, Fulda played a dominant role in the history of other texts: our only surviving medieval manuscript of Valerius Flaccus (Vat. lat. 3277) was written there; of the two Carolingian manuscripts of Columella, one was written at Corbie (Leningrad, Class. Lat. F. v. 1), the other at Fulda (Ambros. L. 85 sup.); the prime source for the *Historia Augusta* (Val. Pal. lat. 899), which was itself written in northern Italy, must have reached Fulda, for a direct copy of it (Bamberg Class. 54) is of Fulda origin; books 1–6 of the *Annals* of Tacitus have come down to us in a manuscript (Laur. 68.1) written at Fulda and preserved at Corvey, a daughter-house of Corbie; finally, to end on a lighter note, while one of the early manuscripts of the cookery book of Apicius is a show-piece of the script of Tours (Urb. lat. 1146), the other (written in a mixture of Anglo-Saxon minuscule and continental script) points almost certainly to Fulda (New York, Acad. Med., MS. Safe).

Tours has already been mentioned as the source of some of our earliest and finest Carolingian manuscripts; to these may be added the oldest extant copy of Suetonius (Paris. lat. 6115). Tours itself stood at the head of a chain of abbeys strung along the valleys of the Loire and the Yonne—Fleury, Ferrières, Auxerre—that provided a major artery for the circulation of classical learning. Fleury played an important part in the transmission of Quintilian and Caesar's *Gallic War*. Together with Auxerre—the two are so closely connected through the circle of Lupus and Heiric that their respective contributions are often difficult to distinguish—Fleury looms large in the history of Petronius' text, and the fertile interaction of this whole group of monasteries can be seen at work in such traditions as that of Nonius Marcellus and Macrobius' *Commentary*. The rich deposits of books in the area of the Loire in time helped to fuel both the literary revival of the late eleventh century and the progress of scholarship in the sixteenth.

Two of the great Vergil codices, the Augusteus and Romanus (Vat. lat. 3256 + Berlin lat. 2° 416; Vat. lat. 3867) have the *ex libris* of the abbey of Saint-Denis at Paris and may have been preserved there from this early period. The monasteries of Lake Constance, in particular Reichenau and Saint Gall, close to the heart of the Carolingian revival and yet in a position to have fruitful contact with northern Italy, made an enormous contribution to the preservation of classical texts. Such scarce items as Ovid's *Metamorphoses* and *Ars amatoria*, Silius Italicus, and the *Natural Questions* of Seneca are recorded for Reichenau or a neighbouring centre, and Murbach, a daughter-house of Reichenau, had a collection of manuscripts that rivalled its own, among them an early and perhaps influential copy of the *Appendix Vergiliana* and the lost archetype of Velleius Paterculus. The rich holdings at Saint Gall will become clear when we see what Poggio was able to find there.

Bobbio, to the south of Milan, belongs to a rather different context; it had been gathering in classical texts long before the Carolingian revival and was vital in preserving a large body of ancient grammar. But it also had some rare poetic texts, Lucretius, Manilius, and Valerius Flaccus; its copy of the last may well have been the archetype of our extant manuscripts. Some of the many texts to which it had given refuge did not emerge until the fifteenth century, others only recently.

If one were to take stock at the end of the ninth century of the classical books available, it would be clear that some authors were so well entrenched in the literary and educational tradition and so

thick on the shelves of the libraries that their survival was no longer
in question: to this group we can assign Vergil and Horace (the
Satires and *Epistles* rather than the lyrics, which were less popular in
the Middle Ages), Lucan, Juvenal and Persius, Terence, the epics of
Statius, some of the rhetorical and philosophical works of Cicero
(the *Letters* and *Speeches* were still rare or unknown), the *Catilina*
and *Jugurtha* of Sallust, the Elder Pliny, Justinus, and Vitruvius. The
Elder Seneca and Valerius Maximus were available, as were Aulus
Gellius and the *Letters* of Seneca, but Gellius and Seneca both
circulated in two separate parts, of which one was much less
common than the other, and at this period complete copies were
rare or non-existent. Quintilian was less common than one would
expect (his place had been usurped by the *Ad Herennium* and the *De
inventione*), and he too was incomplete; most of the manuscripts
were *mutili*, though a complete text was to be found in Germany in
the tenth century. Martial and Suetonius were not common, though
Einhard's *Life of Charlemagne*, thanks to a happy connection with
Fulda, is a brilliant adaptation of Suetonius' literary method and a
milestone in the development of secular biography. Plautus,
Lucretius, Livy, and the Younger Pliny were even scarcer, and the
great age of Ovid was still to come. Some authors existed in so few
copies—sometimes only one—that their future was still precarious:
Cicero's *Letters*, Tacitus, Columella, Petronius, Apicius, Valerius
Flaccus, and Ammianus were all copied at this time, but not on a
scale that would ensure their survival through wars and acts of God
and the less dramatic but ever-present evils of mice and mould; it
was going to need another *renovatio* to make their position secure.
The few or unique copies of Tibullus and Catullus, Seneca's *Tragedies* and Statius' *Silvae*, were virtually in hibernation, while
Propertius, Seneca's *Dialogues*, Apuleius' *Golden Ass*, much of Tacitus, Manilius, Nepos, and Velleius Paterculus had shown no sign of
animation.

One cannot consider these facts without marvelling at the
slenderness of the thread on which the fate of the Latin classics
hung. In the case of many texts a single copy survived into the
Carolingian period, and often a battered one at that. When the
great period of the revival was over, some of the great works of

Latin literature were still but a single manuscript on a single shelf. The slightest accident could still have robbed us of some of our most precious texts, of Catullus and Propertius, Petronius or Tacitus. There are some extraordinary examples of survival: the fifth-century manuscript of Livy's fifth decade which found a home at Lorsch (Vienna lat. 15) survived until the sixteenth century without ever being copied. A mere mishap, and five more books of Livy would have disappeared without trace.

VIII. CAROLINGIAN SCHOLARSHIP

One of the more obvious aspects of the Carolingian age is the staggering amount of parchment it consumed: there was a tremendous spate of publication, ranging from creative poetry, through history, biography, hagiography, theology, philosophy, and biblical exegesis, to the handbooks on rhetoric, dialectic, metrics, and grammar. All of this has its relevance, for anything that involved a more sophisticated study and exploitation of the Latin language and literature furthered the classical tradition. But if, for our present purpose, we confine our attention to the study of classical literature and put some weight on the word scholarship, there are only a few men who need engage our attention.

One of the earliest glimpses of scholarly activity expended on a classical text in the Carolingian period is provided by the most celebrated manuscript of Lucretius, the codex Oblongus (Voss. Lat. F. 30), written in the palace scriptorium of Charlemagne about the year 800. This has been corrected and at times—where the original scribe had left blank spaces—supplemented in an insular hand by the once intriguing 'corrector Saxonicus', who proved to be no Saxon at all, but the Irish scholar Dungal. He spent periods at the court and was regarded by Charlemagne as an authority on astronomy; it is hardly surprising to see him taking a personal interest in the text of Lucretius. A much larger place in the history of scholarship has been won by another Irishman, Sedulius Scottus, who was active at Liège in the middle of the century. Versatile and gifted, theologian and versifier as well as the author of grammatical commentaries on Priscian and others, Sedulius interests us most as the compiler of a *Collectaneum*, a collection of excerpts from various authors. This is largely a moral rag-bag of the type one meets frequently in the Middle Ages, but he shows some interest in the style of the authors excerpted and is truly remarkable for the range of his reading: he excerpts a large number of Ciceronian works (including the *Philippics*, *Pro Fonteio*, *Pro Flacco*, *In Pisonem*), Valerius Maximus, Macrobius, the military manuals of Frontinus and Vegetius, and the *Historia Augusta*. For Cicero's *Speeches* he seems to have used one of the important extant manuscripts (Vat. Arch. S. Pietro H. 25), copied in Italy and probably from an uncial original. A similar collection has been left to us by Hadoard, the *custos librorum* at Corbie, written almost certainly in his own hand (Vat. Reg. lat. 1762 of the mid-ninth century). Hadoard shows much less respect for his authors: his moral maxims are torn from their context, denuded of the names and historical references that tie them to place and period, and Christianized where necessary. But his range is again noteworthy, particularly of Ciceronian works—*Academica priora*, *De natura deorum*, *De divinatione*, *De fato*, *Paradoxa*, *De legibus*, *Timaeus*, *Tusculanae disputationes*, *De officiis*, *De amicitia*, *De senectute*, *De oratore*. He is of less textual importance than one might imagine, for some of the manuscripts he used are still extant. A more fascinating document, since it reflects the whole career and personal interests of the compiler, is the scrap-book (St. Gall 878) of Walafrid Strabo (808-49), poet, tutor to the future Charles the Bald, and abbot of Reichenau. The extracts themselves fail to reveal his literary interests: the only pagan works of the classical period he chose to excerpt were Columella and the *Letters* of Seneca, the first a not surprising choice for the author of a charming poem on his monastery garden. But the scrap-book has helped to demonstrate a more active intervention in the transmission of classical authors than is normal with an excerptor by revealing that the elegant hand which has supplemented and in places written or rewritten our oldest manuscript of Horace (Vat. Reg. lat. 1703 = R) belongs to Walafrid himself.

But the scholar who towers over his contemporaries is Lupus of Ferrières (c. 805-62). Author of the famous dictum *propter se ipsam appetenda sapientia* (*Epist.* 1), he alone of the men of his age gives a foretaste of the Renaissance. He was educated at Ferrières and completed his studies at Fulda under the greatest teacher of the post-Alcuinian period, Hrabanus Maurus (780–856); he returned to Ferrières in 836 and was abbot from 842 until his death. His letters are of great interest; despite his involvement in the affairs of the world, his correspondence is dominated by his scholarly interests. Anxious to increase the resources of the library at Ferrières, which had been modest enough in his student days, he writes far and wide in his search for books, to Einhard (who had now left the court and retired to Seligenstadt), to Tours, to York, to the Pope himself. However, he was not the only manuscript-hunter in the ninth century: his distinction rests on the fact that he is avid to obtain manuscripts of works which he already possesses, so that by collation he can correct and supplement his own text. He succeeded in filling up some of the gaps in the incomplete Valerius Maximus that had survived from antiquity by drawing on the rare epitome made by Julius Paris in the fourth century. The following extract from a letter written in 847 to a monk at Prüm will illustrate his practice (*Epist.* 69):

> Tullianas epistolas quas misisti cum nostris conferri faciam, ut ex utrisque, si possit fieri, veritas exculpatur. Tu autem huic nostro cursori Tullium in Arato [the *Aratea*] trade, ut ex eo quem me impetraturum credo, quae deesse illi Egil noster aperuit, suppleantur.

Glad to give as well as to receive, Lupus willingly replies to queries on points of grammar, prosody, or exegesis, and gives us a vivid glimpse of the intellectual life of a circle of Carolingian scholars. He wrote little, and the main monument of his humanism, apart from his letters, are the manuscripts of classical authors—more than a dozen in number—which reveal his handiwork. The most important of these in one respect is a manuscript of Cicero's *De oratore* in the British Museum (Harley 2736), written by Lupus himself; those he has annotated include texts of Cicero, among them the oldest manuscript of the Leiden corpus of the philosophical works (Vienna lat. 189), Livy (VI–X), Valerius Maximus, Aulus Gellius, Macrobius (on the *Somnium Scipionis*), and Donatus (on *Aeneid* I–V,

X). We know that Einhard sent a Gellius to Fulda at Lupus' request and that Hrabanus was busy having it copied in 836 (*Epist.* 5). A manuscript of Gellius written at Fulda did come to light (Leeuwarden, Prov. Bibl. van Friesland 55), but the hope that it might prove to have been the manuscript used by Lupus to correct his own copy of Gellius (Vat. Reg. lat. 597) was disappointed. His practice of leaving spaces where lacunae are established or suspected, marking corruptions, and recording variants, reveals a sound scholarly approach to classical texts that outweighs the modest quality of his own critical contribution. In the field of biblical studies Lupus' practice of collating manuscripts had been strikingly anticipated by Theodulfus, bishop of Orléans and abbot of Fleury. Before his death in 821 he had made an edition of the Vulgate in which he foreshadowed modern editorial methods by using sigla in the margin to distinguish the sources of his variants, such as ā for the Alcuinian reading, ŝ for the Spanish recension.

Lupus was important as a teacher, and among his pupils was Heiric of Auxerre (c. 841–76), himself the teacher of such important figures in the next generation as Hucbald of Reims and Remigius of Auxerre. When one reflects that Lupus was taught by Hrabanus and Hrabanus in turn by Alcuin, one can clearly see one of the threads in the continuity of Carolingian education. Heiric occupies an important place in the history of classical texts. He published collections of excerpts from Valerius Maximus and Suetonius which he had taken down at Lupus' dictation. Lupus' manuscript of Valerius has come down to us (Berne 366). There were texts of Suetonius in the early ninth century at both Tours (Paris lat. 6115) and Fulda, and it was from Fulda that Lupus had tried, and probably succeeded, in obtaining his copy. Heiric is also the first person known to have used the excerpts of Petronius which began to circulate in the ninth century, and he is responsible for a collection of rare texts which have survived in a manuscript written at Auxerre in the years 860–2 and annotated by Heiric himself (Vat. lat. 4929). This odd little collection of texts is extremely interesting because we know something of both its earlier and its later history. Among its varied contents are two texts, Julius Paris' epitome of Valerius Maximus and the geography of Pomponius Mela, which both have a subscription recording that they were edited at Ravenna by Rusticius Helpidius Domnulus, probably a man of that name known to have lived in the fifth century. As we have seen, Ravenna was probably an important source of books for the Carolingians. It was Heiric who in turn passed on Helpidius' little encyclopedia to posterity: via a twelfth-century copy the contents of the Vaticanus reached Petrarch, who then ensured their wide distribution in the Renaissance.

IX. THE CAROLINGIAN TWILIGHT

The intellectual life of the Carolingian revival had been closely connected with the cohesion and security of Charlemagne's political achievement. During the course of the ninth and tenth centuries his empire suffered repeated attacks on all sides from the Vikings, Saracens, and Hungarians; whole regions were devastated and monasteries sacked, while internal disagreement led to its being split up in 843 into the separate political units that already foreshadow the fragmented face of modern Europe. However, the educational machine that Charlemagne and Alcuin had set in motion, working through the monastic and cathedral schools, had sufficient momentum to keep going until a new age could take over the classical tradition and exploit it more fully.

The tenth century was very much a period of transition from the Carolingian age to the economic and intellectual expansion of the eleventh and twelfth centuries. There was a general sagging in the cultural level and a falling off in the production of classical manuscripts, but this of course varies from area to area as new centres increase in importance and others decline; the classics went on being copied and new texts were added to the range of authors in circulation. Indeed, among the scholars of the age there were two whose breadth of learning could not have been paralleled in the previous century: these were Ratherius (c. 887–974), bishop of Liège and thrice bishop of Verona, and Gerbert of Reims (c. 950–1003).

Ratherius was one of the most turbulent figures in a turbulent century. Indeed, he doubtless owes much of the breadth of his classical knowledge to his varied changes of location, and these in turn to an impetuous temper and a vitriolic tongue, more heavily indebted to the Latin satirists than was comfortable for his fellow clergy, which forced him to scuttle in almost picaresque fashion to and fro across Europe. He claims our special attention for his knowledge of two rare texts, Plautus and Catullus. It is probable that he met the plays of Plautus in France, which was the original home of the Palatine family of manuscripts, and the same may be true of Catullus. For although the great discovery of Catullus' poems took place in Verona, the first sign that they had survived was the inclusion of poem 62 in the *florilegium Thuaneum* (Paris lat. 8071), written in France in the late ninth century. A monument to Ratherius' devotion to the classics still remains in the shape of the most important single manuscript of Livy's first decade (Laur. 63.19 = M), which was copied at Verona on his instructions. Some of the more explosive marginalia readily betray their author. A twin manuscript, possibly copied at the same time and presented to Otto I, found its way to the cathedral of Worms.

The Carolingian tradition was perhaps best maintained in Germany, especially under the Ottonian dynasty (936–1002). Otto III was a highly cultivated man, and the increased contact between Germany and Italy resulting from the revival of the Holy Roman Empire injected some fresh vigour into the classical learning of the north. As tutor and counsellor to Otto III Gerbert was a central figure on this scene. He was a great teacher, a pioneer in mathematics, and an active collector of manuscripts; he was at different times abbot of Bobbio, archbishop of Reims and Ravenna, and finally Pope Sylvester II. He knew such rare authors as Celsus and Manilius—the latter he found at Bobbio—and one of our extant manuscripts of Cicero's *De oratore* (Erlangen 380) was written for him. With Gerbert's help and through his contacts in Italy Otto III was able to revive the great tradition of imperial libraries by building up a fine collection of his own; some of these books passed via his successor Henry II to the cathedral library at Bamberg, and in Bamberg they still are. He succeeded in acquiring at Piacenza a fifth-century uncial manuscript of Livy's fourth decade. All we have of this is a few strips that were used to strengthen a binding (Bamberg, Class. 35a), but at least two copies had been taken from it and one of them, written at Bamberg in the eleventh century, is our main source for the text (Class. 35). Other manuscripts acquired from Italy are our earliest copy of the pseudo-Quintilian *Declamationes maiores* (Class. 44) and a very valuable historical collection containing Florus, Festus, and Eutropius (Class. 31). The presence at Bamberg of magnificent manuscripts of Pliny and Seneca attributed to the scriptorium of Louis the Pious suggests that Otto III had also acquired books from the libraries of his imperial predecessors.

Among other contributions made by the German abbeys and schools of this period may be mentioned our earliest and best manuscript of Cicero's *De finibus* (Vat. Pal. lat. 1513), written at Lorsch in the eleventh century, and an important omnibus volume of Cicero's works. The latter, which is now in the British Library (Harley 2682), was written in Germany in the eleventh century and formerly belonged to Cologne Cathedral. It contains a number of the speeches, letters, and philosophical works, and is a valuable textual witness for some of them.

There was a steady growth in the number of classical works available as texts that had achieved little or no circulation in the full flush of the Carolingian revival were taken down from the shelves and read and copied. Evidence has accumulated of a strong local revival in the area of Liège. A number of manuscripts now in Brussels were written in this region, apparently at the instigation of Olbert, abbot of Gembloux and St. James's Liège. Among these are the earliest manuscripts of both Cicero's *Pro Archia* (Brussels 5348–52, later rediscovered by Petrarch) and Manilius (MS. 10012, from Gembloux); also an important collection of Claudian's poetry (MS. 5381) that appears to descend from a book at one time in the Carolingian palace library. The monastery of Lobbes, not far from Gembloux, had a similar Claudian and copies, all now lost, of such rare texts as Lucretius, Tibullus, and Valerius Flaccus. This looks like the unearthing of texts that had lurked in that area since the Carolingian period.

The stocks of classical books in Britain had been devastated by the Viking raids and other disorders of the ninth century and recovery was slow. Two manuscripts written in Wales, one of the late ninth century and containing Book I of Ovid's *Ars amatoria* (Oxford, Bodl. Auct. F. 4.32, part IV), the other a copy of Martianus Capella (Cambridge, Corpus Christi College 153) of similar date, suggest that the Welsh, using continental exemplars, had initiated a modest revival while their English neighbours were still in disarray. But thanks to the monastic reforms of Dunstan and Ethelwold and the establishment of contacts with such centres as Fleury and Corbie, England began in the tenth century to import books from the continent and with them the continental script. The most important manuscript of Cicero's *Aratea* (Harley 647), written in France in the Carolingian period, had arrived in England by the end of the century and soon produced a whole brood of offspring on English soil. Manuscripts of Juvenal and Persius survive from tenth-century England, including an attractive one in insular minuscule (Cambridge, Trinity College O. 4.10), which must be among the last of the classical manuscripts written in this script.

X. THE RESURGENCE OF MONTECASSINO

The most dramatic single event in the history of Latin scholarship in the eleventh century was the phenomenal revival of Montecassino; the mother monastery of the Benedictine order had her most brilliant hour at a time when Benedictinism was rapidly declining as the cultural force of Europe. The great efflorescence of artistic and intellectual activity that reached its peak under abbot Desiderius (1058–87) was accompanied by a renewed interest in the classics, and in the late eleventh and early twelfth century there was written at Montecassino and allied centres a wonderful series of important Beneventan manuscripts of classical and other authors. At one swoop a number of texts were recovered which might otherwise have been lost for ever; to this one monastery in this one period we owe the preservation of the later *Annals* and *Histories* of Tacitus (Plate XIV), the *Golden Ass* of Apuleius, the *Dialogues* of Seneca, Varro's *De lingua latina*, Frontinus' *De aquis*, and thirty-odd lines of Juvenal's sixth satire that are not to be found in any other manuscript.

XI. THE TWELFTH-CENTURY RENAISSANCE

As we have already noted incidentally, education was gradually passing from the monks and the monasteries to the secular clergy in the cathedral and urban schools. The monasteries remained important for their libraries and scriptoria and indeed as cultural centres, but more creative intellectual life passed to the cathedral schools, which rapidly increased from the middle of the eleventh century and in a few cases later developed into the first universities. By then the intellectual map of Europe had changed dramatically. The great centre for the revival of Roman law was Bologna; the first medical school came into being at Salerno; the Norman kingdom of southern Italy and Sicily fostered the translation of Greek technical works into Latin, and with the reconquest of Spain from the Muslims Toledo emerged as the chief centre for the translating activity that brought Arabic science and scholarship within the reach of the West. To the north the main scene of intellectual activity had shifted to Norman France and Norman England, with Bec and Canterbury to the fore, though it took the English schools a long time to catch up with those of France. The literary side of the classical revival was mainly carried on in the schools of Orléans and Chartres, while philosophy and dialectic chose Paris for their home and made it the intellectual capital of Europe. The literary output of ancient Rome continued to be the basic stuff of education and remained the chief source of literary inspiration, but now it had a new role—to cater for the specialized needs of a complex society with a professional interest in law and medicine, rhetoric and logic. The exciting books for this age were Euclid and Ptolemy, the Digest, and such works of the Aristotelian and medical corpus as were rapidly becoming available. The intellectual energy and self-confidence of the revival, the thirst for new knowledge and the urge to restructure the old, combined with the fundamental changes taking place in education and society to create new approaches to the ancient world. Increased wealth and elegance, together with the secularizing trends in art and letters, enabled people to take a more robust interest in a literature that had not been designed for the cloister. The twelfth century also marked a turning point in the development of a reading public. Lay literacy had almost disappeared with the end of antiquity and in general only the clergy and members of the ruling families were able to read. But now the vitality of the literary renaissance and the increasing use of written documents in commerce and administration testify to a cultural change. Literacy, at first confined to the Anglo-Norman nobility, began to percolate to other classes of society and was widespread by the end of the thirteenth century. It is significant that until the middle of that century the term *litteratus* denotes the ability to read and write Latin; from then òn it implies a certain familiarity with Latin literature and is closer in meaning to 'cultured'.

An age that had a rapidly developing literature of its own, both Latin and vernacular, was able to explore with understanding the techniques of ancient epic and history. Love poetry and the moral writings of the satirist were in the greatest demand: ancient literature catered for both the senses and the conscience. In the process it became transformed: Vergil was allegorized, Ovid moralized, the satirists encrusted with glosses and comment rarely in keeping with the original intention. The results were various. In his *De amicitia* Aelred of Rievaulx was able to rethink the problem of human relationships in Christian terms and rework Cicero's dialogue in a way that does no real violence to the model nor detracts from the charm and originality of his own treatment. Seneca, subtly blended with material from Christian writers, could inspire some noble passages, as in William of Saint Thierry, though he loses his identity in the process; in Gautier of Saint Victor, suitably twisted, he could be made to denounce the study of pagan authors. Borrowings from Ovid sparkle through some of the most erotic scenes in the elegiac comedy of the period, but he is commonly exploited as a manual on morals and much else, his tone and intention so grotesquely distorted that the *Remedia amoris* could become a school text and even the poet's nose, reputedly large for obvious reasons, be transformed into an organ supremely capable of discriminating between virtue and vice.

Vergil, Horace, Ovid, Juvenal, Persius, Cicero, Seneca, Sallust were the staple literary diet of the twelfth century; Statius (excluding the *Silvae*) and Terence were popular, Quintilian was known but not much used, Martial increased in favour, while some Plautus (the first eight plays) and Livy began to circulate. No age would have taken greater delight in the poetry of Catullus, Tibullus, and Propertius, but the rare or unique copies of these authors that were in existence were slow to stir; Tibullus and Propertius were just beginning to emerge, but Catullus was still unknown. Tacitus remained on the shelf, and Lucretius is a striking example of how a text can circulate in the ninth century and then virtually disappear from sight for the rest of the Middle Ages. The classical emphasis of the revival can be gauged from the fact that in the extant palimpsests the ancient authors begin to appear more frequently in the upper texts: the tables have turned, but attacks on the educational use of the classics continued.

Some notion of the acquaintance with Latin literature enjoyed by the foremost intellects of the period can be derived from the works of two Englishmen, William of Malmesbury (died c. 1143) and John of Salisbury (c. 1110–80), the first the greatest historian of the period, the second the finest representative of the literary revival of the twelfth century. As librarian of Malmesbury, William had at his disposal an excellent library, which he did much himself to improve, and an easy access to the world of books; in addition to the usual run of school texts, he had read Caesar's *Gallic War*, Aulus Gellius, Suetonius, Martial, and such an uncommon text at this time as the *Apocolocyntosis* of Seneca; he was also the first person in the Middle Ages to quote from the whole corpus of Seneca's *Letters*. A real researcher, with strong historical and antiquarian interests, William has earned an honoured place in the history of classical scholarship. His particular concern was to seek out related texts and put them together, and some of his collections, often autograph, still survive. One of his historical collections, containing Vegetius, Frontinus, and Eutropius (Oxford, Lincoln College, Lat. 100), is a good example. His impressive attempt at an omnibus Cicero still exists in

a later copy (Cambridge, University Library, Dd. 13.2); it contains
an explicit defence of his classical interests and what is perhaps the
first attempt at an edition of the fragments of the *Hortensius* and *De
republica*, carefully culled from the works of Augustine. John of
Salisbury, educated at Chartres and Paris and unrivalled in the
Middle Ages as a stylist, not only absorbed a great deal of patristic,
medieval, and classical literature, but was also able to bring it to
bear on the practical problems of his day. His favourite reading was
Cicero, Seneca, and the *exempla* of Valerius Maximus, but his strong
classical interest led him to authors not commonly found: he quotes
from the *Strategemata* of Frontinus and was remarkable in knowing
the whole extant text of Petronius. He used Heiric's excerpts for
Suetonius and may at times be dependent on other *florilegia*. His
caustic attacks on the encroachment of dialectic show that the
purely literary revival is on the wane.

William of Malmesbury and John of Salisbury were of course
exceptional, and among their contemporaries were many who were
content to give their writings a spurious air of learning by pillaging
the encyclopedists, the grammarians, and the *florilegia*: second-
hand learning had come to stay. Robert of Cricklade dedicated to
Henry II a nine-book *defloratio* of the Elder Pliny, William of
Malmesbury compiled a *Polyhistor*, Étienne of Rouen prepared an
abridgement of Quintilian. Some of the miscellaneous *florilegia*,
when they were put together by someone who had access to a wide
selection of books, are of considerable textual importance in that
they tap a tradition at an earlier stage than that represented by the
extant manuscripts and draw on a different source. The *florilegium
Gallicum*, put together in northern France in the twelfth century, is
a good example; it contains extracts from a large number of authors
and has some contribution to make to the text of Tibullus,
Petronius, Valerius Flaccus, and others. An early thirteenth-century
florilegium of mainly classical authors (Paris lat. 15155, with portions
elsewhere) contains extracts from Propertius and the *Laus Pisonis*.
Wibald, abbot of Stavelot and later (1146–58) of Corvey, like William
of Malmesbury before him, had the ambitious notion of putting the
whole of Cicero into one volume, and he almost succeeded, for
there can be little doubt that the most comprehensive manuscript

of Cicero's works, written at Corvey in the twelfth century (Berlin lat. 2° 252), is the very volume. Containing oratorical and philosophical works, an imposing range of speeches, and part of the *Epistulae ad familiares*, it is an important textual source and an impressive witness to the humanism of the twelfth century.

If one were to ask how the Renaissance of the late eleventh and twelfth century affected the textual transmission of our classical texts, the answer seems to be that it consolidated the gains of the Carolingian revival. Authors central to medieval education or agreeable to the taste of the time simply poured from the scriptoria; in the case of popular writers like Ovid and Seneca, we have four or five times as many manuscripts from the twelfth century as from all previous centuries put together. Many of these manuscripts are textually worthless, containing nothing of value that is not found in a purer form in earlier witnesses, but often the twelfth-century broadening of the tradition has resulted in gains to the text. The best manuscript of Cicero's *Ad familiares* belongs to the ninth century (Laur. 49.9); but the errors and gaps in its text have to be remedied by calling in the other branch of the tradition, Carolingian in origin but largely represented by manuscripts of the twelfth century. Other texts survive entirely in manuscripts of this period: such texts of Seneca's *Natural Questions* as existed in the Carolingian era have perished and it is the descendants of this tradition, copied in the twelfth and thirteenth centuries, that have preserved the text for us.

XII. THE SCHOLASTIC AGE

In the late twelfth and throughout the thirteenth century the schools and universities were more concerned with assimilating and organizing the material and ideas brought to the surface by the recent intellectual ferment than with making fresh discoveries. The skills employed in the systematization of acquired knowledge and the unification of dogma were those of dialectic and logic, and these subtle sciences dominated not only philosophy, theology, and the fields of specialized knowledge, but grammar and literary exegesis as well. When the classical heritage was absorbed into the systems of contemporary thought, with its strong tendency to allegorize and elaborate, it was bound to become distorted. It also suffered in other ways. With so much else to occupy the mind, the wide reading of ancient authors gave way to the more practical manuals, the *auctores* to the *artes*, and the new grammars and rhetorics that came into use were often scholastic in character. The classics still remained a valuable quarry for moral anecdote and could provide a curious age with information of all sorts; but form and style were no longer part of the attraction, and matter could be more easily assimilated when reduced to excerpts and *exempla*. At the same time the writers of the twelfth and thirteenth centuries took their place alongside the ancient authors; although they did not displace them, the monopoly of the past had been broken.

For these reasons the century that witnessed the final triumph of the Middle Ages in many fields is not a particularly enticing one for the classical scholar. Manuscripts pour on to the market, but the text of those authors who have been copied for generations is getting more and more corrupt; the proportion of grain to chaff is getting smaller, and the manuscripts themselves, with their heavy Gothic appearance, are less alluring than those of previous centuries. Despite all this, the classics survived the tide of scholasticism and made significant advances where least expected. The heroes of the period were the builders of the mighty philosophical and theological systems, but amongst those intent on the organization of knowledge were some who gave an important place to pagan literature. Vincent of Beauvais, who died about 1264, is the most monumental encyclopedist of the Middle Ages; his *Speculum maius* was an attempt to put the whole sum of knowledge into one corpus. Like so many others, he was anti-pagan in principle, but he saw the value of profane texts and defends his use of them with a good conscience. He draws heavily on classical authors; Ovid and Seneca far outdistance the others, Vergil is eclipsed. A large part of his classical quotations are taken from secondary sources, and the appearance of rare authors like Tibullus is explained by his dependence on earlier compilations, in particular the *florilegium Gallicum*.

About 1250 and within a few years of the publication of the

Speculum maius Richard of Fournival, a native of Amiens and later chancellor of its cathedral, was compiling his *Biblionomia*. In it he lays out the literature and wisdom of the world for the guidance of his fellow citizens in the form of an elaborate garden in which the various branches of knowledge each have their plot. This charming analogy quickly crystallizes into a picture of a library in which the books are laid out on desks according to their subject. This systematic bibliography is not, as has sometimes been thought, the imaginary projection of a bibliophile, but the actual catalogue of Fournival's own carefully collected library. It must have contained about 300 volumes and in size and range could challenge the monastic and cathedral libraries of his day. It contained some rare classical texts and among the most noteworthy are three items in the *opera poetarum*: Tibullus, Propertius, and Seneca's *Tragedies*. His copy of Tibullus may have descended ultimately from the manuscript at one time in the palace library of Charlemagne, for one of the earliest of the *florilegia* in which Tibullus occasionally surfaces also contains a collection of the poetry of the Carolingian court circle. His manuscript passed in 1272, with the bulk of his collection, to the library of the Sorbonne, but it is now lost; had it survived, it would have been our oldest manuscript of Tibullus, if not the source of much of the Renaissance tradition. But Fournival's manuscripts of Propertius and the *Tragedies* do survive and have now been identified. Seneca's *Tragedies* had shown signs of life; some excerpts had appeared in the *florilegium Thuaneum* (Paris lat. 8071), written in France in the ninth century, and our oldest complete manuscript, the codex Etruscus (Laur. 37.13 = E), goes back to the eleventh, but the plays had remained almost unknown. It is not until the thirteenth century that manuscripts of the other and main stream of the tradition (known as A) begin to appear; this re-emerged in northern France, though the oldest of its representatives (Cambridge, Corpus Christi College 406) appears to have been written in England. The manuscript known to editors as P (Paris lat. 8260) was written for Richard of Fournival. His copy of Propertius, written by the same scribe as the Seneca, is the manuscript known as A (Voss. Lat. O. 38), the second oldest witness to the text and one of the two parents of the humanist tradition. One of the greatest Roman poets had to wait a long time to come to life again; and for his poems we are heavily indebted, as with so many discoveries to come, to a new phenomenon, the wealthy private book collector.

The *Tragedies* were not the only text of Seneca to achieve circulation in northern Europe at this time. The *Dialogues* reached the schools of Paris in the first half of the thirteenth century, having worked their way north from Montecassino. They were known to John of Garland as early as 1220 and fifty years later, somewhat tardily but with tremendous excitement, their 'discovery' was announced by Roger Bacon. Though this text too begins to circulate again in northern France, among the first to make use of it were Roger Bacon and John of Wales, both Franciscans and both as much at home in Oxford as in Paris. They serve to draw attention to the less spectacular but not inconsiderable contribution to the promotion of classical studies already being made by the English friars. Some of the English Franciscans actually compiled in the thirteenth century a *Registrum librorum Angliae*, a union catalogue of books available in English libraries, a remarkable bibliographical project in which some classical authors were included. John of Wales's treatises, such as the *Communiloquium* and *Compendiloquium*, were full of references to the ancients and opened a wide and flattering window on classical antiquity; they were intended not only as aids for the teacher and preacher, but also as manuals for polite conversation. Somewhat later Nicholas Trevet, a Dominican but again mainly associated with Oxford and Paris, achieved such a wide reputation for erudition and the exegesis of antique texts that he received commissions from Italy to write commentaries on Livy and Seneca's *Tragedies*. These prepared the way for the classicizing group of friars who have been shown to have been active in England in the early fourteenth century. This loosely knit group, of which the most important are perhaps Thomas Waleys and Robert Holcot, did much to popularize a knowledge of the ancient world by introducing classical allusions to illustrate their biblical commentaries and sermons and helping to create an audience with a taste for ancient history and myth. With his classical scholarship, seen at its best in his commentary on the first ten books of the *De civitate dei*, completed in 1332, his admiration for the ancients, and his knowledge of rare texts, Thomas Waleys comes very close to being a humanist and doubtless owes much of his special quality to periods spent at Bologna and Avignon. He claims to have seen a copy of Apuleius' *Metamorphoses* and can quote from Livy's rare fourth decade, thanks to a book lent to him by the bishop of Modena. The fondness for classical learning common to the group might have developed into humanism had circumstances been different; as it was, their lack of stylistic sophistication, their medieval ways of thinking, their profession, and their lack of contact with a leisured highbrow milieu prevented this from happening; the movement took a different direction and faded out.

Thus more and more was added to the vast body of classical books and learning which had been accumulating over the centuries. Classical studies survived and advanced and were successfully adapted to new tastes and conditions, but in a context in which they were never really emancipated, could never really catch fire. It was left to the humanists of the Renaissance, who drew on this great medieval heritage with curiously little sense of debt, to exploit what had been achieved in a new and vital way.

XIII. GREEK IN THE WEST IN THE MIDDLE AGES

Under the Roman empire Italy had been to all intents and purposes a bilingual country, but with the decline of the empire Greek fell out of use except in the south of Italy and Sicily, where many towns were by origin Greek colonies. Cassiodorus' monastery Vivarium near Squillace is known to have had a collection of Greek books, but there is no sign that they contributed in any tangible way to the preservation of Greek. And in all the other parts of Western Europe, where the language had never been so firmly established, if indeed it was spoken at all, a knowledge of Greek became an attainment of exceptional rarity throughout the Middle Ages. Even diplomatic correspondence was sometimes delayed for lack of suitably qualified translators and interpreters. Though the importance of the language was often recognized, the history of Greek in the Latin West is a series of brief episodes which never led to the establishment of a lasting school.

The first of these episodes took place in England with the arrival of the Greek-speaking missionaries Theodore (d. 690) and Hadrian (d. 710). Interlinear glosses in about half a dozen manuscripts prove that they taught some Greek in Canterbury, confirming the reports in Bede's *Ecclesiastical History*.

The Carolingian revival of the ninth century created some interest in Greek. A few bilingual biblical manuscripts survive, proved by their handwriting to be products of the Latin world; they are thought to come from the scriptorium at Saint Gall. In 827 the Byzantine emperor sent a copy of Pseudo-Dionysius the Areopagite to the French king (still preserved as Paris gr. 437), which served as the basis for a translation of this highly popular forgery into Latin. A few years later the Irishman John Scottus Eriugena used the manuscript for his own translation of these works, and he also made some translations from Gregory of Nyssa, Gregory of Nazianzus, and Maximus the Confessor. But though some of his versions were widely read he did not create a tradition of Greek learning, and few other Greek texts were accessible for the time being except Boethius' versions of some of Aristotle's writings on logic and a version of Plato's *Timaeus* made in the fourth century by Chalcidius. In Rome a powerful figure at the papal court, Anastasius Bibliothecarius, added some historical and theological texts to the stock of accessible Greek authors.

In the twelfth century the range of translations was increased substantially. Much of the credit belongs to Burgundio of Pisa (1110–93), who had spent the years 1135–8 in Constantinople as an interpreter and returned there later, taking the opportunity to collect books. Copies of Galen which he used for his translations can be identified by marginal annotations in his own hand. A more obscure figure is James of Venice, a canon lawyer whose version of Aristotle's *Analytica posteriora* was known to John of Salisbury in 1159. Slightly better known are the inelegant and literal versions of Plato, Euclid, and Ptolemy made in Sicily c. 1160 under the aegis of Henricus Aristippus, archdeacon of Catania (d. 1162), who is said to have acquired some manuscripts sent as a gift by the Byzantine emperor to the Norman king of Sicily. Aristippus himself translated Plato's *Phaedo* and *Meno*, some works of Aristotle, and perhaps Hero's *Pneumatica*, which discusses steam-engines, 'penny-in-the-slot' machines, and other gadgets which have a surprisingly modern ring about them. He is praised also for his assistance in making the versions of Euclid, Proclus, and Ptolemy. Another important figure in this circle was the admiral Eugenius, who translated Ptolemy's *Optics* from the Arabic into Latin (the Greek is now lost). The main interests of these men were clearly scientific.

Yet the influence of these translators was perhaps slightly less than would have been expected, for Gerard of Cremona seems to have translated Ptolemy's *Almagest* from the Arabic in Toledo c. 1175, apparently in ignorance of the existing version. For the diffusion of Aristotelianism the work of Arabic scholars in Spain who did not know the original Greek text was also important. Arabic versions and commentaries by Avicenna and other scholars, especially Averroes (d. 1198), were turned into Latin in Toledo in the middle and late twelfth century. A large proportion of the Aristotelian corpus became known and circulated rapidly to other parts of Europe.

In the thirteenth century a few eminent men show more than a passing acquaintance with Greek. Robert Grosseteste (c. 1168–1253), though he learnt it late in life and always needed help from native speakers, studied Aristotle and translated the *Ethics*; he also translated Pseudo-Dionysius the Areopagite (his copy of the Greek text is in the Bodleian Library, Canonici gr. 97). His pupil Roger Bacon (c. 1214–94) wrote a Greek grammar (Oxford, Corpus Christi College 148), but despite his insistence that texts should be studied in the original rather than the often unintelligible translations he had few if any followers. A Flemish contemporary, William of Moerbeke (c. 1215–c. 1286), translated parts of Galen, Archimedes, and Aristotle, the last of these perhaps at the request of Thomas Aquinas. He lived for a time in Greece and can be traced at Thebes and Nicaea in 1260; later he became the Latin archbishop of Corinth. In Greece he had the good fortune to find some Neoplatonic writings which are now lost or fragmentary. Another figure of importance was a Greek from Reggio called Nicholas (fl.

c. 1308–45), who settled at the court of the Angevin kings at Naples, taking a doctorate at the university there in 1319, and made versions of many works ascribed to Galen. Some of these survive in his Latin text only.

It should be noted that as a rule medieval translations were made word for word, and quite often the translator was out of his depth when dealing with technicalities or the finer points of idiom. Nor was Latin the ideal medium for rendering all the subtleties of the originals. The lack of a definite article made it impossible to deal with many abstract expressions, and from 1266 onwards Moerbeke decided to make good the deficiency by using the French 'le'.

4

THE RENAISSANCE

1. HUMANISM

It will be convenient for the purpose of this brief survey to regard
the Renaissance as the period extending from about 1300 to the
middle of the sixteenth century. A cultural movement which is
recognizable as humanism, the stimulating force of the Renaissance, was at work in certain parts of Italy by the end of the
thirteenth century; by the middle of the sixteenth it had spread to
most of Western Europe and had transformed, among so many
other things, the transmission and study of classical antiquity. The
scholar of the late Renaissance had at his disposal almost as much
of the literature of Greece and Rome as we possess ourselves; most
of it he could read, at ease and at no great cost, in print; and the
translation of Greek into Latin, and of both into the vernacular
languages, had made a large part of ancient literature available to
the public at large. On the scholarly side, the foundations of historical and textual criticism had been securely laid.

Although humanism eventually acted upon all areas of intellectual and artistic life, it was primarily a literary activity and was
closely connected with the study and imitation of classical literature. The origin of the nineteenth-century term 'humanism' has
been traced to the word *umanista*, coined in the student slang of the
Italian universities of the late fifteenth century, on the analogy of
such words as *legista* and *iurista*, to denote the professional teacher
of the humanities, the *studia humanitatis*, which by this time had
crystallized as the study of grammar, rhetoric, history, poetry, and
moral philosophy, a canon as important for what it excluded as for
what it contained. The philosophical overtones humanism later
developed are only in part the result of its originally classical
emphasis—the teaching, study, and promotion of classical literature.

Many humanists, particularly in the fifteenth century, were professional teachers of the humanities; in this capacity they stepped into the place of the medieval *dictatores*, the men who had taught the art of composing letters, speeches, and other documents essential to diplomacy and public life. But the *dictamen* was an essentially medieval phenomenon, elaborate, stereotyped, smelling of the handbook and fair copy. The cultivation of style depended very little on the use of classical models, poetry was neglected, and classical studies generally in Italy seem to have been in some respects considerably less 'humane' than elsewhere. It is therefore not easy to see why humanism should have emerged from precisely this stable. There appears to be no simple answer, but it has been pointed out that most of the early humanists were notaries or lawyers or in some way associated with the legal profession. The law schools of Italy held a dominant position and the revival of Roman Law at Bologna had reforged a link with antiquity. The *dictatores* had been particularly active in the twelfth and thirteenth centuries, and the strongly grammatical and rhetorical emphasis of the education which lawyers would have received as a preliminary to their legal training, however much it may have lost its classical flavour, would impart a good command of Latin and a strong sense of style. Other important factors were the secular nature of Italian education, the existence of a sophisticated urban culture and of a professional class who had the training and the means and the leisure to pursue their classical interests and yet were sufficiently involved in civic life to make practical use, when the opportunity offered, of the new rhetoric. Some allowance must be made too for the personality of some of the individuals concerned, a Lovato or a Petrarch, who were gifted with the ability to communicate to others their enthusiasm and sense of excitement, and to the simple fact that there were libraries within reach which could provide the right sort of text to give humanism a new direction and emphasize the break with the past. Nor, as humanism broadened and extended its influence to other fields, was the practical aim of the *dictator* superseded, but the way to speaking and writing well was seen to lie in the use of classical models; the Latin classics were revived, not only as an academic study, but as the stuff of which eloquence was made, and it was this command of the Latin tongue that enabled the Renaissance man to impress his peers, denounce his enemies, thunder in defence of creed or city. In turn this led to a more sympathetic and comprehensive study of all aspects of ancient life and to that feeling of identification, however illusory, with the men and ideals of the ancient world which is the mark of neoclassicism.

This attempt to get closer to the classical spirit and to relive and rethink the past in terms of the present completely transcends the medieval approach to ancient letters. At last Latin literature was emancipated from the role for which it had been so badly cast, that of playing second-fiddle to religion; humanism was fundamentally secular, and the thin but unbroken tradition of lay education in Italy had doubtless contributed to this. The humanists were men of the world, sometimes teachers of grammar or literature, more commonly notaries, papal secretaries, chancellors of cities. They were usually book collectors, often on a large scale, and the growth of private libraries and a commercial book trade helped to break the long ecclesiastical monopoly of learning. At the same time the movement quickly gained a foothold within the Church and soon humanists were to be found in the highest positions of its hierarchy.

II. THE FIRST HUMANISTS

The beginnings of humanism are clearly detectable in a small literary coterie which grew up in Padua in the second half of the thirteenth century. The leader of these prehumanists was a Paduan judge, Lovato Lovati (1241-1309), who had a keen interest in classical poetry, a remarkable flair for unearthing texts unknown for centuries, and the ability to communicate his enthusiasm to a circle of friends. His surviving works are some collections of poems, in particular his *Metrical Epistles*. It is evident from these that Lovato was at best a mediocre poet, despite a freshness in his attempt to capture the spirit of his classical models; what is remarkable about these poems is the range of Latin poetry they reveal and the intricate way in which it is reworked. Since the clues to his classical models are echoes rather than direct quotations, the evidence is not always as clear cut as one would wish, especially as Latin poets are fond of echoing each other and the nature of poetic diction is such that coincidence cannot always be ruled out. It has been claimed that Lovato knew Lucretius, Catullus, the *Odes* of Horace, the whole of Tibullus, Propertius, Seneca's *Tragedies*, Martial, the *Silvae* of Statius, Valerius Flaccus, and Ovid's *Ibis*. Some of the items in this list have succumbed to a more sceptical scrutiny: the evidence for Lovato's knowledge of Catullus and Propertius has largely dissolved, though Catullus, soon to surface at Verona, was known to later prehumanists, and the evidence for Lucretius looks dubious; but precision is impossible and the acceptance that they may not have known certain texts does not materially affect the importance of Lovato and his circle. Other members of the group were acquainted with a similar range of Latin poets, and among the prose authors they studied evidence has emerged of a strong interest in Cicero.

A clue to the source of some of Lovato's texts may lie in a manuscript in the British Library (Add. 19906), which contains *inter alia* Justinus' *Epitome* and a collection of Lovato's poems. At the end of the *Epitome* the scribe has copied the subscription that he had found in his exemplar, and this reveals that the manuscript he was using was written in the monastery of Pomposa, in the Po delta, just before 1100. It was one of the books produced when the library was being enlarged at the instigation of abbot Hieronymus. Whether or not Add. 19906 was copied by Lovato himself, about 1290, as has been suggested, this manuscript establishes a link between Lovato and Pomposa which can be supported by other evidence. Among the classical texts known from the inventory to have been at Pomposa as early as 1093 was a great rarity, the *Tragedies* of Seneca, and this was probably none other than the extant eleventh-century 'codex Etruscus' of the *Tragedies* (Laur. 37.13 = E). Its parent may well have come from Montecassino. Lovato's use of an E-type text suggests that he had access to the Etruscus or something very close to it. Thus Pomposa appears to have been one of the libraries on which the prehumanists were able to draw, the Chapter Library at Verona was clearly another, and Bobbio, which is known to have had copies of Lucretius and Valerius Flaccus in the ninth century, may ultimately explain their knowledge of other texts. But not all the questions raised by their acquaintance with such a body of poetry have been answered; when these texts were rediscovered later, they came to light in France and Switzerland and Germany, with the Alps between them and the Veneto. Padua is a somewhat isolated and still obscure chapter in the story of the rediscovery of antiquity.

Lovato has also left us a short note on the metre and prosody of Senecan tragedy, remarkable in that it is derived, not from the medieval manuals, but from an intelligent study of Seneca's own practice. It was elaborated by his successors and is an indication of the intense interest which the prehumanists took in Roman tragedy. He also tried his hand at archaeology, and identified a skeleton which some workmen had turned up as the remains of the legendary founder of Padua, the Trojan Antenor, a gorgeous error. From all this it is clear that something new had begun.

Something of a contrast is provided by another Paduan judge of the same circle, Geremia da Montagnone (c. 1255–1321), who had no literary ambitions and trod the well-beaten path of the didactic florilegist: his *Compendium moralium notabilium*, probably put together in the first decade of the fourteenth century, enjoyed a wide circulation and was eventually printed in Venice in 1505. Geremia is more typical of his period; but in some respects his compendium plants him firmly in the humanist group. His reading is vast, his excerpts are systematically arranged, with chapter and verse added, and he seems to be quoting at first hand from the authors themselves; his notions of chronological sequence are not bad for his time, and he makes a nice distinction (e.g. *poeta* and *versilogus*) between classical and medieval writers. His quotations from Catullus and Martial, from Horace's *Odes* and Ovid's *Ibis*, together with his lavish use of Seneca's tragedies, show clearly the influence of the local humanism.

Lovato's spiritual successor was his friend and fellow townsman Albertino Mussato (1262–1329). A notary by profession, Mussato achieved distinction in the worlds of politics, diplomacy, and literature. Strongly influenced by Lovato, he read the same Latin poets and delved more deeply into Senecan tragedy; he also wrote

Historiae modelled on Livy, Sallust, and Caesar. His greatest literary success came in 1315: in order to open the eyes of the Paduans to the danger of falling into the clutches of the lord of Verona, Cangrande della Scala, he wrote a Senecan tragedy, the *Ecerinis*, which dealt in lurid colour with the rise and fall of Padua's own former tyrant, Ezzelino III. His play, the first tragedy to be written in classical metres since antiquity, was a tremendous literary and political success; the Paduans crowned its author with laurels and so revived a Roman custom which caught the imagination of the Renaissance and was a fitting compliment for the pioneer of modern classical drama.

Although limited in its influence by the weakness in communications and the fragmentation of political life in Italy, Paduan humanism soon percolated to the neighbouring town of Vicenza, where the notary Benvenuto Campesani (1255–1323) composed in the early years of the fourteenth century his famous and enigmatic epigram celebrating the return to Verona of her long-lost poet Catullus. Verona fostered a more scholarly tradition of humanism, which was nourished by the Chapter Library. Among its treasures were two important prose texts, the lost Veronensis of Pliny's *Letters* which had been known to Ratherius, and the ninth-century manuscript of the *Historia Augusta* (Vat. Pal. lat. 899), which had travelled down to Verona in time to have an enormous influence on Renaissance historiography. Both were used by Giovanni de Matociis (fl. 1306–20), custodian of the cathedral, who, in addition to his major work, the *Historia Imperialis*, produced the first critical work on literary history to be written in the Renaissance, his *Brevis adnotatio de duobus Pliniis*. Basing himself on the Verona Pliny and a text of Suetonius, he was able to split the composite Pliny of the Middle Ages into the Elder and the Younger. The Chapter Library also had its own florilegist: in 1329 someone who had access to the books put together a *Flores moralium auctoritatum* (Verona CLXVIII (155)) which, while being partly derived from other florilegia, contained excerpts from rare texts known to have been at Verona, from Catullus, the Younger Pliny, the *Historia Augusta*, Varro's *Res rusticae*, and Cicero's *Letters to Atticus and Quintus*.

III. THE CONSOLIDATION OF HUMANISM: PETRARCH
     AND HIS GENERATION

Although recent research has shown that the prehumanists had
advanced much further along the road to humanism than had been
supposed, especially in their acquisition of a new body of Latin
poetry, the éclat with which Petrarch (1304–74) makes his dramatic
entry has hardly been dimmed. He dwarfs his precursors in every
respect: he was an immeasurably greater poet and greater man than
any. of them; his horizons were wider and his influence, never
cramped within the limits of town or province, extended over most
of Western Europe; he had the vision and the ability to unite the
two existing strands of humanism, the literary and the scholarly,
and to combine aims which reached for the moon with the capacity
for painstaking research; he went further than anyone else in trying
to revive within the framework of a Christian society the ideals of
ancient Rome, and his attempts to get close to the great figures of
the past, and indeed to rival their achievement, though flirting with
the vainglorious, unleashed passions and ambitions which were to
reanimate the whole cultural legacy of the ancient world and bring
it to bear upon contemporary modes of thought and literature.

It was fortunate for Petrarch, and indeed for the continuity of the
classical tradition in the West, that for a critical period in the fourteenth century (1309–77) the papal curia transferred its seat from
Rome to Avignon. Avignon was well placed to be a point of cultural
contact between the north and the south, and the attraction to the
papal court of men of different nationalities and intellectual outlook
had important consequences. In particular, educated churchmen
and lawyers, whose growing interest in classical texts demanded
more knowledge of the ancient world than their schooling had
provided, began to draw on the medieval legacy of the north. The
monastic and cathedral libraries of France lay within reach, and for
help in reading the more difficult classical texts they turned to
Oxford, to the polymath Nicholas Trevet, who wrote at the express
request of a pope and a cardinal his commentaries on Livy (c. 1318)
and the *Tragedies* of Seneca (c. 1315). Thus when Petrarch arrived at

Avignon he found an older generation with an active interest in texts which had been little read for centuries. Petrarch owed much to this stimulating society; at the same time he had the imagination and the historical sense to see the inadequacy of looking at antiquity through the eyes of the Middle Ages and broke away to recreate it for himself.

The importance of Avignon as a point of contact between France and Italy, the Middle Ages and the Renaissance, is illustrated by the history of a group of texts that includes Julius Paris' epitome of Valerius Maximus and the *De chorographia* of Pomponius Mela. As we have seen (pp. 105-6), this little body of utilitarian texts was edited and probably put together at Ravenna in the fifth century by Rusticius Helpidius Domnulus and survives in a copy made in the ninth century at Auxerre and annotated by Heiric (Vat. lat. 4929). These texts had a long and important career in the Renaissance, and all the humanist copies derive from the Auxerre archetype via a twelfth-century manuscript, now lost, which Petrarch had acquired at Avignon. We know this because Petrarch's notes were often copied along with the text, and in the earliest of the humanist copies (Ambros. H. 14 inf.) we find, for instance, the revealing remark: *Avinio. Ubi nunc sumus 1335.* The textual history of Propertius too illustrates a similar pattern. The oldest manuscript of this author (Gud. lat. 224 = N), written in northern France and at one time in the region of Metz, does not appear to have been used in Italy until the 1470s; another old manuscript, no longer extant, was to arrive with Poggio in the 1420s; but the earliest manuscripts in the humanist tradition derive in direct line from the other early Propertius manuscript still extant (Voss. Lat. O. 38 = A), which never left northern Europe. The link between the Vossianus and the humanist manuscripts is a copy of A which had belonged to Petrarch. Via Petrarch's copy we get back to A; and A takes us back, via the Sorbonne library—where it was at the time of Petrarch's trip to Paris in 1333—to the booky garden of Richard of Fournival, and through him to the medieval libraries of northern France. Amid the gay distractions of papal Avignon the young Petrarch once again became the converging point of threads of transmission which stretched back through the Middle Ages to antiquity itself, and forward again, with complex ramifications, into the High Renaissance.

The manuscript that everyone immediately associates with Petrarch and Avignon is a famous Livy now in the British Library (Harley 2493, Plate XV). This volume, which originally contained books 1–10 and 21–40, was put together by Petrarch; parts of it he copied in his own hand. The nucleus of the book is a manuscript of Livy's third decade, written in Italy about 1200 and ultimately derived, as are all the complete manuscripts that have survived, from the extant Puteanus; to this Petrarch added a copy of the first and fourth decades. The various books of Livy's voluminous work, usually in units of ten, had followed their separate fates through the Middle Ages and it was no mean achievement to have put three decades under one cover, especially as the fourth was rare in Petrarch's day; the remaining books of Livy (41–5) were not discovered until the sixteenth century. The text was supplemented, annotated, and corrected by Petrarch himself; of special interest are the variants recorded in his notes to books 26–30 of the third decade, for these were taken from a manuscript independent of the Puteanus. It is evident that for these books, as for the fourth decade, Petrarch had drawn on a manuscript of the Spirensian tradition. This tradition, so called because one of its early representatives had belonged to the Cathedral of Speyer, descends stage by stage from the fifth-century uncial manuscript that was at Piacenza when Otto III acquired it and carried it off to Germany (see pp. 107–8). Thus Petrarch succeeded in bringing together, though not for the first time, two great textual traditions whose history we can trace from antiquity to the Renaissance. According to an attractive theory that has been widely accepted Petrarch's source for the Spirensian tradition was ultimately an old manuscript that Landolfo Colonna, a member of the Colonna family whose patronage Petrarch enjoyed and who was for a long time a canon of Chartres, had borrowed from the Cathedral library. But it has long been known that the Spirensian tradition of the fourth decade, in a form close to that used by Petrarch, had circulated among the prehumanists in Padua, and the hypothesis that he had tapped this source via an old manuscript at Chartres has become uneconomical and for various reasons difficult to maintain. Thus the geographical location of Avignon, within the reach of French medieval libraries, may be less significant in the case of Livy than at one time appeared, and Petrarch's assembling of such a remarkable book would owe more to his youthful flair and enthusiasm, the scholarly intercourse that Avignon offered, and the deposits of Livy already available in Italy. Petrarch's Livy later passed into the possession of Lorenzo Valla, whose famous emendations can be seen in its margins.

This happy conjunction of book collector and scholar meant that in time Petrarch acquired a classical library which for breadth and quality had no equal in his day. We can to a certain extent reconstruct his collection of Cicero texts, an author whom he regarded as his *alter ego* and for whom he scoured the whole of Europe. It is an impressive list: almost all the philosophical works, most of the *rhetorica*, the *Letters to Atticus and Quintus*, and a remarkable range of speeches which he had built up over a lifetime, extending from the *Pro Archia*, which he discovered at Liège in 1333 and copied himself, to the *Pro Cluentio*, which Boccaccio transcribed for him in 1355 from an eleventh-century manuscript in Montecassino (Laur. 51.10). The *Letters to Atticus* were a discovery of supreme importance to him, worthy of an immediate letter to Cicero himself. He found them, as had others before him, in the Chapter Library at Verona, in 1345. It is on these letters, and in practice still more on those of Seneca (whose works he possessed *in toto*), that his own letters, the most charming and valuable of his prose writings, are modelled.

More significant than the mere range of his books was the intensity with which he read and re-read those he thought important; for it was easy in the Renaissance to degenerate into a mere book collector. The patience with which he corrected and annotated his texts can be seen in the embryonic editions of the Harleian Livy and the Ambrosian Vergil (S.P. 10/27, *olim* A. 79 inf.), his own copy of his favourite poet. By a stroke of good fortune, in addition to reconstructing much of Petrarch's library and seeing him hard at work on his books, we have an intimate record of his literary tastes, for on the flyleaf of a manuscript in Paris (lat. 2201) we have what a brilliant piece of decipherment proved to be Petrarch's own list of his favourite books. The list is instructive, both for the works it contains and their order of priority, and for those it does not contain; but it must be remembered that the list belongs to the earlier period of his life and that some of the books that he prized were among his later discoveries. Cicero not unexpectedly heads the list, his 'moral' works taking precedence. Next comes Seneca: the *Letters* have pride of place; the *Tragedies* come later, and in a second and more select list on the same page they are explicitly excluded from the inner circle. The next main section is devoted to history, headed by Valerius Maximus and Livy; there is a special category of *exempla*, in which Macrobius and Gellius find their home. Poetry follows, with Vergil, Lucan, Statius, Horace, Ovid, and Juvenal; Horace is qualified *praesertim in odis*, a complete reversal of medieval taste. At the end come the technical works, grammar, dialectic, and astrology. Augustine is favoured with a list to himself, and with Boethius' *De consolatione Philosophiae* he makes up the sum of the Christian content. The only Greek work is Aristotle's *Ethics* (in Latin, of course), and this disappears from the select list. Of the law, in which Petrarch received his formal education at Bologna, nothing; the writers of the Middle Ages are likewise rejected, made redundant by direct contact with antiquity.

One of the first to fall under the influence of Petrarch's humanism was his younger contemporary Boccaccio (1313–75). Under the patronage of its ruler, Robert of Anjou (1309–43), Naples had emerged as an important intellectual centre quite early in the century and it was here that Boccaccio spent his youth. His early works, written in Italian, belong to the medieval tradition of rhetoric and romance; it was largely his admiration for Petrarch, whom in 1350 he got to know personally, that made him turn from the vernacular to Latin, from literature to scholarship. As a scholar he fell far behind Petrarch; he lacked the patience even to be good at copying manuscripts. He was in the main a gatherer of facts about ancient life and literature, and his encyclopedic treatises on ancient biography, geography, and mythology, enjoyed a considerable vogue in the Renaissance and did much to promote the understanding of classical literature. He had a passionate interest in poetry, and this led him along the lesser-known paths of Latin literature to poetry unknown to Petrarch, to Ovid's *Ibis*, and the *Appendix Vergiliana*; our oldest manuscript of the *Priapea* (Laur. 33.31) is in his hand.

Among the prose works which he possessed was a group which clearly indicate that a new stream of the medieval tradition had broken through to the surface: his acquaintance with the *Annals* and *Histories* of Tacitus, Apuleius' *Golden Ass*, and Varro's *De lingua latina*, can only mean that someone had unlocked the riches of Montecassino. Knowledge of these Cassinese texts began to percolate beyond the walls of the monastery and within a few years the manuscripts themselves had been spirited away from their medieval home and were in the hands of the Florentine humanists. It is not surprising that the details of this process, and the men responsible, remain something of a mystery. Boccaccio may himself have taken a hand in the affair; he apparently visited Montecassino in 1355 and may there have made or obtained a copy of two unknown texts contained in the Beneventan manuscript Laur. 51.10, Varro's *De lingua latina* and Cicero's *Pro Cluentio*, for later that year he was able to send Petrarch a copy of these works written in his own hand. At some stage he acquired Laur. 51.10 itself, and his library also contained copies of Tacitus and Apuleius. He was able to draw on Apuleius when writing his own *Decameron*, and his autograph copy of the *Golden Ass* (Laur. 54.32) is still extant. The Cassinese manuscripts of both Apuleius and Tacitus turned up in Florence, and there they remain; they came into the possession of Niccolò Niccoli, passed to the Library of San Marco and, bound together, they now sit under one cover in the Laurentian Library (Laur. 68.2). Varro and the *Pro Cluentio* followed a similar route. It has been suggested that an important part in this operation may have been taken by a humanist known to both Boccaccio and Petrarch, Zanobi da Strada. As secretary to the bishop in whose jurisdiction Montecassino lay, he had access to the monastery and lived there from 1355 to 1357; marginalia in all three of the early manuscripts of Apuleius (including the mysterious *spurcum additamentum* at *Met.* 10.21.1) are in his hand and testify to his strong personal interest in that particular text.

Although he was not in the front rank as a scholar, Boccaccio put his genius and enthusiasm behind the humanist movement and helped to mark out the lines along which it was to develop. He naturalized humanism in Florence and made the first attempt, even if for the time being an abortive one, to establish Greek studies in the city which was to become the centre of the teaching of Greek in the West.

IV. COLUCCIO SALUTATI (1331–1406)

The combination of creative genius and humanist drive gives Petrarch and Boccaccio an aura which has eluded Coluccio Salutati. But he is a man of solid and enduring achievements, a great administrator and public figure, a writer and thinker who struggled with the difficulties of combining pagan poetry and Christian ethic, the past and the present, into a harmonious whole, and a scholar with a substantial and distinctive contribution to make to classical studies. He was a powerful and critical link in the development of humanism, second in importance only to Petrarch, and contributed decisively to its establishment as one of the great movements of European culture. He had corresponded with Petrarch in his later years, knew Boccaccio well, and was strongly influenced by both. Inspired by the previous generation, he passed on the torch to the next great wave of humanists, many of whom he could claim as his disciples, among them Poggio and Leonardo Bruni. From the death of Petrarch in 1374 until his own death in 1406 Salutati presided over the humanist movement.

Although a disconcerting taste for allegorical exegesis makes it clear that Salutati had one foot still in the Middle Ages, he possessed in full measure the characteristic qualities of the humanist. As chancellor of Florence for over thirty years, he was able to consummate the powerful alliance that had grown up between humanism and politics, to use his Latin and his learning to lash his antagonists, whether enemies of Florence or detractors of classical literature. He read the ancient authors passionately and at first hand and achieved the easy intimacy with them that we have seen in Petrarch. Like other humanists, he combined his enthusiasm for ancient literature with a serious concern for scholarly detail: he was an active collator of manuscripts, showed remarkable grasp of the ways in which texts are corrupted, made some creditable contributions to textual criticism (his emendation of Scipio Nasica to Scipio Asina in Valerius Maximus (6.9.1) is well known), and has been recognized as a pioneer in this field. Above all, it was he who invited Chrysoloras to Florence (see p. 147) and so made possible, in 1397, the real beginning of Greek studies in Western Europe.

Not the least thing about Salutati was his library; more than a hundred of his books have been identified. One of them is a classical text copied throughout in his own hand, the *Tragedies* of Seneca (Brit. Mus. Add. 11987), to which he had added Mussato's *Ecerinis*. Although his books have less intrinsic interest than those of Petrarch, this fine collection was an important cultural instrument both during his lifetime and after it was dispersed. Among his more remarkable volumes were the oldest complete manuscript of Tibullus (Ambros. R. 26 sup. = A), one of the three primary witnesses to the text of Catullus (Ottob. lat. 1829 = R), and—his greatest find—a copy of Cicero's *Ad familiares*. Cicero's *Letters* had a special significance for the early humanists; they felt that they now knew Cicero intimately, that they could travel back in time to the classical period and relive moments with the person who was for them the greatest of the Romans. The *Ad familiares* were found in the cathedral library at Vercelli by Pasquino Cappelli, chancellor of Milan, who had instituted a search at Salutati's instigation. Salutati was really looking for a manuscript of the *Letters to Atticus*, which Petrarch had known, and he was beside himself with joy to receive (in 1392) the unexpected bonus of a completely unknown collection. In the following year he obtained a copy of the *Letters to Atticus*, and so became the first person for centuries to possess both collections; his copies still survive (Laur. 49.7 and 49.18; the second is the important manuscript M of the *Ad Atticum*). The Vercelli codex was eventually taken to Florence and there it remains (Laur. 49.9), the only complete surviving Carolingian manuscript of Cicero's *Letters*. It is interesting to observe that the rounded picture of Cicero that emerged from his letters provoked very different reactions from Petrarch and Salutati. While Petrarch was upset to discover that

Cicero had left philosophy for a life of action and intrigue, it was his
blending of intellectual pursuits with a political career that roused
the admiration of Salutati and the later Renaissance.

V. THE GREAT AGE OF DISCOVERY: POGGIO
(1380–1459)

The gradual rediscovery of ancient literature runs like a powerful
current through the Renaissance from the days of Paduan prehumanism into the second half of the fifteenth century and beyond.
Lovato, Petrarch, Boccaccio, and Salutati had been pre-eminent
among those who had added to the list of classical works made
accessible to the writers and thinkers of their time; but for sheer
ability in turning up lost texts they were all outdone by Poggio, an
arresting person, who found time as papal secretary to indulge in a
variety of literary pursuits, ranging from history and moral essays to
polemic and pornography of such accomplished scurrility that it
becomes clear that the more robust writings of antiquity had not
been rediscovered for nothing.

The great opportunity for another break-through in the discovery of classical texts came when the Council of Constance
(1414–17) was summoned to heal the Great Schism and settle other
ecclesiastical problems. The whole papal court moved to Constance, and the humanists who were assisting at the conference
soon perceived, as men do, that there were interesting activities not
included in the agenda; they devoted their spare time to the search
for classical texts. Poggio made a number of expeditions, the first in
1415 to the monastery of Cluny in Burgundy, where he found an
ancient manuscript of Cicero's speeches, containing the *Pro Cluentio*, *Pro Roscio Amerino*, *Pro Murena*, *Pro Milone*, and *Pro Caelio*. The
Pro Roscio and *Pro Murena* were previously unknown. This manuscript, which was at least as early as the eighth century, is known as
the *vetus Cluniacensis*, and its partial reconstruction from copies and
extracts in 1905 is perhaps the greatest achievement of the English
Ciceronian scholar A. C. Clark. The text of the lost Cluniacensis is
most accurately mirrored in a manuscript which was in part

copied from it before it was carried off to Italy by Poggio (Paris lat. 14749). This manuscript has now yielded up its secret and revealed the hand of the French humanist Nicholas of Clamanges.

His next foray was in the summer of 1416, this time to Saint Gall in company with three humanist friends, Bartolomeo da Montepulciano, Cencio Rustici, and Zomino da Pistoia. The result was three major discoveries: a complete Quintilian (previous humanists had had to make do with *mutili*), Asconius' *Commentary* on five of Cicero's speeches, and a manuscript containing four books (i–iv.377) of the *Argonautica* of Valerius Flaccus. Poggio's manuscript of Quintilian is of little value, but for Asconius we depend on three copies which resulted from this trip, one made by Poggio, one (and the best) by Zomino (Pistoia A. 37), and one derived from Bartolomeo's autograph (Laur. 54.5). The lost Sangallensis of the *Argonautica* has to be reconstructed from a similar trio, one certainly in Poggio's hand (Madrid, Bibl. Nac. 8514, *olim* X. 81, which also contains his Asconius); but for Valerius we have a complete and more important ninth-century manuscript from Fulda (Vat. lat. 3277), which was itself eventually taken to Italy.

Early in 1417, armed with official sanction, Poggio and Bartolomeo made a highly organized expedition to Saint Gall and other monasteries of the area: their finds included Lucretius, Silius Italicus, and Manilius. The manuscripts which they found have perished, but their legacy remains. The copy of Manilius which Poggio had made is an important witness to the text (Madrid, Bibl. Nac. 3678, *olim* M. 31); his Lucretius fathered the whole race of *Itali*, and all our manuscripts of Silius go back to the copies made as a result of this expedition. At the same time Poggio acquired from Fulda their famous manuscript of Ammianus (Vat. lat. 1873), which he carried off to Italy; he also set eyes on their Apicius, and this too was eventually taken to Rome, by Enoch of Ascoli in 1455 (New York, Acad. Med. MS. Safe). Now or at some later date he also obtained a manuscript of Columella (an author already known in Italy), and his manuscript was probably the insular codex at Fulda, which reached Italy in the fifteenth century (Ambros. L. 85 sup.).

In the summer of 1417 Poggio went on more extended travels in France and Germany. He made two important discoveries. The first was eight unknown speeches of Cicero: the *Pro Caecina*, *Pro Roscio comoedo*, *De lege agraria* i–iii, *Pro Rabirio perduellionis reo*, *In Pisonem*, *Pro Rabirio Postumo*. He found the *Pro Caecina* at Langres, the others probably in Cologne cathedral. His autograph copy of these speeches has now been discovered (Vat. lat. 11458) and so done away with a tedious process of reconstruction. The second find was one of the rarest of texts, the *Silvae* of Statius; our manuscripts of these poems all descend from the copy that was made for him (Madrid, Bibl. Nac. 3678, *olim* M. 31).

When the Council was over, Poggio spent some years in England, where he found what he described as a *particula Petronii*, i.e. the *excerpta vulgaria*; it is from this manuscript that all the fifteenth-century copies descend. On his way home in 1423 he found at Cologne a second manuscript of Petronius containing the *Cena Trimalchionis*, and from the copy that he commissioned descends our unique source for the complete *Cena* (Paris lat. 7989). It disappeared from view while on loan to Niccolò Niccoli, fortunately to reappear at Trogir in Dalmatia about 1650. The Propertius that he sent to Niccoli in 1427 may have been another of the fruits of this expedition.

Poggio's achievements in the field of discovery were prodigious; his personal intervention in the history of many important texts was decisive and influential. He also occupies a notable place in the history of handwriting; though he may not have invented the new humanistic script, as was once thought, he was one of its first and finest exponents (Plate XVI). As time went by, and particularly from the beginning of the thirteenth century, Caroline minuscule had become more angular and thick and considerably less attractive, developing into what is known as the Gothic hand. The humanistic script was a deliberate return to an earlier form of Caroline minuscule; it appears to have been developed about 1400 in Florence, with Salutati and his two protégés Niccolò Niccoli and Poggio all playing a part. Niccoli seems to have developed the cursive form of the new script. With the advent of printing the formal hand provided the model for the roman fount, the cursive for italic.

The bulk of Latin literature known to us had now been recovered. The more important of the remaining discoveries may be mentioned more briefly. In 1421, in the cathedral of Lodi, to the south-east of Milan, Gerardo Landriani found a collection of *rhetorica*, including the *De oratore* and *Orator* (previously only known through *mutili*) and an unknown work, the *Brutus*. In 1429 Nicolaus of Cues brought to Rome an eleventh-century German manuscript of Plautus (Vat. lat. 3870), which contained, among others, the twelve plays which were still unknown. The unique manuscript of Tacitus' *Opera minora* (Iesi lat. 8) had been known to Poggio as early as 1425, but attempts to entice it from Hersfeld had failed: in 1455 it was finally brought to Rome, probably by Enoch of Ascoli. The remaining unknown part of Tacitus, *Annals* 1–6, was filched from Corvey and arrived in Rome in 1508. Other fifteenth-century discoveries included Cornelius Nepos, Celsus, Frontinus' *De aquis*, and the *Panegyrici Latini*.

With the finding of a large number of grammatical works at Bobbio in 1493 ended what Sabbadini called the heroic age of discovery. But important texts continued to see the light. In 1501–4 Sannazaro found in France the archetype of the pseudo-Ovidian *Halieutica* and the *Cynegetica* of Grattius (Vienna lat. 277) and its no less interesting and important copy (for the Vienna manuscript is now incomplete) containing the *florilegium Thuaneum*. But most of the discoveries of the early sixteenth century were associated with the scholarly activity now centred at Basle, the home at this time of Erasmus and Beatus Rhenanus and such printers as Froben and Cratander. This included a vigorous and perhaps more systematic search for new manuscripts. Beatus Rhenanus discovered Velleius Paterculus at Murbach in 1515 and produced the *editio princeps* in 1520. By using an important new manuscript Cratander was able to print in 1528 an edition of Cicero which contained five letters to Brutus never seen before and for which his book remains the unique source. In 1527 Grynaeus found the surviving books of Livy's fifth decade at Lorsch. Such finds were rarely to be the lot of later generations of scholars, but the excitement of discovery continued, buoyed up by two new sources, palimpsests and papyri.

It should be remembered in this context that the humanists also had a capacity for losing manuscripts. Once they had carefully copied a text, they were liable to have little interest in the manuscript which had preserved it. The Cluny and Lodi manuscripts of Cicero, the Veronenses of Catullus and Pliny have perished; only a few leaves survive of the Hersfeld Tacitus; the *Cena Trimalchionis* was nearly lost again for ever. Other manuscripts unnamed and unsung survived into the Renaissance (their existence can be inferred from their humanist progeny), but not beyond it. Nor does the situation appear to have been much better in the sixteenth century. Manuscripts were often treated with scant respect by the printers to whom they had been entrusted and faced an uncertain future when they had served their purpose. There were some sad casualties. The Murbach codex of the *Historia Augusta* lent to Erasmus survives as a few scraps in a binding (Nuremberg, Fragm. Lat. 7); the fifth-century manuscript of Pliny's *Letters*, the unique source for book X, now reduced to a fragment (Pierpont Morgan Lib., M. 462), had triumphed over every hazard until borrowed by Aldus from the abbey of Saint-Victor at Paris; the two manuscripts from Worms and Speyer which Beatus Rhenanus and Gelenius used for their edition of Livy disappeared from sight. But these two scholars do not appear to have been as culpable as was once thought. The Hersfeld manuscript of Ammianus Marcellinus that Gelenius used for the Froben edition of 1533 survived until later in the century, when it was dismembered not far from Hersfeld to provide covers for account books (we still have six leaves: Kassel, Philol. 2° 27); and the Murbach codex of Velleius Paterculus used by Rhenanus seems to have survived into the late eighteenth century, being last heard of in a sale-room in 1786.

VI. LATIN SCHOLARSHIP IN THE FIFTEENTH CENTURY:
     VALLA AND POLITIAN

The quickened interest in all aspects of ancient life and literature, fostered by the continual excitement of new discoveries, led to a vigorous growth in all the main disciplines and techniques that are necessary to a full understanding of classical antiquity. While archaeology, numismatics, epigraphy, and the study of Roman institutions were launched along sound lines by such men as Flavio

Biondo (1392–1463), historical and textual criticism, which are fundamental to the study of classical texts, were developed with singular brilliance by two humanists who may be regarded as representing what was best in the scholarship of the fifteenth century, Lorenzo Valla (1407–57) and Angelo Poliziano (1454–94). As attention will be focused on these two figures, it should be emphasized that they are in a class apart. The average scholar of the time did not reach these heights, though there is evidence that a great deal of sound and scrupulous work was done on Latin texts during this period. A glance at the apparatus criticus of many classical texts—Catullus is a good example—will show how frequently scholars of this period were able to correct errors in the tradition; and their successors of today, sometimes chagrined to find that their emendation had been anticipated long ago by some anonymous pedant, are not always justified in assuming that luck rather than judgement had produced the answer. But there were also the dabblers, men whose confidence in emending and elucidating classical texts had outstripped their scholarly equipment and whose facile jottings, even when they were not intended to infect the traditional text, might easily do so. There was a temptation to embellish, to produce the readable and elegant text which the customer expected. Hence the caution with which editors use the manuscripts of this period, often disappointed to find that a splendidly produced book contains an inferior or specious text.

It was now possible to study the works of Latin literature with greater ease and in greater depth. A contributory factor of supreme importance was the increasing number of splendid libraries, founded or enriched by generous and influential patrons, among them the Visconti in Pavia, Duke Federigo of Urbino, Alfonso V in Naples, the Medici in Florence, Pope Nicholas V in Rome. In the train of the library-builders came the highly organized entrepreneur like the bookseller Vespasiano da Bisticci (1421–98), who was prepared to lay on forty-five scribes when a library was on order; and, as the manuscript gave way to the printed book, classical texts and the scholarly work that began to gather around them could be disseminated without restriction or limit. The invention of printing would soon have a profound effect on the progress and conduct of scholarship. Classical texts moved into the public domain, scholars had at their disposal the same standardized text against which to pit their wits or collate their manuscripts, and there was now an international forum for learned debate or polemic.

The critical standards of this surging humanism were carefully probed by Lorenzo Valla. Trained in Latin and Greek by the best teachers of his day, among them Aurispa and Leonardo Bruni, and gifted with exceptional ability, Valla was clearly destined to make his mark. But his vain and aggressive nature, which prompted him to tilt at every sacred cow and was to involve him in a series of venomous polemics, particularly with Panormita and Poggio, might have seriously hampered his career, had it not been for the protection and patronage, first of Alfonso V, then of Nicholas V. Nicholas opened the doors of the Curia to this *enfant terrible*, and under his successor he became papal secretary. From 1450 he held a chair of rhetoric at Rome.

An early victim of his critical powers was the Donation of Constantine, a notorious document, fabricated as early as the eighth or ninth century, which strengthened papal claims to temporal power by recording the legendary gift of Rome and the provinces of Italy by Constantine to the Pope: in 1440 Valla proved, on historical and linguistic grounds, that the Donation was a forgery. It is not surprising that he likewise attacked the authenticity of the spurious correspondence between Seneca and Saint Paul, which had had an undeserved run since the days of Jerome. His most famous work is his *Elegantiae*, dealing with points of Latin style, usage, and grammar. Composed while he was at Naples, it was first printed in 1471; by 1536 it had appeared in no less than 59 editions, a standard authority on the Latin language for both the fifteenth and sixteenth centuries. Its critical and independent scholarship marks the highest point that the study of Latin had so far attained. It was followed, in 1446-7, by his *Emendationes sex librorum Titi Livi* (books 21–6). Written with a scathing brilliance recurrent in later works of this sort, this philological masterpiece was designed to discredit two other scholars at the court of Alfonso, Panormita and Facio, and made it painfully clear that only the best could play at the fashionable game of emending Livy. One of the weapons in his arsenal was the great Livy volume which had been put together by Petrarch, and his autograph notes can still be seen in its margins (Plate XV). He dared to emend the Vulgate itself, and his notes and corrections (1449), based on a study of the Greek original and early patristic texts, were fully appreciated by Erasmus, who had them printed in 1505. He also found time to be a prolific translator from the Greek. He firmly belongs to the first half of the century, and it is significant that full recognition of his talents had to wait until his works were put into print.

Politian was born at Montepulciano and educated at Florence. He showed a precocious talent and was taken at an early age into the household of Lorenzo de' Medici, who made him tutor to his children and remained his lifelong friend and patron; by the age of thirty he was a professor of such repute that he attracted scholars from all over Europe to his lectures on Greek and Latin literature. As well as being an influential teacher, he was the finest poet of his time, both in Italian and in Latin; and as a scholar he at times transcends his age and moves out of reach of any of his contemporaries.

Politian won his prominent position in the history of the classical tradition both by his exact scholarship and by the way in which he opened the eyes of his contemporaries to the full perspective of ancient literature. Valla had recommended the study of Quintilian, but his insistence on a classical norm in the writing of Latin had tended to foster the predominant cult of Ciceronian Latin. Politian firmly rejected Ciceronianism and chose to create an eclectic style of his own which exploited the whole range of Latin: *'non exprimis' inquit aliquis 'Ciceronem'. Quid tum? Non enim sum Cicero, me tamen (ut opinor) exprimo* (*Epist.* 8.16). In the same way he was the first to give serious attention to the prose and poetry of the Silver Age.

Politian's great work of scholarship was his *Miscellanea*, a collection of studies of varying length on different points of scholarship. The elegant and original format of this miscellany, which put as much distance as possible between itself and the line by line commentary on a specific text that had formerly been the fashion, was well chosen to display the many sides of his learning. The first part (*Centuria prima*) was published in Florence in 1489; an autograph draft of a second series of chapters came to light only recently. The work is similar in style to the *Attic Nights* of Aulus Gellius; again the influence of late authors is evident. A few examples of the topics discussed will show the character of the book: the origin of the names of the days of the week, the original meaning of the word 'panic', the significance of a coin struck by Brutus showing his portrait with a cap and two daggers are typical problems. To settle the question of how to spell the name Vergil Politian invokes the evidence of some inscriptions and the spelling of very old manuscripts. He uses the text of Callimachus to emend a corrupt passage in Catullus (66.48), a typical example of his use of Greek sources to correct and illustrate Latin texts. In an important chapter for the development of textual criticism (*Misc.* xviii) he points out that the manuscript of the *Epistulae ad familiares* which was made for Salutati in 1392 (Laur. 49.7 = P) is a copy of the Vercelli manuscript (Laur. 49.9 = M), and demonstrates that P itself, in which a number of leaves have been displaced through an error in binding, must be the parent of a whole family of later manuscripts in which the sequence of a group of letters has been disturbed. He made a similar inference about the manuscripts of Valerius Flaccus. This methodical application of the principle of *eliminatio codicum descriptorum* (see p. 210) is not found again until the nineteenth century. In the *Letters to Atticus* (15.14.4) he emends the vulgate reading *cera* to *cerula* on the strength of the reading *ceruia* in M, the best of the Italian manuscripts (Laur. 49.18). The principle that conjectural emendation must start from the earliest recoverable stage of the tradition, employed more than once by Politian, was not fully exploited until the age of Lachmann.

Although his conviction that later manuscripts are derivative was too sweeping, Politian's constant recourse to the oldest manuscripts available and his distrust of humanist copies was bound to produce solid results. In this he was helped enormously by the improved library facilities of his day and the advent of the printed book; between 1465 and 1475 the bulk of the Latin classics were put into print. He made full use of libraries, both public and private, in Florence and elsewhere, particularly that of the Medici; no less than thirty-five Medicean manuscripts were out on loan to him at the time of his death. Among the many great classical manuscripts he is known to have examined or collated were such important witnesses as the Bembinus of Terence (Vat. lat. 3226 of the fourth to fifth century), the Romanus of Vergil (Vat. lat. 3867 of the fifth to sixth century), the Etruscus of Seneca's *Tragedies*, an old Propertius, possibly the Neapolitanus, possibly Poggio's discovery, and the lost archetype of Valerius Flaccus. Some of the manuscripts he used have been lost and his careful collations, usually entered (by him or for him) into his copy of an early printed edition, have the status of important witnesses to the text. Examples are the Parma edition of Ovid in the Bodleian Library, with his autograph readings from the lost Marcianus of the *Tristia*, and his *editio princeps* of the *Scriptores rei rusticae*; this contains collations of an early manuscript of Columella (doubtless Ambros. L. 85 sup. from Fulda), and, more important, of the lost archetype of the agricultural works of Cato and Varro. The variants that he entered in his copy of the first edition of the *Silvae*, however, are now thought to have been taken from Poggio's manuscript (Madrid 3678) rather than from its exemplar and so have no independent value.

His keen interest in the more technical writings of antiquity is further illustrated by a massive edition of the Elder Pliny (Rome, 1473) now at Oxford; this contains a transcript of Politian's notes and collations, the latter taken from five different manuscripts (carefully distinguished with the sigla *a b c d e*) and the important critical work of a contemporary scholar, the *Castigationes Plinianae* of Ermolao Barbaro. For Apicius he was able to collate the two ninth-century manuscripts on which the text is based (E and V), from Fulda and Tours respectively. The Fulda manuscript is now in the Academy of Medicine in New York (MS. Safe), while a fragment of Politian's own manuscript of Apicius, complete with his collations of E and V, eventually came to light in Russia (Leningrad 627/1), a remarkable and colourful history for a cookery book. He studied and copied important medical texts, including the manuscript of Celsus discovered by Giovanni Lamola in Milan in 1427 (Laur. 73.1); and the copy which he caused to be made of an old manuscript of the *Ars veterinaria* of Pelagonius is now the unique source for the text (Riccardianus 1179). Its *subscriptio*, which is typical, demonstrates

the sound and scholarly way in which Politian dealt with manuscript evidence:

> Hunc librum de codice sanequam vetusto Angelus Politianus, Medicae
> domus alumnus et Laurenti cliens, curavit exscribendum; dein ipse cum
> exemplari contulit et certa fide emendavit, ita tamen ut ab illo mutaret nihil,
> set et quae depravata inveniret relinqueret intacta, neque suum ausus est
> unquam iudicium interponere. Quod si priores institutum servassent, minus
> multo mendosos codices haberemus. Qui legis boni consule et vale. Floren-
> tiae, anno MCCCCLXXXV, Decembri mense.

VII. GREEK STUDIES: DIPLOMATS, REFUGEES AND
      BOOK COLLECTORS

The introduction of Greek studies to the city states of central and
northern Italy might have been expected to come about at an early
date and without difficulty through contact with the Greek-
speaking communities of the extreme south and Sicily. But the
south was quite isolated from the rest of the peninsula and had not
shared the growth in wealth and other progress of the bigger
northern cities, a state of affairs which was not altered until well
into the present century. Occasionally men of ability from these
regions travelled to the north on diplomatic missions, and in the
fourteenth century two of them received an enthusiastic welcome
from the leading scholars and writers of the day. It is well known
how Petrarch took lessons from the monk Barlaam, whom he met
at the papal court at Avignon. But though the monk was admitted
by his most bitter theological opponents to be a master of theology
and logic, his ability as a teacher left something to be desired, and
Petrarch never succeeded in learning enough Greek to read the
copy of Homer that a Byzantine ambassador gave him (Ambros. I.
98 inf.). Another opportunity to learn Greek arose in 1360, when
Barlaam's pupil Leonzio Pilato was intercepted by Boccaccio at
Florence on his way north to Avignon; he was induced to stay and
lecture on Greek, in return for an annual stipend from the Florentine government, but being a man of restless and impatient character he did not stay many years. For Boccaccio he translated Homer

together with about four hundred lines of Euripides' *Hecuba*; he also studied the Greek sections in the Florentine Pandects of Justinian's *Digest*. Shortly afterwards a translation of one of Plutarch's essays was undertaken for Coluccio Salutati. The style of these versions was very rough, and humanists with a feeling for Latin style, Salutati himself included, did their best to make improvements. The opening lines of the *Iliad* ran as follows in Leonzio's version:

> iram cane dea Pelidae Achillis
> pestiferam quae innumerabiles dolores Achivis posuit,
> multas autem robustas animas ad infernum antemisit . . .

More fruitful than the contacts with the south of Italy were those with Constantinople itself. The declining fortunes of the Greek empire made it necessary to send frequent diplomatic missions abroad to beg help against the Turkish invader; monarchs as far distant as the king of England received these appeals. We have already seen how a knowledge of Latin literature was made available to the Byzantines through Maximus Planudes, who had served on an embassy sent to Venice. It was almost exactly a century later that another Byzantine diplomat, Manuel Chrysoloras, became the first man to give regular lectures on Greek in Italy. He began in Florence in 1397, which is therefore a date of fundamental importance in the cultural history of Europe, and continued his courses for about three years before moving to Pavia for an equally brief stay. He had several notable pupils including Guarino and Leonardo Bruni. One important result of his teaching was that Latin translations of Greek texts were prepared, and he insisted that the old word-for-word style of translation should be abandoned, and that attention should be given to ensuring some literary merit in the version. An indication of his influence as an instructor is that his textbook of Greek grammar entitled *Erotemata* gained a considerable circulation, and eventually became the first Greek grammar to be printed (in 1471); it was later used by such famous men as Erasmus and Reuchlin.

During the fifteenth century the opportunities for an Italian to learn Greek improved. A number of Byzantines came to live in Italy, and after the defeat of their country in 1453 there was a stream of refugees, who generally reached Italy by way of Crete and Venice, and who were all anxious to earn a living by teaching their native language or copying texts. Fortunately for them the revival in knowledge of classical Latin caused a widespread desire to read the Greek authors so frequently quoted or mentioned in it. A famous school at Mantua, directed by Vittorino da Feltre from 1423 to 1446, laid emphasis on the value of Greek. But it is difficult to estimate how many Italians in fact learnt Greek to a standard which permitted them to read a text with ease. Enthusiasm for the new language might soon be lost through the lack of a gifted teacher or the irritating drawbacks of unsystematic grammatical textbooks; even Erasmus complained of the effort required to master the language. Some Italians, including Politian, are known to have taught themselves by taking a Latin translation, for example the traditional version of the Bible or Theodore Gaza's rendering of Aristotle, and using it as a key to elucidate the Greek text. In the absence of a teacher or a satisfactory grammar this was an exceptionally difficult undertaking. Many would-be scholars must have been obliged to content themselves with reading Latin translations: a great number of these were produced, especially under the patronage of Pope Nicholas V (1447–55), who commissioned versions of Thucydides, Herodotus, Xenophon, Plato, Aristotle, Theophrastus, Ptolemy, and Strabo. A small minority of students had the energy or the means to seek instruction in Constantinople itself; two of the more famous fifteenth-century figures who did this were Filelfo (1398–1481) and Guarino (1374–1460).

Another reason for travel to the East was the chance of bringing back manuscripts which might well include new texts. Some collectors had remarkable success, and Giovanni Aurispa came back to Italy in 1423 with 238 volumes of Greek pagan texts (Plate IV); an equally large modern collection of printed texts would be considered substantial, but one must not exaggerate the merits of the Aurispa library, since it doubtless contained a large number of duplicated titles. Probably Filelfo's collection of forty Greek books was more typical of the private libraries formed at the time. Rulers of Italian states collected also. From Florence Lorenzo de' Medici dispatched Janus Lascaris, one of the scholar refugees, on a journey to various Byzantine provinces in 1492 in search of manuscripts. The papal collections also grew rapidly. Venice acquired the basis of its large collection rather differently in 1468 through the gift of Cardinal Bessarion; he had collected for some time with the object of forming a complete library of Greek literature, giving his agents instructions to search in many territories of the former empire, and it is known that a part of his collection, including the newly discovered text of Quintus of Smyrna and perhaps the famous codex Venetus of Aristophanes (Marc. gr. 474), was acquired from the monastery of Saint Nicholas at Otranto.

VIII. GREEK SCHOLARSHIP IN THE FIFTEENTH CENTURY: BESSARION AND POLITIAN

A comprehensive account of Greek studies in the fifteenth century would need to deal with several of the more eminent humanists, but for this short introduction it must suffice to select two of the most notable scholars as typical of the aims and achievements of the period. One of these two represents the learning of the Greeks, the other shows what the Italians were able to learn from their masters.

The earlier of the two figures is Cardinal Bessarion (1403–72). He was born in Trebizond and educated in Constantinople at the school run by George Chrysococces, where he first met the Italian Filelfo with whom he was to correspond frequently in later life. He became a monk in 1423, and spent the years 1431–6 at Mistra in the Peloponnese in the circle of the freethinker George Gemistus Plethon, from whom he probably acquired his admiration for Plato. Through Plethon he was introduced to the emperor and came to be employed on government business; the emperor made him abbot of a monastery in the capital in 1436 and in the following year promoted him to the see of Nicaea. In 1438 he came to Italy as a member of the delegation sent to the Council of Florence and Ferrara to negotiate a union between the Greek and Roman churches. More than one attempt had been made to restore church unity, and now the need to end the schism was made acute by the rapid disintegration of the Byzantine empire, which governed no more than a tiny proportion of its former territories; hopes of Western military aid might be realized after a reunion of the church. The proceedings of the council were protracted, but in the end an agreement was reached between the two parties, very largely owing to the forceful arguments of Bessarion, who had to overcome determined opposition from members of his own delegation. The union was abortive, since the mass of the population in the Greek empire, encouraged by many of the clergy, refused to accept the act of union as a just compromise; the minority who accepted the union became a separate sect, known as the Greek Uniate Church, which thus owes its existence to Bessarion. Despite the failure of the council to have any lasting political effect Bessarion's services to the Church did not pass unnoticed by the pope; he became a cardinal and resided permanently in Italy, taking a considerable part in church affairs, and on more than one occasion he was nearly elected pope.

The cardinal's house in Rome was a centre of literary activity, where Greeks and Italians mixed freely; of the former the two most famous were Theodore Gaza and George Trapezuntios, who translated various works into Latin, while among the Italians were Poggio and Valla. Bessarion's wide knowledge and expert command of Latin caused him to be dubbed by Valla '*Latinorum Graecissimus, Graecorum Latinissimus*'. His library was exceptionally large; the Greek books alone amounted to some five hundred volumes towards the end of his life and included many important copies of classical texts, for his tastes were not confined to theology and philosophy. He took great care over them, as may be seen from the possession-notes, shelf-marks, and other notes he inserted on the flyleaves. He had not always been a keen collector, since he had relied on the book trade in Constantinople as an adequate source of supply; but one of his letters states that the fall of the Greek empire in 1453 made him form the plan of building as complete a collection as possible of Greek books, in the intention of placing it eventually at the disposal of those Greeks who survived the fall of the empire and reached Italy. This statement of his plans shows one of his main reasons for presenting his collection during his own lifetime (1468) to the city of Venice to form the basis of a public library, for it was in Venice that a high proportion of Greek refugees tended to congregate.

Bessarion's own literary work included a Latin translation of Aristotle's *Metaphysics*, and a long book against the critics of Plato. A good many pamphlets and letters also survive. Two of the former are of interest for our present purpose. The first arose out of the negotiations for church unity. The crucial point in the argument between the Greeks and the Latins concerned the procession of the Holy Spirit: is it of the same or merely similar nature to God the Father? Bessarion's great success was that he found a passage in Saint Basil's tract *Against Eunomius* which clearly enunciated the view of the Latin Church, and should therefore have formed the basis of a reconciliation, since the authority of Saint Basil in the Greek Church was beyond criticism. Bessarion's opponents at the council, members of the Greek delegation who wanted a successful conclusion to the discussions only if everything went their own way, claimed that the passage was not a genuine statement by Saint Basil, that an earlier Greek church reformer or the Italians had forged it, and that they had manuscripts which omitted the words in question. Though sure of his ground Bessarion was temporarily at a loss to prove his point and had to rely on other less decisive evidence to convince the opposition. But when he returned briefly to Constantinople he determined to settle the matter to his satisfaction and began to examine all the copies of the text that he could lay his hands on. At the time of the council only one of the six copies of the work that could be found appeared to favour Bessarion's opponents, and that gave every sign of having been tampered with, for the vital passage had been deleted and other words substituted for it. Research in the monastic libraries of the capital soon yielded two old copies of the text, one on paper dated to the middle of the twelfth century, and the other on parchment of still greater age; the text of both these copies supported Bessarion, while only very recent copies of the text, which appeared to have been written at the time of the council or just after, supported the other view. Bessarion used the age of the two old copies as his decisive argument; they were both older than the date of certain earlier Greek churchmen who had favoured union with the West, and so could not have been forged by them; and as to the notion that they had been forged by the Italians, the high quality of the Greek was sufficient reply to the suggestion.

After this example of scholarly method used to refute the unscrupulous manipulation of texts we come to Bessarion's other short work which shows his scholarship to advantage, and here too the context is theological. After a reading from Saint John's Gospel as part of the liturgy conducted in his house in Rome, lively conversation began as to the correct text of John 21: 22. The reading had been performed from the Latin Vulgate, which erroneously gave the word *sic* instead of *si* (the Greek has ἐάν). Bessarion pointed out in discussion that this was a simple case of a copyist's error, involving only one letter. His audience was not completely persuaded, and so he wrote a pamphlet to prove his point. Here several important principles are enunciated, and the whole matter is discussed with a common sense that seems natural to us but was not welcome to the narrow-minded conservatism of men who regarded every word of Saint Jerome's translation as sacred. Bessarion states that the Greek text is the original and must have precedence over the Latin translation, and is able to claim Augustine's authority for this proposition. He also shows that early quotations of the Greek text in Origen, Cyril, and Chrysostom all have the same wording. Then he shows that the whole context of the passage is not suited to the reading of the Vulgate. The work is of great importance and anticipates the attitude of Erasmus in regarding the Greek text of the New Testament as the only proper basis for interpretation. It may owe something to Valla, who frequently met Bessarion and had previously written but not published a tract entitled *Adnotationes in Novum Testamentum*, in which he called into question the Vulgate's accuracy.

To the Greek bishop who settled in Italy and whose scholarly activity was devoted mainly to theology and philosophy Politian (1454–94) offers a striking contrast. He is famous as a poet in his vernacular language and in Latin, but was equally distinguished as a scholar. Though primarily interested in ancient literature he had a proper understanding of the subsidiary branches of knowledge, such as epigraphy and numismatics, which make a contribution to our general understanding of the ancient world. The combination of poet and scholar in Politian has an interesting analogy in the Hellenistic world; the same description suits Callimachus and Eratosthenes, and it is perhaps not entirely a coincidence that Politian was the first scholar to give serious attention to Hellenistic poetry.

His ability as a Latinist and his appreciation of the importance of old manuscripts have been described above. It may merely be worth remarking in passing that he changed the direction of Greek and Latin studies in rather the same way, by encouraging an interest in post-classical authors; just as in Latin he had pointed out the merits of Quintilian, Suetonius, and the Silver Latin poets, so in Greek he lectured on Callimachus and Theocritus. As a Greek scholar he was the first Italian of whom it was generally agreed that he equalled native Greeks in knowledge of the language. Such a claim appears in his own works. In a letter to Matthias Corvinus, king of Hungary (*Epist.* 9.1), where he offers his literary services, either as a translator of classical texts or official panegyrist of the king's successes, he states that he knows as much Greek as the Greeks themselves, and is the first Italian to do so for a thousand years. The same boast is implied in the opening of his inaugural lecture on Homer. Whatever vanity there may be in this claim, it can easily be justified. Politian is the first Italian of the Renaissance who did work of permanent value on a Greek text, so that his name can still be found in the apparatus criticus of a modern edition (Valla's contributions to the text of Thucydides must reflect the high quality of the manuscript he used and not, as was once thought, his own ingenuity.) One other notable testimony to Politian's linguistic talent is that from the age of seventeen he composed epigrams in Greek. About fifty of these survive in various metres, and though they are faulty in a number of matters of scansion and prosody they display considerable knowledge of the language, especially in the use of a wide vocabulary.

His works include several translations from the Greek. There is a fluent version of the late historian Herodian and some short essays by Epictetus and Plutarch. But most important prose authors had already been translated, and so Politian could turn his energy in other directions. The work which best displays the many sides of his learning is the *Miscellanea*. Most of the chapters deal with matters of Latin scholarship, but numerous Greek authors are quoted as evidence to justify or reinforce an argument. One example already mentioned is his use of the text of Callimachus to emend a corrupt passage in Catullus (66.48). Perhaps the most significant chapter is the one which gives a text of Callimachus' fifth hymn, *The bath of Pallas*, accompanied by a translation into elegant elegiacs. Here he prints the Greek text without accents in order to avoid anachronism, a point of scholarly precision in which he has not been followed by later generations, and makes a very good job of preparing the first edition of the hymn.

IX. THE FIRST PRINTED GREEK TEXTS: ALDUS
MANUTIUS AND MARCUS MUSURUS

While the new art of printing soon led to a spate of editions of Latin classics from the seventies of the fifteenth century onwards, for Greek texts the situation was quite different. Part of the reason for this may have been the difficulty of designing a suitable fount of type, in which the number of sorts would not be unreasonably increased by the various combination of letters with accents and breathings. Certainly some of the early printers, in a mistaken desire to reproduce in print the appearance of contemporary Greek script, devised founts of type that were expensive to operate with and unsatisfactory in appearance. Even the famous Aldine founts, which served for a very long time as the models for later typographers, are open to both these criticisms. But not all early printers failed in this way; the type-face designed by the famous Frenchman Nicholas Jenson, who worked in Venice, was an excellent piece of work, and still better in some ways was that used for printing passages of Greek in Politian's *Miscellanea*: here the accents and breathings were omitted and ligatures avoided, so that the text bore no close resemblance to written script but was far more easily legible. It is surprising that one of these simpler founts was not immediately accepted as the standard.

More serious than the typographical difficulty was the lack of demand for Greek texts in sufficient numbers to make an edition pay. Knowledge of Greek was quite restricted, and Latin translations could be printed instead in editions large enough to be profitable. A striking example of this is that Plato was not printed in Greek until 1513, but Marsilio Ficino's translation appeared in 1484 in an edition of 1,025 copies. Not only was this an uncommonly large edition, for the average number of copies of all publications at this date is thought to have been 250 or a little more, but it was sold out within six years, and another printing took place. But in contrast to this the Greek text of the *editio princeps* of Isocrates, which appeared in Milan in 1493, sold so slowly that in 1535 the remaining copies were reissued with a new title-page. Before the Aldine press was set up the total number of volumes printed in Greek was scarcely more than a dozen. Several of these were grammars by Chrysoloras and Constantine Lascaris, and the only major classical texts apart from Isocrates were Homer, Theocritus, and the Greek Anthology.

Aldus Manutius (1449–1515) had the idea of setting up a publishing house primarily for the printing of Greek texts. The notion came to him while he was living in Carpi, a town near Modena, acting as tutor to the sons of the ruler. Florence might seem to be the obvious place for the location of this enterprise, in view of its intellectual pre-eminence, but the death of Lorenzo de' Medici had removed the most influential patron of learning and letters. On the other hand Venice, thanks to Bessarion's legacy, possessed a larger library of Greek books than had been assembled by the Medici family, and Aldus may have hoped, wrongly as it turned out, to be able to use it. The most important factor may have been the great reputation of Venice as a centre of the printing trade; more than half the books printed in Italy before 1500 were published there. Skilled and experienced workmen would be available for the new firm.

From 1494 to 1515 the Aldine press issued a great series of editions of classical texts: with the death of Aldus in the latter year the firm declined. The printing of Latin texts had advanced to the point that Aldus' books include only one first edition of a Latin text, and an unimportant one at that. But in Greek he was responsible for the first printing of nearly all the major authors, and during his twenty years in business he had almost a monopoly of preparing Greek texts. In Venice and its territories he had privileges from the government which amounted to a patent for the exclusive right to use type-faces designed or commissioned by himself.

His great project could not have been realized without the help of numerous scholarly friends, both Greek and Italian. The man who undertook much the most significant single share of the scholarly work was the Cretan Marcus Musurus (c. 1470–1517). Aldus himself must probably be counted a considerable scholar in his own right. But it is not always easy to tell how much of the work was done by him or Musurus or some other members of the circle. The title-pages of Aldine books and the dedicatory letters written by Aldus often do not name the editor of the text. In such cases the most likely solution to the problem is that the work was shared by several of the publisher's friends. By 1502 at the latest the title-pages refer to the Academy or Neakademia, a club formed by Aldus for the promotion of Greek studies. It had a set of rules drawn up in Greek, one of which was that at meetings Greek should be the only language permitted. About thirty or forty members can be identified. Permanent residence in Venice was not necessary for membership, since Musurus, who taught at Padua and at Carpi for a time, appears to have been a member. Visiting foreign scholars were welcomed; the most famous example was Erasmus.

The quantity of first editions brought out by the press during its most active periods testifies to the enthusiasm of the collaborators and the efficient organization of the printing. The first Greek book to appear was a short text, Musaeus, doubtless chosen as an easy experiment before proceeding to more difficult ventures. After this came a text of Theocritus and Hesiod more complete than the one already in print. Then the press settled to the enormous task of editing Aristotle and Theophrastus, the result being a series of five folio volumes brought out between 1495 and 1498. The only interval in the activity of the firm was caused by the war of the League of Cambrai against Venice, and no Greek books could be produced during the years 1505–7 and 1510–12. The most remarkable years for the publication of major classical texts were 1502–4, which saw the first editions of Sophocles, Euripides, Herodotus,

Thucydides, and Demosthenes. But Aldus did not confine himself to major authors: he published Herodian's *History*, Pollux, Stephanus of Byzantium, and Philostratus' *Life of Apollonius*, to mention only a selection. In the preface to the last of these he stated bluntly, with a candour not normal among publishers, what a worthless text he believed this to be (*nihil unquam memini me legere deterius*). Nearly all the Aldine books were classical texts; Christian writers only occasionally appeared. At one time Aldus seems to have projected an Old Testament in Hebrew, Greek, and Latin, together with a New Testament in Greek and Latin, but nothing came of this during his own lifetime.

The task of an editor at this date was full of difficulties. Manuscripts had to be obtained to serve as copy for the typesetters, and if, as often happened, the text was corrupt, the editor might attempt either to emend it or to find better manuscripts. The prefaces give some indications of these hardships. Aldus tells us that in the whole of Italy he had been able to find only one copy of Theophrastus. This remark is one of the proofs that he was unable to exploit the riches of Bessarion's library. At the end of his introduction to Thucydides he says that he would willingly have added Xenophon and Gemistus Plethon to the same volume, but had to postpone it for lack of manuscripts. Musurus in his preface to the epistolographi says that some passages in Alciphron were so corrupt that he could not put them right, and asks readers to excuse the unintelligible state of the text as printed. Musurus' procedure can be observed a little more closely in some of his other books. The first large volume for which he was undoubtedly responsible is the Aristophanes of 1498 (Plate VIII), and it can be established that he worked from at least four manuscripts in preparing it. One of these survives in Modena (Estensis *a.* U. 5.10). A text of the comedies had to be constructed from these four books and submitted to the typesetter. An equally substantial task was the redaction of the scholia, which were printed in the margins in just the same position as they had in a medieval manuscript. The scholia in the manuscripts at Musurus' disposal were of different types, and he had an enormous task in selecting and combining the notes into a form that could be printed. To this clerical labour was added the need to restore the correct text, which he did in a number of passages. Similar clerical labour awaited him a number of years later, when he came to edit the lexicon of Hesychius, a Greek dictionary compiled in the sixth century. This survives in only one manuscript (now Marc. gr. 622). Rather than write out the whole text afresh to provide the printer's copy Musurus himself wrote in the manuscript all the necessary corrections and instructions to the printer. As the script contained numerous abbreviations Musurus wrote out in full, either above the line or in the margin, each abbreviated word. He also corrected a large number of mistakes, and the most recent editor has remarked that every page has some emendation which shows Musurus' skill and linguistic knowledge. One rather amusing instance of his skill, which shows him going to greater lengths than modern critics would think necessary, arises in another text, the third pastoral poem of Moschus. Here there is a gap in the text between lines 92 and 93, which Musurus filled by six hexameter lines of his own. Though these lines consist largely of echoes from the similar poems of Theocritus, and were probably not intended to do more than indicate the general sense required by the context, they have sometimes been regarded as genuine lines of the poem, supposedly recovered by Musurus from a unique manuscript that is now lost.

Musurus' contribution to classical scholarship is not easy to estimate exactly, because in many cases the copy which he submitted to the printer is lost, and the best potential source of evidence is thereby denied to us. But if he was personally responsible for all the good readings which appear for the first time in editions that he saw through the press, there can be no doubt that he was the most talented classical scholar ever produced by his nation.

X. ERASMUS (C.1469–1536)

We must now turn to consider the level of scholarship that could be achieved by a native of northern Europe. The figure who commands attention is Erasmus. Though originally a monk at Steyn near Gouda, he contrived to obtain permanent leave from his monastery, and it was in Paris that he began to take up Greek. He found the language difficult, and did not benefit much from the tuition of a Greek refugee called George Hermonymus. In 1506 he went to Italy with the intention of improving his knowledge of the language, and in due course made contact with Aldus. Erasmus was by this time tolerably well known in literary circles through the publication of the first edition of the *Adagia*, a collection of proverbs with accompanying comments, and the *Enchiridion militis Christiani*, in which the blunt expression of his view of piety had caused some offence to ecclesiastical authorities. Erasmus had added fuel to the flames in 1505 by supervising the printing of another book that was not welcome to the clerical establishment, Lorenzo Valla's *Adnotationes in Novum Testamentum*, which treated the text of the Bible not as if it were sacred but like any other literary monument. It was therefore natural that Erasmus should soon be in touch with Aldus, and in due course he visited Venice, staying as a guest in the printer's house for several months. In one of his later *Colloquia*, called *Opulentia sordida*, he gives a vivid description of the miserable food and housekeeping, but there is reason to think that this is much exaggerated by Erasmus for the purpose of replying to a scurrilous polemic by Alberto Pio of Carpi. In Venice he naturally had the chance to acquire all the Greek he needed, and read the many texts that Aldus' private library could offer. One immediate result of his stay was the publication of a greatly enlarged version of the *Adagia*, incorporating material from the Greek sources that he had just begun to know well.

Much later in his career he wrote a pamphlet on the correct pronunciation of Greek, which led to the widespread adoption of what is called the Erasmian pronunciation. As a rule the Greek exiles taught classical Greek in the pronunciation of the modern language, which certainly is quite different from that used in the ancient world. Evidence to prove this had already been noted by the Spanish scholar Antonio Nebrija (1444–1522) and some members of the Aldine circle. The epithet Erasmian therefore fails to give credit for the discovery where it is due; but it is only fair to add that Erasmus himself did not claim to be the inventor of the new system, which he may be presumed to have met for the first time while staying with Aldus.

Fruitful and important though Erasmus' association with Aldus had been, he is better remembered for his long collaboration with one of the great printing houses of the north, that of Froben at Basle. Erasmus found the milieu congenial, took an active share in the editorial side of the business, and formed with Froben a friendship of considerable importance for the promotion of Christian humanism. One of the earliest and most spectacular fruits of this alliance was the first publication of the Greek text of the New Testament in 1516. By coincidence the Greek text was being set up in type at the same time in Spain at Alcalá (this edition also included the Old Testament with the Greek and Hebrew texts); but difficulties of various kinds prevented publication until 1520. It is worth noting that while Cardinal Ximénez, the chief editor of the Complutensian Polyglot, as it is sometimes known, recommended study of the Bible in the original languages, his views were perhaps not shared by all his collaborators; in one of the prefatory letters there is at least a hint that the Latin text is more to be trusted than the others. Erasmus, however, was quite clear in his own mind of the importance of establishing the original text of the New Testament. A good deal is known about his editorial procedure. He began working seriously at his projected edition during his stay in England in 1512–13, and had four manuscripts of the Greek text for consultation; one of these has been identified as the Leicester codex, a fifteenth-century copy. During the printing at Basle in 1515–16 he had five manuscripts by him, and one which has marks indicating that it was used as copy for the printer is still preserved (Basle AN iv.1). This is a twelfth-century manuscript of no particular value. It seems that Erasmus was aware of the likely value of really old manuscripts, but his palaeographical knowledge was inadequate for his need. In this respect he was clearly inferior to Politian and almost certainly to Bessarion; in general he relied on rather late books of no great merit, despite the evident possibility of discovering better and older texts by inquiry from his many correspondents. Though he rightly regarded codex B (Vat. gr. 1209) as of amazing age, and for a reprint of his edition obtained some collations of it through a friend, it does not seem that he ever used it systematically for the whole text. On the other hand he had a grossly exaggerated regard for a manuscript of the Apocalypse, which he thought might even date back to the apostolic age; modern scholarship has identified it as a twelfth-century codex (formerly Schloss Harburg, I 1, 4°, 1). One positive aspect of his work is that he appears to have understood the principle *difficilior lectio potior* (see below, Ch. 6 VII).

Among many points arising out of the edition two may be mentioned here. In the book of Revelation his only manuscript lacked the last few verses and was unintelligible at other points; being determined to print a Greek text, Erasmus consulted the Vulgate in these passages and made his own Greek version of it. In so doing he exceeded the duty of an editor as it is now understood, and made some mistakes in his Greek. In the first epistle of John (5: 7) Erasmus had followed the Greek in omitting the so-called *comma Johanneum*, a statement of the doctrine of the Trinity which was found in the Vulgate. This caused some controversy, during which Erasmus unwisely offered to insert the words into any reprint of his edition if they could be found in a Greek manuscript. Not surprisingly a manuscript was written for the purpose without delay (Trinity College Dublin 30), and the promise had to be made good. But Erasmus took the chance of indicating his suspicions about the authenticity of the book. The episode shows how a lack of a set of logical principles for the evaluation of manuscripts handicapped scholars in their dealings with opponents who were willing to descend to forgery. Bessarion had had a similar experience at the Council of Florence, but it was easier for him to refute his opponents in controversy, since his aim was to prove a certain passage genuine by showing that it occurred in manuscripts earlier than the date of potential forgers; whereas Erasmus had no equally neat argument at his disposal, and could only appeal to the good authority of very old manuscripts.

Despite its shortcomings in these matters Erasmus' edition of the Greek New Testament represents a very great step forward in scholarship. Against stubborn opposition it established the principles that texts are to be studied in the original language rather than translations, and that texts of scripture are to be discussed and interpreted according to the same rules of logic and common sense as any others. The work of Valla and Bessarion had come to fruition.

Erasmus had been attracted to Basle in the first place because it had already become a centre for the publishing of patristic texts. His New Testament was immediately followed by his first edition of Jerome, and that by a long series of editions of the Fathers which he produced either alone or in collaboration with others, often returning again and again to revise the same author. These include Cyprian, Hilary, Ambrose, and Augustine, and are an impressive monument to his energy and learning, both on account of the massive labour involved and because the patristic writers had received comparatively little critical attention from early editors. While engaged on these mammoth operations, Erasmus still found time to work on classical texts, an essential part of his humanist program. His services to classical Greek are comparatively small, though he produced a number of translations and edited Aristotle and Demosthenes; the only author of whom he produced the *editio princeps* was Ptolemy (1533). His contribution to Latin literature is much greater; the authors he edited include Terence, Livy, Suetonius, the Elder Pliny, and Seneca. The last, which he edited twice (1515, 1529), has been recognized as representative of both his strength and his failings. The first edition was marred by characteristic haste. It went through the press in the absence of its editor, who in any case had enough on his plate with Jerome and the New Testament both in their last stages; the distinction between editor, copy-editor, and proof corrector being more than somewhat blurred, too much was left to others, whom Erasmus afterwards blamed for incompetence and worse. The text benefited from a refreshingly critical approach, but Erasmus knew how much better it should have been and returned to retrieve what he regarded as a disgrace in 1529. The second edition, prefaced by an admirably balanced and sensible essay on Seneca, produced two successful emendations for every one in the first edition and provides convincing proof of the judgement and scholarship of its editor. But again the printing was carried out in something of a fluster, with manuscripts continuing to arrive when parts of the book were already in print. He made judicious use of such manuscripts as he could muster, but they seem to have been an indifferent lot, with one signal exception. He had access to readings from the Lorsch manuscript of the *De beneficiis* and *De clementia* (cf. p. 99), the archetype of the whole tradition. But he was inhibited by the critical methods of his day: instead of basing his text of these works upon this prime witness, he drew on it spasmodically to emend what he had before him, and a great opportunity was lost.

5

SOME ASPECTS OF SCHOLARSHIP
SINCE THE RENAISSANCE

I. THE COUNTER-REFORMATION; THE HIGH RENAISSANCE IN ITALY

The progress of scholarship in the sixteenth century was hampered by continuing religious controversy. Although Bessarion had been stimulated by such controversy to write two short books of great importance for the development of critical method, it is not easy to discover equally fruitful controversies among the contemporaries of Erasmus or in the next generation. Erasmus himself, though he had exploited the work of Valla and Bessarion for his edition of the New Testament and was aware of Politian's eminence as a scholar, did not possess the palaeographical skill that might have led to further advances; and as he settled at Basle, while most of the best working libraries with manuscript collections were still at that date to be found south of the Alps, he could scarcely hope to add greatly to his experience in dealing with manuscripts. Religious disputes took up much of his time and energy in later years, and in 1524 we find him complaining (*Epist.* 1531) that the struggle between Luther and his opponents had become such a preoccupation in literary circles that the book trade was affected, and in the German-speaking parts of Europe it was hardly possible to sell books on any other topic. Elsewhere, and especially in Italy, the energies of literary men were consumed by another controversy in which Erasmus was once again a leading figure: the question was whether Cicero should be regarded as the one and only suitable model for Latin prose, and though the discussion had been going on intermittently since the days of Poggio and Valla, Erasmus succeeded in giving new life to the argument by publishing at Basle in 1528 a dialogue entitled *Ciceronianus*, in which he held up to ridicule many of the absurdities committed by unduly enthusiastic admirers of Cicero. The debate did not end with Erasmus, whose moderate view failed to win general acceptance. In the middle of the century the extreme pro-Ciceronians seem to have been in the majority, but later there was a change of taste, which affected reading habits and prose style. Literary men became more interested in the works of Seneca and Tacitus than in Cicero and allowed this interest to affect their manner of writing both in Latin and the vernaculars; one of the most important representatives of the new movement was the classical scholar Justus Lipsius.

The prospects for classical and biblical scholarship were not improved by the Counter-Reformation. The abolition of intellectual freedom implicit in the decisions of the Council of Trent (1545–63) did nothing to encourage the free pursuit of classical scholarship. The authority of the Vulgate as the text of the Bible was reaffirmed. Erasmus' books were put on the index of prohibited literature, and although the Church did not make a systematic attempt to have them destroyed, the intellectual atmosphere of Catholic countries was not conducive to classical scholarship. The dispute between Catholics and Protestants was still being carried on bitterly at the beginning of the next century, and one indication of its power to deflect able minds from what might have been more profitable concerns is that Casaubon devoted two years or more to a refutation of the ecclesiastical history compiled by Cardinal Baronius.

However, the dark side of the picture must not be exaggerated. Although most Latin texts had by now appeared in printed editions, there were still some Greek authors of importance that had not been made generally available in the original language by the time of Erasmus' death, and these gradually appeared in the course of the century. In 1544 Josephus and Archimedes came out in Basle. There is good reason to think that the ancients' achievements in mathematics and some other sciences were only just beginning to be fully understood. It is worth noting that Marcus Musurus' successor in the chair of Greek in Venice spent most of his time at the shipyards designing new types of galley; he achieved great fame as a naval architect, and claimed, probably wrongly, that one of his best ideas came from an ancient source. Meanwhile in Paris the king's printer Robert Estienne (1503–59) was very active. His house produced the first editions of the church history of Eusebius and the Roman histories by Dionysius of Halicarnassus and Dio Cassius. He had already made a name by publishing his Latin dictionary in 1531, and he increased his reputation, and equally his unpopularity with the theological faculty at the Sorbonne, by a series of editions of the Bible. Between 1532 and 1540 he is known to have made some search for good manuscripts of the Vulgate, and in the preface to the 1551 edition, which is otherwise famous for the division of the text into verses universally adopted since that date, he makes an interesting comment on the value of the Vulgate. He asserts, not without justice, that in the New Testament it can be taken to represent the Greek text at a very early stage of its history. Despite an apparatus criticus reporting the variants of fifteen manuscripts his edition is critically disappointing in other respects.

The value of a relatively early translation had been correctly assessed in 1549 by the best Italian scholar of the day, Pier Vettori (1499–1585). In his edition of Aristotle's *Rhetoric* he used the medieval Latin version by William of Moerbeke, citing about 300 of its readings. In his preface he shows that its literal and inelegant form can be exploited to reveal precisely the Greek text of the exemplar used by the translator, and its use is chiefly that by being older than the Greek copies it has not suffered as much of the corruption that results inevitably from copying by hand. Vettori notes the frequent agreement of Moerbeke's version with the oldest and best Greek manuscript (Paris gr. 1741), whose readings he was able to use. Though he shows no knowledge of stemmatic theory as such and apparently did not realize that the Paris codex is even older than Moerbeke's version (though not therefore older than his exemplar), his procedure in dealing with this indirect or secondary tradition is of a scholarly competence that deserves mention in even the briefest survey.

Vettori was in touch with the Estienne family, and after Robert had been obliged to leave Paris and set up his printing house in Geneva, Vettori published with his son Henri (d. 1598) an edition of Aeschylus which was the first to include the full text of the *Agamemnon* (previously lines 323–1050 had been omitted). The younger

Estienne was a figure at least as important as his father, but as far as classical scholarship is concerned his main achievement was the completion in 1572 of a work begun by his father, the *Thesaurus linguae graecae*. He produced an edition of the *Anacreontea*, which had a vogue among the poets of the time, but he was not responsible for the first Greek editions of the few remaining authors not yet printed, the most notable of these being Plotinus (1580), Photius' *Bibliotheca* (1601), Sextus Empiricus (1617), and the mathematician Diophantus (1621).

Vettori's most able and active contemporary in Italy was Francesco Robortello of Udine (1516–67). He is generally best known for the *editio princeps* of Longinus *On the sublime* (1552) and an important edition of Aristotle's *Poetics* (1548), but he deserves notice here for another reason. In 1557 he wrote a short dissertation *De arte critica sive ratione corrigendi antiquorum libros disputatio*, which is apparently the first attempt to write a brief manual of textual criticism. Robortello claims to be the first to have devised a theory of emendation. After a short and rather slight section on the value of old manuscripts, in which he shows an awareness of the value of Latin texts written in 'Longobardic' script, by which he probably means pre-Caroline minuscule rather than Beneventan, he turns to the principles governing the art of conjecture. The critic is to test his ideas in the light of palaeography, style, and a general understanding of the subject-matter. Then follows a series of eight headings under which emendations can be classified, mostly illustrated with a few examples. The classification is not as clear as might be wished, but it deals with such essential notions as the intrusive gloss that has displaced the original reading and the possibility of error arising from incorrect division of words. The illustrations are mostly taken from Latin authors, but there are a few from Plutarch and Aristotle's *Rhetoric*, where he may have learnt from Vettori. There is no trace of stemmatic theory anywhere in the argument, and the palaeographical knowledge shown is rather disappointing in view of the many good manuscript collections accessible to him. Nevertheless it is very much to his credit that he attempted a systematic account of the way that the critic should go about his task of restoring classical texts to their original state.

The study of the broader aspects of classical antiquity in Italy during this period is well represented by Fulvio Orsini (1529–1600). Cold-shouldered as an illegitimate adjunct to the great family whose name he bore, Orsini owed the bent of his interests and his preferment in the first place to Gentile Delfini, a learned canon of the church of Saint John Lateran, where Orsini began as a chorister, and later to the patronage of the Farnese family, three of whose cardinals he served as librarian. A scholar and collector in the central Renaissance tradition, he had a number of important and original publications to his credit, such as his *Virgilius illustratus* (1567), which filled in the Greek literary background to Vergil, works on iconography (*Imagines et Elogia*, 1570) and numismatics (*Familiae Romanae*, 1577), and the *editio princeps* of the greater part of the fragmentary books of Polybius (1582). It was the breadth of his enthusiasms, ranging over the whole antiquarian world of art, sculpture, inscriptions, coins, and gems, which marked out his contribution to classical studies. He was well placed to make fruitful contacts with scholars of other countries, so that he knew Lipsius, helped Gruter, entertained Daniel and de Thou. His great archaeological collection ended up at Naples, but his books and manuscripts became one of the most important of the early acquisitions of the Vatican. These included a valuable collection of autograph manuscripts of the great humanists, from Petrarch to his own day, but also a number of books of great antiquity, the Augusteus of Virgil (Vat. lat. 3256), a present, not entirely unsolicited, from Claude Dupuy, and others obtained after protracted haggling from the legacy of Pietro Bembo, an important Pindar (Vat. gr. 1312), the Vaticanus of Virgil (Vat. lat. 3225), and the great Terence in rustic capitals which we still call the Bembinus (Vat. lat. 3226). But his activity at the centre of the antiquarian movement of his time was of no less significance than his achievements in the literary field.

Work on patristic authors also made some limited progress in the latter part of the sixteenth century. In 1550 appeared the first edition of Clement of Alexandria, edited by Vettori and printed in Florence but with a dedication to Cardinal Cervini, the future Pope Marcellus II. The cardinal was interested in setting up a press at Rome, in order to produce theological texts in editions that would rival and if possible replace those of Erasmus, whose commentaries on the Scriptures and the Fathers were regarded as dangerous if not downright heretical. The creation of the Index in 1558 gave an impetus for several decades to the production of editions in full conformity with orthodoxy, but the results were variable both in quality and in quantity. The fight against heresy could not be entirely beneficial to scholarship, which received a setback in 1587 when Pope Sixtus V, at the foundation of the Typographia Vaticana, decreed that problems of textual criticism too difficult for the editorial staff to solve by their own efforts must be referred to himself. On the other hand it is known that the staff were capable of careful and intelligent work when left to their own devices, as can be deduced from surviving papers relating to a new edition of Saint Augustine.

The most notable literary event of Sixtus V's pontificate was the publication of the Latin Vulgate in 1590, accompanied by the threat of excommunication to anyone who should subsequently dare to change its readings or print the variants from the manuscripts. Notwithstanding the threat his successor Clement VIII in 1592 recalled the unsold copies and issued another edition differing in many passages, which became and remained the official text of the Roman Catholic Church until it began to be replaced by the Benedictine edition published in Rome from 1926 onwards.

The best achievements in patristic studies at this period fall a little later and come from an utterly different milieu. In Oxford, Thomas James (1573–1629), the first librarian of the Bodleian, who took a delight in showing the inadequacy of editions prepared by Catholic scholars on the continent, organized in 1610–12 a team of helpers to collate manuscripts of Gregory, Cyprian, and Ambrose. They found an extremely large number of erroneous or dubious readings in the printed texts and James compared his task to that of cleansing the Augean stables. He and his team are known to have worked on more than fifty manuscripts and he planned without success a series of patristic texts based on the best manuscripts. In this he foreshadowed the work of the Benedictines of Saint Maur, who were able to use some of his material. Still more significant is the edition of Saint John Chrysostom by Sir Henry Savile (1549–1622),

Warden of Merton College Oxford and Provost of Eton, published
at Eton in 1612 in eight folio volumes. To a considerable extent this
edition of one of the most popular and influential of all the Fathers,
both Greek and Latin, has not been superseded. Savile's papers for
the edition amount to nearly 16,000 pages, and were by no means
the only product of a busy life of scholarship in many fields. An
indication of his industry is perhaps given by his wife's remark to
him: 'Sir Henry, I would I were a book too, and then you would a
little more respect me.'

11. THE BEGINNINGS OF HUMANISM AND SCHOLARSHIP IN FRANCE

The speed and vitality with which humanism had taken root and
flourished in Italy was unparalleled elsewhere. In France classicism
remained more traditionalist and made no such dramatic leap
despite its being open to Italian influence, particularly through
Avignon, from the early fourteenth century onwards. But the
strength and vitality of French medieval culture meant that French
humanism could absorb what it needed from Italy without being
too dependent on it and could strike out along its own path within
the broad lines of its own tradition. The sensitivity of French
scholars on this issue and the frequent signs of a reaction against
Italian scholarship reflect both their debt to Italian humanism and
the pride they took in the originality of their own achievement.

Pierre Bersuire (d. 1362) had been one of the first to benefit from
the cultural interaction fostered at Avignon and from personal
contact with Petrarch himself, who gave him his friendship and
help with his classical studies. His translation of Livy into French
was an important step in reinforcing the historian's new-found
popularity and his *Ovidius moralisatus* shows some Petrarchan influence; but his medieval ways of thinking were too strong for even a
Petrarch to change and he fell far short of being a humanist. But a
powerful group who thoroughly deserved the name had emerged in
France towards the end of the century, among them Jean de Montreuil (1334–1418) and his intimate friend Nicholas of Clamanges

(c. 1360–1437). Though they owed their wide familiarity with classical authors, particularly Cicero, to contact with Italian humanists and imported texts, their humanism was firmly rooted in the north and they were well able to discover new texts on their own account. Cluny in particular had proved a rich source. Not even a Poggio can turn up a new text every time without being told where to look, and the presence of Jean de Montreuil at the Council of Constance may have had important side-effects. It can hardly have been a coincidence that Poggio found the *Pro Caecina* at Langres, where Nicholas of Clamanges, the great connoisseur of Cicero's speeches, had been canon and treasurer to the cathedral chapter. And although Poggio claims credit for the discovery of the vetus Cluniacensis of the speeches and indeed had it sent to Italy, the best and most conscientious copy of the lost manuscripts is the one made before it went to Italy, by Nicholas of Clamanges.

The apparently intermittent progress of French humanism was strengthened by two events which took place in the second half of the fifteenth century, the appearance of the first teachers of Greek and the setting up of the first printing press in France. Earlier attempts to organize Greek studies at Paris had proved abortive and Gregorio Tifernate, who arrived in 1456, stayed only a few years. George Hermonymus of Sparta, who came to France in 1476, is best known for his failure to give much help as a teacher to either Budé or Erasmus. But with the arrival of Janus Lascaris in 1495 and Girolamo Aleandro in 1508, Greek studies began to flourish and became an important element in French humanism. The first printers were German, the first book was a collection of the model letters of the Italian humanist Gasparino Barzizza, but the promoter of the first press to operate in France was Guillaume Fichet, master in theology and librarian of the Sorbonne, who in 1470 obtained authorization to set up a printing press in the College itself. It made a decisively humanistic début; it used the Roman letter exclusively and its first publications were either straight Latin texts, Sallust, Cicero, Juvenal, Terence, and the like, or works bearing on the cultivation of Latin style, such as Valla's *Elegantiae* and Fichet's own *Rhetorica*. The first Greek book to be printed in France appeared in 1507.

The first great classical scholar of France is Guillaume Budé (1468–1540). Born into a wealthy family and not disinclined in his earlier years to the traditional pursuits of the upper class, Budé did not get down to serious study until he was well into his twenties and appears to have been largely self-taught. Years of hard work finally bore fruit. In 1505 he produced his translation of three of Plutarch's treatises into Latin and in 1508 a work of prime importance which established him as one of the founders of legal science. This was his commentary on part of the *Digest*, his *Annotationes in XXIV libros Pandectarum*, an attempt to cut through the medieval accretion of commentary and gloss and reconstitute the text and spirit of Roman law. Neither diplomatic and administrative duties nor a large family nor his fearful headaches stood in the way of Budé's dogged scholarship. In 1515 came his *De asse*, a study of ancient coinage and measures as much a pain to read as a milestone in the establishment of classical studies as a serious discipline. Thanks to a thorough knowledge of the ancient sources, and a practical bent which allowed him to use a balance and consult the local baker, he outstripped previous essays in the field and produced one of the scholarly masterpieces of the century. His *Commentarii linguae graecae* was more lexicographical in character and much of it was afterwards incorporated in the *Thesaurus* of Henri Estienne. His later works, such as his *De philologia* and *De transitu Hellenismi ad Christianismum*, were attempts to define the place of classical, and particularly Greek, studies in contemporary Christian society and justify the position, still somewhat uncomfortable, of the Christian humanist. A monument to one of his many services to scholarship still stands, the Collège de France; it was largely due to the firm pressure applied by Budé that Francis I was finally persuaded in 1530 to institute its precursor, the Collège des Lecteurs Royaux, which gave the study of the ancient languages a certain independence and emancipated them from the prejudices and traditionalist curricula of the university. By giving concrete expression to his view that there is more to humanism than elegance of form Budé initiated a strong trend in the French scholarship of the period, which accorded high respect to solid learning and a thorough understanding of all aspects of ancient life. Though interested primarily in illuminating the content of ancient texts, Budé knew that this depended on a close criticism of the sources themselves and his numismatic researches, for instance, have left an abiding mark on the text of the relevant parts of the Elder Pliny.

While Budé had been reluctantly drawn into the Ciceronian controversy, the Elder Scaliger (Julius Caesar, 1484–1558) had chosen, rather late in life, to make a quick reputation by writing two poisonous orations against the *Ciceronianus* of Erasmus. Though of Italian origin (whether high or low became a matter of lively international dispute), he had left Italy in 1525 to become physician to the bishop of Agen, settled there, and acquired a French wife and fifteen children, one of whom became even more famous than he. His work extends from commentaries on botanical and zoological works of Aristotle and Theophrastus, inspired by his professional interest in medicine, to philology and literary criticism. His *De causis linguae latinae* (1540) is remarkable for its time in aiming at a scientific analysis of the principles of the Latin language, but the work that earned him the fame for which he thirsted was his *Poetice*, published posthumously in 1561. In this he tries in a lucid and coherent manner to produce a theory of poetry relevant to Latin literature viewed as a continuum and extending from the classical poets down to his contemporaries Erasmus and Dolet; nor is it less interesting as an essay in practical criticism.

Budé and Scaliger had not been primarily interested in textual criticism. But they were followed by a series of scholars who conspicuously advanced both the standard and the technique of editing classical texts. The first of these was Adrianus Turnebus (1512–65), who held chairs at Toulouse and Paris and was Royal Reader in Greek from 1547 until his death. As director of the Royal Press (1552–6), he published a series of Greek texts, including Aeschylus, Philo, and Sophocles. He also worked on Latin authors and produced an important edition of Cicero's *De legibus* which included a reconstruction of its Greek sources. His most substantial work is his *Adversaria*, in thirty books, a miscellany of passages from ancient authors emended and explained, criticized by Joseph Scaliger as an *abortivus foetus*, not so much for its content, in which he found much to admire, but because it continued the Italian fashion of *Adversaria*

promoted by Politian and Vettori. Turnebus is admired for his
acumen, judgement, and conjectural gifts. He has made an abiding
impression on the text of Aeschylus. His edition of Sophocles
(1553) is also the *editio princeps* of the scholia of Triclinius. His text
shows too much Triclinian influence; still, he posed the problem of
the Triclinian recension, gave the text of Sophocles a new look, and
added to the corpus of scholia available in his day. Though his
editorial method was the standard *emendatio ope codicum* of his time,
he saw the need to use older and better manuscripts than had
generally been used for the early printed editions and knew a *codex
vestustus* when he saw one. To him we owe our knowledge of an
important manuscript of Plautus, the *Fragmenta Senonensia*, better
known as the codex Turnebi. This was a fragmentary manuscript
from the monastery of Sainte Colombe at Sens, which Turnebus
had in his possession for a time and which may have perished when
the monastery was burnt by the Calvinists in 1567. Apart from the
readings quoted in his *Adversaria*, a transcript of part of Turnebus's
collation made by the jurist François Duaren in the margins of a
contemporary edition of Plautus came to light in the Bodleian
Library in 1897 (8° D 105 Linc.). Turnebus's manuscript or his collation of it was known to Lambinus and Scaliger, and the book in
which his collation is preserved is itself a commentary on the
period, having passed from Duaren to the poets Tabourot and
Belleau, to Scaliger and Daniel Heinsius.

Turnebus's counterpart in Latin scholarship was Denys Lambin,
or Lambinus (1520–72). Before being appointed Royal Reader in
1561, Lambinus had been able to spend considerable periods in
Italy, had met such scholars as Faernus and Muretus, and taken the
opportunity to collate manuscripts in Italian libraries. This bore
fruit when he came to publish his great series of Latin texts, of
which the most celebrated are Horace (1561), Lucretius (1563), and
the whole of Cicero (1565–6); not the least remarkable feature of
these editions is the shortness of the interval between them.
Lambinus had an unrivalled knowledge of the literature of the
Golden Age, an acute intellect, and a fine feeling for language exemplified in the exquisite elegance of his own Latin style. He had a
particular predilection for Lucretius and his masterly edition held

the field until Lachmann. One of the five manuscripts he used was the ninth-century codex Quadratus (Leiden, Voss. Lat. Q. 94 = Q), one of the two manuscripts on which the text is still based; it was then at the monastery of Saint Bertin, near Saint Omer, and he had access to a collation made for Turnebus. For Cicero's letters he used a manuscript of outstanding merit which belonged to the Lyons printer Jean de Tournes and was last heard of in 1580; for its readings we are dependent on three French scholars of this period, Lambinus, Turnebus, and Bosius.

The manuscript collectors of this age, often scholars and editors themselves, made a signal contribution to classical studies. Conspicuous among them is Pierre Daniel (c. 1530–1603), a jurist of Orléans, whose great coup was to succeed in buying manuscripts from Fleury after its sack by the Huguenots in 1562. His collection, now mainly at the Vatican or Berne, contained such important relics of the scholarly heritage of that region as Lupus's copy of Valerius Maximus (Berne 366). He also published *editiones principes* of the *Querolus* (1564) and the longer version of Servius (1600), still often referred to as Servius Danielis. Another was Pierre Pithou (1539–96), who published the first editions of the *Pervigilium Veneris* (1577) and the *Fables* of Phaedrus (1596), both based on ninth-century manuscripts which remain prime witnesses to the text. His use of good manuscripts enabled him to publish important editions of Petronius, and he was the first to use the Lorsch manuscript for the text of Juvenal and Persius (1585), the famous codex Pithoeanus, now to be found, with many other of his manuscripts, at Montpellier. Equally important was Jacques Bongars (c. 1554–1612), whose enormous library, partly derived from the collections of Daniel and Cujas and now at Berne, included such choice items as the famous Irish manuscript of Horace (Berne 363) and our best manuscript of Petronius (Berne 357). Indeed, the complicated history of the text of Petronius in the latter half of the sixteenth century epitomizes the activity of a group of French scholars of this period, Pierre Daniel, the Pithou brothers, Bongars, Scaliger, and the great professor of jurisprudence who had taught them all and may have inspired this particular interest, Jacques Cujas. Its complexity is also an indication of the difficulty of piecing together the

elaborate web formed by the interrelationship of men and manuscripts in this period, even in the case of central texts, and of how
much remains to be discovered about the ramifications of this type
of scholarship.

At the end of the century the classical scholarship of Europe was
dominated by two great Huguenots, Joseph Justus Scaliger (1540–
1609) and Isaac Casaubon (1559–1614). Scaliger was as fortunate as
Casaubon was ill-starred. Launched into Latin by his father, Scaliger
enjoyed for thirty years the patronage of a French nobleman and
when offered the chair at Leiden vacated by Lipsius his eminence as
a scholar was such that he was allowed to accept the chair but
decline the customary duties attached to it. His scholarship owes its
strength to a massive learning in a number of fields and the capacity
to treat an author or a subject as an organic whole. It is best seen in
his great edition of Manilius (first edition, 1579), a worthy precursor
to those of Bentley and Housman, and in the series of studies,
extending from 1583 to 1606, in which he reconstructed the
chronological systems of the ancient world and made a fundamental contribution to the study of history. His early interest in
archaic Latin is exemplified in his edition of Festus (1575), a
lacunose and difficult text, to which he was able to apply not only
his conjectural brilliance but also the legal and antiquarian training
he had received at the hands of Cujas and such recent discoveries as
Daniel's Servius. While over-cleverness, or too much confidence in
his erudition or methodology, often induced him to take unjustifi-
able liberties with the tradition, he left a powerful and permanent
mark on the texts he edited, Manilius in particular, and contributed
to a more scientific approach to the editing of texts. In his edition of
Catullus he sought to prove from the nature of the corruptions in
the manuscripts (such as the confusion of open *a* and *u*, long *i* and
l) that they were descended from a common parent in what he
called 'Lombardic' script; by this he appears to have meant something like the Visigothic hand he had encountered when working
on Ausonius. Though he was wrong, he had gone further than anyone in trying to reconstruct the details of a lost archetype and in
making the history of a particular text an important criterion in
establishing it.

Scaliger was far from untouched by the religious troubles of his day, but the way they bedevilled the scholarship of the sixteenth century is more starkly illustrated in the case of his friend and younger contemporary Casaubon. Born in Geneva of refugee Protestant parents, obliged to learn his Greek hiding in a cave in the French mountains, unable to avoid being drawn into the wrangle because of his distinction as a scholar and forced to spend much of his time and talents on arid polemic, this great French scholar finally found rest as a naturalized Englishman in Westminster Abbey. With him the French scholarship of the period ended, as it had begun, on a chalcenteric note. He was a man of vast industry and erudition, but had the rarer gift of being able to use his learning as a commentator to illumine rather than impress. He appears to have chosen to work on those texts that offered the most scope to his wide knowledge, such as Diogenes Laertius, Strabo, and Athenaeus. His choice of difficult and often diffuse texts, with which most students of the classics have but a passing acquaintance, means that his services are not always recognized. For Casaubon is still with us. His *Animadversiones* on Athenaeus formed the core of Schweighäuser's commentary of 1801, Strabo is still usually cited by reference to Casaubon's pages, his notes on Persius loom large in Conington's commentary. Son-in-law to Henri Estienne and for a time sub-librarian to de Thou at the royal library, Casaubon was most at home in the world of books and manuscripts, able to find material for his own needs and to supply scholars all over Europe. His use of manuscript material has not been properly appraised, but he seems to have made no dramatic advances, except that his second edition of Theophrastus' *Characters* (1599) added five more characters (24–8) to those then known. Some of his most distinguished work was long buried in his unfinished commentary on Aeschylus.

III. THE NETHERLANDS IN THE SIXTEENTH AND
SEVENTEENTH CENTURIES

Although Erasmus could speak with disgust of the ignorance which obtained in the Netherlands in his youth, it is likely that there was a more widespread general level of literacy than elsewhere. A large measure of the credit for this must go to the Brothers of the Common Life, the members of a community founded at Deventer in the later fourteenth century who devoted a large part of their energy to educational projects and the copying of books. Among the many schools which owed their existence or excellence to them were those attended by Erasmus at Deventer and Hertogenbosch. The general level of literacy and the growth of prosperous mercantile towns helped to create conditions in which learning could flourish despite a late start.

It was the universities and the printing houses, often working closely together, that were largely responsible for the powerful classical tradition of the Netherlands. The university of Louvain was founded in 1425 and the establishment of the Collegium Trilingue for the study of Latin, Greek, and Hebrew in the same town about 1517 further strengthened its claim to be for a time one of the greatest intellectual centres of northern Europe. A similarly dominating position in the northern Netherlands was achieved by the university of Leiden, founded in 1575 to commemorate the heroic resistance of its inhabitants to siege by the forces of Spain. Just as the Protestant north and the Catholic south had their respective centres of higher learning, so they had equally famous traditions of printing. Although the early history of Dutch printing is obscure, it is interesting to observe that such a standard schoolbook as Donatus' *Ars minor* was printed in Holland about 1470, while in the south at Louvain John of Westphalia issued a number of standard classical authors as early as 1475. His successor in the business, Thierry Martens, was himself a scholar and a friend of Erasmus. From 1512 onwards he began to produce classical books to meet the needs of the university and printed the first Greek texts to be published in this part of Europe. In the great age of printing in the Netherlands, in the later sixteenth and seventeenth centuries, it was Plantin who held sway in the south and Elzevir in the north. Christopher Plantin settled in Antwerp in 1550; on his death in 1589 the business passed to his son-in-law Jan Moerentorf (Moretus) and continued on the same premises and in the same family for three centuries, when it was transformed into the Musée

Plantin-Moretus. Though his most famous production was the eight-volume Polyglot Bible (1568–73), his vast and varied output contained an enormous number of classical editions, some of them magnificently produced. The Plantin Horace of 1566, edited by Theodore Poelman, is the first to use sigla in the modern manner. He was closely associated with such scholars as Canter and Lipsius, and published a number of *editiones principes* of Greek authors, including Nonnus (1569) and Stobaeus (1575). Louis Elzevir had established himself at Leiden, initially as a bookseller, in 1580. His first book, a text of Eutropius (1592), heralded a strong preoccupation with classical books which fortunately coincided with the great period of Dutch scholarship and so ensured a series of good scholarly texts. Particularly influential was the charming little duodecimo series of classical authors, inaugurated by his sons in 1629. At a guilder a volume they appealed to the student and carried both the name of Elzevir and a sound tradition of classical scholarship all over Europe, much as the great series of Greek and Latin texts begun in 1824 was to make the name of B. G. Teubner a household word and provide a sound basis for modern scholarship.

Although the greatest classical scholar to emerge in the Netherlands in the sixteenth century is undoubtedly Justus Lipsius, there were others whose special interests claim our attention. One of these is Wilhelm Canter (1542–75), whose speciality was Greek textual criticism. He is mainly known for his editions of the three tragedians, but he also edited the *editio princeps* of the *Eclogae* of Stobaeus for the Plantin Press. He makes a special claim for his treatment of the lyrics, and his edition of Euripides, printed by Plantin in 1571, is the first to pay particular attention to responsion and its role in emendation. He also wrote a short manual on textual criticism, *Syntagma de ratione emendandi scriptores Graecos*, appended to his Latin translation of the speeches of Aelius Aristides (1566). This is a systematic classification of the different types of error in Greek texts, brought under such headings as the confusion of certain letters, wrong word-division, omissions, additions and transpositions, errors arising from assimilation or the misunderstanding of abbreviations, and illustrated with examples taken almost exclusively from Aristides. He provides a brief but businesslike guide to

the errors of scribes and, though little that he says would come as
news to the great critics of his day, it is a gain to have certain valid
principles of emendation explicitly set out, even if the details need
refinement. Franz Modius (1556–97) is less noteworthy for his
scholarship, though he edited a number of Latin texts, than for his
insistence that conjecture alone is useless and even dangerous, that
there must be a proper balance between manuscript authority and
emendation, that recension is an essential preliminary to editing. In
this conviction, and also obliged by the political unrest of the
Netherlands to be on the move, he systematically explored the
manuscript collections of a wide area, extending from northern
France through the Low Countries to Fulda and Bamberg. His
activity is remarkable for its scale and his reports of manuscript
readings, found in his *Novantiquae lectiones* (1584), acquire great
value when the manuscripts themselves have been destroyed, as in
the case of the Cologne manuscript of Silius Italicus. The only other
first-hand report of the Cologne Silius is provided by his friend and
later enemy, Ludovicus Carrio (1547–95), who was similarly active
on a smaller scale. Jacob Cruquius worked almost exclusively on
Horace and owes his fame to his invention of the ghostly 'commentator Cruquianus', now exorcized, and to his timely examination of four Horace manuscripts at the monastery of Saint Pierre au
Mont-Blandin, near Ghent, just before its destruction in 1566. One
of these was the very important, if controversial, *Blandinius
vetustissimus*, which assures the Bruges professor a fractional share
of the immortality that Horace so confidently forecast for himself.

It was a singular piece of good fortune for the new university of
Leiden that it should have attracted so soon after its inauguration
one of the most brilliant Latinists of the century. Justus Lipsius
(1547–1606) was a Catholic by upbringing and associated in his
early years with the university of Louvain, but his conversion to the
Protestant faith had opened the way for his being invited to the
chair of history at Leiden, which he held from 1579 to 1591, just as
his reconversion led to his return to Louvain in 1592, where he was
Professor of History at the university and of Latin at the Collegium
Trilingue. His achievement was based on a thorough knowledge of
the history and antiquities of Rome, reflected in his monographs

and discussions on various topics from ancient warfare to dinner parties, and a close reading of the texts, which combined to produce a commentator and critic of the first order. Though he worked with good effect on Plautus and Propertius and Seneca's *Tragedies*, his main contribution was to the prose writers of the imperial period and he is best remembered for his editions of Tacitus (1574, frequently revised) and Seneca (1605). His interest in this period led him to modify his own prose style, initially Ciceronian in character, and to develop a pointed style which had considerable influence on both Latin and vernacular prose writing. His Tacitus is his greatest achievement and a random glance at the apparatus criticus of any modern edition, where his name appears with devastating regularity, will show how he was able to transform the text, despite a basically cautious approach to emendation. As a young man he had spent two years in Italy doing the fashionable things, studying the antiquities, exploring the libraries, and meeting Muretus, but he was luckier with his monuments than his manuscripts. He failed to examine the two Medicean manuscripts of Tacitus and had to rely on copies until his last edition, which appeared posthumously in 1607, where he was able to make use of the collations published in 1600 by an important and rather neglected scholar, Curzio Pichena, gratified to discover how often his conjectures had been confirmed. His Seneca is a magnificent folio volume, published, as were so many of his works, by Plantin. He relied on poor manuscript material and his Seneca generally lacked the brilliance of his Tacitus, but it remains a fitting culmination to the labours of a man who had made such a thorough study of Stoicism in preparation for the work that he had been able to revive it as a living force in the troubled days of the Netherlands. His *Manuductio ad Stoicam philosophiam* and *Physiologia Stoicorum* (1604) give the first full account of Stoicism, while his own *De constantia* (1584), which owes much to Seneca in both thought and style, went through thirty-two editions and was translated into several languages.

In the seventeenth century the Netherlands were unaffected by the general decline in the level of classical scholarship which can be discerned in other countries. It maintained its flourishing tradition well into the eighteenth century, when the influence of Bentley, working through Hemsterhuys, contributed to a brilliant revival of Greek studies that more than compensated for the dogged industry of the Elder Burman and the incompetence of Havercamp. Leiden attracted powerful scholars from abroad and Dutch scholarship was enhanced by their influence. Joseph Scaliger had succeeded in 1593 to the chair at Leiden vacated by Lipsius, and occupied it until his death. The same chair, vacant from 1609 to 1631, was then again filled from abroad, to the chagrin of Vossius, by the appointment of the erudite but somewhat dilettante Salmasius (Claude de Saumaise, 1588–1653). He is known for his polemic with Milton, owned the famous codex Salmasianus of the Latin Anthology (Paris lat. 10318), and played a part, much smaller than has at times been supposed, in making known the contents of the famous manuscript of the Greek Anthology at Heidelberg (Heidelberg gr. 23 + Paris suppl. gr. 384); but he had done his best work before moving to Leiden.

G. J. Vossius (1577–1649) helped to give Dutch scholarship a broader basis by treating a wide range of subjects in a systematic and encyclopedic way. He was Professor of Rhetoric at Leiden for ten years until 1632, when he accepted the Chair of History at the newly founded Athenaeum at Amsterdam. He also became a non-resident prebendary of Canterbury. He wrote a comprehensive treatise on rhetoric and later a more influential *Poetic institutions* (1647), two notable contributions to Latin grammar and usage, his *Aristarchus* and *De vitiis sermonis et glossematis latinobarbaris*, while his *De historicis graecis* and *De historicis latinis* (1624, 1627), dictionaries of historians from antiquity to the sixteenth century, took him into the neglected field of literary history. His *De theologia gentili*, still almost medieval in its misconceptions, can claim to be one of the earliest books on classical mythology. His interest in the theory of poetry was shared by his contemporary Daniel Heinsius (1580–1655), the devoted protégé of Scaliger, who in 1611 published an edition of Aristotle's *Poetics* and a short treatise *De tragoediae constitutione*. The latter is a succinct and authoritative restatement of the Aristotelian view of tragedy, filled out with references to Horace's *Ars poetica* and illustrations from Greek tragedy and Seneca, and it had considerable influence on neoclassical drama and the French theatre in particular. He was an elegant versifier and a stimulating teacher, but he had a very mixed success as a textual critic and his greatest gift to this branch of classics was his son.

The editing of Latin authors continued to be the central activity of Dutch scholarship and it was carried on with distinction in the latter half of the seventeenth century by two great friends, J. F. Gronovius (1611–71) and Nicolaus Heinsius (1620–81), who dominated respectively the fields of prose and poetry. Gronovius was born in Hamburg and had travelled in England, France, and Italy before settling at Leiden. During his travels he had taken the opportunity to examine Latin manuscripts. It was in Florence in 1640 that he came across the codex Etruscus of Seneca's *Tragedies*, neglected since the Renaissance: he immediately recognized its worth and in his edition of 1661 firmly established its authority. He did other useful work on Latin poetry, but is best known for his numerous editions of the prose writers of the imperial period, including Livy, the Elder Pliny, both Senecas, Tacitus, and Gellius, an enormous output distinguished, as was his miscellaneous *Observationes*, by wide knowledge, good judgement, and balanced scholarship. Heinsius was more gifted. He held no academic post and could give to study only such time as remained from an active career in diplomacy and public life. His diplomatic missions had given him the chance to investigate many of the manuscript collections of Europe and his great store of accurate collations stood him in good stead. But his strength lay in his fine feeling for the elegance of Latin poetry, partly derived from his own skill in writing verse, a precise understanding of the niceties of diction and convention which made him a sensitive and almost uncanny critic. This combination of divinatory skill with the capacity for careful collation and a fund of common sense acquired in the world at large helped to make him one of the greatest critics of Latin poetry. His main editions were of Ovid, Vergil, Valerius Flaccus, and the later poets Claudian and Prudentius, but he left notes on others which were published after his death and he did some work on Silver Latin prose.

Isaac Vossius (1618–89) is best remembered as a bibliophile, or indeed as the free-thinking Anglican convert who dared to read

Ovid during divine service in Saint George's Chapel. He had come to England in 1670, was given a doctorate at Oxford and a prebend at Windsor, and became a well-known if somewhat odd figure in the London society of Charles II. His versatile forays into the by-ways of erudition have left no permanent mark, but he had a decisive hand in shaping some of our greatest manuscript collections. Like Salmasius and Heinsius and Descartes, he had been invited to Stockholm by that extraordinary monarch, queen Christina of Sweden, and enjoyed her patronage from 1649 to 1652. Apart from tutoring her in Greek, he aided her in her ambition to build up a library comparable with that of the other courts of Europe. Among the manuscripts he acquired for her were those of his father, Gerard Vossius, and the French jurist Paul Petau, who had himself bought part of Pierre Daniel's collection. The majority of the queen's manuscripts are now in the Vatican and constitute the Reginenses. But Vossius was not slow to exploit his expertise on his own behalf and he left behind a magnificent library. The Vossiani were offered to the Bodleian Library and Bentley was energetic in trying to promote their purchase, but they went instead to Leiden, and with them the two great manuscripts of Lucretius which, had they not been removed at a critical moment from Bentley's reach, might have changed the course of textual studies.

IV. RICHARD BENTLEY (1662–1742): CLASSICAL AND THEOLOGICAL STUDIES

The next figure of commanding importance in the history of textual criticism is Richard Bentley, who was Master of Trinity College Cambridge from 1699 onwards. Much of his time in that position was taken up by the academic intrigues that were endemic in Oxford and Cambridge colleges in the seventeenth and eighteenth centuries, but his amazing self-control enabled him to avoid being entirely distracted from scholarship, and the list of his works would be more than creditable to many men who enjoyed an undisturbed career. He began to make a name for himself in 1691 by the publication of the *Epistula ad Joannem Millium*. This was a series of observations on the text of John Malalas, an obscure and mediocre Byzantine chronicler of the sixth century, then being printed for the first time. Bentley's extraordinary learning allowed him to emend the text in many places and in passing he offered explanations and emendations of other and better-known authors. It was probably these, in conjunction with the attractive vivacity of his Latin style, which made the work well known in a short time, and his fame spread to a wider public than professional scholars, for in 1697 we find him a member of a small circle that included Newton, Wren, Locke, and John Evelyn.

A few years later Bentley distinguished himself again with his work on the epistles of Phalaris. Once again it was an obscure text of no literary merit that called forth his best efforts, but, as will be seen below, he cannot be accused of confining himself to a pedantic delight in the study of trivial authors. The letters, which purport to be by the early tyrant of Acragas, are in fact a composition of the Second Sophistic age, and there is no explicit testimony to their existence earlier than the anthology of John Stobaeus in the fifth century A.D. Bentley was by no means the first person to cast doubts on their authenticity; Politian had done so already. But there were still some scholars who believed them genuine, and when a new edition appeared the argument began again. It formed a small part of the controversy between the Ancients and the Moderns, and there were some who maintained that irrespective of their dubious authenticity the letters of Phalaris were one of the best literary products of antiquity. Bentley's *Dissertation*, although its conclusions did not win universal acceptance for a long time, was a masterly proof that the letters were a miserable and worthless forgery, marred by every kind of anachronism and composed in a dialect unknown to the supposed author, and the display of learning employed in order to demonstrate the conclusion made it clear that Bentley had no serious rival as a critic or commentator anywhere in Europe.

As a textual critic Bentley is perhaps best known for the work he did on Latin authors at a later stage in his career. His zest for emendation, which is relatively easy in authors whose texts are badly preserved and who have never received the attentions of a good critic, led him astray in dealing with such authors as Horace, and he earned notoriety by the amusing change he proposed to make in the fable of the fox caught in the granary (*Epistles* 1.7.29). Insisting that a fox will not eat grain Bentley proposed to read 'field-mouse' (*nitedula* instead of *vulpecula*), quite oblivious of the consideration that the author of the fable chose the animal as the representative of cunning greed at the expense of the facts of natural history. This insistence on logic, without consideration of poetic and other forms of literary licence, mars Bentley's contributions to the emendation of leading authors that he edited, namely Horace in 1711 and Terence in 1726, and the same is even more true of his attempt to restore the works of Milton to what he supposed to be their original state before a putative interpolator imposed on the blind poet with a series of alterations of the text. On the other hand, where hard facts were at a premium, as in the astronomical poem by Manilius, Bentley's gifts were given a great opportunity, and the opinion of experts is that he made contributions of the utmost brilliance to the interpretation of the hardest passages of this very hard poem, the edition of which appeared in 1739 although the work for it had been done long before. It should also be recorded that in dealing with Terence he displayed a notable command of the principles of metre; in this field, however, he acknowledged the importance of a sixteenth-century Italian predecessor, Gabriele Faerno.

Bentley made many emendations in the text of other authors, of which a high proportion have been accepted or seriously considered by subsequent editors. But two of his most valuable activities were projects that never came to fruition, editions of Homer and the New Testament. As far as Homer is concerned, his most notable discovery was that the metre of many lines could be explained by postulating the existence of the letter digamma, a notion which contributed as much as any other single discovery to the understanding of this text.

Though Bentley is commonly thought of as a classical scholar pure and simple because of his striking achievements in that field, he was also of sufficient competence in theology to be appointed Regius Professor of Divinity in 1717. Three years later he published a tiny pamphlet called *Proposals for an edition of the New Testament*, in which he announced explicitly that the text would be based on the oldest manuscripts of the Greek text and of the Vulgate. Bentley knew that in English libraries he could lay hands on more than one manuscript a thousand years old, and he arranged for some collations of equally old manuscripts in foreign libraries to be made. With the aid of this information he reckoned to be able to restore the text as it was in the best copies circulating at the time of the Council of Nicaea (A.D. 325). It is interesting to note that he did not hope to establish the authors' text exactly as it stood in the autographs, and in passing it should be said that one of his most distinguished followers, Lachmann, writing in 1830, announced his intention of restoring the text as it was c. A.D. 380. Bentley had already begun collations, and although the work never made much progress he was able to state in the *Proposals* with characteristic confidence 'I find that by taking 2,000 errors out of the Pope's Vulgate, and as many out of the Protestant Pope Stephens', I can set out an edition of each in columns, without using any book under 900 years old, that shall so exactly agree, word for word, and, what at first amazed me, order for order, that no two tallies, nor two indentures, can agree better' (the reference to order is an allusion to the many manuscript variants involving the order of words). He continued, however, with the much less characteristic promise 'I alter not a letter of my own head without the authority of these old witnesses', which is far from the principle he adopted in the textual criticism of secular authors.

Since his edition was never completed, the so-called *textus receptus*, in other words the text in the form which Erasmus and Estienne had given it, continued to be printed. Only very rarely did a bold critic show independence of mind and risk the annoyance of churchmen at large by printing other readings or his own conjectures, and it was not until 1881 that the principles of recension and textual criticism were rigorously applied to the New Testament in the edition of B. F. Westcott and F. J. A. Hort.

While Bentley would therefore appear to be a century and a half ahead of his time, it is only fair to record that his *Proposals* scarcely mark any advance on the work of the cantankerous French priest

Richard Simon (1638–1712). For our purpose Simon's chief work is his *Histoire critique du texte du Nouveau Testament*, published in Rotterdam in 1689 (censorship and *odium theologicum* prevented publication in his own country) and translated into English in the same year. This seems to be the first attempt to write a monograph on the transmission of an ancient text, and despite its unattractive appearance and concern with polemic it contains important exemplifications of critical principles in the chapters on the manuscripts, and it is impossible to believe that Bentley did not know and approve of them. After observing that there is nothing in the Greek tradition like the Masoretic system for ensuring textual stability he states as his policy the investigation of the Greek manuscripts, the various versions and the scholia. There follows a survey of the history of the New Testament text from the time of Valla onwards, with comments on the printed editions, chiefly concerned with their success or otherwise in providing a satisfactory apparatus of variant readings. He knows that the great age of a manuscript does not automatically guarantee the truth of its readings, and he follows previous critics in the view that the Greek text should be tested by comparison with early patristic citations, since these are earlier than the schism of the Greek and Roman churches, as a result of which, according to some critics, the Greek text had been deliberately falsified. His use of the versions is admirably shown by his discussion of John 7: 39, where he exploits the Vulgate and Syriac versions in order to arrive at a view of the passage. It leads him to the surprisingly modern and sophisticated view that obscure or ambiguous texts were explained by scholia, and when these scholia were short they easily came to be incorporated into the text. As to the use of early Greek manuscripts, much of his time is spent on readings of the codex Bezae (Cambridge, University Library, Nn. 2. 41, commonly known by the symbol D), which has a text very different from most other witnesses and presents some of the most awkward problems of criticism. But he was also aware of the importance of the Vatican codex B (Vat. gr. 1209) and the Alexandrinus (British Library, MS. Royal I D viii).

V. THE ORIGINS OF PALAEOGRAPHY

The first steps towards establishing the study of manuscripts on a firm basis were not taken until the end of the seventeenth century. Bessarion and Politian may be credited with some palaeographical knowledge, and the former at least found it useful in refuting his opponents at the Council of Florence. While the technique of editing and the art of textual criticism made steady progress in the late Renaissance and the following century, little or no interest was taken in the date and origin of the manuscripts being used for editions of classical and Christian texts. Once again it was religious controversy that led to progress. A quarrel broke out between the Jesuits and the Benedictines; a Jesuit called Daniel van Papenbroeck (1628–1714, otherwise known as Papebroch) proved in 1675 that a charter supposedly issued by the Merovingian king Dagobert in 646 and guaranteeing certain privileges to the Benedictines was a forgery. The French Benedictine order, which had recently been revived under the title of the Congregation of Saint Maur and was devoting itself to various scholarly enterprises, treated van Papenbroek's work as a challenge. One of its most able members, Dom Jean Mabillon (1632–1707), spent several years in studying charters and manuscripts, drawing up in a systematic way for the first time a series of criteria for testing the authenticity of medieval documents. The result was *De re diplomatica* (1681), to which we owe the word diplomatic, normally used as the technical term for the study of legal and official documents. Mabillon's work dealt also to a lesser extent with manuscripts, but was restricted to Latin. It was immediately recognized as a masterpiece, even by van Papenbroeck, who had a cordial exchange of letters with Mabillon, acknowledging that his attempt to prove the spuriousness of all Merovingian charters was an excess of scepticism. On the other hand his thesis about the charter of 646 was upheld.

Among the projects of the Congregation of Saint Maur were new editions of the Greek and Latin Fathers. A large group of monks was at work at the Parisian house of Saint-Germain-des-Prés. A knowledge of medieval charters had only limited application, but

Mabillon's remarks on manuscripts stimulated one of his junior colleagues to look more closely at the writing of Greek manuscripts. Dom Bernard de Montfaucon (1655–1741) had been ordained in 1676 after illness had enforced his retirement from the army. Since 1687 he had been working on the edition of the Greek Fathers, and particularly on Athanasius. In the year after the death of Mabillon he produced *Palaeographia graeca*, and in this case too the title of his book invented a word that has been standard ever since. In its own field it was in some ways a greater achievement than Mabillon's book, since it remained the best book on the subject for about two centuries and it made the first attempt to understand the history of individual letter forms, which is fundamental to palaeography. The scope of the book is rather different, since very few medieval Greek charters or other documents were available to Montfaucon (they are still mostly to be found in the archives of the monasteries of Mount Athos, which Montfaucon never visited), and in any case the authenticity of these documents raised no issues for Montfaucon and his contemporaries. So he was able to devote himself to studying the manuscripts, and his examination of examples that can be dated with little or no doubt from the subscriptions of the scribes themselves was of permanent value. His other contribution to palaeography was *Bibliotheca Coisliniana* (1715), one of the first systematic descriptions of a complete collection of manuscripts, in this case the fine collection of about 400 items that had been inherited by Coislin, the prince-bishop of Metz, from Séguier, Chancellor of France under Louis XIV. It may be worth adding in passing that Montfaucon was by no means a narrow specialist, concerned with nothing but manuscripts. His other works include a dictionary of classical antiquities in ten folio volumes, to which a further five were subsequently added as a supplement. It appeared in 1719 under the title of *Antiquité expliquée*; 1,800 were sold within ten months, and a second edition of 2,200 copies was called for.

Despite the enormous bulk of their writings, Mabillon and Montfaucon found time to travel, especially in Italy, to visit other manuscript collections that could offer material for their works. In Verona, where the wealth of the Chapter Library had been known to humanists of the Renaissance, the visitor of the late seventeenth century was told that the books could no longer be found. This tantalizing state of affairs roused the curiosity of a local aristocrat and antiquarian, the marquis Scipione Maffei (1675-1755). Besides making a name for himself by writing the tragedy *Merope*, which was a landmark in the revival of the Italian theatre, he found himself involved in historical controversy in 1712, when he wrote a pamphlet against the duke Francesco Farnese. Farnese had been duped into purchasing the grandmastership of an order of Saint John supposedly set up by the emperor Constantine. The pope and the Austrian emperor swallowed the bait as well, and Farnese was assigned for the use of his order the beautiful church of Santa Maria della Steccata in Parma. Maffei demonstrated that the order must be bogus, since all such orders were of medieval date, a fact which did not save his book from being placed on the index of prohibited literature.

Maffei let it be known to the canon librarian of the cathedral in Verona that he was very anxious to discover the fate of the manuscripts it had once possessed. One morning in 1712 the librarian found them; they had been piled on top of a cupboard in order to avoid damage from flooding, and then had been entirely forgotten. The news was taken at once to Maffei's house, and he rushed over to the cathedral in his night clothes and slippers. When he set eyes on the books, a wonderful collection mostly of very early date, he thought that he must be dreaming, but the dream proved to be a reality and it was not long before he was studying the manuscripts in his own home. The result of this study was a very important theoretical improvement in the understanding of Latin book-hands. Mabillon had divided them into five independent categories, Gothic, Langobardic, Saxon, Merovingian, and Roman. But he had said nothing about any possible relation between them. Maffei hit on the fact that the explanation of the diversity of Latin scripts in the early Middle Ages must be that in late antiquity there were certain basic types, majuscule, minuscule, and cursive, and when the Roman Empire broke apart variations of these scripts arose independently. It was this flash of insight which made palaeography a subject with a clear theoretical basis. The only major advance subsequently is the one associated with the name of Ludwig Traube

(1861–1907), whose great contribution was to show that manuscripts, apart from being the primary sources for the texts of classical and medieval literature, can be treated as documents illustrating the history of medieval culture. A manuscript which may be proved utterly useless as a copy of an author's text may none the less be of the greatest value in another way, since if it can be assigned with certainty to its place of origin, or better still, if the scribe of it can be identified with certainty, it will tell us something about the intellectual history of the Middle Ages.

VI. DISCOVERIES OF TEXTS SINCE THE RENAISSANCE

(a) *Palimpsests*

The recovery of an unknown ancient text produces a special sense of excitement and one which the learned world was rarely in a position to experience in the centuries following the Renaissance. But a new series of discoveries, less glamorous but by no means unrewarding, began with the realization that some classical texts still lay hidden in the lower script of palimpsests. Although such palimpsests had long existed in some of the best-known European libraries, in Paris and Rome, Milan and Verona, they were not really exploited until the nineteenth century, when the great discoveries of Mai and Niebuhr conferred an aura of romance on the humble rescript and allowed it to make a spectacular entry into the story of classical scholarship.

The first palimpsest text to be brought to the notice of the public was an early and important manuscript of the Greek Bible, the fifth-century codex Ephraemi (Paris gr. 9, lower script), discovered by Jean Boivin, the sub-librarian of the Royal Library in Paris, in 1692. The first new classical text to emerge from a palimpsest was again Greek and likewise discovered at Paris, by J. J. Wettstein in 1715–16, though he failed to attribute it correctly: the sixth-century codex Claromontanus of the Pauline Epistles (Paris gr. 107B) had at some stage been patched up by the insertion of two leaves from a fifth-century manuscript of Euripides' *Phaethon*, which was then in part reused. This manuscript, which can be supplemented from papyri and the indirect tradition, provides substantial fragments of Euripides' play. Other scholars of the eighteenth century succeeded in anticipating some of the later discoveries, but their ignorance of the chemical means later used to restore faded writing or their reluctance to employ such aids meant that they failed to realize the full significance of their finds. Scipione Maffei had discovered some of the Verona rescripts, including both the palimpsested part and the one unpalimpsested leaf of Gaius' *Institutes* (Verona XV (13)), but it was not until 1816 that the text was correctly attributed. In the middle of the century Dom Tassin, one of the Maurist authors of the *Nouveau traité de diplomatique*, a revised and improved version of Mabillon's work, suggested that one of the primary scripts of a manuscript rewritten at Corbie (Paris lat. 12161) contained a fragment of the then completely unknown writer Fronto. His anticipation of Mai's discovery is hardly more remarkable than the fact that the sixth-century fragment which he had detected was not properly appreciated until 1956, almost exactly two centuries later, when it was identified by Bernard Bischoff as a fragment of one of Fronto's epistles (*Ad Verum* 2.1). In 1772 P. J. Bruns discovered the substructure of Vat. Pal. lat. 24, a rich patchwork of ancient codices, and from it he edited a fragment of Livy Book 91. In the following year G. Migliore extracted from the lower scripts of the same manuscript two fragmentary texts which he took to be Cicero but which were in fact the remains of the *De amicitia* and *De vita patris* of Seneca, later re-edited by Niebuhr and Studemund.

So considerable steps had been taken, faltering though they were at times, to salvage palimpsested texts before the dramatic second decade of the nineteenth century. Then, owing to a combination of circumstances, there was a great leap forward. The main contributory factors were the untiring and almost ruthless energy of Angelo Mai (1782–1854) and his good fortune in being appointed successively librarian of the Ambrosian and of the Vatican, the two libraries which housed the particularly rich collection of palimpsests from Bobbio. He was also the first to make successful use of reagents, which facilitated the detection of palimpsested texts, made the writing more legible, and aided identification; a great measure of his success must be attributed to this. In the space of a few years, beginning in 1814, he published a whole series of new texts, including fragments of some of Cicero's speeches and the *scholia Bobiensia* (Ambros. S.P. 11.66, *olim* R. 57 sup.), the letters of Fronto (S.P. 9/1-6, 11, *olim* E. 147 sup.), and, from the great Ambrosian palimpsest of Plautus (S.P. 9/13-20, *olim* G. 82 sup.), what remains of the hitherto unknown *Vidularia*. In 1819 he moved from Milan to the Vatican and towards the end of that year crowned his achievements by finding the text for which men like Roger Bacon and Petrarch had passionately searched and which even the most optimistic scholars had given up as lost for ever, the *De republica* of Cicero (Plate X). He published the *editio princeps* in 1822.

Others were quick to enter the palimpsest field, many of them more careful and better scholars than Mai, who had been hasty and uncritical and not over-scrupulous; but he had creamed the collection. One of them was the great German historian Barthold Georg Niebuhr (1776–1831), who arrived in Rome as the Prussian ambassador in 1816, having made on his way to the capital the only find to rival the more spectacular discoveries of Mai. At Verona he succeeded in reading with the use of a reagent the lower script of the Gaius palimpsest, in parts *ter scriptus*, and so made possible the eventual publication in 1820 of the first edition of the complete *Institutes*. Though his greater acumen made relations with Mai somewhat strained, he did contribute to Mai's edition of the *De republica*.

No account of the decipherment and publication of palimpsests, however brief, could omit the name of Wilhelm Studemund (1843–89), who devoted years of an active scholarly life and finally his sight to the patient and meticulous transcription of palimpsest texts. The best known are his transcripts of Gaius (1874) and the Ambrosian Plautus (1889); the latter bears the touching inscription, taken from Catullus 14, *ni te plus oculis meis amarem*. The work of such later scholars was hampered by the earlier employment of reagents, which stained and sometimes corroded the parchment, often with disastrous results. The first reagent to be known was gallic acid and this was the one used by Mai, sometimes with a heavy hand; later scholars used potassium bisulphate or the recipe of a Turin chemist Giobert, which consisted of successive applications of hydrochloric acid and potassium cyanide. They were all harmful in some degree (but infinitely more slowly than might have been expected of such deadly compounds) and had the result that manuscripts so treated are rarely susceptible to the safer and more advanced techniques possible today, especially that of ultra-violet photography, which were perfected in particular by Alban Dold at the Palimpsest Institute of the Abbey of Beuron, in south-west Germany. Unless modern techniques of electronic photography and image processing produce significant results, the editions and transcripts of the nineteenth century will retain their value.

Early in the present century J. L. Heiberg found in Constantinople a palimpsest copy of Archimedes which yielded two works of note (Metochion of the Holy Sepulchre, MS. 355). One, *On floating bodies*, was known already in the Latin translation by William of Moerbeke, but the other, *Method*, was entirely new and of great significance for the history of mathematics, since it showed that Archimedes devised a procedure similar to the integral calculus. Two other fairly recently discovered palimpsests may be worth notice. One is in Jerusalem (Patriarchate MS. 36), and contains part of several Euripidean plays, written probably in the middle of the eleventh century. It is one of the earliest copies with a substantial portion of Euripides' works, but despite its date it does not improve the text much. The other is in Leiden (B.P.G. 60 A), and yields parts of some Sophoclean plays. It is the twin brother of the famous Laurentian codex, seemingly written by the same scribe.

(b) *Papyri*

Until the end of the last century our knowledge of ancient texts depended almost entirely on copies made during the Middle Ages, whereas manuscripts dating back to the later centuries of the ancient world formed only a tiny proportion of the total number known. From the Renaissance onwards such discoveries as were made of new texts, or more commonly, better manuscripts of texts already known, usually consisted in the unearthing of neglected medieval manuscripts. The only significant exception was the recovery of the charred remains of papyrus rolls from the excavations of Herculaneum; most of these contained the abstruse writings of the Epicurean philosopher Philodemus. Because of their poor state of preservation not much use was made of them, and it is only in very recent times that technology has made advances which allow us to read them with relative ease. But a remarkable change was brought about when the archaeologists working in Egypt brought to light quantities of ancient books, often generically known as papyri even though a substantial minority of them are in fact written on parchment. The biggest finds were made at Oxyrhynchus in Upper Egypt by B. P. Grenfell and A. S. Hunt. For the first time scholars could consult a mass of ancient books, which are on average about a thousand years older than the textual witnesses that they had to rely on before. Discoveries and their publication have continued ever since. Even though the papyri of literary content are outnumbered by documents of various kinds in the ratio of perhaps ten to one, there are many early manuscripts of known texts and a significant number which add to the stock of extant Greek literature. Not all these texts are complete or of the highest quality as literature, but among them are such important books as Aristotle's *Athenian constitution* (P. Lit. Lond. 108), the *Odes* of Bacchylides (P. Lit. Lond. 46), and substantial fragments of Sophocles' satyr-play the *Ichneutae* (P. Oxy. 1174), Euripides' *Hypsipyle* (P. Oxy. 852), Menander's *Dyscolus* virtually complete (P. Bodmer 4), *Epitrepontes* and *Samia* (P. Cairo inv. 43227), and *Sicyonius* (P. Sorbonne 72, 2272, 2273). The authors best represented, however, are those of the school-room, and against the handful of really interesting papyri must be set the hundreds of Homer that have survived. Other fascinating discoveries include many important biblical papyri, the most notable being the scrap measuring two and a half by three and a half inches from the Gospel of Saint John that can be dated to the early second century (P. Rylands 457), and the unsavoury documents of ancient racial prejudice known as the *Acts of the pagan martyrs*. The Manichaean heresy is illuminated by a fascinating miniature codex now in Cologne (P. Colon. inv. 4780).

Nearly all the papyri come from Egypt, though there are a few from Dura-Europos on the Euphrates and Nessana in the Negev desert. The vast majority of the Egyptian papyri have been found in a district some way from the capital. The number and variety of the literary finds are rather surprising, since one might not expect to find such evidence of wide reading in a country district. The survival of the papyri was made possible because in the villages refuse, including waste paper, was thrown onto huge rubbish dumps, which rose high enough to make their contents immune from any effects of moisture from the annual inundation or irrigation; with the dryness of the climate the papyri often avoided further damage. A few of them come not directly from the rubbish dumps, but from tombs, like Timotheus' *Persae* (P. Berol. 9875), or from cartonnage, the casing in which mummies were enclosed. This substance was made from layers of papyrus stuck together rather like papier mâché, and unwanted papyri were evidently bought up in quantity to make it. Many of these were damaged books no longer of any use to their owners, and we owe our knowledge of Menander's *Sicyonius*, a hundred lines of Euripides' *Antiope* (P. Lit. Lond. 70), and the end of his *Erechtheus* (P. Sorbonne 2328) to this fortunate habit of the Egyptian undertakers. Archaeological excavation has recently uncovered some very interesting Latin texts, nine lines of the poet Gallus (see p. 247) and what appears to be a fragment of Livy, Book 11; the latter was found in the ruins of what was once a late antique Coptic monastery.

(c) *Other manuscript discoveries*

Since the end of the Renaissance there has been no great stream of discoveries of unknown texts except among the papyri. But for a long time research in manuscript collections was far from systematic, with the result that from time to time it was possible for a fortunate scholar to uncover an ancient text of more than trivial importance, and it is worth recording here the most notable examples.

In 1743 Prosper Petronius, working in the Vatican library, lit upon a unique codex of Theophrastus' *Characters*, which is still the only known witness to the text of nos. 29 and 30 (Vat. gr. 110), and thereby completed the text of this attractive and influential little book. The Homeric Hymn to Demeter came to light in 1777 when C. F. Matthaei unearthed a manuscript now in Leiden (B.P.G. 33H); originally it had been in the Moscow Imperial Archive, and Matthaei claimed that he had found it in a farmhouse where for years it had been lying among pigs and chickens; not everyone has believed him. Soon after this a much greater discovery was made in Venice. In 1788 Villoison published the marginal scholia to the *Iliad* found in the codex now known as Venetus A (Marc. gr. 454). They contained a vast fund of new information about the Alexandrian critics of Homer, and this information stimulated F. A. Wolf to write *Prolegomena ad Homerum*, one of the most important books in the whole history of classical scholarship (1795). While Robert Wood, in his *Essay on the original genius of Homer*, had already seen in 1767 that the usual picture of a literate Homer writing down his poems could not be a complete explanation of the present form of the Homeric poems, it was left to Wolf to demonstrate, with the help of the newly found scholia, that the textual problems in Homer were not of the same type as in other authors, and that an explanation for this state of affairs could be provided on the assumption that the text of Homer was not written down until the time of Solon or Pisistratus. Wolf's book marked the beginning of serious discussion of what is traditionally called the Homeric Question.

From the history of Greek scholarship in the nineteenth century it is worth mentioning the discovery of the verse fables by Babrius, found by Mynas Minoides in a manuscript on Mount Athos that is now in the British Library (Add. 22087). The same scholar recovered some previously unknown essays of Galen (MSS. Paris supp. gr. 634 and 635). Sometimes, however, hopes of discovery were deceived. In 1823 the famous Italian poet Giacomo Leopardi, who was also the best Italian classical scholar of his day, found in the Vatican what seemed to be a new piece of classical Attic prose. But the absence of a title in the manuscript and the lack of adequate works of reference conspired to delude his hopes; the text turned out to be a relatively common work of patristic literature written in the best imitation Attic, i.e. Atticist Greek; it was the address of Saint Basil to his nephews on the merits of reading classical literature.

In Latin there is less to record, since most of the great finds of modern times have been made in palimpsests as described above. A significant exception is Petronius' *Cena Trimalchionis*, which, although known for a fleeting moment in the Renaissance, was first printed at Padua in 1664. In 1899 an Oxford undergraduate examining an eleventh-century copy of Juvenal in Beneventan script (Canonici Class. Lat. 41) found that in satire VI it contained thirty-six additional verses, and though the text is extremely corrupt the balance of opinion now favours the view that they are genuine. And it may be just worth mentioning that an unknown letter of Saint Cyprian came to light not long ago in Holkham lat. 121, and though the letter itself is of no consequence its source at one remove may be a manuscript from Montecassino, a possibility which once again shows how important that one religious community was for the transmission of texts. Another recent find is the collection of Latin poems known as the Epigrammata Bobiensia, because the manuscript is a Renaissance apograph of a Bobbio codex (Vat. lat. 2836). Some of the authors represented are Augustan or of the first century, while nos. 2–9 are by Naucellius, a prominent literary figure of the end of the fourth century. Among still more recent finds are some lines of Rutilius Namatianus, recovered from a strip of parchment used for binding, also from Bobbio, and no less than twenty-nine unedited letters of Augustine that had lain unobserved in two manuscripts, one in Paris and one in Marseilles.

(d) *Epigraphic texts*

While books in their various forms have provided the main vehicle for the transmission of the vast legacy which the Greeks and Romans committed to writing, the large and increasing collections of inscriptions are themselves monuments to the enormous number of texts which have reached us inscribed on bronze, stone, and the like. The valuable contribution which epigraphy and numismatics can make to the illumination of ancient life was appreciated as early as the Renaissance and is in general beyond the scope of this book, but some of the texts which have been preserved by these means should be mentioned, for they are in some cases extensive, of major importance, or useful in that they augment or complement or correct the purely literary tradition.

An obvious example is the *Res gestae Divi Augusti*, a document of crucial importance for the study of Augustus and the early principate. This is the record of his achievements which Augustus left behind him with the express wish that it be engraved on bronze and placed in front of his Mausoleum. Both the original manuscript, which he deposited with the Vestal Virgins, and the original inscription have perished without trace, but copies were set up in the provinces, sometimes with a Greek paraphrase for the benefit of the local population, and the bulk of the text can be recovered from three fragments discovered in Galatia, the largest one, which has been known since 1555, on the walls of a temple in Ankara. Though it is a rather special and grandiose example, the *Res gestae* belong to the wider tradition of the *laudatio*, or obituary notice, and for obvious reasons this genre is particularly well represented by epigraphic texts, ranging from grandiloquent orations to humble and touching records of personal affection. A famous one is the so-called *Laudatio Turiae* (*ILS* 8393), the funeral oration for a Roman matron of the late first century B.C., a substantial piece of writing. But even stones, as the ancients never tire of telling us, have their own mortality, and much of this stout matron's virtuous career would have been lost to fame had not the pen finally come to the aid of the chisel; for of the six fragments that have turned up in various parts of Rome since the seventeenth century, three have disappeared and now survive only in manuscript copies, which we mainly owe to the Jesuit scholar Jacques Sirmond and to J. M. Suárez, the librarian of Cardinal Barberini (Paris lat. 9696, Vat. lat. 9140).

The bronze tablet at Lyons (*ILS* 212) which preserves the speech which the emperor Claudius made to the Senate in A.D. 48 advocating the admission of Gallic nobles is of literary as well as historical interest. For this text, discovered in 1528, gives us the unique opportunity of being able to compare Claudius' actual speech, rambling and pedantic, with the taut literary adaptation that Tacitus provides (*Ann.* 11.24). The monument of Antiochus I of Commagene, which was discovered towards the end of the last century on the lofty slopes of an extinct volcano at Nemrud Dagh in eastern Turkey, has won itself an important place in literary history. Its florid text, as elevated in style as in its place of rest, has filled a crucial gap in our knowledge by providing the only example of the ornate 'Asianic' style of oratory which featured so largely in the rhetorical polemic of Cicero's day.

We owe a remarkable philosophical text to the philanthropic urge of Diogenes of Oenoanda, who was so impressed with the efficacy of the Epicurean philosophy that about the year A.D. 200 he had his exposition of the doctrines of Epicurus set up in the market-place of Oenoanda, in Lycia, for the benefit of his fellow citizens. Fragments of this unique text, forty metres long, which number almost a hundred and are still being discovered, lie scattered among the ruins of Oenoanda and provide editors with a jig-saw puzzle of truly monumental proportions. A remarkable feature of the inscription is the way in which its disposition in columns and concern for the convenience of the reader reproduce on an enlarged scale the conventions of the contemporary book. The earliest known example of a Christian hymn in the metrical form characteristic of Byzantium comes from an equally unexpected source: it is an inscription from a catacomb at Kertsch in the Crimea which can be dated to the year 491. It is part of the service for baptism. A statue of Socrates in Naples has inscribed on it a sentence from Plato's *Crito* (46b4–6); there is a divergence from the text offered by the manuscripts and J. Burnet in the Oxford Classical Text accepted the reading on the stone.

More informal contributions to our store of ancient literature have been made by those who write on walls. These include a not inconsiderable body of original poetry, but often graffiti are only quotations from works which have already reached us via more orthodox channels. These are occasionally of interest to textual critics as evidence of indirect tradition. In this way a potsherd of the second century B.C. (Berlin ostrakon 4758) can find its way into the apparatus criticus of Euripides (*Hipp.* 616ff.) and the frequency with which *arma virumque cano* is scrawled on the walls of Pompeii helps to prove that this, and not *ille ego qui quondam*, is the true beginning of the *Aeneid*. A notable example is a distich of Propertius (3.16.13f.)

found on a basilica at Pompeii. While the oldest manuscripts are united in reading

> Quisquis amator erit, *Scythicis* licet *ambulat* oris,
> nemo *deo* ut *noceat* barbarus esse volet

the inscription (*CIL* iv. 1950) offers

> Quisquis amator erit, *Scythiae* licet *ambulet* oris,
> nemo *adeo* ut *feriat* barbarus esse volet

and is right in at least two of the four places in which it differs from the direct tradition.

VII. EPILOGUE

It is now time to draw together the threads of this rather selective account of the progress of scholarship between the end of the Renaissance and the beginning of what may be properly regarded as modern scholarship in the nineteenth century. Our purpose throughout this book has been to show how the existence of literary texts has been dependent both on material factors, such as the form of the book and the supply of writing materials, and on intellectual movements and changes in educational practice, and how the survival and quality of literary studies have been assisted by the gradual evolution of methods of scholarship. Once printing was established as the means of disseminating texts (and there was some resistance on the part of men such as Federigo duke of Urbino who declared that no printed book should ever form part of his library), one part of our story is at an end, since the survival of texts was assured. But it seemed worth while to pursue the history of scholarly method further, at least as far as the study of texts is concerned, and to highlight some of the developments which permitted a better and fuller use of the legacy of the past. The generally poor quality of the early printed editions shows how much remained still to be done for the theory of textual criticism, how the process of sifting manuscript resources had only just begun, how editing was hampered by a failure to appreciate the complexity of the study of classical civilization as a whole (*Alter-tumswissenschaft*).

Although material progress made the leading states of the period from the Renaissance to the Counter-Reformation much richer and therefore able in principle to devote greater resources to scholarship, there were still many obstacles to be overcome. In some countries limitations on intellectual freedom existed. Printing was not yet so cheap that a profit could be made by the publication of highly specialized works. Co-operation between scholars was often an honourable manifestation of an effort to create a 'republic of letters', an expression used in English by Addison (1672–1719) and found on the first page of the *Journal des Sçavans* for 1665–6. Yet the enormous correspondence conducted by a giant such as Erasmus needed further support if it was to be effective. Learned societies and universities should have provided it, but although they sometimes made creditable efforts, the net result was generally disappointing. Learned men of the Renaissance also formed academies. Of these numerous clubs the one which receives an honourable mention in our account is the group which worked with Aldus Manutius. Many others appear to have no claim on our attention, at any rate so far as this branch of scholarship is concerned. The universities also failed for a long time to co-ordinate their efforts and run their own publishing houses. And Oxford and Cambridge, which did have university presses active from the sixteenth century onwards, were institutions as much concerned with producing a supply of recruits for the ministry of the Church of England as with the advance of scholarship, a state of affairs not altered until reform began in the middle of the nineteenth century. It is a great pity that one of the most distinguished and productive academies, the Royal Society, was founded in London, where there was no university, and as late as 1660. By that time the concept of useful knowledge, which formed part of its full title, had been seriously affected by the scientific revolution and was about to be affected still further by the so-called dispute between the ancients and the moderns. The relative merits of ancient and modern achievements in the arts and sciences had already been an issue in the fifteenth century, and the advances of modern science were now

manifest. Even in medicine Galen's authority had begun to be
undermined by Berengario of Carpi and Vesalius. As a result the
early volumes of the Royal Society's *Philosophical Transactions* do not
contain any contribution that could be described as classical philology; later there are occasional exceptions to the rule, for instance a
note by the astronomer Halley on the point where Caesar landed in
Britain, and an essay by the librarian Humphrey Wanley entitled
'The age of MSS'. A pleasant contrast is offered by the wider range
of contents of the *Journal des Sçavans*; they had more interest in
literature and in 1666 found room for a review of the first edition of
the *Cena Trimalchionis* and of a dissertation which had been
stimulated by the new publication.

But as Dr Johnson said when considering how far the expecta-
tions expressed at the foundation of the Royal Society had been
realized, the course of progress is naturally slow. The application of
his remark to scholarship becomes apparent if we try to trace the
early history of one feature of the academic world which is now
taken for granted, editions of texts published in a uniform series.
Perhaps these go back to P. D. Huet (1630–1721), tutor to the
princes of the French royal house. Either he or the Duc de
Montausier is to be given credit for organizing the production of a
set of nearly sixty volumes of Latin authors *in usum Delphini*. A sign
of the times is that Leibniz, then living in Paris, was invited to contribute the edition of Vitruvius but asked to be excused because he
did not have the necessary knowledge of architecture and offered
instead to edit the obscure Martianus Capella. Perhaps it was this
series which inspired the most famous of all, begun by the firm of
B. G. Teubner in Leipzig in 1824 at the instigation of F. Passow.
Classical studies, in so far as they were concerned with literature
rather than archaeology, which gathered strength in the eighteenth
century, had had to recover from the blow they received from the
dispute between the ancients and the moderns. They had taken on
a new lease of life when in 1777 F. A. Wolf succeeded in his request
to be matriculated at Göttingen not in the faculty of theology but
as a *studiosus philologiae*.

The refinements of editorial technique which have until recently
been exclusively associated with the name of Lachmann made it

possible to envisage a new stage of scholarship in which classical texts would be reliably established as far as the extant evidence permitted. The invention of photography began towards the end of the nineteenth century to remove many obstacles from the realization of the new ideal. These advances occurred at just the right time to give an extra impetus to scholars concerned with the ideal implicit in the Teubner enterprise. No edition can now be taken seriously if it does not make clear the nature of the manuscript tradition and the criteria by which the witnesses are to be evaluated; and now scholars are almost always able to obey literally the advice of the Vice-Chancellor of Cambridge University who refused an application for a travel grant to visit Florence and said, 'Let Mr. Porson collect his manuscripts at home.' With the modern conveniences of microfilm and quick and comfortable travel, it is easy to forget the difficulties which our predecessors faced. The systematic description of manuscripts has also become a branch of scholarship, and the official catalogues of the leading libraries are a source of primary material for the modern scholar that his predecessors generally lacked. Another very important contribution to scholarship has been the decreasing mobility of the manuscript collections. Most manuscripts of Latin and Greek texts are now owned by institutions that may be confidently expected to retain them in perpetuity. But at least up to the end of the last century manuscripts were almost as likely to travel as they had been in the unsettled days of the Middle Ages and Renaissance. In our account we have occasionally alluded to these movements, and some others are explained in the notes to the index of manuscripts. They form a minor but not entirely insignificant facet of the history of culture and scholarship. The accumulation of the primary source material needed to provide the best attainable texts of the ancient authors is now well advanced and parallel to this process is the accumulation and evaluation of the objects, whether inscriptions, documentary papyri, or works of art, unearthed by the archaeologists and serving to throw light on the history, art, and material culture of the ancient world. The interaction between these various fields, the promotion of which was one of the great contributions of German scholarship in the nineteenth century, is the basis of the modern concept of the study of antiquity as a whole and promises a rich and continuing supply of themes as long as classical studies retain their place as an intellectual discipline.

6

TEXTUAL CRITICISM

I. INTRODUCTORY

The foregoing chapters have attempted to give some idea of the ways in which the Greek and Latin classics were handed down through the Middle Ages to the modern world, and to outline some of the more important historical and cultural phenomena which affected the transmission of these texts. The business of textual criticism is in a sense to reverse this process, to follow back the threads of transmission and try to restore the texts as closely as possible to the form which they originally had.

Since no autograph manuscripts of the classical authors survive, we are dependent for our knowledge of what they wrote on manuscripts (and sometimes printed editions) which lie at an unknown number of removes from the originals. These manuscripts vary in their trustworthiness as witnesses to the original texts; all of them have suffered to some degree in the process of transmission, whether from physical damage, from the fallibility of scribes, or from the effects of deliberate interpolation. Any attempt to restore the original text will obviously involve the use of a difficult and complex process, and this process falls into two stages.

The first stage is recension (*recensio*). The object of recension is to reconstruct from the evidence of the surviving manuscripts the earliest recoverable form of the text that lies behind them. Unless the manuscript tradition depends on a single witness, it is necessary (1) to establish the relationships of the surviving manuscripts to each other, (2) to eliminate from consideration those which are derived exclusively from other existing manuscripts and therefore have no independent value (*eliminatio codicum descriptorum*), and (3) to use the established relationship of those which remain (ideally expressed in the form of a *stemma codicum* or family tree) to reconstruct the lost manuscript or manuscripts from which the surviving witnesses descend. When the most primitive state of the text that is recoverable from the manuscripts has been reconstructed, the second main stage of the critical process begins. The transmitted text must be examined and the critic must decide whether it is authentic or not (*examinatio*); if not, his duty is to emend it (*emendatio*), if this can be done with a reasonable degree of certainty, or to isolate the corruption. The task is often complicated by the presence of two or more variant readings, each with a claim to be the transmitted text. The whole of this second stage is sometimes still given its traditional, though misleading, name—*emendatio*.

II. THE DEVELOPMENT OF THE THEORY OF TEXTUAL CRITICISM

The invention of the printed book, and in particular the appearance of the first printed editions of Cicero in 1465, meant that for the first time the future of classical texts was secure. But it had one unfortunate side-effect: the early printers, by the act of putting a text into print, tended to give that form of the text an authority and a permanence which in fact it rarely deserved. The *editio princeps* of a classical author was usually little more than a transcript of whatever humanist manuscript the printer chose to use as his copy, a replica in print of the current manuscript article. The repetition of this text, with only minor changes, from one edition to another soon led to the establishment of a vulgate text; and while there was nothing to prevent one from improving the vulgate by piecemeal emendation, the forces of inertia and conservatism made it difficult to discard it in favour of a radically new text.

Emendation continued to do its work, as it had done in every age; and although the critic's basic equipment—common sense and judgement and taste—were natural rather than acquired gifts, the development of some of the more useful principles of emendation and the rapid progress of classical scholarship in general enabled him to make a sharper attack on textual corruption. But emendation cannot be used to the greatest effect until recension has done its work, and scholars right up to the nineteenth century were in most cases obliged to exercise their critical gifts, which were often of the highest order, not upon the transmitted text as it is properly understood, but upon an entrenched vulgate. This they tried to emend, not only by conjecture, but also by the use of such manuscripts as they could find. There were some very remarkable discoveries, but more often the new manuscripts were no better than those on which the vulgate had originally been based. For in the days when libraries were largely uncatalogued, travel difficult, photography unknown, and palaeography in its infancy, this was a hit or miss process. Worse still, when good manuscripts were found, their usefulness was limited because their aid was sought only when the vulgate was manifestly unsatisfactory.

The first step towards more scientific textual criticism was the rejection of the vulgate text as the basis for discussion and with it the illogical conservatism which regarded the use of manuscripts as a departure from the tradition rather than a return to it. In this, as in other departments of criticism, the first impulse came from New Testament studies, where the problem was more obvious: the wealth of manuscript evidence left little scope for conjectural emendation and the task of choosing the truth from the variant readings was hampered by the almost divine sanction which was attributed to the *textus receptus*. In 1721 Richard Bentley, known to classical students more for the untrammelled boldness of his conjectures, projected an edition of the New Testament based exclusively on the ancient manuscripts and the Latin Vulgate. The conservative attitude of theologians prevented the project from being realized until Lachmann's edition of 1831, but the attack on the *textus receptus* was renewed a few years later by J. J. Wettstein, and in the course of a few decades the same radical approach had percolated to the field of classical philology, where Johann August Ernesti and Friedrich August Wolf restated in the firmest terms the need to make the manuscripts the basis of any critical text.

The relentless accumulation of manuscript evidence through the seventeenth and eighteenth centuries accentuated the need to work out a valid method of sorting the grain from the chaff. Many scholars contributed to the elaboration of the stemmatic theory of recension; this had been formulated in all its essentials by the middle of the nineteenth century and, although his own contribution is much slighter than had been supposed, it is still associated with the name of Karl Lachmann. For all its limitations, it revolutionized the editing of classical texts. There were glimmerings of the genealogical method as early as the humanist age. Politian, as we have seen, saw that manuscripts which derived from an older surviving exemplar were of no value, and effectively applied the principle of *eliminatio* to some of the manuscripts of Cicero's *Letters*. In 1508 Erasmus postulated a single archetype from which all the surviving manuscripts of a text descended; and although his notion of an archetype was less precisely defined than ours, he was able to explain how easy it is for all the manuscripts to be wrong. The notion of the medieval archetype seems to have been first entertained by Scaliger, who in 1577 tried to prove from the nature of the corruptions in the manuscripts of Catullus that they were derived from a common parent written in a pre-Caroline minuscule.

Scaliger was far ahead of his time. No great advance was made towards a theory of recension until the eighteenth century and then the impetus came, once again, from New Testament scholarship. In the thirties J. A. Bengel perceived that the manuscripts of the New Testament could be classified on a genealogical basis. More than that, he spoke of the day when they would be reduced to what he called a *tabula genealogica*, and saw clearly the potentialities of his *tabula* as an instrument for the critical evaluation of variants. His genealogical approach was adopted with varying success by classical scholars of the late eighteenth and early nineteenth centuries, and brought to fruition in a brilliant burst of scholarship in the 1830s. In 1830 Lachmann, preparing the way for his edition of the New Testament, gave a more detailed formulation of the rules which Bengel had expounded for the choice of variants; in 1831 Carl Zumpt, in his edition of the *Verrines*, drew what appears to have been the first *stemma codicum* of a classical text, and gave it the name which has won general acceptance; the great editions published by Ritschl and Madvig over the next few years refined and established the method. The most famous of all stemmata, that of Lucretius, was constructed by Jacob Bernays in 1847, and it remained for Lachmann, in his edition of 1850, to apply his rules for the mechanical application of the stemma and to give a classic demonstration of the validity of the hypothetical archetype by reconstructing its physical form and telling his astounded contemporaries how many pages it had, and how many lines to the page.

III. THE STEMMATIC THEORY OF RECENSION

The classic statement of the theory of stemmatics is that of Paul Maas. In practice the stemmatic theory has serious limitations, as Maas was well aware, since its successful operation depends on the tradition being 'closed'; these limitations are discussed below. The essentials of the theory are as follows:

(a) *The construction of a stemma.* Of fundamental importance in stemmatics are the errors which scribes make in copying manuscripts; for these errors provide the most valid means of working

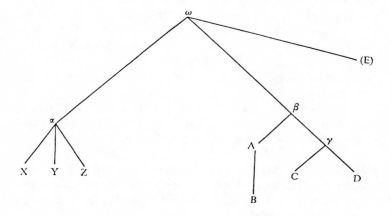

out the relationships of the manuscripts. Special attention is paid to errors of omission and transposition. For stemmatic purposes these errors can be divided into (*a*) those which show that two manuscripts are more closely related to each other than to a third manuscript (conjunctive errors), and (*b*) those which show that one

manuscript is independent of another because the second contains
an error or errors from which the first is free (separative errors).
Care is taken to see that these errors are 'significant', i.e. not such
mistakes as two scribes are likely to make independently, or such as
a scribe could easily remove by conjecture. On this basis the inter-
relationships of the various manuscripts and manuscript groups are
worked out step by step until, ideally, a stemma of the whole manuscript tradition has been reconstructed.

(*b*) *The application of the stemma.* The mechanical application of
the stemma to reconstruct the reading of the archetype is best illustrated by a hypothetical stemma, as shown above. ω represents the
archetype; the intermediate lost manuscripts from which the
survivors descend are indicated, as is customary, by Greek letters.
The extant manuscripts are eight in number (ABCDEXYZ); for the
sake of the illustration, it is assumed that E is a fragment available
only for a small part of the text.

1. If B is derived exclusively from A, it will differ from A only in
   being more corrupt. The first stage, therefore, is to eliminate B.
2. The text of γ can be inferred from the agreement of CD or from
   the agreement of one of them with an outside witness (A or α).
3. The text of β can be inferred from the agreement of ACD or of
   AC against D or of AD against C or from the agreement of either
   A or γ with α.
4. The text of α can be inferred from the agreement of XYZ or of
   any two of them against the third or from the agreement of one
   of them (provided the other two disagree with each other)
   with β.
5. When the texts of the two hyparchetypes (α and β) have been
   reconstructed, the readings peculiar to the individual witnesses
   ACDXYZ can be eliminated from consideration (*eliminatio
   lectionum singularium*).
6. If α and β agree, they may be assumed to give the text of the
   archetype (ω). If they disagree, either of the two readings may be
   the text of the archetype. It is the task of *examinatio* to decide
   which of these two variants is authentic.
7. If at some point in the text we have the evidence of a third in-

dependent branch of the tradition (E), then the principle of two against one will operate and the text of the archetype will only be in doubt if all three disagree or if two of them are likely to have fallen into the same error independently.

The application of these principles is sometimes a simple matter. The relationship of the manuscripts may be made clear by one or more glaring faults. Particularly striking examples are afforded when a book has suffered physical damage which is reflected in the copies made from it, whether directly or at more than one remove. The first scholar to use this form of argument was Politian, in his discussion of Cicero's letters, but the utility of the method remained unappreciated by other scholars for a very long time. In the tradition of Lucretius important inferences were made by Lachmann from physical damage that must have taken place in a lost book. It is evident that at one time there was a copy with twenty-six lines to the page. Some leaves of this fell out and were incorrectly replaced, thus causing serious dislocation of the text in some surviving copies. A more far-reaching conclusion can be drawn from the manuscripts of Arrian's work on Alexander's expedition to India. There are about forty of these, and all have a substantial gap in the text at one point. As a rule this lacuna occurs in the middle of a page and the scribes have copied the text without noticing its existence. But in one manuscript (Vienna, hist. gr. 4) it occurs between the end of one verso page and the beginning of the next recto page, and further investigation shows that there is one leaf missing at this point. All other manuscripts evidently descend from this book after it had suffered mutilation. In this case, therefore, the archetype is preserved. Another preserved archetype is the Oxford Epictetus (Auct. T. 4.13, Plate V); here a smudge of dirt has obscured a few words of text, which are missing from all other copies.

But such methods of inference cannot be applied in the majority of traditions. In general it may be possible to establish a few facts about the relation of the later manuscripts of an author from minor textual omissions, but for the main outline of the stemma it will be necessary to classify and arrange the manuscripts by reference to a series of significant errors.

IV. LIMITATIONS OF THE STEMMATIC METHOD

The apparent simplicity and finality of the stemmatic method as outlined above is deceptive. Though it often answers the editor's problem of selecting the right manuscript or manuscripts for his text, there are circumstances in which its utility is restricted. The theory assumes that readings and errors are transmitted 'vertically' from one manuscript to another, that is to say directly from one book to the copies that are made from it. But it has become increasingly evident as scholars have pursued more detailed inquiries that the tradition of many texts, including some of the highest interest and importance, cannot be elucidated by the application of the stemmatic theory. In these cases the manuscripts cannot be assigned to classes or families characterized by groups of errors because there has been contamination or 'horizontal' transmission. Readers in ancient and medieval times did not necessarily copy a text from a single exemplar; as their texts were often corrupt, they compared different copies, entering in their own manuscripts good readings or interesting variants as they found them. In some traditions—an example is Xenophon's *Cyropaedia*—the process was undertaken so often that the tradition has been hopelessly contaminated by the date of the earliest extant manuscripts. Scholarly activity naturally led to this result, and in many manuscripts the process can be observed, since variant readings are quoted in the margins or between the lines. It follows that the texts most commonly read, including those prescribed for the school syllabus, are most likely to show serious contamination. But the tradition of more recondite authors is not exempt from this feature, as the example of Diogenes Laertius shows.

A further difficulty in the theory lies in its assumption that all surviving manuscripts can be traced back to a single archetype, datable to the late ancient world or early Middle Ages. In practice thorough examination of manuscript variants has often suggested that this is not so, but that the tradition is 'open'. It may be possible to account for almost all the variants on the assumption of a stemma leading back to an archetype, but some readings refuse to fit the pattern, and if they are apparently ancient readings (a question of judgement arises here), another source has to be postulated for them. This source may be one or more manuscripts representing a different branch of tradition, which ceased to be copied as a whole but was consulted by scholars for some readings; these readings became variants within the main tradition, whether incorporated into its 'archetype' or at a later stage (see pp. 60–1). The plays of Aeschylus and Euripides which came to be prescribed for school reading probably went through this process.

Occasionally the facts are even more puzzling. In 1899 an Oxford manuscript of Juvenal (Canonici class. lat. 41) was found to contain thirty-six lines in satire VI that appear nowhere else, except that two of them are quoted by a scholiast. The passage has been regarded as spurious, but it is probable that interpolators would have lacked the powers or the motive to insert it; on the other hand if it is genuine, how are we to explain its survival in an otherwise mediocre copy and in only one of some five hundred manuscripts? A similar puzzle arises in the letters of Saint Cyprian. Recent work revealed the existence in a single copy (Holkham lat. 121) of a letter hitherto unknown and yet beyond all reasonable doubt genuine. Here too the tradition is copious and contaminated. No satisfactory explanation has yet been devised, but one feature is common to both cases: the Juvenal manuscript was written at Montecassino, while the Cyprian manuscript is very closely related textually to another book from the same monastery, which possessed so many unique texts.

One final complicating factor is the possibility that the ancient author himself made corrections or alterations to his original text after publication. Sometimes these would be extensive enough to justify us in speaking of a second edition. Under the conditions of the ancient publishing trade a second edition was much less likely to supplant its predecessor than in the modern world. Cicero's attempts to revise or eliminate errors in his works did not affect all the copies from which our archetypes descended (see p. 24). The two versions circulated side by side throughout antiquity with horizontal transmission taking place. Where a stemma cannot now be worked out this may be the reason. One or two examples can also be given in which authors' revisions are visible but have not affected the stemma so seriously. At Martial 10.48.23 it looks as if the name of a charioteer stood in the first edition of the book, but for the second edition, prepared after his death, the no longer topical name was replaced by a word indicating the team to which he belonged. A possible explanation of the incoherence of a scene in Aristophanes' *Frogs* (1437–53) is that some of the lines come from a revised version of the play. Similarly Galen (15.624) attributes the confused state of one of Hippocrates' works to marginal additions and revisions by the author.

V. AGE AND MERIT IN INDIVIDUAL MANUSCRIPTS

The notion of a best manuscript is sometimes found in discussions of textual problems, and there was a time when an appeal to the authority of the *codex optimus* was the normal or the most common way of discriminating between variant readings. But this procedure has rightly been criticized, since it was frequently used without regard to stemmatic method, and in any case it involves an error of logic. One cannot hope to identify the best manuscript of an author until one has considered the readings of all the significant manuscripts at all the points where they diverge; significant manuscripts are those extant or reconstructed books which the stemmatic method, in so far as it is applicable, proves to be of use for constituting the text.

When this has been done it is possible to draw up lists of passages in which the various manuscripts individually offer the reading which is best for literary, linguistic, historical or other reasons, and the manuscript which has the largest tally of such readings to its credit has a right to be termed the best manuscript. The utility of the term is often limited, particularly if there are one or more other manuscripts which have an almost equal number of good readings. In textual traditions where the term may reasonably be employed its use is confined to passages where there is a variety of readings among the manuscripts and there are no grounds for preferring one of these readings to another. Since the best manuscript is that which gives the greatest number of correct readings in passages where there are rational grounds for decision, it is more likely than the others to give the correct reading in passages where no such grounds exist. It is this argument from probability which justifies the appeal to the best manuscript in the circumstances indicated.

Here it is necessary to mention a variation of the faulty argument referred to above. This consists of an appeal to the authority of the oldest manuscript, usually implying that the antiquity of a manuscript guarantees its merit; conversely manuscripts of the Renaissance are dismissed as unimportant merely because of their date. There is of course no doubt that in general a certain relation exists between the age of a manuscript and the quality of the text that it offers, since it is a reasonable supposition that a late manuscript is separated from the original text by a larger number of intervening transcripts, each of which is to be presumed more corrupt than its predecessors. In many textual traditions investigation will show that the oldest manuscript is the best. But there are some exceptions which serve to show that the generalization must not be carelessly applied. A general argument may be drawn from the evidence of the papyri; though these are many centuries earlier than the medieval manuscripts, they do not as a whole offer markedly superior texts, and one of the most famous and important, containing Menander's *Dyscolus* (P. Bodmer 4), is astonishingly corrupt. Medieval manuscripts yield a number of instructive examples. Several manuscripts of Greek authors which date from the Palaeologan Renaissance (see p. 73) are of much the same value to editors as the more famous manuscripts of the same texts that are as much as three centuries earlier (e.g. Vienna supp. gr. 39 of Plato, Paris gr. 1734 of Thucydides, Laur. 32.16 and Wolfenbüttel Aug. 2996 of Apollonius Rhodius). A more extreme example is the sixteenth-century Vienna manuscript of the minor works of Xenophon (phil. gr. 37), which is clearly at least equal in importance to the other witnesses, being the unique source of many correct readings. The same phenomenon may be observed among Latin texts. Late manuscripts and indeed printed texts or collations made by modern scholars are often of great importance. A longish section of

Sallust's *Jugurtha* is missing in the earliest manuscripts, fragments of Gellius are only found in a few fifteenth-century witnesses, and for some of the letters of Cicero and Pliny we are wholly dependent on printed editions. There are also traditions in which the relationship between the older manuscripts and some of the more recent witnesses is complicated and obscure, as for example in the case of Juvenal, Persius, and Ovid, so that the truth may on occasion surface in comparatively late manuscripts. In the case of Seneca's *Tragedies* the family A was for a long time undervalued, partly because its representatives were of later date than the main witness of the E branch of the tradition, the codex Etruscus (Laur. 37.13). As a result of the discovery of these late witnesses that are of interest to the editor and textual critic a principle has been established, which is usually expressed by the formula *recentiores, non deteriores*.

These late manuscripts pose a problem for the editor: what is the source of their good readings? In some cases it is clear beyond any reasonable doubt that they represent a branch of the tradition that cannot otherwise be traced; the good readings are such that they could not possibly have been invented by a scholar of the Middle Ages or Renaissance. The copy of Xenophon mentioned above is a case in point: it supplies words missing from the text, in some places where the gap had not even been demonstrated beforehand. But often it is not so easy to come to a conclusion. Renaissance scholars were capable of acute conjectures, at least in Latin texts—two humanist manuscripts that long persuaded critics that they had some independent value are a copy of Lucretius in Florence (Laur. 35.31) and the Leiden Tacitus (B.P.L. 16 B)—and it is often impossible to say with any certainty whether or not a particular conjecture would have been within their powers. The same considerations apply to Byzantine scholars, but recent investigations have tended to suggest that their ability in conjectural restoration of a text was rather more limited than has sometimes been assumed in the past.

VI. INDIRECT TRADITION

Apart from ancient and medieval books (and occasionally translations into other languages) the editor and critic sometimes has
another source of help in the secondary or indirect tradition. This is
the term applied to quotations of one author by another, who may
on occasion preserve the correct reading when all the ordinary
manuscripts of the author quoted are in error. There are one or two
famous examples of this phenomenon. In Vergil's fourth *Eclogue*
(62–3) the manuscripts give

> cui non risere parentes,
> nec deus hunc mensa, dea nec dignata cubili est.

But Quintilian (9.3.8; though his MSS. too are corrupt) evidently
read *qui* at the beginning of the relative clause, which led to the
necessary conjecture:

> qui non risere parenti.

And it is not only ancient authors whose quotations hint at the right
text. Some good manuscripts that are now lost survived until late in
the Middle Ages and were consulted by scholars of that period. A
medieval source of secondary tradition which is often important is
the *Suda* lexicon. Two examples may be given of good readings that
it offers in quotations of Aristophanes: (*a*) *Knights* 254, where it has
ἔφευγεν, whereas the manuscripts have the unmetrical ἔφυγε. (*b*)
Clouds 215, where the manuscripts give πάνυ φροντίζετε, whereas
the Suda has μεταφροντίζετε, an amusing new coinage, probably
correct (the Ravenna scholiast also apparently had this reading).

It should not be supposed, however, that secondary tradition is
an unfailing source of correct readings. Ancient and medieval
writers were even less inclined than their modern counterparts to
follow the advice of Dr. Routh, president of Magdalen College,
Oxford, from 1791 to 1854, who when asked by Dean Burgon
whether after a long career he had any advice to offer young
scholars replied 'Always verify your references'. Quotations were
usually made from memory and there were good reasons for this

practice. Ancient books of the roll type did not facilitate quick reference, and when the codex form was adopted readers still could not count regularly on such aids as page numbering, chapter division, and line numbering, which are part of every modern text. These considerations must be borne in mind in cases where the manuscripts of an author offer one reading, and there is an acceptable but not absolutely certain alternative in the secondary tradition. Either reading may be what the author wrote. But in the majority of cases editors will probably be right to follow the primary tradition; the divergent reading of a quotation is likely to be right only if the purpose of the quotation was to emphasize or illustrate the divergent words or phrases, whereas if the divergence is incidental to the quotation it is probably due merely to lapse of memory.

The difficulty of enunciating firm principles may be shown by a few examples:

(*a*) Aristophanes, *Acharnians* 23: the MSS. have οὐδ' οἱ πρυτάνεις ἥκουϲιν, ἀλλ' ἀωρίαν | ἥκοντεϲ κτλ. The *Suda* lexicon quotes the line with the reading ἀωρίᾳ, in the article which is devoted to this word. In principle there is some reason to hope that this might be an accurate quotation, but the dative is less idiomatic than the accusative in this type of adverb and for that reason is rejected by the editors.

(*b*) In the same play at 391–2 the MSS. offer:

> εἶτ' ἐξάνοιγε μηχανὰϲ τὰϲ Ϲιϲύφου,
> ὡϲ ϲκῆψιν ἀγὼν οὗτοϲ οὐκ εἰϲδέξεται.

These lines are quoted in the *Suda* article on Sisyphus, but with two differences: in the first line εἶτα is replaced by ἀλλὰ, and in the second εἰϲδέξεται by προϲδέξεται. Since the quotation is not intended to illustrate either of these words, there is not much reason to trust in its accuracy. Yet on other grounds ἀλλὰ may well be right, and προϲδέξεται is as likely to be right as the rather puzzling εἰϲδέξεται.

(*c*) Lucretius 3.72 is given in the MSS. as:

> crudeles gaudent in tristi funere fratres.

Macrobius quotes the line in a passage where he is comparing Lucretius and Vergil (6.2.15), and gives the variant *fratris*. This is clearly superior, but the quotation was not made to illustrate any single word in the line.

(*d*) In the same book at 676 the MSS. have:

> non, ut opinor, id a leto iam longius errat.

The grammarian Charisius (p. 265, Barwick[2]) quotes the line with the variant *longiter*, and says that it was his purpose to exemplify the form by this quotation. For this reason editors usually, though not invariably, adopt the reading.

VII. SOME OTHER BASIC PRINCIPLES

The critic may find himself in a position where he has to choose between two readings that are equally acceptable in respect of the sense and the linguistic usage of his author, but feels that it is unsafe or impossible to argue from the merits of the manuscripts. In such situations there are two maxims that are frequently invoked, *utrum in alterum abiturum erat* and *difficilior lectio potior*. The first of these is a general principle, and the basis of it can be easily explained. Given the tendency of scribes to corrupt texts it is reasonable to suppose that careless copying or a desire to simplify a difficult passage encouraged certain types of alteration. The maxim *difficilior lectio potior* is strictly speaking no more than an application of this general principle. It embodies the notion that if one of the available readings is more difficult to understand, it is more likely to be the correct reading. The justification of this view is that scribes tended, sometimes consciously, sometimes inadvertently, to remove from the text the rare or archaic linguistic forms that were no longer readily understood, or to simplify a complex process of thought that they could not master. Alternative terms to describe these activities are interpolation and trivialization. Many references to the maxim *difficilior lectio* will be found in commentaries, and there is no doubt of its value. But it has probably been overworked, for there is a temptation to use it as a defence of anomalous syntax or usage; in

such cases the more difficult reading may be more difficult because
it is wrong.

VIII. CORRUPTIONS

In order to extract the truth from the manuscript evidence the
scholar needs to have some acquaintance with the various types of
corruption that occur. The primary cause of these was the inability
of scribes to make an accurate copy of the text that lay before them.
The majority of errors were involuntary, but at the end of this
section we refer to an important category of which this is not true.
Although it seems surprising at first sight that the concentration of
the scribes should have failed so often, anyone may soon verify for
himself by experiment how difficult it is to make an entirely accurate copy of even a short text. If due allowance is made for the length
of time during which copying by hand was the only means of transmission, it is perhaps remarkable that more ancient texts were not
reduced to an unintelligible condition. Many different pitfalls lay in
the path of the scribe if he once allowed his attention to wander.
Some of the possibilities are indicated in the list below. They are to
be regarded as a small selection divided into rough and ready
categories. It must be emphasized that scribal errors have never been
made the subject of a statistical study, and so it is not possible to
establish with any degree of precision the relative frequency of the
various types. Another important warning is that the assignment of
an error to a class is not always as easy as it might appear. Cases
arise in which it is possible to attribute a mistake to one of several
causes or to a combination of them. A third consideration to be
borne in mind is that not all causes of error were active at all times.
A case in point is that the use of some abbreviations which were
liable to cause difficulty to scribes can be set within chronological or
geographical limits.
    A. Mistakes induced by any feature of ancient or medieval
handwriting may be taken as a first class of error. It might be
supposed that this class is much more numerous than any other,
but the careful study of an apparatus criticus casts doubt on this

view. Typical causes of error within this class are (i) the lack of division between words in many manuscripts, (ii) a close similarity of certain letters in a script which results in their being confused, (iii) the misreading of an abbreviation; apart from ordinary signs representing syllables or common short words there was a special method of abbreviation for certain key terms of Christian theology; these are known as *nomina sacra*, and are frequent in both Greek and Latin texts. In both languages abbreviations are so numerous and complex that the study of them forms a subject in itself (Plate V). (iv) Since numerals were represented by letters in both languages they were often incorrectly transmitted, a fact which is a serious hindrance to students of economic and military history. Perhaps one may add here (v) the confusion of two words of similar shape or spelling even when there is no immediate cause of confusion in the forms of the individual letters.

(i) 1. Petronius, *Cena* 43.

    Quid habet quod queratur? *abbas secrevit.*

    ab asse crevit   Scheffer. (Cf. also G (i).)

  2. Aeschylus, *Eumenides* 224.

    δίκας δ' ἐπ' ἄλλας τῶνδ' ἐποπτεύcει θεά.

    δὲ Παλλὰς Sophianus.

(ii) The following letters are commonly confused in Latin scripts:

    In capitals: ILT EF PT PF PC BR HN OQ COG and such combinations as M NI.

    In uncials: ILT FPR CEOGU and such combinations as U CI. Characteristic of uncial, as opposed to capital, is the confusion of EU (now rounded in form) with the group COG.

    In minuscule: *au oe cld nu sf ct* and various letters or combinations of letters made of one or more downstrokes (minims), e.g. the letters in *minimum*. The confusion of *pr rn ns* is characteristic of insular script; in Visigothic the peculiar *t*, and in Beneventan both the *t* and the *a* cause difficulty (see Plate XIV).

  1. Seneca, *Epist.* 81.25.

    Manifestum etiam *contuenti* discrimen est.

    coniventi codd. recc.

2. Lucretius ii.497.

> quare non est ut credere possis
> esse infinitis distantia *femina* formis.

semina O^c

Groups of letters liable to be confused with each other in Greek script are:

In uncials: *ΑΔΛ ΕΘΟϹ ΙϹΚ ΓΤ.*

In minuscule: βκμ μν α ευ.

1. Aristotle, *Poetics* 1462 b 3.

> λέγω δ᾽ οἷον εἴ τις τὸν Οἰδίπουν θείη τὸν Ϲοφοκλέουϲ ἐν ἔπεϲιν ὅϲοιϲ
> ἢ ἰδίαϲ.

ἢ ἰδίαϲ MSS.: ἡ 'Ιλιάϲ a humanist corrector (confusion of *Δ* and *Λ*).

2. Julian, *Epist.* 23.

> δόϲ μοί τι κατὰ τοὺϲ μελικτὰϲ εἰπεῖν ῥήτοραϲ.

μελικτὰϲ Aldine edition: μελητὰϲ VL: μελίτουϲ N: βελτίϲτουϲ Jackson. β and μ are very similar in minuscule; here the corruption is aided by the uncial confusion of IC and K.

(iii) 1. Curtius Rufus, vi.11.30.

> Intellego non prodesse mihi quod praesentis sceleris *expressum.*

expers sum   codd. recc.

The symbols for *per pro prae* (usually ꝑ ꝓ p̄) are one example of the many *notae* which are open to misinterpretation.

2. Seneca, *Epist.* 76.7.

> Quare *autem* unum sit bonum quod honestum dicam.

autem] ħ V: hoc M: om. P: in b. The manuscript V has preserved the insular abbreviation for *autem* which has been the undoing of MPb.

3. Scholium on Aristophanes, *Knights* 505.

> τοῦτο πρῶτον τὸ δρᾶμα δι᾽ αὑτοῦ καθῆκε, τὰ δ᾽ ἄλλα δι᾽ ἑτέρων
> ἀπων.

ἀπων V: προϲώπων ΕΓΘΜ. In V's exemplar there were two compendia, α (= προ) and ~ (= ω).

4. Aeschylus, *Eumenides* 567–8.

> †ἥ τ᾽ οὖν διάτοροϲ† Τυρϲηνικὴ
> ϲάλπιγξ βροτείου πνεύματοϲ πληρουμένη.

οὖν may well conceal the *nomen sacrum* οὐρανόν (ο̄ῡνο̄ῡ), which has been further corrupted.

(iv) 1. Cicero, *Att.* i.13.6.

Messalla consul Autronianam domum emit HS CXXXIIII.

Other MSS. offer CXXXVII or CXXXIII or XXXIII. HS 13,400,000 is an astronomical price for a house. A plausible emendation is X̄X̄X̄ĪĪĪ = 3,300,000 (Constans), but certainty is in the circumstances unattainable.

2. Thucydides, iii.50.1.

τοὺς δ᾽ ἄλλους ἄνδρας οὓς ὁ Πάχης ἀπέπεμψεν ὡς αἰτιωτάτους ὄντας τῆς ἀποστάσεως Κλέωνος γνώμῃ διέφθειραν οἱ Ἀθηναῖοι (ἦσαν δὲ ὀλίγῳ πλείους χιλίων), καὶ Μυτιληναίων τείχη καθεῖλον καὶ ναῦς παρέλαβον.

χιλίων MSS.; but this number seems too large for the ringleaders of a revolt in Mytilene, and τριάκοντα has been suggested instead. χιλίων would be written ‚Α (in uncials), τριάκοντα Λ΄ (cf. A (ii) above).

(v) 1. Seneca, *Epist.* 102.22.

Tempus hic ubi inveni relinquam, ipse me diis reddam.

corpus   Pincianus.

2. Pindar, *Pythians* 4.90.

καὶ μὰν Τιτυὸν βέλος Ἀρτέμιδος θήρευσε κραιπνόν.

κραιπνόν correctly most MSS.: τερπνόν C.

B. Other corruptions arose out of changes in spelling and pronunciation. For instance in late Latin the sounds *ae* and *e* became identical, while *b* came to be sounded as a fricative and was confused with *v*. In Greek several vowels and diphthongs were reduced to the single sound of iota, as in the modern language. Error resulting from this change is known as iotacism. Beta became fricative as in modern Greek, and so did upsilon in diphthongs. The distinction between omicron and omega was lost. The diphthong alpha-iota became identical with epsilon. Orthographical errors are of extreme frequency, but the majority of them are of no consequence for the establishment of the text and are not recorded in the apparatus.

1. Quintilian 6.3.93 (quoting Domitius Afer).
   Pane et aqua *bibo.*
   vivo   Haupt. (Most MSS. inevitably have *panem et aquam bibo.*)
2. Diogenes Laertius, *Vita philosophorum* ix.10.
   (ἔφη) ἡμέραν τε καὶ νύκτα γίνεϲθαι καὶ μῆναϲ καὶ ὥραϲ αἰτίουϲ καὶ
   ἐνιαυτοὺϲ ὑετούϲ τε καὶ πνεύματα καὶ τὰ τούτοιϲ ὅμοια κατὰ τὰϲ δια-
   φόρουϲ ἀναθυμιάϲειϲ.
   αἰτίουϲ BP: ἐτείουϲ F.

C. Omissions constitute a third large class of error. Here again subdivision is possible. Sometimes we find (i) omission of not more than a few letters; if this occurs in a passage where the scribe has written a sequence of letters only once when they should be repeated, the term haplography is used. This mistake arises if the scribe is moving ahead too quickly with his task, and an extended form of the same mistake is sometimes referred to as (ii) *saut du même au même.* Here the scribe, finding the same word twice within a short space, copies the text as far as its first occurrence; then looking back at the exemplar to see what he must copy next he inadvertently fixes his eye on the second occurrence of the word and proceeds from that point. As a result the intervening words are omitted from his copy. Mistakes are also caused if two words in close proximity have the same beginning or ending; the technical terms for these are homoearcton and homoeoteleuton. The same fault of eyesight was responsible for similar errors which it is convenient to list as a slightly different category, (iii) the omission of a whole line of text. This error is often found in the manuscripts of the poets, and its informative value to scholars trying to establish a stemma is obvious. Examples can be found in prose texts also. It should be added, however, that a large number of omissions occur for no apparent reason except the carelessness of the scribe; this is particularly common with small words.

(i) I. Lucretius, iii.135.
   Quidquid ⟨id⟩ est, habeant; tu cetera percipe dicta.
   id   suppl. *l* 31.

2. Aristophanes, *Acharnians* 221–2.

μὴ γὰρ ἐγχάνοι ποτὲ

μηδέ περ γέροντας ὄντας ἐκφυγὼν Ἀχαρνέας.

ὄντας is omitted by most MSS., but is clearly necessary.

(ii) 1. Cicero, *Att.* vii.9.4.

Praeteriit tempus non legis *sed libidinis tuae, fac tamen legis*; ut succedatur decernitur; impedis et ais 'habe meam rationem'.
sed . . . legis C: om. Ω.

2. Aristophanes, *Acharnians* 692–5.

ταῦτα πῶς εἰκότα, γέροντ᾿ ἀπο(λέ-
cαι πολιὸν ἄνδρα περὶ κλεψύδραν,
πολλὰ δὴ ξυμπονήcαντα καὶ θερμὸν ἀπο-)
μορξάμενον ἀνδρικὸν ἱδρῶτα δὴ καὶ πολύν.

The MS. A omitted the section enclosed in parentheses.

(iii) 1. Seneca, *de ira* 3.7.1.

tenerique iam visa cum ipso cadunt ita fit ut frequenter inrita sit eius voluntas

These words form one line of the Ambrosianus: they are omitted by a number of the later manuscripts, which in this way reveal their derivation from A.

2. The omission of Sophocles *Antigone* 1167 in all the manuscripts has been mentioned already in connection with Eustathius and the importance of the secondary tradition. A stemma of the Sophocles manuscripts is facilitated by the omission of *Oedipus Tyrannus* 800 from the famous Medicean MS. (Laur. 32.9) and its twin brother, the Leiden palimpsest (Leiden, B.P.G. 60 A).

D. A fourth group may be termed errors of addition. The simplest of these are no more than the repetition of a few letters or syllables, which is referred to as (i) dittography. More substantial is the addition to the text of explanatory or illustrative material. The most frequent type in this category is (ii) the addition of a gloss. Most Greek manuscripts have a number of brief interlinear notes explaining rare or difficult words. These glosses were easily added to the text in the course of transcription. In poetry a simple addition of this kind may be immediately obvious because of the violence it does to the metre; but sometimes the word used as a gloss had the same metrical value as the word in the text and replaced it without impairing the metre, and examples of this process are not easy to detect. The detection of (iii) glosses in a prose text is often of the greatest difficulty. Many passages contain explanatory phrases which are not strictly required for the sense but offer no offence to grammar or syntax. These phrases present problems which may remain insoluble. Two texts which scholars have recently discussed in detail in the light of these questions are Petronius' *Satyricon* and Cicero's *Tusculan Disputations*. (iv) A rare but interesting corruption is the addition to a text of a parallel passage originally written in the margin of a book by a learned reader. This may happen in verse or prose. Cases are known from Greek tragedy, and Galen (17(1).634) noticed that it had happened in one of the Hippocratic treatises.

(i) 1. Seneca, *Epist.* 78.14.

Quod acerbum fuit ferre, *retulisse* iucundum est.

tulisse Bartsch.

2. Song quoted by Athenaeus 694d.

γελάceιαc, ὦ Πάν, ἐπ' ἐμαῖc
εὐφροcύναιc ταῖcδ' ἀοιδαῖc, ἀοιδέ, κεχαρημένοc.

εὐφροcύναιc A: εὔφροcι Wilamowitz
ἀοιδαῖc ἀοιδέ A: ἀοιδαῖc Hermann

(ii) 1. Aeschylus, *Agamemnon* 549.

καὶ πῶc; ἀπόντων τυράννων ἔτρειc τινάc;

So F: Triclinius restored the metre by substituting κοιράνων for τυράννων.

2. Plautus, *Truculentus* 278.

Cumque ea noctem in stramentis pernoctare perpetim [totam].

The Ambrosian palimpsest gives both the gloss (*totam*) and the word which has been glossed (*perpetim*); the Palatine family give the correct text.

(iii) 1. Seneca, *Epist.* 42.4.

Eadem velle [subaudi si] cognosces: da posse quantum volunt.

The words *subaudi si* ('understand *si*'), corrupted to *subaudis* and worse in the MSS., were put in the margin to help the reader with the paratactic conditional sentence and then incorporated into the text.

2. Diogenes Laertius, *Vitae philosophorum* v.76.

λέγεται δ' ἀποβαλόντα αὐτὸν τὰς ὄψεις ἐν Ἀλεξανδρείᾳ
κομίσαςθαι αὖθις παρὰ τοῦ Cαράπιδος.

ἀποβαλόντα BP: τυφλωθέντα F, which is a gloss.

(iv) 1. In the margin of the Medicean Aeschylus at *Persae* 253 the line Sophocles *Antigone* 277 has been written. In copies of M this line has been incorporated into the Aeschylean text.

2. Vergil, *Aen.* ii.76.

ille haec deposita tandem formidine fatur.

Sinon is about to explain himself. This line is omitted in P and added at the foot of the page in M by a later hand. It is a doublet of iii.612, where it is in place, and has been added here because of the similarity between this passage and that in book iii.

E. Errors of transposition are another well-known class. (i) Transposition of letters is common. (ii) In poetry verses are often copied in the wrong order. (iii) In all kinds of text word order is subject to fluctuation. The number of variants of this kind is large enough to suggest that inferences about the word order of Latin and Greek prose should be made with great care.

In Greek texts of both verse and prose there were special causes leading to corruption of word order during the Middle Ages. (iv) One of these affected the text of tragedy. A common metre in Byzantium was a twelve-syllable line rather like the classical iambic line but subject to different rules, the most important being that the penultimate syllable must carry an accent (at this date a stress accent). As a result some scribes altered, probably unconsciously, lines of tragedy in order to make them conform to this rule. The process is known as *vitium Byzantinum*. (v) In Byzantine prose there was a rule affecting the order of words; in general it was necessary that the last two stressed syllables of a sentence should be separated by two or four unstressed syllables (in special cases by none or six). The effect of this is sometimes visible in manuscripts of classical prose writers.

(i) 1. Lucretius, iii.170.

   Si minus offendit vitam vis horrida *leti*
   ossibus ac nervis disclusis intus adacta . . .
   teli Marullus.

2. Aeschylus, *Agamemnon* 1205.

   βαρύνεται γὰρ πᾶς τις εὖ πράccων πλέον.

   So Triclinius' autograph; but F has the correct reading ἀβρύνεται.

(ii) This extremely frequent error may be found exemplified in the text of
   any author.

(iii) 1. Seneca, *Epist.* 117.24.

   Deos vitam et salutem roga.

   So Bθ. Other manuscripts read *vitam roga et salutem* or *salutem et vitam
   roga*. Manuscript authority and rhythm (double cretic) decide.

2. Pindar, *Nemeans* 7.37.

   ἵκοντο δ᾽ εἰc Ἐφύραν πλαγχθέντεc.

   So the MSS.; Boeckh restored metrical responsion by reading πλαγχθέντεc δ᾽ εἰc Ἐφύραν ἵκοντο.

(iv) Aeschylus, *Agamemnon* 1106.

   ἐκεῖνα δ᾽ ἔγνων. πᾶcα γὰρ πόλιc βοᾷ.

   So M, correctly, but F and Triclinius have βοᾷ πόλιc.

(v) Plutarch, *de curiositate* 13 (522).

   ὁμοίωc οὐδ᾽ Ἀλέξανδροc εἰc ὄψιν ἦλθε τῆc Δαρείου γυναικὸc
   ἐκπρεπεcτάτηc εἶναι λεγομένηc.

   So most MSS.: the Λ-family alter to give a Byzantine clausula: τῇ
   Δαρείου γυναικὶ εὐπρεπεcτάτῃ λεγομένῃ τυγχάνειν.

F. In a sixth group one may include errors induced by the
context. (i) The inflection of a word may be wrongly assimilated to
that of an adjacent word. (ii) The scribes allowed themselves to be
influenced by words or phrases that they had recently copied or
were just about to copy.

(i) 1. Catullus, xxxiv. 17.

   tu cursu dea *menstrua*/metiens iter annuum
   rustica agricolae bonis/tecta frugibus exples.
   menstruo   B. Guarinus.

2. Euripides, *Helen* 1243.

κενοῖϲι θάπτειν ἐν πέπλοιϲ ὑφάϲμαϲιν.

πέπλοιϲ L: πέπλων Scaliger.

(ii) 1. Seneca, *Epist.* 114.9.

Ubi luxuriam late felicitas fudit, *luxus* primum corporum esse diligentior incipit.

cultus   Muretus.

2. Euripides, *Rhesus* 776–7.

ἤπυϲα δ᾽ αὐτοῖϲ μὴ πελάζεϲθαι ϲτρατῷ,
κλῶπαϲ δοκήϲαϲ ϲυμμάχων πλάθειν τινάϲ.

At 776 V has πλάθειν for πελάζεϲθαι by anticipation.

G. Some mistakes betray the influence of Christian thought. As all readers in the Middle Ages were more or less devout Christians it would be very surprising if they had succeeded in copying thousands of manuscripts without committing mistakes of this kind.

1. Petronius, *Cena* 58.

Sathana tibi irata sit curabo.

Sathana H: Athana   Heinsius. (Cf. also D (i). As the previous sentence ends with *habeas*, this could be a case of dittography.)

2. Aristophanes, *Knights* 1302–4.

οὐδὲ πυνθάνεϲθε ταῦτ᾽, ὦ παρθένοι, τὰν τῇ πόλει;
φαϲὶν αἰτεῖϲθαί τιν᾽ ἡμῶν ἑκατὸν εἰϲ Καρχηδόνα,
ἄνδρα μοχθηρὸν πολίτην, ὀξίνην Ὑπέρβολον.

Καρχηδόνα RVΦ: Χαλκηδόνα Γ² and a scholiast.

Carthage is more likely to be right than Chalcedon, a city of little importance in the Athenian empire but well known to every orthodox Greek in the Middle Ages because of the famous church council held there in A.D. 451.

H. There is a class of mistakes that derives from the deliberate activity of the scribe. As has been seen above, ancient and medieval readers tried to emend passages that they found difficult or corrupt, and their attempts were sometimes misguided or ill informed. A typical example is that Triclinius mutilated some Euripidean lyrics because he knew that metrical responsion ought to be restored, but was not well enough acquainted with the language of classical poetry to make the correct emendations. Such faulty corrections are often referred to as interpolations, though the term is not quite apt. Deliberate alteration on a larger scale can be seen in attempts to bowdlerize. This process was not as widespread, however, as might be expected. It seems that schoolmasters of late antiquity and the Middle Ages were not as anxious to suppress obscene or otherwise embarrassing passages as more recent editors have been. The excisions found in some modern school editions of Aristophanes do not seem to be anticipated in medieval manuscripts. But there are manuscripts of Herodotus which omit the account of sacred prostitution at 1.199, and there is a family of Martial manuscripts in which some of the blatant obscenities have been replaced by less offensive words. Another type of interpolation, for which scribes were not responsible, is that made by the actors in the texts of Greek tragedy (see p. 15).

1. Juvenal, viii.148.
    Ipse rotam adstringit sufflamine mulio consul.

In some manuscripts this has been, not unnaturally, corrupted to *sufflamine multo*. At this point deliberate interpolation steps in and restores the metre: other manuscripts read *multo sufflamine*.

2. Tacitus, *Annals* 13.39.1.
    Et Corbulo, ne irritum bellum traheretur utque Armenios ad sua defendenda cogeret, exscindere parat castella.

So M. In the Leiden Tacitus interpolation has run riot, producing specious nonsense:

    Et Corbulone irritum bellum trahente ut Armenios ad sua defendenda cogeret exinde repetit castella.

3. Euripides, *Electra* 435-7.
    ἵν' ὁ φιλάδελφος ἔπαλλε δελ-
    φὶς πρῴραις κυανεμβόλοι-
    ϲιν εἱλιϲϲόμενος.

So the first hand in L; Triclinius used his knowledge of strophic responsion and the quotation of this passage at Aristophanes *Frogs* 1314ff. to make one good alteration (φίλαυλος), but then committed a bad error (κυανεμβόλοις εἰειλισσόμενος).

4. Plutarch, *de curiositate* 7 (518).

φέρε γὰρ Ἡρόφιλον ἢ Ἐρασίστρατον ἢ τὸν Ἀσκληπιὸν αὐτόν, ὅτ᾽ ἦν ἄνθρωπος, ἔχοντα τὰ φάρμακα καὶ τὰ ὄργανα, κατ᾽ οἰκίαν παριστάμενον ἀνακρίνειν, μή τις ἔχει σύριγγα περὶ δακτύλιον ἢ γυνὴ κάρκινον ἐν ὑστέρᾳ.

The Λ-family here alter δακτύλιον to δάκτυλον and delete ἐν ὑστέρᾳ.

The diversity of the causes of error brings with it a consequence of great importance to the critic. He cannot approach his task in the belief that any one class of error is predominant. In practice many scholars appear to have assumed that errors arising from palaeographical causes are the commonest; certainly this is the conclusion to be drawn from the numerous and often elaborate palaeographical justifications that accompany proposed emendations. The only safe method is to follow the rule explicitly enunciated by Haupt, and reiterated by Housman: 'the prime requisite of a good emendation is that it should start from the thought; it is only afterwards that other considerations, such as those of metre, or possibilities, such as the interchange of letters, are taken into account. ... If the sense requires it I am prepared to write *Constantinopolitanus* where the MSS. have the monosyllabic interjection *o*.' In order to drive home their lesson Haupt and Housman quoted an extreme example. In fact when a critic has decided on grounds of sense how a corrupt passage might be restored, he considers various possibilities in the light of the types of error listed above, and is influenced by them in his choice between different restorations of the text. When really serious corruption has taken place it may well be necessary to print between obeli (††) the text of the archetype and indicate in the apparatus the best conjectures; in such passages certainty is unattainable even with the critic's sharpest weapons.

IX. FLUID FORMS OF TRANSMISSION: TECHNICAL AND POPULAR LITERATURE

Since we have been concerned mainly with the transmission of literature, the texts on which we have concentrated are for the most part works of art, and these may legitimately be expected to retain the form the writer put upon them. In this case the proper object of transmission is to reproduce the text as accurately as possible, and on the whole the fidelity with which the classics are transmitted is remarkable. Even texts of a more technical nature may be safeguarded by the prestige attached to ancient authors. But some types of writing lend themselves to more fluid forms of transmission; the text evolves with time to suit changed needs or circumstances. Among these are handbooks of various sorts, texts in which the literary intention is subsidiary or negligible and the primary aim is to provide the reader with a body of useful, practical information, whether it be legal material, a body of grammar, or technical instruction in one of the applied sciences. Planudes' treatment of some passages in Aratus' *Phaenomena* is a case in point. Less striking, but perhaps more typical, is the example of the manual by Menander Rhetor of c. A.D. 300: at least two manuscripts exhibit substantial variants of a type which are much more likely to be late alterations than the author's second thoughts. The late medical text by Aetius of Amida furnishes another example. Such books fail in their purpose if the information they contain is out of date, if it is insufficient—or conversely too elaborate—for the needs of the reader. The emphasis may need to be changed to meet a new demand; even the style may be too rough or indeed too sophisticated for a new age. Commentaries and scholia are particularly susceptible to such a process. The later Byzantine scholars such as Demetrius Triclinius demonstrate this clearly: he reduced the bulk and complexity of existing scholia to suit the needs and abilities of his students. Sometimes the epitomes and the expanded or variant versions which such conditions generate replace the original text; sometimes they survive alongside it, and may combine with it or other versions to produce still more forms. Translation is primarily designed to make a work available to those who cannot read the original; but if the translation is freely executed and the opportunity is taken to correct, bring up to date, or otherwise modify the original, then a new version comes into being.

This process can easily be exemplified from antiquity itself. When Faventinus made his epitome of Vitruvius in the late third or early fourth century, he redesigned it as a short manual on private architecture; it is intelligently organized, he made useful additions, and the ancient agriculturist Palladius used it in preference to the larger work. M. Gavius Apicius was a gastronome of the age of Tiberius, but the cookery book that bears his name, compiled in the late fourth or early fifth century, reveals strands and layers which have been selected and combined from various sources, medical and agricultural as well as purely gastronomic, and successively added, as time went on, to what remains of the original Apician recipes. The *Excerpta* of the Ostrogoth Vinidarius, made a little later, is a highly abbreviated version of a similar compilation. These works were subsequently transmitted, except for the inevitable excerpting, essentially in the forms in which they existed in antiquity. But other texts went on mutating. The various treatises on surveying which make up the *Corpus Agrimensorum* descend from a collection made in the fifth century, but most of the manuscripts preserve, not the original collection, but a variety of later compilations in which the material has been reorganized and condensed or augmented to suit the needs of the time or its potential users. The *De compendiosa doctrina* of Nonius Marcellus circulated in three versions in the Carolingian period; in one of these it has clearly been adapted to form a Latin dictionary for monastic use. Vibius Sequester's treatise *De fluminibus* has the literary polish of a telephone directory, and it was valued for what it was, a simple list of rivers and other geographical features: a twelfth-century reader in the Loire valley, mortified no doubt to discover that his own great river was among its more obvious omissions, saw to it that those who came after him should have a more complete list than the author had provided. The process by which the remains of Verrius Flaccus' *De verborum significatu* have come down to us has already been mentioned (p. 22). The freedom with which Paul the Deacon treated the already epitomized version made by Festus when he produced his own epitome as a gift for Charlemagne's library is candidly described in the dedicatory letter:

> Cupiens aliquid vestris bibliothecis addere, quia ex proprio perparum valeo, necessario ex alieno mutuavi. Sextus denique Pompeius Romanis studiis affatim eruditus ... opus suum ad viginti usque prolixa volumina extendit. Ex qua ego prolixitate superflua quaeque et minus necessaria praetergrediens et quaedam abstrusa penitus stilo proprio enucleans, nonnulla ita ut erant posita relinquens, hoc vestrae celsitudini legendum conpendium obtuli. (K. Neff, *Die Gedichte des Paulus Diaconus*, Munich 1908, p. 124.)

Although history has its Muse to protect it, it remains a practical source of information and may on occasion be condensed or expanded. Few would have the nerve to continue the work of a historian of Tacitus' stature and individuality, but Eutropius' *Breviarium* did not command the same respect: Paul the Deacon expanded it by adding material from other writers and indeed six books of his own composition, thus bringing down to the time of Justinian a history which had originally stopped in the late fourth century; about the year 1000 Landolfo Sagax treated Paul the Deacon's *Historia Romana*, as it was called, in a similar fashion by adding more books and carrying the tale down to the ninth century.

When we move into the world of folklore and romance, the controlled transmission which normally operates in the case of ancient texts gives way to a profusion of protean forms. The works of antiquity are not immune, and a classic example of one which generated a whole industry of popular literature is the Alexander romance of pseudo-Callisthenes, written sometime after A.D. 200. This survives in numerous forms, in Greek and Latin and a host of other languages, in versions of antique and medieval date, prose and verse. The main Greek tradition runs to five recensions, the last four derived in various ways from the first, and the medieval Latin translation, the *Historia de preliis Alexandri Magni* of Leo Archipresbyter, itself gave birth to three derivative versions.

Such transmissions pose problems for an editor. He has to work out the interrelationship of the various recensions as well as that of the manuscripts which transmit any one of them. The text of one version, perhaps descended from an earlier or better source, may allow the editor to correct that of another, but it is not always easy to decide whether a version is wrong or simply different. And which does he choose to edit? In some cases he will print the original or dominant version, and then add additional or divergent passages at the foot of the page. If typography and format permit, he may produce a synoptic edition in which the different recensions are printed alongside each other in parallel columns. Or it may be advisable to edit each version separately. The choice will depend on the merits and conditions of each particular text.

X. CONVENTIONS IN THE APPARATUS CRITICUS

Having followed our account of the material and cultural facts which lead to the existence of an apparatus criticus the reader may still feel not entirely at ease when confronted by the apparatus for the first time. This feeling is all the more justified if he or she is reading a text which has a complicated transmission, as is generally true of the authors included in the school curriculum of the Middle Ages.

It is necessary to familiarize oneself with certain conventions, in particular the use of Latin technical terms which tend to be abbreviated, e.g. coni(ecit), suppl(evit), secl(usit), del(evit). While cod./ codd., ms./mss., om., add., and P. or Pap. for papyrus are not likely to puzzle, it may not be obvious to beginners that gl. is used in relation to interlinear glosses (which often displace the genuine reading from the text); that sch. refers to scholia (which may preserve or hint at a better reading); that lm. indicates the lemma, that is to say the word or words quoted from the text; and whereas edd. refers to editors, ed. pr. is a common way of referring to the first printed edition (editio princeps). Another useful abbreviation is cett. (ceteri codices). The symbol ς (stigma) is often used to indicate one or more of the later manuscripts, also cited as 'recc.', when these are deemed to be less important than the earlier tradition or dependent on it. In dealing with quotations from ancient or medieval dictionaries such as the *Suda* or Hesychius it is common to use s.v. (sub voce) to indicate the entry in question.

Not all readings can be reported in a straightforward fashion. It may be necessary to say that a word is written above the line; hence the use of s.l. (supra lineam). Manuscripts were often corrected, and M^{ac}, M^{pc} (ante correctionem, post correctionem) indicate this fact; it is desirable that the editor should say somewhere, if he can, who the corrector was. M^1 may be used instead of M^{ac}, and M^2 is the usual way of indicating the reading of a second hand; again it is useful to know whether the hand is that of a contemporary of the main scribe, and it may require great palaeographical skill to form an opinion. There is also the question of variant readings. When these are given in the scholia, v.l. (varia lectio) is a common formula. But many variants are given in the manuscripts, in Greek usually with the letters γρ or the unabbreviated γράφεται, in Latin with ℓ (*vel*) or *al* (*alias*).

It is important to understand that brackets of the form ⟨ ⟩ enclose something which the manuscripts omit and has therefore had to be supplied by scholars. By contrast the square brackets [ ] mark portions of text transmitted in all or at least the great majority of the witnesses but which are deemed by the editor to be spurious later additions. Unfortunately it has to be stated here that the conventions used for the editing of papyri are more complex and not entirely consistent with what has just been explained; for details consult the explanatory note in any recent volume of the Oxyrhynchus Papyri.

If the apparatus criticus is set out fully, a word or words of the text will be repeated as the beginning of each entry. Sometimes an editor saves space by not doing this; instead he lists only the deviant readings which he is rejecting. This abbreviated procedure can at times lead to obscurity. Important manuscripts are referred to by sigla, usually a capital letter; but lower-case letters and Greek letters have to be used sometimes when there are very large numbers of witnesses to be cited. It is a great help when editors can use special sigla to indicate groups or families of manuscripts; a Greek letter or bold type is an efficient way of doing this.

In many editions the apparatus is difficult for the average reader to use because it contains far more detail than is necessary. Editors who are not very familiar with the behaviour of ancient and medieval scribes often report many trivial mistakes of spelling. These are not valuable unless one is making a survey of scribal habits, which is an important but highly specialized branch of study, not part of the brief of the average editor. Sometimes, however, an editor may feel justified in adopting a compromise position: he will perhaps come to the conclusion that if there is one manuscript of much greater importance than any other single witness to the text, even the minor errors of this manuscript should be recorded. A case in point would be L (Laur. 32.9) of Sophocles, Aeschylus, and Apollonius Rhodius.

XI. CONCLUSION

In this account of the function and methodology of textual criticism we have described some of the principles and criteria which have been most commonly and most usefully employed by those who attempt to reverse the process of transmission and restore the words of the ancients as closely as possible to their original form. In order to reduce to the length of a chapter a subject which normally fills a book and even then is no more than a guide, we have confined our account to basic and well-tried techniques. This will inevitably give the impression that textual criticism is a tidier and more cut-and-dried process than it proves to be in practice. While general principles are undoubtedly of great use, specific problems have an unfortunate habit of being *sui generis*, and similarly it is rare to find two manuscript traditions which respond to exactly the same treatment.

One omission is obvious. While giving space to the limitations of the stemmatic theory, we have not explored the complicated and sometimes controversial methods which have been devised to deal with contaminated traditions. The more open a tradition is, the less fruitful the stemmatic approach is likely to be, and other methods must be tried. These range from empirical, common-sense approaches which accept the necessities of an imperfect world, to elaborate statistical techniques which aim at more objective results. In some cases it is possible to adopt a flexible modification of the genealogical method. The manuscripts are classified as far as is possible into broad groups and the editor chooses his readings eclectically, persuaded more by their intrinsic merit than by considerations of affiliation and authority and taking care to balance these factors to suit the nature of the tradition. But if contamination has gone so far that, in the words of Housman, 'the true line of division is between the variants themselves, not between the manuscripts which offer them,' various approaches may be adopted which all tend to concentrate on the variants themselves rather than on the manuscripts which carry them. These may involve sophisticated mathematical techniques, which are particularly tempting at the present time, now that the development of computers and allied mechanical and electronic devices have made them more feasible. We have given no account of distributional and statistical methods, which would be a study in itself, nor of their automatization, which is generating a large body of literature, not all of which is readily intelligible to students of the humanities. It is not yet clear whether these elaborate techniques, however valid as a theoretical study, will yield practical results which justify the labour and expense entailed or are markedly superior to those produced by traditional means and 'nature's own computer, located between the ears of the investigator'. In any case their future seems to lie more in the biblical and patristic fields and with vernacular languages than with classical texts, where the material is more easily controlled and not usually unmanageable by traditional methods accompanied by the limited use of scientific aids. Ultimately, the basic essential equipment is taste, judgement, common sense, and the capacity to distinguish what is right from what is wrong in a given context; and these remain the perquisite of human wit. But where the tradition is large and complex, computers can be usefully employed in building up a provisional picture of the interrelationship of texts. Outside the field of recension computers have been used in stylistic studies and for the making of concordances, and they are particularly valuable for information retrieval. The *Thesaurus Linguae Graecae*, an electronic repository of Greek literature from Homer to the sixth century A.D., contains approximately 8,000 works and 61 million words and is being extended to cover the period down to A.D. 1453. A more modest, pilot disk is already in use for Latin literature. The enormous potential that such instruments have for various forms of research is obvious, and they are already bearing fruit in the field of textual criticism.

ABBREVIATIONS

AJA	*American Journal of Archaeology*
AJP	*American Journal of Philology*
BEC	*Bibliothèque de l'École des Chartes*
BICS	*Bulletin of the Institute of Classical Studies of the University of London*
BZ	*Byzantinische Zeitschrift*
C&M	*Classica et Mediaevalia*
CLA	*Codices Latini Antiquiores*
CPh	*Classical Philology*
CQ	*Classical Quarterly*
CR	*Classical Review*
CSEL	*Corpus scriptorum ecclesiasticorum latinorum*
GIF	*Giornale italiano di filologia*
GRBS	*Greek, Roman, and Byzantine Studies*
HSCP	*Harvard Studies in Classical Philology*
IMU	*Italia medioevale e umanistica*
JHS	*Journal of Hellenic Studies*
JöBG	*Jahrbuch der österreichischen Byzantinischen Gesellschaft*
JRS	*Journal of Roman Studies*
JTS	*Journal of Theological Studies*
JWI	*Journal of the Warburg and Courtauld Institutes*
MGH	*Monumenta Germaniae Historica*
MH	*Museum Helveticum*
Mnem.	*Mnemosyne*
MS	*Mediaeval Studies*
NGG	*Nachrichten von der Gesellschaft der Wissenschaften zu Göttingen*
PBA	*Proceedings of the British Academy*
PCPhS	*Proceedings of the Cambridge Philological Society*
PG	*Patrologia Graeca*
PL	*Patrologia Latina*
RE	*Paulys Real-Encyclopädie der classischen Altertumswissenschaft*
REA	*Revue des études anciennes*
REG	*Revue des études grecques*
RhM	*Rheinisches Museum für Philologie*
RHT	*Revue d'histoire des textes*
Settimane	*Settimane di studio del Centro italiano di studi sull' Alto Medioevo*
SIFC	*Studi italiani di filologia classica*

TAPA	*Transactions of the American Philological Association*
VCh	*Vigiliae Christianae*
YCS	*Yale Classical Studies*
ZPE	*Zeitschrift für Papyrologie und Epigraphik*

NOTES

I. *Ancient books*

The growth of the book trade in classical Athens is described by E. G. Turner, *Athenian books in the fifth and fourth centuries B.C.*, London 1977[2]. The exact period at which it becomes legitimate to speak of a trade is uncertain, but it is worth emphasizing that Xenophon, *Anabasis* 7.5.14, speaks of books (βίβλοι γεγραμμέναι) as forming part of the cargo of ships wrecked off Salmydessos on the north coast of Thrace; the inference seems inescapable that books were an article exported (from Athens?) to the cities of the Euxine coast as early as the year 399 B.C. If this is so, our inability to extract more precise information from the passages of Eupolis and Plato cited in the text is of little importance.

On the form and appearance of books in Greece from the classical period until the end of the Roman Empire the reader should consult E. G. Turner, *Greek papyri*, Oxford 1980[2], and his companion volume, *Greek manuscripts of the ancient world*, London 1987[2], which offers a well-chosen album of plates with commentary.

The supply of papyrus was precarious in the classical period, if we can trust the evidence of the letter from Speusippus to Philip of Macedon (p. 50 in L. Köhler's ed., *Philologus Supplement-Band* 20, Leipzig 1928); the text indicates a shortage of papyrus c. 342 B.C. owing to the Persian occupation of Egypt. But though this letter is now regarded as genuine by many authorities, its status is not entirely above suspicion. The standard account of the production and use of papyrus is given by N. Lewis, *Papyrus in classical antiquity*, Oxford 1974. T. C. Skeat, in *Scritti in onore di Orsolina Montevecchi*, Bologna 1981, pp. 373–6, has suggested that the tension in papyrus would simplify the task of re-rolling a book. For fresh thoughts about the technique of manufacture as described by Pliny see I. H. M. Hendriks, *ZPE* 37 (1980), 121–36.

It is possible to calculate the length of some *volumina* from Herculaneum (see G. Cavallo, *Libri scritture scribi a Ercolano*, Naples 1983, pp. 14–16, 47). P. Herc. 1497 was about 10½ metres long, P. Herc. 1423 about 10 metres, P. Herc. 1471 about 11½ metres. Among other papyri it has been argued that P. Petrie 1 5–8 of Plato's *Phaedo* and P. Oxy. 225 of Thucydides II would each have measured some 15 metres if the text was complete in one roll (which is not certain). It has been suggested that P. Oxy. 3672 of Plato, *Laws* vi will have been about 12 metres long.

The use and gradual refinement of punctuation are still debated; apart from Turner's book cited above see R. Pfeiffer, *History of classical scholarship*, Oxford 1968, pp. 178–81; another useful survey is given by M. Geymonat in the *Enciclopedia Virgiliana*, s.v. interpunzione, vol. 2 pp. 998–1000. H.-I. Marrou, *Histoire de l'éducation dans l'antiquité*, Paris 1965⁶, p. 602 n. 30, suggested that books with full punctuation never passed into general use but were confined to teachers and pupils (his remark applies particularly to books in the Roman period). An interesting example of a conjecture that finds part of its justification in the absence of punctuation from ancient texts is given by H. Lloyd-Jones, *The justice of Zeus*, Berkeley 1983², p. 213 n. 23. Horace, *Epistles* 1.15 presents a problem: the syntax is so complicated that the modern reader is bound to ask how his ancient counterpart could find his way through the text.

II. *The library of the Museum and Hellenistic scholarship*

The standard work on Alexandrian scholarship is R. Pfeiffer, *History of classical scholarship: from the beginnings to the end of the Hellenistic age*, Oxford 1968, reviewed by N. G. Wilson, *CR* 19 (1969), 366–72. This is the first volume of a work intended to replace J. E. Sandys, *History of classical scholarship*, vols. 1–3, Cambridge 1903–8 (some volumes subsequently revised), reprinted 1958, which is still valuable as a reference book. On the Museum and library see P. M. Fraser, *Ptolemaic Alexandria*, Oxford 1972, chapter 6.

The monograph of Lloyd W. Daly, *Contributions to a history of alphabetization in antiquity and the Middle Ages*, Brussels 1967 (=Collection Latomus, vol. 90), is of interest; since it is there shown that Zenodotus and Callimachus used the principle of alphabetical order in some of their writings, one may conjecture that the same principle was employed to some extent in the arrangement of the library in the Museum.

The so-called 'wild' papyri of Homer were re-edited by S. R. West, *The Ptolemaic papyri of Homer*, Cologne 1967.

G. P. Goold, *TAPA* 91 (1960), 272–91, expressed extreme scepticism about the idea that copies of Homer in the old Athenian alphabet found their way into the Alexandrian library; but his conclusion if right does not necessarily apply to all other authors.

Accentuation is discussed by C. M. Mazzucchi, *Aegyptus* 59 (1979), 145–67.

The general rule that commentary was written in a separate book has been upset by the discovery of P. Lille 76d of Callimachus, probably of the third century B.C., in which text and notes alternate in the column (see plate 75a in Turner, *Greek manuscripts*).

The primary sources about the use of the critical signs are corrupt and confused, but the facts were reasonably well sorted out by A. Gudeman in *RE*, s.v. Kritische Zeichen. See also R. L. Fowler, *ZPE* 33 (1979), 17–28, esp. 24 f.

The statistics of Aristarchan emendations generally adopted in the text of Homer come from T. W. Allen's edition of the *Iliad*, Oxford 1931, vol. 1, pp. 199–200; on pp. 201–2 similar calculations are given for readings ascribed to Zenodotus and Aristophanes. Subsequent publications will not have altered the figures substantially.

On Aristarchus' principle of interpreting Homer from Homer see N. G. Wilson, *CR* 21 (1971), 172; A. G. Lee, *PCPhS* 201 (1975), 63–4; N. G. Wilson, ibid., 202 (1976), 123.

The Lille Stesichorus is shown on plate 74 of Turner, *Greek manuscripts*.

The actors' interpolations are discussed by D. L. Page, *Actors' interpolations in Greek tragedy*, Oxford 1934; on the passage mentioned in the text see A. M. Dale, *Wiener Studien*, 69 (1956), 103–4 (= *Collected papers*, Cambridge 1969, pp. 126–7), M. D. Reeve, *GRBS* 13 (1972), 263–4, and the editions of C. W. Willink, Oxford 1986, and M. L. West, Warminster 1987. The scale of the problem becomes clear from E. Fraenkel's study of Euripides' *Phoenissae* in the *Sitzungsberichte* of the Bavarian Academy for 1963, pp. 1–120.

III. *Other Hellenistic work*

For the archaeological discoveries at Pergamon see E. Akurgal, *Ancient civilisations and ruins of Turkey*, Istanbul 1978[4], pp. 69–111.

There is controversy about the authenticity of Dionysius Thrax (see H. Erbse, *Glotta* 58 (1980), 244–58) and even the interpretation of his phrase κρίϲιϲ ποιημάτων has been questioned (see N. G. Wilson, *Studi classici e orientali* 33 (1983), 107–8).

Didymus' commentary on Demosthenes was edited by H. Diels and W. Schubart, Berlin 1904; for the exact definition of the type of literature to which it belongs see F. Leo's review in *NGG* (1904), 254–61 (= *Kleine Schriften*, vol. 2, pp. 387–94), but note also the reservations of S. West, *CQ* N.S. 20 (1970), 288–96.

On the Epicureans see E. Puglia, *Demetrio Lacone: Aporie testuali ed esegetiche in Epicuro*, Naples 1988, esp. pp. 82–4.

IV. *Books and scholarship in the Roman Republic*

The Latin book does not receive very much specific treatment in the standard works on books in the ancient world, since it is similar in all its essentials to its Greek counterpart and the bulk of our evidence comes from Egypt, where there was comparatively little interest in Latin. But we now have E. J. Kenney's chapter on 'Books and Readers in the Roman World' in *The Cambridge history of classical literature*, vol. 2, *Latin literature*, ed. E. J. Kenney and W. V. Clausen, Cambridge 1982, pp. 3–32; and Egypt has compensated for its comparatively small contribution to our knowledge of Roman books by producing one of the most dramatic finds of recent years. This is the discovery of fragments of Gallus' poetry in a Roman outpost at Qaṣr Ibrîm, part of a book which must have belonged to a Roman officer serving in the very province that Gallus had ruled and which may have been written in the author's own lifetime. This affords us a wonderful glimpse of the lay-out of a Latin book in the classical period. Of particular note is the spacing, the indentation of the pentameters, and the systematic use of interpunction to mark word-division, a convenience which had been abandoned by the end of the first century A.D. On the Gallus fragments see R. D. Anderson, P. J. Parsons, R. G. M. Nisbet, 'Elegiacs by Gallus from Qaṣr Ibrîm', *JRS* 69 (1979), 125–55 and plates IV–VI. It is hardly surprising that some have thought this remarkable book too good to be true. F. Brunhölzl has declared it to be a fake: 'Der sogennante Gallus-papyrus von Kasr Ibrîm', *Codices Manuscripti*, 10 (1984), 43–50; there is a reply by F. Blänsdorf, 'Der Gallus-papyrus: — eine Fälschung?', *ZPE* 67 (1987), 43–50.

More information about writing habits in the early second century A.D., particularly useful in that it relates to the opposite corner of the Empire, has come from the Roman fort of Vindolanda (Chesterholm), where hundreds of fragmentary tablets have been unearthed. The majority of these are not the usual waxed tablets, incised with a stylus, but thin slivers of alder or birch written with pen and ink and specially prepared for this purpose. The use of such wooden leaves, which could be folded and fastened together to make notebooks, was more widespread than had been thought, particularly in parts of the empire far removed from the source of papyrus. They were mainly used for letters and accounts. For further information, see A. K. Bowman and J. D. Thomas, *Vindolanda: The Latin writing tablets* (Britannia Monograph Series, 4), London 1983.

These discoveries, and the Gallus fragment in particular, provide new evidence for interpunction and hence the readability of books in the classical period. On interpunction, see Parsons, op. cit., 131. The view that Latin books, down to the end of the first century A.D., were provided with more in the way of punctuation and aids to the reader than was generally customary in antiquity was propounded by R. P. Oliver, *TAPA* 82 (1951), 241–2, and further developed by E. O. Wingo, *Latin punctuation in the classical age*, The Hague 1972. A more sceptical view is taken by G. B. Townend, who discusses the difficulties of punctuating Latin texts, with particular reference to hexameter poetry and Vergil: *CQ* 19 (1969), 330–44, *Proceedings of the Virgil Society*, 9 (1969–70), 76–86. See too W. Müller, *Rhetorische und syntaktische Interpunktion* (Diss. Tübingen 1964), and the literature cited in section I above. Other aspects of Roman books and their production are discussed below.

There is no full and comprehensive account of scholarship during the Roman period. The primary material can be found in G. Funaioli, *Grammaticae Romanae fragmenta*, vol. 1, Leipzig 1907, and its continuation, A. Mazzarino, *Grammaticae Romanae fragmenta aetatis Caesareae*, vol. 1, Turin 1955. Brief accounts are given by A. Gudeman, *Grundriss der Geschichte der klassischen Philologie*, Leipzig 1909² (reprinted Darmstadt 1967); F. Leo, *Geschichte der römischen Literatur*, vol. 1, Berlin 1913, pp. 355–68; G. Funaioli, *Studi di letteratura antica*, vol. 1, Bologna 1946, 206ff. Much can also be derived from Leo's *Plautinische Forschungen*, Berlin 1912², and G. Pasquali's *Storia della tradizione e critica del testo*, Florence 1952². The aspects of scholarship in the Roman period that most concern us here have been examined by J. E. G. Zetzel in *Latin textual criticism in antiquity*, New York 1981, which deals with a number of topics treated in this and the following sections; for important additions and qualifications, see the reviews by H. D. Jocelyn, *Gnomon*, 55 (1983), 307–11, and M. D. Reeve, *CPh* 80 (1985), 85–92.

The history of the text of Plautus in antiquity throws some much needed light on the beginnings of Roman scholarship, murky though that story sometimes is: cf. W. M. Lindsay, *The ancient editions of Plautus*, Oxford 1904; F. Leo, *Plautinische Forschungen*, pp. 1–62, Pasquali, *Storia della tradizione*, pp. 331–54. The history of the text of Terence in antiquity has been the subject of recent studies, where reference to earlier work may be found: J. N. Grant, *Studies in the textual tradition of Terence* (Phoenix, Suppl. Vol. 20), Toronto 1986, pp. 1–96; H. D. Jocelyn, 'Two questionable areas of the directly transmitted text of Terence's *Adelphoe* (vv. 115–19; 584–6)', in S. Prete (ed.), *Protrepticon. Studi classici ed umanistici in onore di G. Tarugi*, Milan 1989, pp. 45–54. On the composite nature of the prologue to the *Poenulus*, see Jocelyn, '*Imperator histricus*', *YCS* 21 (1969), 97–123; for the date of the alternative ending to the *Andria* of Terence, O. Skutsch, 'Der zweite Schluss der *Andria*', *RhM* 100 (1957), 53–68. There is a good account of the history of the text of the dramatic poets in ancient times, with particular reference to Ennius, in Jocelyn, *The tragedies of Ennius*, Cambridge 1967, pp. 47–57. Recent critics have attributed the disorder of the *De agri cultura* to Cato himself: for a résumé of the question, see A. E. Astin, *Cato the censor*, Oxford 1978, pp. 191–203.

On the *Anecdoton* and the critical activity of Aelius Stilo and his circle, see S. F. Bonner, 'Anecdoton Parisinum', *Hermes*, 88 (1960), 354–60. The *Anecdoton* and the whole subject of critical *notae* and their use have been re-examined in a series of articles by H. D. Jocelyn, 'The annotations of M. Valerius Probus', *CQ* 34 (1984), 464–72, 35 (1985), 149–61, 466–74. The composite nature of the material in the *Anecdoton* rules out derivation from a single source, such as Suetonius' *De notis*.

Attention focuses on Atticus because of the wealth of information in Cicero's letters, in contrast to our ignorance of the book trade at Rome before his time. His precise role has been discussed by R. Sommer, *Hermes*, 61 (1926), 389–422; see further R. Feger, *RE*, Suppl. 8 (1956), 517–20, K. Büchner in *Geschichte der Textüberlieferung der antiken und mittelalterlichen Literatur*, vol. 1, Zürich 1961, 328. The evidence is conveniently presented (and interpreted with predictable bias) by J. Carcopino, *Les Secrets de la correspondence de Cicéron*, vol. 2, Paris 1947, pp. 305–29.

A very lucid account of the process of 'publication' in Roman times is given by Raymond J. Starr, 'The circulation of literary texts in the Roman World', *CQ* 37 (1987), 213–23. See also B. A. van Groningen, *ΕΚΔΟΣΙΣ*, *Mnem.* Ser. 4, 16 (1963), 1–17; Kenney, op. cit., 19.

V. *Developments under the early Empire*

For a general account of the book trade in Rome see T. Kleberg, *Buchhandel und Verlagswesen in der Antike*, Darmstadt 1967, pp. 22–68. M. H. L. M. van der Valk, 'On the edition of books in antiquity', *Vigiliae Christianae*, 11 (1957), 1–10, emphasizes the part *bibliopolae* played in the publication of books, particularly in the time of Martial.

The relationship between libraries and literature is discussed by A. J. Marshall, 'Library resources and creative writing at Rome', *Phoenix*, 30 (1976), 252–64.

On education at Rome in the Republic and early Empire see S. F. Bonner, *Education in ancient Rome*, London 1977.

The history and the quality of the scholarly work on Virgil has been re-examined by S. Timpanaro, *Per la storia della filologia virgiliana antica*, Rome 1986 (reviewed by N. Horsfall, *CR* 37 (1987), 177–80; H. D. Jocelyn,

Gnomon, 60 (1988), 199–202). On Hyginus he takes issue with the negative view expressed by e.g. G. P. Goold, *HSCP* 74 (1970), 161–2, Zetzel, ibid. 77 (1973), 237–8. On the transmission of Vergil, see too E. Courtney, 'The formation of the text of Vergil', *BICS* 28 (1981), 13–29; Zetzel, *Latin textual criticism*, pp. 246–8.

The nature and importance of Probus' work on ancient texts has been subjected to renewed scrutiny: see the important articles by Jocelyn in *CQ* (1984–5) cited above; Timpanaro, *Per la storia*, pp. 77–127; M. L. Delvigo, *Testo virgiliano e tradizione indiretta. Le varianti probiane* (Biblioteca di Materiali e discussioni per l'analisi dei testi classici, 5), Pisa 1987. His alleged influence on the text of Horace has been examined by C. O. Brink, *Horace on poetry: the 'Ars Poetica'*, Cambridge, 1971, pp. 35–8. These provide a full bibliography of earlier literature, where more negative assessments of Probus' philological activity will be found. The codex Palatinus of Virgil shows traces of Probus' influence.

VI. *Archaism in the second century*

On the second-hand book trade, see T. Kleberg, 'Antiquarischer Buchhandel im alten Rom', *Annales Acad. Reg. Scient. Upsaliensis*, 8 (1964), 21–32. The fictional nature of much of what Gellius relates, first exposed by L. A. Holford-Strevens, casts suspicion on the remarkable volumes he mentions: Zetzel, 'Emendavi ad Tironem: some notes on scholarship in the second century A.D.', *HSCP* 77 (1973), 225–43; Holford-Strevens, 'Fact and Fiction in Aulus Gellius', *Liverpool Classical Monthly*, 7.5 (1982), 65–8; *Aulus Gellius*, London 1988, pp. 139–41.

The subscriptions of Statilius Maximus in *De lege agraria* have given rise to considerable discussion: Zetzel, 'Statilius Maximus and Ciceronian studies in the Antonine Age', *BICS* 21 (1974), 107–23; O. Pecere, 'La subscriptio di Statilio Massimo e la tradizione delle Agrarie di Cicerone', *IMU* 25 (1982), 73–123; D. E. Martin, 'The Statilius subscriptions and the editions of late antiquity', in D. F. Bright and E. S. Ramage (edd.), *Classical texts and their traditions: studies in honor of C. R. Trahman*, Chico 1984, pp. 147–54; Timpanaro, *Per la storia*, pp. 200–9.

VII. *The compendium and the commentary*

There is still much to be written on the scholiasts and grammarians of late antiquity: we have no major study, for instance, of Priscian. Their social status and educational rôle is examined by R. A. Kaster, *Guardians of language: The grammarian and society in late antiquity*, Berkeley and Los Angeles 1987. On aspects of their philological work, we have Zetzel, *Latin textual criticism*, and Timpanaro, *Per la storia*. For a general study of Donatus, L. Holtz, *Donat et la tradition de l'enseignement grammatical. Étude sur l'Ars Donati et sa diffusion (IVᵉ-IXᵉ siècles) et édition critique*, Paris 1981. There is an excellent brief account of the commentators on Horace in R. G. M. Nisbet and M. Hubbard, *A Commentary on Horace: Odes, Book I*, Oxford 1970, pp. xlvii–li.

VIII. *From roll to codex*

C. H. Roberts' classic article on the codex has now appeared in a revised form: C. H. Roberts and T. C. Skeat, *The Birth of the Codex*, Oxford 1983; there is an important review by M. McCormick in *Scriptorium*, 39 (1985), 150–8. For other recent studies of the codex see Roberts, *Manuscript, society and belief in early Christian Egypt*, Oxford 1979; E. G. Turner, *The typology of the early codex*, Philadelphia 1977; B. Bischoff, *Paläographie des römischen Altertums und des abendländischen Mittelalters*, Berlin 1979, pp. 34–8. Rough calculations of the relative cost of roll and codex have been made by Skeat in 'The length of the standard papyrus roll and the cost-advantage of the codex', *ZPE* 45 (1982), 169–75.

For other aspects of the production and circulation of books in late antiquity, see E. Arns, *La Technique du livre d'après Saint-Jérôme*, Paris 1953; G. Cavallo, 'Libro e pubblico alla fine del mondo antico', in G. Cavallo (ed.), *Libri, editori e pubblico nel mondo antico: Guida storica e critica* (Universale Laterza, 315), Bari 1975, pp. 83–132, 149–62; 'La circolazione libraria nell'età di Giustiniano', in G. G. Archi (ed.), *L'imperatore Giustiniano: storia e mito, Giornate di studio a Ravenna, 14–16 ottobre 1976*, Milan 1978, pp. 201–36. Jerome reveals a remarkable awareness of the causes of textual corruption and the problems involved in establishing a correct text: cf. K. K. Hulley, 'Principles of textual criticism known to St. Jerome', *HSCP* 55 (1944), 87–109.

Our brief account of ancient scripts is necessarily over-simplified; for a recent and authoritative treatment, see Bischoff, op. cit., 71–106. It is also confined to the bookhands of antiquity. Evidence that literary texts may in some cases have been transmitted in old Roman cursive has been collected by Bischoff, op. cit., 81 nn. 68, 70, Pecere, *La tradizione* (see below), p. 240, n. 309: to the literature they cite may be added J. G. Griffith, *MH* 25 (1968), 105, Grant, *Studies in the textual tradition of Terence*, pp. 13–15.

IX. *Paganism and Christianity in the fourth century*

Our perception of the conflict between paganism and Christianity in the fourth century has changed considerably in recent years, as the following studies, all relevant to the aspects that most concern us, will illustrate: A. Momigliano, *The conflict between paganism and Christianity in the fourth century*, Oxford 1963, and in particular the contribution by H. Bloch, pp. 193–218; R. A. Markus, 'Paganism, Christianity and the Latin classics in the fourth century', in J. W. Binns (ed.), *Latin literature of the fourth century*, London 1974, pp. 1–21; A. Cameron, 'Paganism and literature in late fourth century Rome', in *Christianisme et formes littéraires* (Entretiens sur l'Antiquité Classique, 23), Geneva 1977, pp. 1–40. Alan Cameron's redating of Macrobius' *Saturnalia* (*JRS* 56 (1966), 25–38) has been generally accepted: for a contrary view, S. Döpp, 'Zur Datierung von Macrobius' *Saturnalia*', *Hermes*, 106 (1978), 619–32. On the Christianization of the senatorial class, see P. Brown, 'Aspects of the Christianization of the Roman aristocracy', *JRS* 51 (1961), 1–11 (reprinted, with additions, in *Religion and society in the age of Saint Augustine*, London 1972, pp. 161–82).

For a more general treatment of the confrontation of the two cultures, see E. K. Rand, *Founders of the Middle Ages*, Cambridge 1929[2]; M. L. W. Laistner, *Christianity and pagan culture in the later Roman empire*, Ithaca, N.Y., 1951 (Cornell Paperbacks, 1967); *Thought and letters in Western Europe, A.D. 500–900*, London 1957[2], pp. 25–53; also H. Fuch's article 'Bildung', in *Reallexikon für Antike und Christentum*, vol. 2 (1954), cols. 350–62. A real assessment of the attitudes and practice of the two most influential figures of the fourth century, Jerome and Augustine, has been made possible by the detailed studies of H. Hagendahl, *Latin fathers and the classics* (Studia Graeca et Latina Gothoburgensia, 6), Göteborg 1958, supplemented by 'Jerome and the Latin Classics', *VCh* 28 (1974), 216–17; *Augustine and the Latin classics* (Studia Graeca et Latina Gothoburgensia, 20), Göteborg 1967. On the last, see J. J. O'Donnell, 'Augustine's Classical Readings', *Recherches Augustiniennes*, 15 (1980), 144–75.

On the question of style and taste, see C. E. Chaffin in *The classical world* (Literature and Western Civilization, ed. D. Daiches and A. Thorlby), London 1972, pp. 461–86.

X. *The subscriptions*

The fundamental work on the subscriptions is still that of Otto Jahn, 'Über die Subscriptionen in den Handschriften römischer Classiker', *Berichte über die Verhandlungen der Sächsischen Gesellschaft der Wissenschaften*, Phil.-hist. Classe 3 (1851), 327–72. J. E. G. Zetzel has provided a useful list of the subscriptions in manuscripts of secular authors in *Latin textual criticism*, pp. 209–31. To the literature on subscriptions already cited in VI above should be added Zetzel, 'The subscriptions in the manuscripts of Livy and Fronto and the meaning of *emendatio*', *CPh* 75 (1980), 38–59; O. Pecere, 'Esemplari con *subscriptiones* e tradizione dei testi latini, l'Apuleio Laur. 68, 2' in C. Questa and R. Raffaelli (edd.), *Il libro e il testo*, Urbino 1984, pp. 111–37; 'La tradizione dei testi latini tra IV e V secolo attraverso i libri sottoscritti', in A. Giardina (ed.), *Tradizione dei classici, trasformazioni della cultura* (Società Romana e Impero Tardoantico, 4), Rome–Bari 1986, pp. 19–81, 210–46. The last contains ample bibliography of the whole subject.

For the imperial fora as intellectual centres, see H.-I. Marrou, *Mélanges d'archéologie et d'histoire de l'École française de Rome*, 49 (1932), 94–110, reprinted and enlarged in *Patristique et humanisme: Mélanges*, Paris 1976, pp. 65–80.

CHAPTER 2

I. *Scholarship and literature under the Roman Empire*

In general see Sandys, *History of classical scholarship*. The ancient grammarians' contributions to syntax are noted by J. Wackernagel, *Vorlesungen über Syntax*, Basle 1950². On Atticism the basic reference book is still W. Schmid, *Der Attizismus in seinen Hauptvertretern*, Stuttgart 1887–96; but a convenient introduction is given by B. P. Reardon, *Courants littéraires grecs des II* et III* siècles après J.-C.*, Paris 1971, pp. 81–91; his book is a valuable survey of the literature of the period. The intellectual life of Oxyrhynchus is attractively described in E. G. Turner's articles in *Journal of Egyptian Archaeology* 38 (1952), pp. 78–93, and *Mitteilungen der Papyrussammlung Erzherzog Rainer* 5 (1956), 141–6.

As a footnote to the picture of scholarship in the second century one may add that in the reign of Hadrian a grammarian called Nicanor wrote a study of the punctuation of the *Iliad*, many fragments of which are preserved in the scholia of MS. Marc. gr. 454. His system was sophisticated and no doubt partly for that reason there is no sign that it ever came to be more widely adopted. In some ways the best scholar of the century was the doctor Galen, on whom it is still worth reading the account given by W. G. Rutherford,

A chapter in the history of annotation, London 1905, pp. 47–57; see also the note *infra* on Erasmus.

II. *The Christian Church and classical studies*

On the Christians and education see H.-I. Marrou, *Histoire de l'éducation*, pp. 451–71. The early Christian apologists are well presented by H. Chadwick, *Early Christian thought and the classical tradition*, Oxford 1966. Other good introductions are W. Jaeger, *Early Christianity and Greek paideia*, Harvard 1961–Oxford 1969, and A. Wifstrand, *Die alte Kirche und die griechische Bildung*, Berne 1967. Origen's scholarship is thoroughly treated by B. Neuschäfer, *Origenes als Philologe*, Basle 1987. A sketch of the influence of the Church on scholarship, mainly in the Byzantine period proper, will be found in N. G. Wilson, *Antike und Abendland*, 16 (1970), 68–77.

Various views have been taken of Saint Basil's intention in what is sometimes called his twenty-second homily (it is in fact addressed to his nephews). Marrou, p. 462, emphasizes that it does not consist of a recommendation to study the classical authors; its advice is rather that, given the existing curriculum of pagan texts, there are ways of ensuring that these do the pupils good instead of harm. On the other hand it is probably wrong to see in Basil no more than a grudging recognition; the tone of the treatise is not unfriendly. There are recent editions by N. G. Wilson, *Saint Basil on the value of Greek literature*, London 1975, and M. Naldini, *Basilio di Cesarea: Discorso ai giovani*, Florence 1984.

The burning of books is discussed by C. A. Forbes, *TAPA* 67 (1936), 114–25, and in the comprehensive monograph by W. Speyer, *Büchervernichtung und Zensur des Geistes bei Heiden, Juden und Christen*, Stuttgart 1981. The documents relating to ecclesiastical censorship in the twelfth century are nos. 1003 and 1008 in V. Grumel, *Regestes des actes du patriarcat de Constantinople*, Istanbul 1947.

III. *The early Byzantine period*

For the topics treated in this section see the fuller account in N. G. Wilson, *Scholars of Byzantium*, London 1983. The genesis of scholia is discussed in the same writer's paper in C. Questa and R. Raffaelli (edd.), *Il libro e il testo, Atti del Convegno internazionale, Urbino 20–23 settembre 1982*, Urbino 1985, pp. 105–10. On the content of scholia see his article referred to above on Ch. 1 III.

Wilamowitz's theory of the selection of plays for use in schools was put forward in his *Einleitung in die griechische Tragödie* (vol. 1 of his edition of Euripides' *Herakles*), 1895[2] and subsequently reprinted, pp. 175–80, 196–8. Its main features had been anticipated by T. Barthold in a Bonn dissertation of 1864. The theory was subjected to a searching examination by W. S. Barrett, *Euripides Hippolytos*, Oxford 1964, pp. 50–3.

The history of the schools or universities of late antiquity is obscure. Some idea of the law school at Beirut may be had from the attractive picture in M. L. Clarke, *Higher education in antiquity*, London 1971, pp. 116–17 (with further references).

IV. *Greek texts in the Orient*

A review of the use of local vernacular languages in the eastern provinces is given by R. MacMullen in *AJP* 87 (1966), 1–16. On the bilingual culture of Egypt and Syria at the end of antiquity see M. Lichtheim, 'Autonomy versus unity in the Christian East', in Lynn White Jr. (ed.), *The transformation of the Roman world: Gibbon's problem after two centuries*, California University Press 1966, pp. 119–46.

Oriental versions of the New Testament are discussed by B. M. Metzger, *The early versions of the New Testament*, Oxford 1967; see the review by J. Barr, *JTS* 30 (1979), 290–303.

Syriac translations of Greek texts are listed by A. Baumstark, *Geschichte der syrischen Literatur*, Bonn 1922. On the schools of Nisibis and Edessa one may consult A. Vööbus, *History of the school of Nisibis*, Louvain 1965. For studies of particular authors see e.g. A. Baumstark, *Jahrbücher für classische Philologie*, Suppl. Vol. 21 (1894), 357–524, *Aristoteles bei den Syrern*, Leipzig 1900, G. Uhlig's edition of Dionysius Thrax, Leipzig 1883, pp. xliv–xlvi, M. Aubineau's edition of Gregory of Nyssa, *De virginitate* (=Sources Chrétiennes, vol. 119), Paris 1966, pp. 223–5, M. D. Macleod and L. R. Wickham, *CQ* 20 (1970), 297–9.

The best introduction to Arabic translations and Hunain ibn Ishaq is by R. Walzer, *HSCP* 63 (1958), 217–31, where further bibliography will be found. There is also quite a useful bibliographical survey by F. Gabrieli, *Al-Andalus*, 24 (1959), 297–318. For an instructive illustration of the difficulties to be overcome and the gains to be expected from the use of an Arabic version, see R. Kassel, *Der Text der aristotelischen Rhetorik*, Berlin 1971, pp. 88–92, 125–6, 141–2. There are editions of the new Diophantus by J. Sesiano, Berlin 1982, and R. Rashed, Paris 1984; the latter is reviewed by I. Bulmer-Thomas, *CR* 34 (1984), 255–8. On Galen see J. S. Wilkie, *JHS* 101 (1981), 145–8, and J. S. Wilkie and D. J. Furley, *Galen on respiration and arteries*, Princeton 1984, pp. 263–9, or their previous announcement in *CR* 22 (1972), 164–7. See also G. Endress (ed.), *Symposium graecoarabicum II* (Archivum graecoarabicum I), Amsterdam 1989.

Joseph Needham, *Science and civilization in China*, vol. 1, Cambridge 1954, p. 219, draws attention to a fascinating episode in the life of the great Arab physician and alchemist Rhazes, who dictated some of the works of Galen to a Chinese scholar visiting Baghdad.

For Armenian translations see M. Leroy, *Ann. Inst. de phil. et d'hist. orient.* 3 (1935), 263–94, who gives the reference to Callimachus; there does not seem to be a more recent survey of the field. For some recent work on the Armenian version of Plato see W. S. M. Nicoll, *CQ* 16 (1966), 70–4.

It may be worth adding that occasionally one has to reckon with a translation into another Oriental language, but these cases are very much rarer, and the number of them discovered so far did not seem to justify a mention of them in the main text. Some passages of Plato's *Republic* are preserved in Coptic in a Gnostic codex from Nag Hammadi; see C. Colpe, *Jahrbuch für Antike und Christentum*, 15 (1972), 14.

A few Greek texts were made available not later than the seventh century in Pehlevi. Reports mention Pseudo-Callisthenes' account of Alexander the Great, the *Geoponica* and two works of astrology, the anthology of Vettius Valens and the *Paranatellonta* of Teucer of Babylon. See C. A. Nallino in *Studies presented to E. G. Browne* (Cambridge 1922) (reprinted in his *Raccolta di scritti editi e inediti*, vol. 6, Rome 1948, pp. 285–303). Even Ethiopic may occasionally be of value to the student of Greek texts. The Greek original of the medieval bestiary known as the Physiologus exists also in an Ethiopic translation. This follows the Greek very closely and must date from the seventh century at the latest, there being little knowledge of Greek after that date. See K. Alpers, *Vestigia Bibliae*, 6 (1984), 57 n. 8. See the same author in *Gnomon*, 56 (1984), 497–500, for a finding of interest to students of the history of the Nicaean creed. Further information on patristic texts is given by G. Lusini, *Studi classici e orientali*, 38 (1988), 469–93.

Some interesting papers on versions in various languages are assembled by M. Pavan and U. Cozzoli, *L'eredità classica nelle lingue orientali*, Rome 1986.

V. *The Renaissance of the ninth century*

The topics dealt with in this section and the next are treated more fully in N. G. Wilson, *Scholars of Byzantium*, London 1983; a few changes of detail are made in the Italian version, *Filologi bizantini*, Naples 1990.

Some questions about Photius are still controversial; very widely differing dates have been proposed for the composition of the *Bibliotheca*, and there is disagreement about the method of composition. The passage in which he describes the meetings of friends at his house is translated and discussed in P. Lemerle's valuable study, *Le premier humanisme byzantin*, Paris 1971, pp. 197–8 (pp. 229–30 in the English tr., *Byzantine humanism: the first phase*, Canberra 1986).

VI. *The later Byzantine period*

On libraries and book production see the essays in *Byzantine books and bookmen: a Dumbarton Oaks colloquium*, Washington D.C. 1975, and N. G. Wilson, *GRBS* 8 (1967), 53–80. The identification of scribes, and very rarely scriptoria, through features of handwriting or book production, is one of the chief means by which our knowledge of Byzantine scholarship advances. Autographs of the leading scholars are still being recognized, and our knowledge of scriptoria is making slow progress. For the methods involved see J. Irigoin, *Scriptorium*, 12 (1958), 208–27 and 13 (1959), 177–209. The objection of principle raised by B. Hemmerdinger, *BZ* 56 (1963), 24, remains a serious difficulty, but need not be held to invalidate all the results of this method of inquiry (known in some circles as codicology). A successful application of the method may be seen in Irigoin's identification of a group of manuscripts of the Greek historians all written with thirty-two lines to the page: *Annuaire de l'École pratique des Hautes Études*, 1968–9, section IV, pp. 137ff.

There is no satisfactory study of Psellus (the article by E. Kriaras in *RE* leaves a good deal to be desired). The two literary essays referred to are now well edited and translated by A. R. Dyck, *Michael Psellus: the essays on Euripides and George of Pisidia and on Heliodorus and Achilles Tatius*, Vienna 1986.

Eustathius' commentary on the *Iliad* has now been edited from the surviving autograph manuscript (Laur. 59.2–3) by M. van der Valk (Leiden 1971–87, with prolegomena of considerable value for assessing Eustathius' sources and methods of scholarship).

CHAPTER 3

I. *The Dark Ages*

Among the most relevant general works on the intellectual and cultural history of the Dark Ages mention should be made of P. Courcelle, *Les Lettres grecques en Occident de Macrobe à Cassiodore*, Paris 1948²; P. Riché, *Éducation et culture dans l'Occident barbare, VIe-VIIIe siècles*, Paris 1972³ (translated into English by J. J. Contreni, *Education and culture in the barbarian West, sixth through eighth centuries*, Columbia, S.C., 1976); B. Bischoff, 'Scriptoria e manoscritti mediatori di civiltà dal sesto secolo alla riforma di Carlo Magno', *Settimane di studio del Centro italiano di studi sull' alto medioevo*, 11 (Spoleto 1963), 479–504, reprinted in his *Mittelalterliche Studien*, vol. 2, Stuttgart 1967, pp. 312–27; also the works earlier cited by Laistner and Marrou. The fundamental work is E. A. Lowe, *Codices Latini Antiquiores*, vols. 1–12, Oxford 1934–71, with Addenda by B. Bischoff and V. Brown in *MS* 47 (1985), 317–66. This contains facsimiles and descriptions of all Latin manuscripts prior to the ninth century.

On the falling off of classical culture during the Dark Ages, see L. D. Reynolds (ed.), *Texts and transmission: a survey of the Latin classics*, Oxford 1983, pp. xiv–xvii.

The passages of Seneca cited by Johannes Lydus may be found in the edition of the *Naturales quaestiones* by A. Gercke, Leipzig 1907, pp. 157–9, and those of Petronius quoted by Fulgentius in the edition of the *Satyricon* by K. Müller, Munich 1961, pp. 185–94; see too V. Ciaffi, *Fulgenzio e Petronio*, Turin 1963. Martin of Braga's *Formula vitae honestae*, dedicated to the Suevic king Mir and written between 570 and 579, is an adaptation of a lost work of Seneca, probably the *De officiis* (cf. E. Bickel, *RhM* 60 (1905), 505–51). Unlike his *De ira*, a carefully constructed mosaic of borrowings from Seneca's treatise of that name, which survives in only one medieval manuscript (Escorial M.III.3, of the tenth century), the *Formula* was an extremely popular work in the Middle Ages and later. Often entitled *De quattuor virtutibus cardinalibus*, it was commonly attributed, with perspicacity if not a sense of poetic justice, to Seneca. For further information see C. W. Barlow, *Martini episcopi Bracarensis opera omnia*, New Haven, Conn. 1950.

For bibliographical material on Cassiodorus see the important article by A. D. Momigliano, 'Cassiodorus and the Italian culture of his time', *PBA* 41 (1955), 207–45, reprinted (with a more select bibliography) in his *Secondo contributo alla storia degli studi classici*, Rome 1960, pp. 219–29, and *Studies in Historiography*, London 1966 (paperback 1969), pp. 181–210. J. J. O'Donnell, *Cassiodorus*, Berkeley 1979, stresses the limited aims that Cassiodorus had in founding Vivarium and seeks to minimize his influence (see the review by Averil Cameron, 'Cassiodorus Deflated', *JRS* 71 (1981), 183–6).

The theory that the oldest Bobbio manuscripts came from Vivarium, advanced by R. Beer in 1911, has crumbled under the attacks of numerous scholars, in particular that of P. Courcelle, *Les Lettres grecques*, 357–88. The identifications proposed by Courcelle are examined by H. Bloch in his review of *CLA* vol. 4 in *Speculum*, 25 (1950), 282–7, and by B. Bischoff in *Mittelalterliche Studien* vol. 3, Stuttgart 1981, p. 152 n. 17. *Cassiodori Senatoris Institutiones*, ed. R. A. B. Mynors, Oxford 1937, provides a critical text of the *Institutiones* and valuable indexes: see too P. Courcelle, 'Histoire d'un brouillon cassiodorien', *REA* 44 (1942), 65–86.

A full-length study of Isidore and his classical sources is provided by J. Fontaine, *Isidore de Seville et la culture classique dans l'Espagne wisigothique*, 3 vols., Paris 1959–83. It seems dangerous to draw firm conclusions about the classical content of the episcopal library at Seville from Isidore's *Versus in bibliotheca* (ed. C. H. Beeson, *Isidor-Studien* (Quellen und Untersuchungen zur lateinischen Philologie des Mittelalters, 4.2, Munich 1913), pp. 157–66). The remarkable story of the dissemination of his works has been most recently and authoritatively treated by B. Bischoff, 'Die europäische Verbreitung der Werke Isidors von Sevilla', *Isidoriana. Estudios sobre San Isidoro de Sevilla en el XIV centenario de su nacimiento*, León 1961, pp. 317–44, reprinted in *Mittelalterliche Studien*, vol. 1, Stuttgart 1966, pp. 171–94.

For the facts and figures about early palimpsests, which can be supplemented from the volumes of *CLA*, see E. A. Lowe, 'Codices rescripti', *Mélanges Eugène Tisserant*, vol. 5, Vatican 1964 (Studi e Testi, 235), pp. 67–112, reprinted in *Palaeographical papers*, Oxford 1972, vol. 2, pp. 480–519. For a detailed study of a famous palimpsest, see J. Fohlen, 'Recherches sur le manuscrit palimpseste Vatican, Pal. lat. 24', *Scrittura e civiltà*, 3 (1979), 195–222.

II. *Ireland and England*

The extent to which the early Irish knew the classics is controversial and the scope of their classical knowledge has at times doubtless been exaggerated. The controversy tends to turn on the rather subjective question of whether Columbanus' familiarity with classical poetry, evidenced for instance in his *Carmen ad Fedolium*, was acquired at home or on the continent. The negative view was put by E. Coccia, 'La cultura irlandese precarolina—miracolo o mito?', *Studi medievali*, 3rd ser. 8 (1967), 257–420. For a judicious defence of Irish classical culture see L. Bieler, 'The classics in Celtic Ireland', in R. R. Bolgar (ed.), *Classical influences on European culture A.D. 500–1500*, Cambridge 1971, pp. 45–9; W. B. Stanford, *Ireland and the classical tradition*, Dublin 1984[2], pp. 1–18. The works of Columbanus have been edited by G. S. M. Walker, *Sancti Columbani opera* (Script. Lat. Hiberniae, vol. 2), Dublin 1957, who however makes some exaggerated statements about classical culture in Ireland: see the review by M. Esposito, *C&M* 21 (1960), 184–203. There are two valuable articles on the scholarly activity of the Irish by B. Bischoff, 'Il monachesimo irlandese nei suoi rapporti col continente', *Settimane*, 4 (Spoleto 1957), 121–38, and 'Wendepunkte in der Geschichte der lateinischen Exegese im Frühmittelalter', *Sacris Erudiri*, 6 (1954), 189–279; both are reprinted in *Mittelalterliche Studien*, vol. 1, pp. 195–205, 205–73. For a handsome introduction to early Irish culture, see L. Bieler, *Irland, Wegbereiter des Mittelalters*, Olten etc. 1961 (English edition, *Ireland, harbinger of the Middle Ages*, Oxford–London 1963).

There is a survey of the whole question of classical learning in the British Isles in T. J. Brown, 'An historical introduction to the use of classical Latin authors in the British Isles from the fifth to the eleventh century', in *La cultura antica nell' occidente latino dal VII all' XI secolo, Settimane*, 22 (Spoleto 1975), vol. 1, pp. 237–99.

There is now firmer evidence for classical texts in Anglo-Saxon England. J. D. A. Ogilvy, *Books known to the English* (Medieval Academy of America Publications, 76), Cambridge, Mass., 1967, still useful but often uncritical, has been overtaken in part by H. Gneuss, 'A preliminary list of manuscripts written or owned in England up to 1100', *Anglo-Saxon England* 9 (1981), 1–60; M. Lapidge, 'Surviving Booklists from Anglo-Saxon England', in M. Lapidge and H. Gneuss (edd.), *Learning and literature in Anglo-Saxon England: studies presented to Peter Clemoes on the occasion of his sixty-fifth birthday*, Cambridge 1985, pp. 33–89. Bede's classical sources are thoroughly studied by M. L. W. Laistner, 'Bede as a classical and a patristic scholar', *Tr. Royal Hist. Soc.*, 4th ser. 16 (1933), 69–94, and 'The library of the Venerable Bede', in *Bede: his life, times, and writings*, ed. A. H. Thompson, Oxford 1935, pp. 237–66; both are reprinted in his collected essays, *The intellectual heritage of the early Middle Ages*, ed. Chester G. Starr, Ithaca, N.Y., 1957, pp. 93–116, 117–49. On Bede see also R. W. Southern, *Medieval humanism and other studies*, Oxford 1970, pp. 1–8.

Alcuin's lines on the contents of the library at York are to be found in his *Versus de sanctis Euboricensis Ecclesiae*, 1535ff., ed. E. Dümmler, *MGH, Poetae latini aevi Carolini*, vol. 1, Berlin 1880–1, pp. 203–4, and now re-edited with a commentary by P. J. Godman, *The bishops, kings, and saints of York* (Oxford Medieval Texts), Oxford 1982.

III. *The Anglo-Saxon missionaries*

W. Levison's *England and the Continent in the eighth century*, Oxford 1946, remains the authoritative work on the missionary activity of the Anglo-Saxons: see especially pp. 132–73. The present location of the fragment of

Justinus at one time in the possession of E. Fischer is unknown. It is therefore particularly fortunate that a second leaf has now come to light: J. Crick,
'An Anglo-Saxon fragment of Justinus's *Epitome*', *Anglo-Saxon England*, 16
(1987), 181–96, and Plate VIII.

IV. *Insular influence on classical texts*

One of the difficulties of assessing the part played by the Irish and the
English in the transmission of classical texts is the imprecise nature of the
term 'insular tradition'. This may be postulated in a variety of circumstances: when one or more manuscripts of a text were actually written
in Britain, or written in insular script on the continent, or associated with
some Irish or Anglo-Saxon foundation, or showing traces, more or less
conjectural, that a lost exemplar belonged to one of these categories.

The route which the flow of cultural life followed from Italy to Britain and
then back again to the continent is very much the *romantische Strasse* for the
transmission of texts and it can be dramatically documented for some
biblical traditions, as in the case of the Fulda and Echternach Gospels
(Fulda, Bonifat. 3; Paris lat. 9389) and, still more clearly, the codex
Amiatinus (Laur. Amiat. 1), where the part played by England in the story is
beyond doubt. This great bible was written at Wearmouth or Jarrow as part
of Ceolfrid's project to produce three complete bibles, or 'pandects', and was
almost certainly used by Bede himself, but much of its decoration was
modelled on that of the lost *codex grandior* of Cassiodorus, written at
Vivarium and brought from Rome to Northumbria by Ceolfrid as one of the
fruits of his journey with Benedict Biscop in 678; he was taking the
Amiatinus to Rome, as a present for the pope, when he died at Langres in
716 (cf. R. L. S. Bruce Mitford, *Journal of the British Archaeological Association*,
3rd ser. 32 (1969), 1–25; J. W. Halporn, 'Pandectes, Pandecta, and the
Cassiodorian commentary on the Psalms', *Revue bénédictine*, 90 (1980), 290–
300, especially 297ff.).

Unfortunately, it is not easy to substantiate such romantic journeys for
classical texts and some of the hastily posited insular traditions once fashionable have evaporated, such as the insular pre-archetype of Lucretius,
an author who does not appear to have reached England before the
fifteenth century (cf. F. Brunhölzl, *Hermes*, 90 (1962), 97–104; V. Brown,
HSCP 72 (1967), 301–10). T. J. Brown (op. cit., 281–9) examines the significance of insular symptoms in classical texts.

V. *The Carolingian Revival*

The educational aims of Charlemagne are fully and explicitly set out in the mandate which he sent to Baugulf, abbot of Fulda, between 794 and 800. This document has been edited and fully discussed by L. Wallach in *Speculum*, 26 (1951), 288–305, reprinted in his *Alcuin and Charlemagne*, Ithaca, N.Y., 1959, rev. ed. 1967, pp. 198–226. Of particular interest is Wallach's demonstration, from the thought and style of the mandate, that Alcuin had taken a hand in its composition. For the educational role of the Palace School, see F. Brunhölzl, 'Der Bildungsauftrag der Hofschule', in *Karl der Grosse, Lebenswerk und Nachleben*, vol. 2, *Das geistige Leben*, ed. B. Bischoff, Düsseldorf 1965, pp. 28–41. For a general study see D. A. Bullough, *The Age of Charlemagne*, London 1973², together with his 'Roman Books and the Carolingian *Renovatio*', *Studies in Church History*, 14 (1977), 23–50. F. Brunhölzl gives a survey of the writers associated with the court in *Geschichte der lateinischen Literatur des Mittelalters*, vol. 1, Munich 1975, pp. 243–315.

VI. *The development of Caroline minuscule*

This brief account of the history of the national hands and the development of Caroline minuscule, complex and at times controversial, has been necessarily simplified. This matters less now that we have the authoritative handbook by B. Bischoff, *Paläographie des römischen Altertums und des abendländischen Mittelalters*, now translated, with additions, into English by D. Ó. Cróinín and D. Ganz, *Latin palaeography: antiquity and the Middle Ages*, Cambridge 1990; and the valuable bibliography of Leonard Boyle, O.P., *Medieval Latin palaeography. A bibliographical introduction* (Toronto Medieval Bibliographies, 8), Toronto 1984. Among other surveys may be mentioned that of J. J. John, 'Latin palaeography', in J. M. Powell (ed.), *Medieval studies: an introduction*, Syracuse, N.Y., 1976, pp. 1–68; B. L. Ullman, *Ancient Writing and its Influence*, New York 1969², reprinted with introduction and additional bibliography by T. J. Brown (Medieval Academy Reprints for Teaching, 10), Toronto 1980.

For Beneventan manuscripts, see E. A. Loew, *The Beneventan script: a history of the South Italian minuscule*, Second edition, prepared and enlarged by Virginia Brown, Rome 1980; also Lowe's *Palaeographical papers*, vol. 1, pp. 70–91, vol. 2, pp. 477–9.

There appear to be at least four Visigothic manuscripts of classical texts: a ninth-century manuscript of Ausonius, actually written by Spanish emigrants at Lyon (Leiden, Voss. Lat. F.111), an eleventh-century Terence

(Madrid, Vitr. 5-4), fragments of another of the twelfth century (León, Cathedral, fragm. 3), and a Lucan of the late eleventh or early twelfth century (Vat. Ottob. lat. 1210 + Vat. Pal. lat. 869).

Two manuscripts in pre-Caroline minuscule are Vienna lat. 277, which now contains Grattius' *Cynegetica* and the pseudo-Ovidian *Halieutica* and once contained a large body of Latin poetry (France, perhaps Lyon), and Munich Clm 29216 (7, a fragmentary Vergil (Italy); both belong to the late eighth century. Lucretius and parts of the tradition of Martial and Statius contain errors which appear to have occurred in a pre-Caroline minuscule.

VII. *Carolingian libraries and the Latin classics*

For the key to the Palace Library see B. Bischoff, 'Die Hofbibliothek Karls des Grossen', in *Karl der Grosse*, pp. 42-62 (= *Mitt. Stud.* vol. 3, pp. 149-69); he has also edited a facsimile of the manuscript containing the book-list, *Sammelhandschrift Diez. B Sant. 66. Grammatici latini et catalogus librorum*, Graz 1973. It is noteworthy that the compiler of the book-list, an Italian, was interested in jotting down only the classical books in the collection. For the attribution of Lucretius and Vitruvius to the Palace School, see *IMU* 15 (1972), 38 n. 3, *Mitt. Stud.* vol. 3, p. 282.

On the libraries of Charlemagne's successors, Louis the Pious and Charles the Bald, see B. Bischoff, 'Die Hofbibliothek unter Ludwig dem Frommen', in J. J. G. Alexander and M. T. Gibson (edd.), *Medieval learning and literature: essays presented to Richard William Hunt*, Oxford 1976, pp. 3-22 (= *Mitt. Stud.* vol. 3, pp. 170-86); R. McKitterick, 'Charles the Bald (823-877) and his library', *The English Historical Review*, 95 (1980), 28-47. Among the books one knows to have been offered to Charles the Bald or written for him was a manuscript of Vegetius which Freculphus, bishop of Lisieux, had specially corrected and prepared for him. A fine copy of Apicius (Vat. Urb. lat. 1146, written at Tours) is thought to have been another present.

The sources on which the Carolingians drew for their books are discussed, with special reference to the *Hofbibliothek*, by Bischoff, 'Das benediktinische Mönchtum und die überlieferung der klassischen Literatur', *Studien und Mitteilungen zur Geschichte des Benediktiner-Ordens und seiner Zweige*, 92 (1981), 165-90, particularly 170ff.; see too L. D. Reynolds (ed.), *Texts and transmission: a survey of the Latin classics*, Oxford 1983, pp. xvii-xxiv.

For Hadoard and the Corbie manuscripts, see B. Bischoff, 'Hadoardus and the manuscripts of classical authors from Corbie', in S. Prete (ed.), *Didaskaliae: studies in honor of Anselm M. Albareda*, New York 1961, pp. 41-57, reprinted (in German) in *Mitt. Stud.* vol. 1, pp. 49-63.

The survey of books in Carolingian libraries is mainly derived from surviving catalogues or the history of the individual texts concerned. The information from the catalogues, though in places out of date, is conveniently assembled in M. Manitius, *Handschriften antiker Autoren in mittelalterlichen Bibliothekskatalogen* (Zentralblatt für Bibliothekswesen, Beiheft 67), Leipzig 1935. See also B. Bischoff, 'Panorama der Handschriftenüberlieferung aus der Zeit Karls des Grossen', *Karl der Grosse*, vol. 2, pp. 233-54 (= *Mitt. Stud.* vol. 3, pp. 5-38); 'Frühkarolingische Handschriften und ihre Heimat' *Scriptorium*, 22 (1968), 306-14.

Further information about the part played by these centres in the transmission of Latin texts, for this and other periods, may be derived from L. D. Reynolds (ed.), *Texts and transmission*, which gives a brief account of the manuscript traditions of all Latin classical texts. A catalogue of some 3,000 manuscripts from the ninth to the end of the twelfth century, with an indication of origin or provenance where known, is provided by B. Munk Olsen, *L'étude des auteurs classiques latins aux XIe et XIIe siècles: catalogue des manuscrits classiques latins copiés du IXe au XIIe siècle*, vols. 1-3, Paris 1982-9. For studies of individual centres, see e.g. B. Bischoff, *Lorsch im Spiegel seiner Handschriften*, Munich 1974; E. Pellegrin, 'La Tradition des textes classiques latins à l'abbaye de Fleury-sur-Loire', *RHT* 14 (1984), 155-67. An account of when classical texts first appear in extant manuscripts is given in *Texts and transmission*, xxviiff.; for their relative popularity see B. Munk Olsen, 'La Popularité des textes classiques entre le IXe et le XIIe siècle, *RHT* 14 (1984), 169-81.

A great deal of information about the part played by libraries and scriptoria in the transmission of texts may be found in the richly documented article by B. Munk Olsen and P. Petitmengin, 'Les Bibliothèques et la transmission des textes, in *Histoire des bibliothèques françaises*, vol. 1, *Les Bibliothèques médiévales. Du vi^e siècle à 1530*, Paris 1989, pp. 415-36.

VIII. *Carolingian scholarship*

The identity of the 'Saxon' corrector was first revealed by B. Bischoff in the catalogue to the 1965 Charlemagne Exhibition at Aachen: cf. *Karl der Grosse, Werk und Wirkung*, Aachen 1965 (= *Charlemagne, œuvre, rayonnement et survivances*, Aix-la-Chapelle 1965), pp. 202-3. For further information on Dungal, see Bischoff, 'Die Bibliothek im Dienste der Schule', *Settimane*, 19 (Spoleto 1972), 410-12; M. Ferrari, 'In Papia conveniant ad Dungalium', *IMU* 15 (1972), 1-32. For Hadoard, see the notes to VII; also C. H. Beeson, 'The Collectaneum of Hadoard', *CPh* 40 (1945), 201-22. Walafrid Strabo's scrapbook is identified and described by Bischoff in 'Eine Sammelhand schrift Walafrid Strabos (Cod. Sangall. 878)', *Aus der Welt des Buches, Festschrift Georg Leyh* (Zentralblatt für Bibliothekswesen, Beiheft 75), Leipzig 1950, pp. 30-48; this article is reprinted and enlarged in *Mitt. Stud.* vol. 2, pp. 34-51, the addenda including the discovery of Walafrid's role in the Horace tradition. For the Seneca excerpt, see L. D. Reynolds, *The medieval tradition of Seneca's letters*, Oxford 1965, pp. 92-3 and Plate 1; for Columella, Å. Josephson, *Die Columella-Handschriften*, Uppsala 1955, pp. 39-41.

There is a good account of Lupus in M. L. W. Laistner, *Thought and Letters*, pp. 252-9. The fundamental work is that of P. E. von Severus, *Lupus von Ferrières, Gestalt und Werk eines Vermittlers antiken Geistesgutes an das Mittelalter im 9. Jahrhundert*, Münster in Westf. 1940. See too Luanne Meagher O.S.B., *The Gellius Manuscript of Lupus of Ferrières*, Chicago 1936; C. H. Beeson, *Servatus Lupus as scribe and text critic* (Medieval Academy of America Publications, 4), Cambridge, Mass., 1930 (an edition of the facsimile of the manuscript of the *De oratore* written by Lupus). For a list of the other books he has annotated or corrected see E. Pellegrin, 'Les Manuscrits de Loup de Ferrières', *BEC* 115 (1957), 5-31; to these may be added a Prudentius (Wolfenbüttel, Aug. 8° 56.18), to which Bischoff drew attention in *Wolfenbütteler Beiträge* 2 (1973), 106 (= *Mitt. Stud.* vol. 3, p. 306) and a manuscript of the Chronicle of Eusebius-Jerome (Berlin, Phill. 1872: cf. R. Schipke, *Studien zur Buch- und Bibliotheksgeschichte, Hans Lülfing zum 70. Geburtstag*, Berlin 1976, pp. 33-8). Lupus' scholarly interests are vividly illustrated by his letters, edited by L. Levillain, 2 vols., Paris 1927-35; there is a Teubner text by P. K. Marshall, *Servati Lupi epistolae*, Leipzig 1984.

On the collations of Theodulfus, see H. Quentin, *Mémoire sur l'établissement du texte de la Vulgate*, vol. 1, *L'Octateuque*, Rome 1922, pp. 290-3, and G. Pasquali, *Storia della tradizione*, p. 155 n. 2.

We now have a good edition of Heiric's *florilegium*: R. Quadri, *I 'Collectanea' di Eirico di Auxerre* (Spicilegium Friburgense, 11), Fribourg 1966. For the story of the transmission of the collection of texts which include Mela and Julius Paris, one of the most fascinating of all since it can be traced almost continuously from antiquity to the Renaissance, see Gius. Billanovich, 'Dall' antica Ravenna alle biblioteche umanistiche', *Annuario dell' Università Cattolica del S. Cuore Milano* (1955-7), 71-107; C. M. Gormley, M. A. Rouse, R. H. Rouse, 'The medieval circulation of the *De Chorographia* of Pomponius Mela', *MS* 46 (1984), 266-320.

IX. *The Carolingian twilight*

For Ratherius and the text of Livy's first decade, see Gius. Billanovich, 'Dal Livio di Raterio (Laur. 63. 19) al Livio del Petrarca (B.M. Harl. 2493)', *IMU* 2 (1959), 103–78. The early history of the Catullus tradition and Ratherius' part in it remains puzzling: see R. J. Tarrant in *Texts and transmission*, p. 43. Ratherius also owned and annotated a copy of Martianus Capella (Voss. Lat. F. 48): cf. C. Leonardi, 'Raterio e Marziano Capella', *IMU* 2 (1959), 73–102.

F. Mütherich has written about 'The library of Otto III', in *The role of the book in medieval culture. Proceedings of the Oxford International Symposium 26 September–1 October 1982* (Bibliologia 3–4), Turnhout 1986, pp. 11–26. For the early history of Livy's fourth decade see Gius. Billanovich, *JWI* 14 (1951), 183ff.; A. H. McDonald in the preface to vol. 5 of the Oxford Classical Text, Oxford 1965, pp. xff.

The discovery of a new catalogue of Lobbes by F. Dolbeau threw fresh light on the contribution made by this area to the transmission of texts: 'Un nouveau catalogue des manuscrits de Lobbes aux XIe et XIIe siècles', *Recherches Augustiniennes*, 13 (1978), 3–36, 14 (1979), 191–248. For the study of Claudian at Lobbes, see R. G. Babcock, 'A revival of Claudian in the tenth century', *C&M* 37 (1986), 203–21.

The manuscript of Ovid's *Ars amatoria* written in early Welsh minuscule later belonged to Dunstan: R. W. Hunt, *Saint Dunstan's classbook from Glastonbury* (Umbrae Codicum Occidentalium, 4), Amsterdam 1961.

X. *The resurgence of Montecassino*

The manuscripts of Montecassino have already been mentioned in connection with the Beneventan script. F. Brunhölzl, *Zum Problem der Casinenser Klassiker überlieferung* (Abhandlungen der Marburger Gelehrten Gesellschaft, 1971, no. 3), Munich 1971, puts forward the theory that some of the unique texts at Montecassino may have come from a late antique private library, perhaps at Casinum. For other important studies see: H. Bloch, 'Monte Cassino's teachers and library in the High Middle Ages', *Settimane*, 19 (Spoleto 1972), 563–605, and 'Der Autor der "Graphia aureae urbis Romae"', *Deutsches Archiv*, 40 (1984), 55–175; G. Cavallo, 'La trasmissione dei testi nell' area beneventano-cassinese', *Settimane*, 22 (Spoleto 1975), 257–424. Bloch's magnificent study of the history of Montecassino and particularly of its buildings and works of art has now appeared: *Monte Cassino in the Middle Ages*, 3 vols., Rome 1986.

Brief accounts, with further bibliography, of the texts in which Monte-cassino intervened decisively will be found in *Texts and transmission*. On the whole, Montecassino seems to have kept its manuscripts to itself during the Middle Ages. With the exception of Seneca's *Dialogues*, the 'Cassinese texts' did not begin to circulate until the Renaissance. For Seneca's *Dialogues*, see L. D. Reynolds, 'The Medieval Tradition of Seneca's *Dialogues*', *CQ* 18 (1968), 355–72; for later humanist discoveries in the monastery, F. Lo Monaco, 'Note su codici cassinesi tra Quattro et Cinquecento' (Miscellanea Cassinese, 48), *Monastica IV*, Montecassino 1984.

XI. *The twelfth-century renaissance*

The classic study of C. H. Haskins, *The Renaissance of the twelfth century* (Cambridge, Mass., 1927), survived to be celebrated and reassessed on the occasion of its fiftieth birthday: see *Renaissance and renewal in the twelfth century*, ed. R. L. Benson and G. Constable, with C. D. Lanham, Cambridge, Mass., 1982 (paperback, 1985). Other general accounts: G. M. Paré, A. Brunet, P. Tremblay, *La Renaissance au XIIe siècle: les écoles et l'enseignement*, Paris and Ottawa 1933; M. de Gandillac and E. Jeauneau (edd.), *Entretiens sur la renaissance su XIIe siècle*, Paris–The Hague 1968; C. Brooke, *The twelfth century Renaissance*, London 1969; P. Weimar (ed.), *Die Renaissance der Wissenschaften im 12. Jahrhundert*, Zürich 1981. England is put into its context by R. W. Southern, 'The place of England in the twelfth century Renaissance', *Medieval humanism and other studies*, Oxford 1970, pp. 158–80. See too R. W. Hunt, 'The deposit of Latin classics in the twelfth-century renaissance', in Bolgar (ed.), *Classical influences*, pp. 51–5.

A large literature is accumulating on the growth of literacy in the Middle Ages. A start can be made with H. Grundmann, '*Litteratus-illiteratus*: der Wandel einer Bildungsnorm vom Altertum zum Mittelalter', *Archiv für Kulturgeschichte*, 40 (1958), 1–65 (= *Ausgewählte Aufsätze*, vol. 3, *Bildung und Sprache*, Stuttgart 1978, pp. 1–66); M. B. Parkes, 'The literacy of the laity', in D. Daiches and A. Thorlby (edd.), *Literature and western civilization*, vol. 2, *The medieval world*, London 1973, pp. 555–77; B. Stock, *The implications of literacy. Written languages and models of interpretation in the eleventh and twelfth centuries*, Princeton 1983.

For John of Salisbury, see H. Liebeschütz, *Medieval humanism in the life and writings of John of Salisbury*, London 1950: Janet Martin, 'John of Salisbury and the classics', summarized in *HSCP* 73 (1969), 319–21; 'Uses of tradition: Gellius, Petronius, and John of Salisbury', *Viator*, 10 (1979), 57–76; 'John of Salisbury's manuscripts of Frontinus and Gellius', *JWI* 40 (1977), 1–26. The last two articles provide an excellent study of John's use of his classical sources. On William of Malmesbury: H. Farmer, 'William of Malmesbury's life and works', *Journal of Ecclesiastical History*, 13 (1962), 39–54, and a series of articles by R. M. Thomson, notably 'The reading of William of Malmesbury', *Revue bénédictine*, 85 (1975), 362–402, 86 (1976), 327–35, 89 (1979), 313–24, and 'The "scriptorium" of William of Malmesbury', in M. B. Parker and A. G. Watson, *Medieval scribes, manuscripts and libraries: essays presented to N. R. Ker*, London 1978, pp. 117–42. William's knowledge of Cicero is particularly impressive, but difficult to estimate precisely, because the corpus of works in the Cambridge manuscript (copied at Cologne in 1444) seems to contain later, continental accretions: see Thomson (1975), 372–7, (1976), 330, (1979), 316.

The *Florilegium Gallicum* has been discussed in relation to the classical texts it contains by B. L. Ullman in a series of articles in *Classical Philology*, 23–7 (1928–32); for a summary see the last, pp. 1–42. Also A. Gagnér, *Florilegium Gallicum*, Lund 1936, and the partial edition by J. Hamacher, *Florilegium Gallicum: Prolegomena und Edition der Excerpte von Petron bis Cicero, De oratore* (Lateinische Sprache und Literatur des Mittelalters, 5), Frankfurt 1975; R. Burton, *Classical poets in the 'Florilegium Gallicum'*, Frankfurt 1983. It was used by the author of another important florilegium, the *Moralium dogma philosophorum*, ed. J. Holmberg, Uppsala 1929, and in the thirteenth century by Vincent of Beauvais (cf. p. 115).

B. Munk Olsen has provided a complete catalogue of florilegia containing excerpts from classical authors up to the year 1200, amounting to more than seventy different compilations: 'Les Classiques latins dans les florilèges médiévaux antérieurs au XIIIᵉ siècle', *RHT* 9 (1979), 47–121, 10 (1980), 115–72. He further analyses their form and purpose in 'Les Florilèges d'auteurs classiques', *Les Genres littéraires dans les sources théologiques et philosophiques médiévales. Définition, critique et exploitation. Actes du Colloque international de Louvain-la-Neuve 25–27 mai 1981* (Publications de l'Institut d'Études Médiévales, 2nd series: *Textes, études, congrès*, vol. 5), Louvain-la-Neuve 1982, pp. 151–64.

For an excellent analysis of the way in which a Latin classical author can be used and adapted for Christian purposes in this period, see J. M. Déchanet's study of Guillaume de Saint-Thierry, '*Seneca Noster*. Des lettres à Lucilius à la lettre aux frères du Mont-Dieu', *Mélanges Joseph de Ghellinck* vol. 2, Gembloux 1951, pp. 753–66. The popularity of Ovid in the twelfth century, less of an *aetas Ovidiana* than had been commonly supposed, is studied by B. Munk Olsen, 'Ovide au Moyen Âge (du XIᵉ au XIIᵉ siècle)', in G. Cavallo (ed.), *Le Strade del testo*, Bari 1987, pp. 67–96.

XII. *The scholastic age*

The *Biblionomia* of Richard de Fournival was edited by L. Delisle, *Le Cabinet des manuscrits de la Bibliothèque Nationale*, vol. 2, Paris 1874, pp. 518–35. For an account of his library see, most recently, R. H. Rouse, 'Manuscripts belonging to Richard of Fournival', *RHT* 3 (1973), 242–69; 'Florilegia and Latin classical authors in twelfth and thirteenth century Orleans', *Viator*, 10 (1979), 131–60, and in particular 138ff. Valuable pioneering work was done by B. L. Ullman, who identified Fournival's Propertius with the extant Voss. Lat. O. 38; cf. in particular 'The library of the Sorbonne in the fourteenth century', *Septicentennial Celebration of the founding of the Sorbonne College in the University of Paris*, Chapel Hill, N.C., 1953, pp. 33–47, reprinted in *Studies in the Italian Renaissance*, Rome 1955, pp. 41–53. Another interesting manuscript that belonged to Fournival is the oldest surviving copy of Aristippus' translation of the *Phaedo* (see p. 120); this is Paris lat. 16581, probably the parent of Petrarch's manuscript (cf. *Plato latinus*, vol. 2: *Phaedo*, ed. L. Minio-Paluello, London 1950, pp. xi–xii).

The most recent and comprehensive study of the manuscript tradition of Seneca's *Tragedies* is O. Zwierlein, *Prolegomena zu einer kritischen Ausgabe der Tragödien Senecas* (Abh. Akad. Mainz, Geistes- u. Sozialwiss. Kl. 1983.3), Wiesbaden 1984. The medieval tradition of the *Dialogues* is treated by L. D. Reynolds, in the article cited in section X.

The activities of the English friars have been illuminated and brought into focus by Beryl Smalley, *English Friars and Antiquity in the early fourteenth century*, Oxford 1960.

The *Registrum librorum Angliae*, of which an edition is forthcoming, is preserved in two manuscripts, Bodleian Library, Tanner 165 and Cambridge, Peterhouse 169.

XIII. *Greek in the West in the Middle Ages*

A useful survey with rich bibliography is offered by W. Berschin, *Griechisches-lateinisches Mittelalter, von Hieronymus zu Nikolaus von Kues*, Berne 1980. For the earlier period there are important contributions in M. W. Herren (ed.), *The sacred nectar of the Greeks: the study of Greek in the West in the early Middle Ages*, London 1988. P. Lemerle, *Le Premier Humanisme byzantin*, Paris 1971, pp. 13–16, underestimates the possibility of some knowledge of Greek at Saint Gall; see L. Bieler's introduction to the facsimile of the Basle Psalter (MS. A.vii.3), published as vol. 5 of Umbrae Codicum Occidentalium, Amsterdam 1960, esp. p. xix. On Burgundio of Pisa see the monograph by

P. Classen, *Burgundio von Pisa, Richter, Gesandter, Uebersetzer*, Heidelberg 1974. His manuscripts of Galen are identified by N. G. Wilson, *Scrittura e Civiltà* 7 (1983), 161–76. James of Venice is dealt with by L. Minio-Paluello, *Traditio*, 8 (1952), 265–304.

Basic information on the twelfth-century translators and much else can be found in C. H. Haskins, *Studies in the history of medieval science*, Cambridge, Mass., 1927[2], pp. 141–241.

Grosseteste's Greek studies are surveyed by A. C. Dionisotti in A. C. Dionisotti, A. Grafton, J. Kraye, *The uses of Greek and Latin: historical essays*, London 1988, pp. 19–39.

Moerbeke's activity can be studied in the various volumes of the *Aristoteles Latinus* series and a convenient résumé of the current state of knowledge is given by B. Schneider, *Die mittelalterlichen griechisch-lateinischen Uebersetzungen der Aristotelischen Rhetorik*, Berlin 1971, pp. 5–9. Moerbeke's translations were very popular; there are 98 surviving manuscripts of his *Rhetoric*, and Dante shows that he knew the work in this version. His ex-libris in MS. Marc. gr. 258, archetype of the *opera minora* of Alexander of Aphrodisias, was discovered by L. Labowsky, *Medieval and Renaissance Studies*, 5 (1961), 155–63. For his version of the *Metaphysics* he appears to have used the celebrated Vienna Aristotle (phil. gr. 100); see G. Vuillemin-Diem in J. Wiesner (ed.), *Aristoteles, Werk und Wirkung*, Berlin 1987, vol. 2, pp. 434–86.

On matters related to this section two papers by B. Bischoff may be recommended: 'The study of foreign languages in the Middle Ages' (*Speculum*, 36 (1961), 209–24) and 'Das griechische Element in der abendländischen Bildung des Mittelalters' (*BZ* 44 (1951), 27–55; both are now reprinted (the first in an enlarged form) in his *Mitt. Stud.* vol. 2, pp. 227–45 and 246–75.

CHAPTER 4

I. *Humanism*

The first important discussions of the origin of the term 'humanist' appeared almost simultaneously: P. O. Kristeller, 'Humanism and scholasticism in the Italian Renaissance', *Byzantion*, 17 (1944–5), 346–74, and A. Campana, 'The origin of the word "humanist"', *JWI* 9 (1946), 60–73. For recent bibliography and further discussion, see R. Avesani, 'La professione dell' "umanista" nel cinquecento', *IMU* 13 (1970), 205–323.

The wider problem of the origin of Italian humanism and its place in the context of the Renaissance is beyond the competence of this book, but some of the more general studies which have influenced the shape of this chapter may be conveniently mentioned here: P. O. Kristeller, various essays and lectures collected together in *Studies in Renaissance thought and letters*, Rome 1956, and *Renaissance thought*, vols. 1-2, New York 1961-5; Kenneth M. Setton, 'The Byzantine background to the Italian Renaissance', *Proc. Amer. Philosoph. Soc.* 100 (1956), 1-76; F. Simone, *Il Rinascimento francese*, Turin 1965² (updated English version by H. Gaston Hall, *The French Renaissance*, London 1969); Beryl Smalley, *English friars*, pp. 280-98; B. L. Ullman, *Studies in the Italian Renaissance*, Rome 1955; R. Weiss, *The dawn of humanisn in Italy*, London 1947, *The spread of Italian humanism*, London 1964, and *The Renaissance discovery of classical antiquity*, Oxford 1969.

Though in many respects out of date, the fundamental works on the rediscovery of classical texts remain those of R. Sabbadini: *Le scoperte dei codici latini e greci ne' secoli xiv e xv*, 2 vols., Florence 1905-14, reprinted with author's additions and corrections and an appreciation by E. Garin, Florence 1967; *Storia e critica di testi latini*, Catania 1914, of which a second edition has now been produced (Medioevo e Umanesimo, no. 11, Padua 1971) with new indexes and a full bibliography of Sabbadini's works.

For a concise account of the development of both *dictamen* and Renaissance rhetoric, see Kristeller, *Renaissance thought and classical antiquity* (ed. M. Mooney), New York 1979, pp. 228ff. A. Grafton and L. Jardine, in their book *From humanism to the humanities*, London 1986, offer a stimulating examination of both the methods and the merits of humanist education.

For the history of humanistic script, together with biographical data on some of the more prominent humanists and samples of their handwriting, see B. L. Ullman, *The origin and development of humanistic script*, Rome 1960; A. C. de la Mare, *The Handwriting of Italian Humanists*, vol. 1, part 1, Oxford 1973. Other works are cited where relevant.

II. *The first humanists*

The first real indication of the strength of Paduan prehumanism was given by Gius. Billanovich in *I primi umanisti e le tradizioni dei classici latini*, Fribourg 1953. The evidence for the wide knowledge of Latin poetry shown by members of this circle was set out by Guido Billanovich, '*Veterum vestigia vatum*' *IMU* 1 (1958), 155-243. For legitimate doubts about some of the claims made for them, see J. L. Butrica, *The Manuscript Tradition of Propertius*, Toronto 1984, pp. 28-9; W. Ludwig, 'Kannte Lovato Catull?', *RhM* 129 (1986), 329-57; and, for Lucretius, M. D. Reeve, *IMU* 23 (1980), 42 n. 8.

A general account of prehumanism at Padua, Verona, and in the Veneto may be found in the articles of Guido Billanovich, R. Avesani, and L. Gargan in *Storia della cultura veneta*, vol. 2, *Il trecento*, Vicenza 1976, pp. 19–170. Among more recent studies, see Guido Billanovich, 'Abbozzi e postille del Mussato nel Vaticano lat. 1769', *IMU* 28 (1985), 7–35; Guido Billanovich and P. L. Schmidt, 'Cicerone e i primi umanisti padovani: il codice Gudiano lat. 2 di Wolfenbüttel', ibid., 37–56. The poetry of Lovato and Mussato is still not properly edited or easily accessible; for a bibliography see Guido Billanovich, '*Veterum vestigia vatum*', p. 181. Mussato's *Ecerinide* was edited by L. Padrin, Bologna 1900, and texts pertaining to the study of Seneca's *Tragedies* at Padua have been edited, with full discussion of this topic, by A. Kh. Megas, Ὁ προουμανιστικὸς κύκλος τῆς Πάδουας (*Lovato Lovati-Albertino Mussato*) καὶ οἱ τραγωδίες τοῦ L. A. Seneca, Thessalonica 1967 (English summary, pp. 229–33). For a good account of Lovato, see R. Weiss, *Italian Studies*, 6 (1951), 3–28. Geremia da Montagnone is dealt with by Weiss, *Il primo secolo dell' umanesimo*, Rome 1949, pp. 15–20, and Ullman, 'Hieremias de Montagnone and his citations from Catullus', *CPh* 5 (1910), 66–82, reprinted in *Studies*, pp. 81–115. For Benvenuto Campesani, see Weiss, *Bollettino del Museo Civico di Padova*, 44 (1955), 129–44. His epigram continues to arouse speculation: for an ingenious solution to the riddle see H. L. Levy, 'Catullus and Cangrande della Scala', *TAPA* 99 (1968), 249–53; for further discussion and bibliography E. Zaffagno, 'L'epigramma di Benvenuto Campesani: "De resurectione Catulli poetae"', in *I classici nel Medioevo e nell' Umanesimo*, Genoa, Istituto di filologia classica e medioevale, 1975, pp. 289–98; Gius. Billanovich, 'Il Catullo della cattedrale di Verona', *Abh. Bay. Akad. d. Wiss.*, Ph.-Hist. Kl., 99 (1988), 35–57.

III. *The consolidation of humanism: Petrarch and his generation*

A. Petrucci, *La scrittura di Francesco Petrarca* (Studi e Testi, 248), Vatican 1967, provides a list of Petrarchan manuscripts and a useful bibliography. See too A. C. de la Mare, *Handwriting*, pp. 1–16, and 'Petrarch's manuscript of the Tragedies', *JWI* 40 (1977), 286–90 (= Escorial T.III.11 of Seneca); Biblioteca Medicea Laurenziana, *Poggio Bracciolini nel VI Centenario della nascita. Mostra di codici e documenti fiorentini*, Catalogo a cura di Riccardo Fubini e Stefano Caroti, Florence 1980. Petrarch's marginalia on Quintilian have been published by Maria Accame Lanzillotta, Florence 1979. The pioneering work of P. de Nolhac, *Pétrarque et l'humanisme*, 2nd. ed., vols. 1–2, Paris 1907, is still useful, though inevitably out of date in many respects.

For Petrarch and Pomponius Mela, see the bibliography cited above

(p. 265). For Propertius, B. L. Ullman, 'The manuscripts of Propertius', *CPh* 6 (1911), 282–301; *Studies*, 181–92; J. L. Butrica, *The manuscript tradition of Propertius*, Toronto 1984, pp. 37ff. The fundamental articles on Petrarch and Livy, though the first needs to be considerably modified in the light of subsequent research by Billanovich and others, is Gius. Billanovich, 'Petrarch and the textual tradition of Livy', *JWI* 14 (1951), 137–208, and 'Dal Livio di Raterio' (cited above, p. 266). Vol. 1, part 1, and vol. 2 of his *La tradizione del testo di Livio e le origini dell' umanesimo* have appeared (Padua 1981); vol. 2 is a complete facsimile of Petrarch's Livy (British Library, Harley 2493). Vol. 1, part 2, is awaited: in the meantime, see his article 'La biblioteca papale salvò le Storie di Livio', *Studi Petrarcheschi*, 3 (1986), 1–115, which includes plates of the important fragments recently discovered at Nancy (Archives Départementales IF 342/3). M. D. Reeve puts forward a radically different view of parts of this story in a series of articles in *Rivista di filologia* 114 (1986), 129–72, 115 (1987), 129–64, 405–40; his main conclusions are summarized in 'The "vetus Carnotensis" of Livy unmasked', in J. Diggle, J. B. Hall, H. D. Jocelyn (edd.), *Studies in Latin literature and its tradition in honour of C. O. Brink* (The Cambridge Philological Society, Suppl. Vol. 15), Cambridge 1989, pp. 97–112.

The importance of Avignon emerges from the study of any text which passed through it. The significance of its role in channelling manuscripts to Italy was pointed out by Ullman in 1941 (*Philological Quarterly*, 20 (1941), 213–17 = *Studies*, pp. 29–33) and recent studies of individual texts have dramatically substantiated his theory. For broader discussions of Avignon as a cultural centre, see F. Simone, *Il Rinascimento*, pp. 9–24; W. Braxton Ross, 'Giovanni Colonna, historian at Avignon', *Speculum*, 45 (1970), 533–45.

Billanovich, *I primi umanisti*, pp. 29–33, deals with the rediscovery of the Montecassino manuscripts and Zanobi da Strada's part in it.

IV. *Coluccio Salutati (1331–1406)*

We are fortunate in having two full-length studies of Salutati: B. L. Ullman, *The humanism of Coluccio Salutati* (Medioevo e Umanesimo, 4), Padua 1963; R. G. Witt, *Hercules at the crossroads: the life, works, and thought of Coluccio Salutati* (Duke Monographs in Medieval and Renaissance Studies, 6), Durham, N.C., 1983. The latter is remarkable for the full picture it presents of Salutati himself and for the light it throws on many aspects of early humanism. For Salutati's influence on the development of humanistic script, see Ullman, *The origin and development*, pp. 11–19; A. C. de la Mare, *Handwriting*, pp. 30–43. An important passage on scribal corruption in Salutati's *De fato et fortuna* is printed by Silvia Rizzo in an appendix to her book *Il lessico filologico degli umanisti* (Sussidi eruditi, 26), Rome 1973, pp. 341-4.

V. *The great age of discovery: Poggio (1380-1459)*

The remarkable story of Poggio's discoveries may still be followed in Sabbadini, though the details need to be checked against recent work on the individual texts concerned: for Poggio's part in the tradition of Ammianus, for instance, see R. Cappelletto, 'Marginalia di Poggio in due codici di Ammiano Marcellino (Vat. lat. 1873 e Vat. lat. 2969)', *Miscellanea Augusto Campana* (Medioevo e Umanesimo, 44-5), Padua 1981, pp. 189-211; for Marius Victorinus, M. De Nonno, 'Tradizione e diffusione di Mario Vittorino grammatico', *Rivista di filologia*, 116 (1988), 5-59. His discoveries come to life in his letters. There is a new edition of these by H. Harth, *Poggio Bracciolini, Lettere*, vols. 1-3, Florence 1984-7; the letters dealing with his manuscript discoveries have been collected and translated by P. W. G. Gordan, *Two Renaissance book hunters: the letters of Poggius Bracciolini to Nicolaus de Niccolis* (Records of Civilization: Sources and Studies, 91), New York 1974. See too A. C. Clark, *Inventa Italorum* (Anecdota Oxoniensia, Classical Series, Part 11), Oxford 1909. Poggio's expedition to Cluny in the spring of 1415 remains dubious: cf. T. Foffano, 'Niccolì, Cosimo e le ricerche di Poggio nelle biblioteche francesi', *IMU* 12 (1969), 113-28.

The works of Ullman and De la Mare cited above deal with Poggio as scribe and calligrapher. It now seems likely that humanistic script was not simply invented by Poggio, but developed about 1400 in Florence, with Poggio, Niccoli, and perhaps Salutati all contributing to its formation: see De la Mare, 'Humanistic script: the first ten years', in F. Kraft and D. Wuttke (edd.), *Das Verhältnis der Humanisten zum Buch*, Boppard 1977, pp. 89-110. Two candidates for Poggio's first attempt at the new script have been put forward: A. C. de la Mare and D. F. S. Thomson, 'Poggio's earliest manuscript?', *IMU* 16 (1973), 179-95 (Venice, Marc. Lat. XII.80 (4167) of Catullus); Gius. Billanovich, 'Alle origini della scrittura umanistica: Padova 1261 e Firenze 1397', *Miscellanea Campana*, 125-40 (Vat. Pal. lat. 903 of Valerius Maximus). Both appear to belong more to the early days of humanistic script than to Poggio himself: on the former, see D. S. McKie, 'Salutati, Poggio and Codex M of Catullus', *Studies in Latin literature* (cited above, section III), pp. 66-96.

The detailed work of C. Questa on Poggio's contribution to the textual tradition of the twelve plays of Plautus permits some assessment of his philological ability: *Per la storia del testo di Plauto nell' umanesimo* 1: *La 'recensio' di Poggio Bracciolini*, Rome 1968; there is an important study of his work on the Basilicanus of Cicero's *Speeches* (Vatican, Arch. S. Pietro H.25) in Silvia Rizzo, *Il lessico filologico*, pp. 327-38. The standard biography is that of E. Walser, *Poggius Florentinus: Leben und Werke*, Leipzig 1914; for a brief and up-to-date account, see the article by E. Bigi and A. Petrucci in *Dizionario bibliografico degli Italiani*, vol. 13 (1971), 640-6.

The discovery that the best copy of the lost vetus Cluniacensis is the handiwork of Nicholas of Clamanges was made by Gilbert Ouy (cf. *Annuaire de l'École pratique des Hautes Études* (IVe Section. Sciences hist. et philol.), 1965-6, 259).

There is increasing respect for Niccolò Niccoli's contribution to humanism, and not least to the recovery, collation, and collecting together of ancient texts; see most recently P. A. Stadter, 'Niccolò Niccoli: winning back the knowledge of the ancients', *Vestigia. Studi in onore di Giuseppe Billanovich* (Storia e letteratura, 162-3), Rome 1984, pp. 747-64. For the personal attacks on Niccoli and a glimpse of the less attractive side of the humanist world, M. C. Davies, 'An Emperor without Clothes? Niccolò Niccoli under attack', *IMU* 30 (1987), 95-148.

The evidence for the survival of the Murbach Velleius into August 1786 was published by A. Allgeier in *Miscellanea Mercati*, 6 (Studi e Testi, 126), 1946, 457ff.

VI. *Latin scholarship in the fifteenth century: Valla and Politian*

Among recent works on the philology of the fifteenth century and later mention must be made of Silvia Rizzo, *Il lessico filologico degli umanisti*; E. J. Kenney, *The classical text*, Berkeley 1974; R. Pfeiffer, *History of classical scholarship 1300-1850*, Oxford 1976; A. Grafton, *Joseph Scaliger. A study in the history of classical scholarship, I. Textual criticism and exegesis*, Oxford 1983; A. Grafton and L. Jardine, *From humanism to the humanities*, London 1986.

On the building up of Renaissance libraries, see: B. L. Ullman and P. A. Stadter, *The public library of Renaissance Florence: Niccolò Niccoli, Cosimo de' Medici and the library of San Marco* (Medioevo e Umanesimo, 10), Padua 1972; C. L. Stinger, *The Renaissance in Rome*, Bloomington 1985, pp. 282-91.

The *Opera omnia* of Valla have been reprinted with a preface by E. Garin and other material, 2 vols., Turin 1962. A different recension of his *Adnotationes in Novum Testamentum* from that printed by Erasmus has been discovered and edited by A. Perosa, Florence 1970. There are recent editions of other works too: *De falso credita et ementita Constantini Donatione*, ed. W. Setz (Monumenta Germaniae Historica, Quellen zur Geistes-geschichte des Mittelalters), Weimar 1976; *Laurentii Valle Antidotum in Facium*, ed. M. Regoliosi, Padua 1981. Good examples of his work on Latin texts are provided by Livy and Quintilian. For Livy see Gius. Billanovich, 'Petrarch and the textual tradition of Livy', *JWI* 14 (1951), 137-51, 'Le *Emendationes in T. Livium* del Valla e il Codex Regius di Livio', *IMU* 1 (1958), 245-64 (with M. Ferraris) and 'Un altro Livio corretto dal Valla (Valenza, Biblioteca della Cattedrale, 173)', ibid., 265-75; M. Regoliosi, 'Lorenzo Valla, Antonio Panormita, Giacomo Curlo e le emendazioni a Livio', *IMU* 24 (1981), 287-316, and 'Le congetture a Livio del Valla. Metodo e problemi', in *Lorenzo Valla e l'umanesimo italiano*, Atti del Convegno Internazionale di Studi Umanistici (Parma, 18-19 Oct. 1984), ed. O. Besomi and M. Regoliosi (Medioevo e Umanesimo, 59), Padua 1986, pp. 51-71. For Quintilian, M. Winterbottom, 'Fifteenth-century manuscripts of Quintilian', *CQ* 17 (1967), 356-63; L. Cesarini Martinelli, 'Le postille di Lorenzo Valla al' "Institutio Oratoria" di Quintiliano, in *Lorenzo Valla e l'umanesimo italiano*, pp. 21-50.

A good idea of the range of Politian's activities is given by the catalogue of an exhibition held at the Biblioteca Laurenziana in 1954 (*Mostra del Poliziano*, a cura di A. Perosa, Florence 1955). See also *Il Poliziano e il suo tempo*, *Atti del IV convegno internazionale di studi sul Rinascimento*, Florence 1957; I. Maier, *Les Manuscrits d'Ange Politien* (Travaux d'humanisme et Renaissance, no. 70), Geneva 1965; V. Branca, *Poliziano e l'umanesimo della parola* (Saggi, 655), Turin 1983.

The recently discovered Centuria has been published as *Angelo Poliziano, Miscellaneorum Centuria Secunda*, ed. V. Branca–M. Pastore Stocchi, vols. 1-4, Florence 1972. We are fortunate in still having the autograph notes which Politian used for his university courses on Suetonius and Statius' *Silvae*: G. Gardenal, *Il Poliziano e Svetonio. Contributo alla storia della filologia umanistica*, Florence 1975 (but see L. Cesarini Martinelli, *Rinascimento*, 16 (1976), 111-31); L. Cesarini Martinelli, *Angelo Poliziano: commento inedito alle Selve di Stazio*, Florence 1978. The Bodleian *postille* on the *Epistula Sapphus* have been published by M. Kubo in *Mediterraneus*, 8 (1985), 3-41 and plates; Livia Castano Musicò is about to publish his notes on the *Georgics*. The Greek epigrams were edited by A. Ardizzoni, Florence 1951.

On his place in the history of scholarship and especially the development of the stemmatic method, see A. Grafton, 'On the scholarship of Politian and its context', *JWI* 40 (1977), 150-88.

More will be found on the scholarship of both Valla and Politian in the works cited at the beginning of this section.

The critical work of Ermolao Barbaro has been published by G. Pozzi, *Hermolai Barbari castigationes Plinianae et in Pomponium Melam*, 4 vols., Padua 1973-9, and studied by V. Branca, in *Storia della cultura veneta*, vol. 3, Vicenza 1980, pp. 123-65.

VII. *Greek studies: diplomats, refugees, and book collectors*

The primary sources for this section, together with an extensive discussion, will be found in A. Pertusi, *Leonzio Pilato fra Petrarca e Boccaccio*, Venice-Rome 1964 (pp. 62ff. deal with his copy of Homer). F. Di Benedetto, 'Leonzio, Omero e le "Pandette" ', *IMU* 12 (1969), 53-112, has shown that Leonzio Pilato owned the Florentine Pandects and translated into Latin the Greek quotations of the *Digest*. Petrarch's copy of Plato has been identified as Paris gr. 1807 by A. Diller, *CPh* 59 (1964), 270-2. One odd fact which needs to be explained is the failure of the Paduan prehumanists mentioned in section II of this chapter to profit from the learning of Pietro d'Abano (fl. c. 1300), who is known to have visited Constantinople and to have done some translations of Greek texts, especially Galen; in one or two cases he completed works left unfinished by Burgundio. For a survey of what is known about him see M. Th. d'Alverny, *Medioevo* 11 (1985), 19-64.

For Chrysoloras see G. Cammelli, *Manuele Crisolora*, Florence 1941. The way that most humanists had to learn Greek is made clear by R. Sabbadini, *Il metodo degli umanisti*, Florence 1922, pp. 17-27, who cites a letter of Ambrogio Traversari about his own experience and a letter of Aldus to Alberto Pio referring to the use of these methods by Ermolao Barbaro, Pico della Mirandola, and Politian. G. Cammelli, *Demetrio Calcondila*, Florence 1954, p. 7, quotes a letter of Giovanni Antonio Campano in which he complains that he has not yet been able to learn Greek for want of a tutor.

On the discovery of manuscripts in general see R. Sabbadini, *Le scoperte dei codici latini e greci ne' secoli xiv e xv*, reprinted with additions, Florence 1967.

VIII. *Greek scholarship in the fifteenth century: Bessarion and Politian*

A short and up-to-date account of Bessarion is given by L. Labowsky in the *Dizionario biografico degli Italiani*. The fundamental work is L. Mohler, *Kardinal Bessarion als Theologe, Humanist und Staatsmann*, Paderborn 1923-42; in the third volume, sub-titled *Aus Bessarions Gelehrtenkreis*, pp. 70-87, will be found the pamphlet expounding his views on the status of the Vulgate translation. His palaeographical researches are outlined in his letter to Alexios Lascaris Philanthropenos. See also J. Gill, *The council of Florence*,

Cambridge 1959. To mark the quincentenary of his donation to Venice an exhibition was mounted; the catalogue, which contains also a text of his act of donation, was published as *Cento codici Bessarionei*, a cura di T. G. Leporace e E. Mioni, Venice 1968.

In connection with the advances made by Valla and Bessarion in New Testament criticism it should be mentioned that Bessarion in due course came to be aware of an important medieval scholar, Nicholas Maniacutia (d. c. 1150), deacon of San Lorenzo in Damaso in Rome. He was an expert critic who took advice from learned Jews in order to be able to appreciate better the meaning of the Old Testament. His activity is usefully surveyed by V. Peri, *Aevum*, 41 (1967), 67–90.

For Valla's *Adnotationes* see the edition by A. Perosa cited above (VI) and in particular p. xxxiv n. 64.

The relevant bibliography on Politian has been given in the notes to section VI.

IX. *The first Greek printed texts: Aldus Manutius and Marcus Musurus*

The authorities on the early printing of Greek are R. Proctor, *The printing of Greek in the 15th century*, Oxford 1900, reprinted 1966, and V. Scholderer, *Greek printing types 1465–1927*, London 1927; see also a paper by the latter on 'Printers and readers in Italy in the fifteenth century', *PBA* 35 (1949), 1–23. The great reduction in book prices brought about by the new invention is made clear by Giovanni Andrea De Bussi, bishop of Aleria, in his preface to the Rome edition of Saint Jerome's letters printed in 1468; he says (fol. 1ᵛ) that books are now available at one fifth of the price that they used to command. But this boast naturally applied to Latin and vernacular texts only. Knowledge of Greek remained for some time a rarity; one may wonder if the frequent tags and quotations of it in the writings of Erasmus, who could count on a very wide readership, imply that the situation had changed for the better in the first two or three decades of the sixteenth century.

On Aldus and Musurus one may consult D. J. Geanakoplos, *Greek scholars in Venice*, Cambridge, Mass., 1962, reprinted 1973 with the title *Byzantium and the Renaissance*. It does not, however, discuss the scholarship of either man in sufficient detail to permit us to form an estimate of their capacities as textual critics, and here further research is required. The activities of the publisher are described well in M. Lowry, *The world of Aldus Manutius*, Oxford 1979, and our understanding of his Greek type is put on a new footing by N. Barker, *Aldus Manutius and the development of Greek script and type in the fifteenth century*, Sandy Hook Conn. 1985. M. Sicherl gives an admirable account of Aldine Greek editions in the exhibition catalogue *Griechische Handschriften und Aldinen*, Wolfenbüttel 1978, pp. 119-49. Aldus' prefaces are edited by G. Orlandi, *Aldo Manuzio editore: dediche, prefazioni, note ai testi*, Milan 1975. The favourable judgement on Musurus' edition of Hesychius comes from K. Latte's edition, vol. 1, Copenhagen 1953, p. xxxiii; the addition to the text of Moschus is dealt with by W. Bühler in his edition (Hermes Einzelschriften 13), Wiesbaden 1960, p. 14; fresh light was thrown on the Aristophanes scholia by N. G. Wilson, *CQ* 12 (1962), 32-47 (Musurus' contribution is less substantial than was once believed).

For the history of the Marciana library, which was very badly housed and difficult of access for more than half a century after Bessarion's donation, see L. Labowsky, *Bessarion's library and the Biblioteca Marciana*, Rome 1979.

X. *Erasmus*

Erasmus' classical scholarship is described in R. Pfeiffer, *History of classical scholarship 1300-1850*, Oxford 1976, pp. 71-81. Pfeiffer cites a revealing aphorism: incorrect punctuation, a tiny detail in itself, is enough to give rise to heresy (*tantula res gignit haereticum sensum*). Although this notion is found in Photius, there is no sign that Erasmus knew his writings. P. S. Allen, *PBA* 11 (1924), 349-68, argues that Erasmus' chief services to learning were in editing patristic texts, mainly of Latin Fathers (his attempts to assemble material for an edition of Chrysostom never made enough progress for printing to begin). One important facet of Erasmus' activity is dealt with by E. Rummel, *Erasmus as a translator of the classics*, Toronto 1985.

For the preparation of the Alcalá Bible and Erasmus' New Testament see the summary in B. M. Metzger, *The Text of the New Testament*, Oxford 1968[2], pp. 96-103. Erasmus' use of manuscripts for his edition and its subsequent revised impressions has to be worked out from various sources, including his letters and passing remarks in his commentaries on the New Testament (the idea of a systematic exposition of the manuscripts used for an edition is relatively modern). The facts stated in the text depend on P. S. Allen's introduction to letter 373 in vol. 2 of *Opus epistolarum Desiderii Erasmi Roterodami*, Oxford 1906-54, pp. 164-6. Allen's account seems to be reliable, with the possible exception of his statement about the Leicester codex. With regard to the Vatican codex B (Vat. gr. 1209), Erasmus had learned of its existence in 1521, and when he was reminded of its importance some years later by the Spanish humanist and theologian Sepúlveda he failed to respond as he should have done. In his reply to Sepúlveda he suggested that a Greek manuscript which supported some readings of the Vulgate had probably been tampered with, not realizing that the great age of B made this relatively implausible; and he advanced the exaggerated but not entirely unreasonable proposition that the only way to be sure of recovering the original Greek was to go back to the text as cited by patristic authorities of the third, fourth, and fifth centuries (letter 2905, written in 1534). An excellent new study of Erasmus is J. H. Bentley, *Humanists and Holy Writ*, Princeton 1983; see pp. 153-4, 158 on the maxim *difficilior lectio potior*. (On this point it is worth recording here a fact kindly communicated to us by Dr R. J. Durling: Galen is very close to this concept. He can be found expressing a preference for old words which are more difficult of explanation (*Corpus medicorum graecorum* 5.10.2.2, p. 178, 17-18) and understands that they would have been changed into something easier if alteration of the text had occurred (ibid., 121.17-18).)

With regard to Erasmus' intentions in editing the New Testament, H. J. de Jonge, 'Novum Testamentum a nobis versum: the essence of Erasmus' edition of the New Testament', *JTS* 35 (1984), 394-413, argues that this work is not to be treated as an edition of the Greek text. But in defence of the conventional view one may say: (1) Erasmus collated MSS. in both languages, so there must be a sense in which he is trying to establish the precise nature of the *graeca veritas*, and that procedure, however incomplete by our standards, was not slapdash by the standards of the time and must be thought of as putting him into the category of editor. (2) It is obvious why he puts emphasis on the Latin rather than the Greek: he wanted to be read and knew that only a tiny fraction of the educated class had enough Greek to follow the original (de Jonge realizes this, pp. 401, 406, without drawing the necessary conclusion). (3) There could have been a prudential reason for Erasmus' presentation of his work as essentially concerned with the Latin, if there were potential critics of his and Valla's idea of concentrating on the *graeca veritas*.

The story of Erasmus and the *comma Johanneum* may have been slightly embroidered; see H. J. de Jonge, *Ephemerides theologicae Lovanienses* 56 (1980), 381-9. But it is clear that Erasmus exposed himself to opponents acting in bad faith.

A good way of approaching the *Adagia* is to read M. M. Phillips, *The 'Adages' of Erasmus*, Cambridge 1964; on pp. 65-9 there is an account of the polemic arising from Erasmus' stay in Aldus' house. His stay is also described by D. J. Geanakoplos, *Greek Scholars in Venice*; see especially pp. 273-5 for the question of the so-called Erasmian pronunciation of Greek.

For further orientation and bibliography, P. Petitmengin, 'Comment étudier l'activité d'Érasme éditeur de textes antiques', *Colloquia Erasmiana Turonensia*, vol. 1 (Paris 1972), pp. 217–22. See also E. Bloch, 'Erasmus and the Froben Press: the making of an editor', *Library Quarterly*, 35 (1965), 109–20.

On Seneca, L. D. Reynolds, *The Medieval Tradition of Seneca's Letters*, Oxford 1965, pp. 4–6, W. Trillitzsch, *Philologus*, 109 (1965), 270–93, M. M. Phillips, op. cit., 15–17.

CHAPTER 5

I. *The Counter-Reformation: the High Renaissance in Italy*

Erasmus' *Ciceronianus* has been edited with substantial prolegomena by A. Gambaro, Brescia 1965. He discusses the history of the controversy, but it is also worth consulting *'Attic' and baroque prose style: the anti-Ciceronian movement*, essays by Morris W. Croll, edited by Patrick-Evans-Wallace, Princeton, N.J., 1966 (paperback 1969). For the Estienne family see especially E. Armstrong, *Robert Estienne, royal printer*, Cambridge 1954. Vettori's work on the Latin Aristotle is discussed by B. Schneider, *Die mittelalterlichen griechisch-lateinischen Uebersetzungen der Aristotelischen Rhetorik*, Berlin 1971, pp. 73–6. Robortello's scholarship has been discussed by A. Carlini, 'L'attività filologica di Francesco Robortello', *Atti dell' Accademia di Udine*, 7 (1967), 36ff. On Fulvio Orsini the standard work is still P. de Nolhac, *La Bibliothèque de Fulvio Orsini* (Bibl. de l'École des Hautes Études, 74), Paris 1887. On the work of Catholic scholars dealing with patristic texts see P. Petitmengin in A. C. Dionisotti, A. Grafton, J. Kraye (edd.), *The uses of Greek and Latin*, London 1988, pp. 127–53. For the Vatican edition of Saint Augustine see P. Petitmengin, 'Le Saint Augustin de la typographie vaticane', *Recherches augustiniennes*, 4 (1966), 199–251. For Thomas James see N. R. Ker, 'Thomas James' collation of Gregory, Cyprian and Ambrose', *Bodleian Library Record*, 4 (1952), 16–32.

II. *The beginnings of humanism and scholarship in France*

For early French humanism one may consult, in addition to F. Simone, *Il Rinascimento francese* and other works mentioned in the notes to the previous chapter: A. H. T. Levi (ed.), *Humanism in France at the end of the Middle Ages and in the early Renaissance*, Manchester 1970; R. Pfeiffer, *History of classical scholarship 1300–1850*, pp. 99–123; G. Ouy, 'In search of the earliest traces of

French Humanism', *The Library Chronicle* (University of Pennsylvania, Philadelphia), 43 (1978), 1–38.

On the early days of printing in France, see now J. Veyrin-Forrer, 'Aux origines de l'imprimerie française: l'atelier de la Sorbonne et ses mécènes, 1470–1473', in *L'art du livre à l'Imprimerie Nationale*, Paris 1973, pp. 32–53. On the importance of printing in the Renaissance generally, E. L. Eisenstein, *The printing press as an agent of change*, Cambrige 1979.

Short accounts of Budé are provided by L. Delaruelle, *Guillaume Budé: les origines, les débuts, les idées maîtresses*, Paris 1907; J. Plattard, *Guillaume Budé et les origines de l'humanisme français*, Paris 1923 (reprinted 1966). See also R. R. Bolgar, 'Humanism as a value system with reference to Budé and Vives', *Humanism in France*, pp. 199–215, and the Catalogue of the Budé Exhibition, *VIIIe Congrès international Guillaume Budé*, Paris 1968. The *De transitu* has been reprinted with a French translation by M. Lebel, Sherbrooke, 1973. There is a classic monograph on the Collège de France by A. Lefranc, *Histoire du Collège de France depuis ses origines jusqu'à la fin du premier Empire*, Paris 1893.

There are not as many recent studies of individual French scholars of this period as one would wish. An exception is V. Hall, *Life of Julius Caesar Scaliger (1484–1558)* (*Trans. Amer. Philosoph. Soc*, N.S. 40, Part 2), Philadelphia, Pa., 1950, and Mark Pattison's classic *Isaac Casaubon*, Oxford 1892[2], reprinted Geneva 1970) retains its value. Detailed bibliography may be found in A. Cioranesco, *Bibliographie de la littérature française du XVIe siècle*, Paris 1959.

For Turnebus' manuscript of Plautus, see W. M. Lindsay, *The Codex Turnebi of Plautus*, Oxford 1898 (reprinted Hildesheim 1970). K. Müller's edition of Petronius (Munich 1961, pp. xiv–xxiv) gives an insight into the complex history of his text in the sixteenth century. Scaliger's classical scholarship has now received full treatment in A. Grafton, *Joseph Scaliger. A study in the history of classical scholarship, I: textual criticism and exegesis*, Oxford 1983. The second volume will examine his studies of ancient chronology; these are to be found partly in his *De emendatione temporum* (1583, 1598[2]), partly in the appendix to his Eusebius of 1606 entitled *Isagogicorum chronologiae canonum libri tres*.

In his 'Dichter und Philologen im französischen Humanismus', *Antike und Abendland*, 7 (1958), 73–83, Pfeiffer studies the interaction between classical scholarship and poetry at the time of the Pléiade; also in his *History of classical scholarship*, pp. 102–7.

For an account of Casaubon's work on Aeschylus, see E. Fraenkel, *Aeschylus, Agamemnon*, vol. 1, Oxford 1950, pp. 36–8 and Appendix I.

III. *The Netherlands in the sixteenth and seventeenth centuries*

The study of the scholarship of the Netherlands is facilitated by some good articles in the *Biographie Nationale*, published by the Académie Royale des Sciences et des Lettres et des Beaux-Arts de Belgique (1866–1944, with later Supplements) and by A. Gerlo and H. D. L. Vervliet, *Bibliographie de l'humanisme des anciens Pays-Bas*, Brussels 1972. Isaac Vossius qualifies for an entry in the *Dictionary of National Biography*. Also useful are L. Müller, *Geschichte der klassischen Philologie in den Niederlanden*, Leipzig 1869; G. Cohen, *Écrivains français en Hollande dans la première moitié du XVIIe siècle*, Paris 1920. On Plantin and his successors, see *The Golden Compass. A history and evaluation of the printing and publishing activities of the Officina Plantiniana at Antwerp*, 2 vols., Amsterdam 1969–72; M. D. Feld, 'The early evolution of the authentic text', *Harvard Library Bulletin*, 26 (1978), 104ff.

It is not surprising, in view of the amount of time and effort expended on editing texts and producing critical miscellanea, that there should be a market for theoretical studies of textual criticism. Canter, who had been anticipated by Robortello, was succeeded in 1597 by a German scholar, Caspar Schoppe, whose *De arte critica* did for Latin texts what Canter had done for Greek; it also attempts a brief history of textual criticism by reviewing critics ancient and modern. Exactly a century later appeared the first edition of the more ambitious *Ars critica* of Jean Le Clerc. On Schoppe see M. D'Addio, *Il pensiero politico dello Scioppio e il machiavelismo del seicento*, Milan 1962; on Jean Le Clerc, A. Barnes, *Jean Le Clerc (1657–1736) et la République des lettres*, Paris 1938. These treatises have been studied by A. Bernardini and G. Righi, *Il concetto di filologia e di cultura classica nel mondo moderno*, Bari 1947 (but cf. A. Momigliano, *Contributo alla storia degli studi classici*, Rome 1955, pp. 393–5); there is a critical account of them in E. J. Kenney, *The classical text*, ch. 2.

Modius' search for manuscripts has been fully documented and discussed by P. Lehmann, *Franciscus Modius als Handschriftenforscher* (Quellen und Untersuchungen zur lateinischen Philologie des Mittelalters, 3.1), Munich 1908.

For two recent views on the Blandinius of Horace, see Pasquali, *Storia della tradizione*, pp. 381ff.; E. Fraenkel, *Horace*, Oxford 1957, pp. 97ff.

Lipsius' methods have been studied by J. Ruysschaert, *Juste Lipse et les Annales de Tacite: une méthode de critique textuelle au XVIe siècle*, Louvain 1949. See too C. O. Brink, 'Justus Lipsius and the text of Tacitus', *JRS* 41 (1951), 32–51; F. R. D. Goodyear, *The Annals of Tacitus*, vol. 1, Cambridge 1972, pp. 8–10; J. Ruysschaert, 'Juste Lipse, éditeur de Tacite', *Studi urbinati*, 53 (1979), 47–61.

For the manuscripts used by Heinsius, see M. D. Reeve, 'Heinsius' manuscripts of Ovid', *RhM* 117 (1974), 133–66; 119 (1976), 65–78. The correspondence of N. Heinsius and Jacques Dupuy (1646–56) has been published by H. Bots, The Hague 1971.

IV. *Richard Bentley (1662–1742): classical and theological studies*

Bentley is treated at considerable length here because of his position in both classical and biblical studies, and it did not seem possible to do justice to him without giving some details of his life and work. Sir R. C. Jebb, *Bentley*, London 1882, is a lively and entertaining account with bibliography. *The Epistola ad Joannem Millium* has been reprinted with an introduction by G. P. Goold, Toronto 1962 (note that the date of Malalas is incorrectly given as the eighth or ninth century).

The history of biblical scholarship is set out by B. Metzger, *The text of the New Testament*, Oxford 1968², pp. 95ff., but we have given here rather more detail of Bentley's *Proposals* and taken a different view of the importance of Richard Simon; on him one may consult the study of Jean Steinmann, *Richard Simon et les origines de l'exégèse biblique*, Desclée de Brouwer 1960, but there too the important details are not always fully brought out. Another useful study is P. Auvray, *Richard Simon 1638–1712, étude bio-bibliographique avec des textes inédits*, Paris 1974. The facts recounted in the text are drawn from chapters 29–33 of the *Histoire critique*, principally from 29. Another good account of New Testament textual criticism is given by J. N. Birdsall in *The Cambridge History of the Bible*, vol. 1, Cambridge 1970, pp. 308–77.

V. *The origins of palaeography*

For a convenient sketch of the history of palaeography one may consult L. Traube, *Geschichte der Paläographie*, printed in vol. 1 of his *Vorlesungen und Abhandlungen*, Munich 1909, pp. 13–80. David Knowles, *Great historical enterprises: problems in monastic history*, London 1963, pp. 33–62, gives an attractive short account of the achievements of the Maurists in scholarship, without giving quite as much detail as one might wish about palaeography. His essay on the Bollandists, ibid., pp. 1–32, should also be consulted for the life and work of van Papenbroeck; he was one of the continuators of Jean Bolland's great project for a comprehensive edition of the lives of the saints, *Acta Sanctorum*; an impressive series of volumes has been, and is still being, produced by a small team of Jesuits in Belgium, who despite some interruptions due to wars and revolutions have maintained an astonishing academic tradition over the centuries. See further P. Peeters, *L'œuvre des Bollandistes*, 2nd ed., Brussels 1961.

Traube and Knowles give all the essential guidance for further reading about the Maurists and Maffei. But on the latter one may also refer to an essay by A. Momigliano, 'Mabillon's Italian disciples', in *Terzo contributo alla storia degli studi classici e del mondo antico*, Rome 1966, pp. 135-52. Maffei's letters, in addition to the works mentioned by Traube, contain some statements about palaeography; see nos. 158 and 160 in the *Epistolario*, ed. C. Garibotto, Milan 1955, pp. 199-201, 203-4. His palaeographical insight is perhaps partially anticipated in Janus Lascaris' letter of dedication prefaced to his edition of the *Greek Anthology*.

Perhaps the earliest catalogue of a manuscript collection is that published as a memorial to the learned Spanish bishop Antonio Agustín, *Antonii Augustini Tarraconensium antistitis bibliothecae graecae anacephaleosis*, Tarragona 1586. A few years later appeared D. Hoeschel's *Catalogus graecorum codicum qui sunt in bibliotheca Reipublicae Augustanae Vindelicae*, Augsburg 1595; this is a scholarly publication with indications in the margins of the extent to which the texts have been published. Also valuable, if somewhat less detailed, was Thomas James' *Ecloga Oxonio-Cantabrigiensis* of 1600, giving an account of the collections of the two English universities.

VI. *Discoveries of texts since the Renaissance*

(a) *Palimpsests.* The first comprehensive account of Latin palimpsests is that of E. Chatelain, 'Les Palimpsestes latins', *Annuaire, École pratique des Hautes Études, Section des sciences hist. et philol.* 1904 (published 1903), pp. 5-42. This has now been largely superseded by E. A. Lowe, '*Codices rescripti*: a list of Latin palimpsests with stray observations on their origin', *Mélanges Eugène Tisserant*, vol. 5, Vatican 1964 (Studi e Testi 235), 67-112, reprinted in *Palaeographical papers*, 2. 480-519. S. Timpanaro provides an excellent account of both Angelo Mai and the early history of palimpsest discovery in 'Angelo Mai', *Atene e Roma*, N.S. 1 (1956), 3-34. For the new palimpsest fragment of Fronto, see B. Bischoff, 'Der Fronto-Palimpsest der Mauriner', *Sitz. Bayer. Akad. der Wiss., Phil.-Hist. Kl.* (1958.2). Further information can be sought in the editions of the texts concerned. For the application of electronic camera and image-processing techniques to erased writing, see J. F. Benton, A. R. Gillespie, J. M. Soha, 'Digital image-processing applied to the photography of manuscripts. With examples drawn from the Pincus MS. of Arnald of Villanova', *Scriptorium* 33 (1979), 40-55.

(b) *Papyri.* On papyri in general see the works cited above on Chapter 1

(I). In addition Sir Harold Bell, *Egypt from Alexander the Great to the Arab conquest*, Oxford 1948, provides an excellent introduction from a cultural and historical point of view.

The codex containing Menander's *Dyscolus* has given us in addition a substantial proportion of his *Aspis* and *Samia*; the fragments of the latter overlap to some extent with those already known, with the result that in these passages we possess two uncommonly early witnesses to the text of a classical author.

Literary papyri, including the very small number of Latin texts among them, are listed with a bibliography by R. A. Pack, *The Greek and Latin literary texts from Greco-Roman Egypt*, Ann Arbor, Mich., 1965. For statistics showing how the main authors are represented at various dates see W. H. Willis, *GRBS* 9 (1968), 205–41. Latin papyri are surveyed in R. Cavenaille, *Corpus papyrorum latinarum*, Wiesbaden 1958. An important recent addition is the scrap of Gallus, published by R. D. Anderson, R. G. M. Nisbet, P. J. Parsons, *JRS* 69 (1979), 125–55. The fragment of Livy has been edited with full description and commentary by B. Bravo and M. Griffin, 'Un frammento del libro XI di Tito Livio?', *Athenaeum* 66 (1988), 447–521. It is now in the Coptic Museum in Cairo (inv. N15/86). Another useful reference work is J. van Haelst, *Catalogue des papyrus littéraires juifs et chrétiens*, Paris 1976.

(c) *Other manuscript discoveries.* A history of the Homeric Question is given by Adam Parry in the introduction to the collected papers of his father Milman Parry, *The making of Homeric verse*, Oxford 1971, pp. xiii–xv.

Matthaei's find is discussed by O. von Gebhardt, *Zentralblatt für Bibliothekswesen* 15 (1898), 442–58.

Leopardi's disappointing experience is recounted by S. Timpanaro in *Differenze*, 9 (*Studi in memoria di Carlo Ascheri*), Urbino 1970, pp. 357–79.

Heiberg's find of Archimedes was announced in *Hermes*, 42 (1907), 235ff. On Juvenal VI and Saint Cyprian see J. G. Griffith, *Hermes*, 91 (1963), 104–14. For the new letter of Saint Cyprian see also M. Bévenot, *The tradition of manuscripts: a study in the transmission of St. Cyprian's treatises*, Oxford 1961. The Epigrammata Bobiensia were edited by A. Campana and F. Munari, Rome 1955. For the new lines of Rutilius Namatianus recovered from Turin F.IV 25, see M. Ferrari, 'Spigolature bobbiesi, I: In margine ai *Codices Latini Antiquiores*, II: Frammenti ignoti di Rutilio Namaziano', *IMU* 16 (1973), 1–41. The newly discovered letters of Augustine have been edited by J. Divjak, *Sancti Aurelii Augustini Opera, Epistulae ex duobus codicibus nuper in lucem prolatae* (CSEL 88), Vienna 1981. The two manuscripts containing the letters are Paris lat. 16861 and Marseilles, Bibl. Mun. 209, of the twelfth and fifteenth centuries respectively.

(d) *Epigraphic texts.* Roberto Weiss, in *The Renaissance discovery of classical antiquity*, Oxford 1969, traces the beginnings of an interest in the tangible remains of antiquity. For the impact of inscriptions on literary texts, see the section 'Rapports avec la littérature' of the 'Bulletin épigraphique' of J. and L. Robert in the *Revue des études grecques.*

The *Res gestae* of Augustus, sometimes referred to as the *Monumentum Ancyranum*, has been frequently edited and it will suffice to mention the editions of J. Gagé, Paris 1935, and P. A. Brunt–J. M. Moore, Oxford 1967. The *Laudatio Turiae* has been edited with a translation and commentary by M. Durry, *Éloge funèbre d'une matrone romaine*, Paris 1950. The Lyons tablet was first published by G. Paradin in his *De antiquo statu Burgundiae*, Lyons 1542.

For the monument of Antiochus of Commagene and its importance for the history of ancient prose style, see K. Humann and O. Puchstein, *Reisen in Kleinasien und Nordsyrien*, Berlin 1890, and E. Norden, *Die antike Kunstprosa*, 2nd ed., Leipzig–Berlin 1909, vol. 1, pp. 140ff.

Diogenes of Oenoanda has been recently re-edited and studied by C. W. Chilton, *Diogenis Oenoandensis fragmenta*, Leipzig 1967; *Diogenes of Oenoanda: The Fragments*, Oxford 1971. There is an important article on the inscription by J. Irigoin, *Studi filologici e storici in onore di Vittorio De Falco*, Naples 1971, pp. 477–85; and for recent progress in the finding of new fragments, see M. F. Smith, *Anatolian Studies* 29 (1979), 68–89 (with, on pp. 87–8, a bibliography of recent finds).

For the early Christian hymn, see P. Maas, *Kleine Schriften*, Munich 1973, p. 315. The statue of Socrates and another epigraphic testimony to the text of Plato are discussed by A. Carlini, *Studi sulla tradizione antica e medioevale del Fedone*, Rome 1972, p. 74.

Pompeian graffiti have been collected and edited by E. Diehl, *Pompeianische Wandinschriften und Verwandtes*, 2nd ed. (Kleine Texte für Vorlesungen und Übungen 56), Berlin 1930. For the corpus of epigraphic poetry, see the relevant parts of the *Anthologia latina* edited by F. Bücheler and E. Lommatzsch, vols. 1–3, Leipzig 1930², 1897, 1926; E. Engström, *Carmina latina epigraphica*, Gothenburg 1911. The occurrence of *arma virumque* on ancient walls is documented by R. P. Hoogma, *Der Einfluss Vergils auf die Carmina Latina Epigraphica*, Amsterdam 1959, pp. 222f. The text of Propertius 3.16.13f. is discussed by M. E. Hubbard in 'Propertiana', *CQ* N.S. 18 (1968), 318f.

VII. *Epilogue*

The role of the classics and the advances of scholarship in the period which saw the growth of modern Europe constitute an exceptionally complex theme, which has not yet been the subject of a comprehensive and satisfying study. Some guidance may be had from Wilamowitz's famous brief sketch of the history of scholarship, *Geschichte der Philologie*, Berlin 1921, revised 1927, translated into English as *History of classical scholarship* by A. Harris, ed. H. Lloyd-Jones, London 1982, and from R. Pfeiffer, *History of classical scholarship 1300–1850*, Oxford 1976. There are also contributions in the two volumes edited by R. R. Bolgar, *Classical influences on European culture A.D. 1500–1700*, and *Classical influences on Western thought*, Cambridge 1976, 1979. A challenging hypothesis about changes in educational practice is put forward by A. Grafton and L. Jardine, *From humanism to the humanities*, London 1986. Readers with an interest in an important period of English scholarship should consult M. L. Clarke, *Greek studies in England 1700–1830*, Cambridge n.d. (1945). Further information is provided by C. O. Brink, *English classical scholarship: historical reflections on Bentley, Porson and Housman*, Cambridge 1986; this study is discussed at length by H. D. Jocelyn, *Philology and education*, Liverpool 1988. Wolf's *Prolegomena* have been translated into English with notes by A. Grafton, G. W. Most, and J. E. G. Zetzel, Princeton 1985.

CHAPTER 6

Our account of stemmatic theory and the history of its evolution depends on P. Maas, *Textual criticism*, Oxford 1958, and S. Timpanaro, *La genesi del metodo del Lachmann*, 3rd edition, Padua 1981. Timpanaro's second and third appendices are also important explorations of areas of stemmatic theory. Maas' exposition is so brief as to verge on the obscure, and some of the finer points of stemmatic theory require a full statement in order to make latent assumptions explicit. Timpanaro, *Maia*, 23 (1970), 289, pointed to one such assumption in the fourth of the inferences from our hypothetical stemma on p. 211, where we have added a parenthesis to meet the case: the agreement of one of the MSS. XYZ with β indicates the reading of α, *provided that* they readings of the other two of the MSS. XYZ disagree with each other; if they agree, as can happen, the tradition has been affected by contamination or emendation. L. Canfora, *Belfagor*, 23 (1968), 361–4, has directed attention to some other obscurities in Maas's presentation of the theory.

Limitations of the stemmatic method were emphasized by G. Pasquali, *Storia della tradizione e critica del testo*, 2nd ed., Florence 1952, and they have been urged more recently, but perhaps too passionately, by R. D. Dawe. *The collation and investigation of manuscripts of Aeschylus*, Cambridge 1964. We have tried to make it clear in our text that controversy on this subject is largely misplaced. Maas knew as well as anyone else that there is no simple answer to the problems of a contaminated tradition, but some critics have failed to notice his explicit statement on the matter. Others, perhaps unduly impressed by the wealth of examples in Pasquali's rather discursive but deservedly famous book, most of which is devoted to unusual traditions, have assumed that contamination is the rule rather than the exception, and that consequently Maas's theory is of no practical use. We doubt whether Pasquali could have wished to create this impression, and it must be stressed that in many traditions the amount of contamination that has taken place is not sufficient to prevent the useful application of stemmatic theory. It may be worth adding here that an interesting *eliminatio codicum* has recently been performed in the stemma of Aristotle's *Rhetoric*, where the tradition is not entirely free from contamination; see R. Kassel, *Der Text der Aristotelischen Rhetorik*, Berlin 1971, pp. 54-5.

An interesting and extremely complicated discussion has been conducted by scholars concerned with classical and medieval texts about the relative frequency of various types of stemma. It was begun by Joseph Bédier, who observed that an extraordinarily high proportion of the stemmata reconstructed by editors of medieval texts have two main branches, in other words they entail the view that two copies, and no more than two, were made from the archetype. Bédier believed that this observation would be found to apply to editions of classical authors. He thought that scholars reached such conclusions because they allowed themselves to be affected by subjective considerations such as the desire to see all questions of textual variation in terms of a dichotomy between truth and error, and he eventually gave up hope of establishing stemmata, preferring to edit on the basis of one manuscript. This is not acceptable as a general principle, however useful or indeed necessary it may be as a procedure in dealing with certain works of medieval literature. Later contributors to the discussion have argued at great length about the possible statistical justification for a predominance of two-branch stemmata. Recently it has been emphasized that proper allowance must be made for cultural conditions during the period of transmission: is it for instance likely that many medieval books were damaged or destroyed before more than two copies could be made from them, or that some books were placed on deposit in central libraries available to students so that a large number of copies were taken? The fact is that some evidence can be adduced for each of these opposing hypotheses, but we do not have much information. A further difficulty is that the ability of scribes to make emendations of obvious errors in the texts, either by collation or by their conjectural skill, can easily lead to a situation in which a scholar may be tempted to posit a two-branched stemma instead of a three-branched one. The same situation arises if scribes independently make identical errors, and stemmatic theory does not give any means of estimating the frequency of this occurrence. The whole matter is exceedingly complicated, and we can only advise the reader to study Timpanaro, *La genesi*, pp. 123–50. What he says applies principally to classical authors; for a recent view of the state of the question in Romance studies see *Romania* 94 (1973), 145–56.

G. B. Alberti, *SIFC* 40 (1968), 44–60, has observed that the term 'open tradition' has come to be used in more than one sense. Pasquali's original use meant that judgement rather than the application of automatic rules was needed in order to infer the readings of the archetype, and in this sense the word can obviously be applied to traditions in which there is no single archetype.

The facts about Saint Cyprian and Juvenal VI have been commented on above in Chapter 5, section (VI) c.

The standard work on second editions in antiquity is H. Emonds, *Zweite Auflage im Altertum*, Leipzig 1941. For the question of author variants in the case of Longus, and for a recent bibliography of the whole subject, see M. D. Reeve, 'Author's variants in Longus?', *PCPhS* 195 (1969), 75–85 (with a reply by D. C. C. Young, ibid. 197 (1971), 99–107); for Ovid, add A. S. Hollis, *Ovid, Metamorphoses Book VIII*, Oxford 1970, pp. x–xi, xxvii. A most instructive discussion of the problems raised by indirect tradition is offered by S. Timpanaro, *Maia*, 22 (1970), 351–9.

Two other critical principles which are useful from time to time may be briefly mentioned here. One is the so-called geographical criterion, which appears in two forms. The first of these involves the notion of survivals on the periphery of a culture, and is an application of a notion that has been fruitful in comparative philology: if there is agreement in striking variants between manuscripts written in two or more peripheral areas of a culture, these readings are probably survivals from a very ancient state of the text. It is not often that we are in a position to know enough about the place of origin of the manuscripts in question, especially if they are Greek, to apply this criterion. The other form of the geographical criterion was worked out by critics of the New Testament, by which one or more manuscripts are assigned to a region, whether peripheral or not, and reference is still frequently made to the Western, Caesarean, and Alexandrian text or family of manuscripts. The basic idea goes back to Jerome, who remarks on variations in the text of biblical manuscripts coming from different regions (*Praefatio in Paralipomena*, *PL* 28.1324–5).

The concept of *recentiores non deteriores* was understood by J. B. de Cardona, bishop of Tortosa (d. 1590); see J. S. Lasso de la Vega in *La crítica textual y los textos clásicos*, University of Murcia 1986, p. 56 n. 35.

Another useful principle in the criticism of prose authors is Wettstein's canon *brevior lectio potior*. This too was devised because of the problems of editing the New Testament, and in particular because of the many additional phrases and sentences found in the Western text, represented notably by the codex Bezae. On both these principles one should consult B. M. Metzger, *The text of the New Testament*.

The derivative nature of the fifteenth-century manuscripts of Lucretius was demonstrated by K. Müller, 'De codicum Lucretii Italicorum origine', *MH* 30 (1973), 166–78; but see also M. D. Reeve, 'The Italian tradition of Lucretius', *IMU* 23 (1980), 27–48. For the Leidensis of Tacitus, see F. R. D. Goodyear, 'The readings of the Leiden manuscript of Tacitus', *CQ* 15 (1965), 299–322; 'On the Leidensis of Tacitus', ibid. 20 (1970), 365–70.

Many of the types of error classified in section VIII of this chapter are discussed, with further examples, in the books and articles listed below. For the texts we cite as exemplifying the problems involved in the detection of glosses, see S. Lundström, *Vermeintliche Glosseme in den Tusculanen*, Uppsala 1964, with the review by G. Williams in *Gnomon*, 37 (1965), 679–87; K. Müller's edition of Petronius (Munich 1961), with the review by R. G. M. Nisbet, *JRS* 52 (1962), 227–38 (who also discussed interpolations in Juvenal). In addition to the cases of bowdlerization we have mentioned, there is one that affects part of the tradition of Lucian's *Asinus*: see H. van Thiel, *Der Eselsroman, Synoptische Ausgabe*, Munich 1972, pp. ix, xix–xxiii.

There is a large literature on the abbreviations which are used in Greek and Latin manuscripts. The classic treatment of *nomina sacra* is that of L. Traube, *Nomina sacra. Versuch einer Geschichte der christlichen Kürzung*, Munich 1907 (repr. Darmstadt 1967), which can be supplemented with A. H. R. E. Paap, *Nomina sacra in the Greek papyri of the first five centuries A.D.*, Leiden 1959, and J. O'Callaghan, '*Nomina sacra' in papyris graecis saeculi III neotestamentariis*, Rome 1970. For abbreviations in Greek medieval manuscripts, see T. W. Allen, *Notes on abbreviations in Greek manuscripts*, Oxford 1889, and G. F. Tsereteli, *De compendiis codicum graecorum praecipue Petropolitanorum et Mosquensium anni nota instructorum* (in Russian), St. Petersburg 1904[2] (repr. Hildesheim 1969). For Latin we have A. Cappelli, *Dizionario di abbreviature latine ed italiane*, Milan 1961[6], with a Supplement by A. Pelzer, Louvain 1964; W. M. Lindsay, *Notae latinae. An account of abbreviations in Latin MSS of the early minuscule period (c.700–850)*, Cambridge 1915, with D. Bains,

A Supplement to Notae latinae (Abbreviations in Latin MSS of 850-1050 A.D.), Cambridge 1936 (reprinted together, Hildesheim 1963).

Valuable advice on dealing with contaminated traditions is given by M. L. West, *Textual criticism and editorial technique* (Stuttgart 1973), pp. 37–46. This book is intended to replace to a great extent both Paul Maas's *Textkritik* and O. Stählin's *Editionstechnik*, 2nd ed., Leipzig 1914.

For other methods of recension, see H. Quentin, *Mémoire sur l'établissement du texte de la Vulgate*, Rome 1922, *Essais de critique textuelle*, Paris 1926; W. W. Greg, *The calculus of variants*, Oxford 1927.

On the transmission of technical manuals through the Middle Ages, see B. Bischoff, 'Die Überlieferung der technischen Literatur', *Settimane*, 18 (Spoleto 1971), 267–96, 496f. (= *Mitt. Stud.* vol. 3, pp. 277–97); on Faventinus, H. Plommer, *Vitruvius and later Roman building manuals*, Cambridge 1973; on Apicius, S. Brandt, *Untersuchungen zum römischen Kochbuche*, Leipzig 1927. For editions of these complicated traditions, see: Eutropius, ed. H. Droysen (*MGH, Auctores antiquissimi*, vol. 2), Berlin 1878; the *Historia de preliis Alexandri Magni*, ed. H.-J. Bergmeister, Meisenheim am Glan 1975; the *Vie de sainte Pélagie*, ed. P. Petitmengin and others, Paris 1981-4.

There is a rapidly increasing number of publications on the use of computers in the classification of manuscripts and related studies, and software that can facilitate many aspects of textual work is continually being developed. Among the pioneer publications in this field we should mention Dom. J. Froger, *La Critique des textes et son automatisation*, Paris 1968; J. G. Griffith, 'A taxonomic study of the manuscript tradition of Juvenal', *MH* 25 (1968), 101-38, and 'Numerical taxonomy and some primary manuscripts of the Gospels', *JTS* 20 (1969), 389-406; *La Pratique des ordinateurs dans la critique des textes* (Colloques internationaux du CNRS, No. 579), Paris 1979; F. Wisse, 'The profile method for classifying and evaluating manuscript evidence' (Studies and Documents, 44), Grand Rapids 1982. But students can best keep abreast of developments in this field by referring to the journals now being published to meet this particular need, such as *Computers and the humanities, Computing and the classics*, and *The humanities computing yearbook*.

Our account of textual criticism may give the impression that once a text has been printed for the first time its form is static except where an editor deliberately alters it. In fact there is sometimes more error and fluctuation than might be supposed: see A. Severyns, *Texte et apparat: histoire critique d'une tradition imprimée*, Brussels 1962 (the *Chrestomathia* of Proclus); R. Laufer, *Introduction à la textologie. Vérification, établissement, édition des textes*, Paris 1972.

In conclusion we mention a small selection of additional books and articles on textual criticism:

(a) M. Bévenot, *The tradition of manuscripts: a study in the transmission of St. Cyprian's treatises*, Oxford 1961.

A. C. Clark, *The descent of manuscripts*, Oxford 1918 (repr. 1969).

A. Dain, *Les Manuscrits*, 2nd ed., Paris 1964.

H. Fränkel, *Einleitung zur kritischen Ausgabe der Argonautika des Apollonius*, Göttingen 1964. The theoretical sections were translated into Italian under the title *Testo critico e critica del testo*, Florence 1969.

L. Havet, *Manuel de critique verbale appliquée aux textes latins*, Paris 1911.

J. Jackson, *Marginalia scaenica*, Oxford 1955.

B. M. Metzger, *The text of the New Testament. Its transmission, corruption and restoration*, Oxford 1968².

R. Renehan, *Greek textual criticism. A reader*, Cambridge, Mass., 1969.

L. D. Reynolds (ed.), *Texts and transmission. A survey of the Latin classics*, Oxford 1983.

B. H. Streeter, *The four gospels*, Oxford 1936⁵. This gives a detailed and ingenious account of the geographical criterion in New Testament criticism.

R. Tosi, *Studi sulla tradizione indiretta dei classici greci*, Bologna 1988.

J. Willis, *Latin textual criticism* (Illinois Studies in Languages and Literature, 61), Urbana 1972.

(b) R. Browning, 'Recentiores non deteriores', *BICS* 7 (1960), 11–21.

W. Bühler, 'Gibt es einen gemeinsamen Archetypus der beiden Überlieferungsstränge von Tertullians Apologeticum?', *Philologus*, 109 (1965), 121–33.

W. Headlam, 'Transposition of words in MSS', *CR* 16 (1902), 243–56.

J. Irigoin, 'Éditions d'auteur et rééditions à la fin de l'antiquité (à propos du "Traité de la virginité" de Grégoire de Nysse)', *Rev. phil.* 96 (1970), 101–6.

—— 'Quelques réflexions sur le concept d'archétype', *RHT* 7 (1977), 235–45.

R. Merkelbach, :Interpolierte Eigennamen', *ZPE* 1 (1967), 100–2.

R. M. Ogilvie, 'Monastic corruption', *Greece and Rome*, 18 (1971), 32–4.

M. D. Reeve, 'Stemmatic method: "Qualcosa che non funziona"?' in *The role of the book in medieval culture*, ed. P. Ganz (Bibliologia 3–4), Turnhout 1986, pp. 57–69.

M. D. Reeve, 'Some applications of Pasquali's *criterio geografico* to 15th-cent. Latin manuscripts', in *Le strade del testo*, ed. G. Cavallo, Bari 1987, pp. 1–10.

—— '*Eliminatio codicum descriptorum*: a methodological problem', in John N. Grant (ed.), *Editing Greek and Latin Texts*, New York 1989, pp. 1–35.

T. C. Skeat, 'The use of dictation in ancient book production', *PBA* 38 (1952), 179–208.

S. Timpanaro, 'Alcuni casi controversi di tradizione indiretta', *Maia*, 22 (1970), 351–9.

N. G. Wilson, 'Variant readings with poor support in the manuscript tradition', *RHT* 17 (1987), 1–13.

D. C. C. Young, 'Some types of error in manuscripts of Aeschylus' *Oresteia*', *GRBS* 5 (1964), 85–99.

—— 'Some types of scribal error in manuscripts of Pindar', *GRBS* 6 (1965), 247–73.

INDEX OF MANUSCRIPTS

Note: the number of collections, both public and private, which contain Greek and Latin manuscripts of direct importance for the subjects treated in this book, is very considerable. Guides to printed descriptions or handwritten catalogues are given for Greek by M. Richard, *Répertoire des bibliothèques et des catalogues des manuscrits grecs*, 2nd ed., Paris 1958, with a *Supplément*, Paris 1965, and for Latin by P. O. Kristeller, *Latin manuscript books before 1600*, 3rd ed., New York 1965. The history of manuscripts since their discovery in the Renaissance is in some cases very complicated. The formation of some of the major libraries has been made the subject of specialized monographs which are outside the scope of the present book. It would be useful if students were able to refer to a short account of the movements of manuscripts from the Renaissance to the present day, which would explain the names and present location of the various collections and would incidentally cast an interesting light on a section of European cultural history. At the moment there does not seem to be a study which precisely fills this need, but the chapter on the 'Nomenclature of manuscripts' in F. W. Hall, *A companion to classical texts*, is still valuable and can now be supplemented by W. Fitzgerald, 'Ocelli nominum. Names and shelfmarks of famous familiar manuscripts', *MS* 45 (1983), 214–97, 48 (1986), 397–421; for a selective treatment of the subject see M. R. James, *The wanderings and homes of manuscripts* (Helps for Students of History no. 17), London 1919, G. Laurion, 'Les Principales Collections de manuscrits grecs', *Phoenix*, 15 (1961), 1–13.

A: MANUSCRIPTS

ATHOS
Almost all the monasteries on Mount Athos have a number of manuscripts; some of the collections are extremely large and have a nucleus of books acquired in the Middle Ages.
Lavra 184: 67
Vatopedi 747: 67

BAMBERG, Staatsbibliothek
Class. 31: 108
    35: 108
    35a: 108
    42: 97, 108
    44: 108
    46: 97, 108
    54: 99

BASLE, Öffentliche Bibliothek der Universität
A VII 3: 269
AN IV 1: 160

ERLANGEN, Universitätsbibliothek
380: 107

ESCORIAL, EL, Real Biblioteca
M.III.3: 258
T.III.11: 272

FLORENCE, Biblioteca Medicea-Laurenziana
Founded in 1444 by Cosimo de' Medici, this became one of the most remarkable Renaissance collections (see p. 275). It is still housed in the building next to the church of San Lorenzo designed for it by Michelangelo (1524; one part was only completed later, in 1571, by Vasari). Early in its history it obtained manuscripts from the Dominican monastery of San Marco, and it has subsequently been enriched by the Conventi Soppressi collections and other acquisitions.

Laur(entianus) 32.2: 76
        32.9: 66, 195, 227, 239
        32.16: 74, 217
        33.31: 133
        35.31: 218
        37.13: 116, 125, 145, 183, 218
        39.1: 36, 39, Plate IX
        48.22: 138, Plate XVI
        49.7: 135, 144
        49.9: 114, 135, 144
        49.18: 135, 144
        51.10: 131, 133

54.5: 137
54.32: 133
59.2–3: 257
59.9: 67
60.3: notes to Plate III
63.19: 107, 266
63.20: 97
68.1: 99, 139, 181
68.2: 109, 133, 181, 253, Plate XIV
73.1: 145
Amiatino 1: 83, 261

FLORENCE, Biblioteca Riccardiana
1179: 145

FULDA, Landesbibliothek
Bonifatianus 3: 261

HEIDELBERG, Universitätsbibliothek
The Heidelberg collection, originally very large, was once owned by the Elector Palatine; hence the designation *Palatini*. After the capture of Heidelberg in 1623 the library was given by Maximilian I, duke of Bavaria, to Pope Gregory XV in return for financial assistance, and most of the manuscripts are still in the Vatican Library. In 1797 Napoleon removed some of the books to Paris (a fate suffered by many other Italian libraries), and when the books were restored in 1815 the University of Heidelberg, aided by the king of Prussia, persuaded Pope Pius VII to let a few volumes return to their original home.
Pal(atinus) gr. 23: 66, 182

HOLKHAM HALL, NORFOLK, Library of the Earls of Leicester
Since 1954 the Greek manuscripts of this collection have been in the Bodleian Library at Oxford.
lat. 121: 199, 215

IESI, Library of Count Balleani
lat. 8: 99, 139

B: PAPYRI

After publication many papyri have been distributed to libraries or other institutions which bore part of the cost of the excavations in Egypt. In such cases they
usually receive a shelf-mark in the library in question, in addition to retaining their
serial number in the original publication.

GENERAL INDEX

Vinidarius, 235
Virgil of Salzburg, 87
Visconti, 141
Visigothic script, 94, 176, 262-3
Visigothic Spain, 79, 84
vitium Byzantinum, 229
Vitruvius, 92, 96, 98, 101, 204, 235, 263
Vittorino da Feltre, 148
Vivarium, 82-3, 118, 258-9
volumen, see Roll
Vossius, Gerard J., 182, 184
Vossius, Isaac, 183-4, 283
Vulgate, 83, 105, 143, 148, 152, 161, 165, 166, 169, 187-8
Vulgate texts, 208-9

Walafrid Strabo, 103, 264-5
Waleys, Thomas, 117-18
Wanley, H., 204
Wearmouth, 88, 261
Westcott, B. F., 187
Wettstein, J. J., 192, 209
Wibald of Corvey, 113
Wilamowitz-Moellendorff, Ulrich

von, 53, 254-5
Wilfrid, bishop of York, 88
William of Malmesbury, 112-13, 268
William of Saint Thierry, 111
Willibrord, 89
Wolf, Friedrich August, 198, 204, 209
Wood, Robert, 198
Word-division, lack of, 4, 9, 223
Worms, cathedral of, 107, 140
Writing tablets, 34, 247
Würzburg, 90

Xenophanes, 9
Xenophon, 48, 148, 157, 214, 217-18, 244
Ximénez, cardinal 160

York, 88, 89, 91, 93, 104, 260

Zanobi da Strada, 133, 273
Zenodotus, 8, 10, 12, 245
Zomino da Pistoia, 137
Zumpt, Carl, 210

NOTES TO THE PLATES

I. Oxford, Bodleian Library, MS. gr. class a.1(P). 2nd cent. The papyrus known as the Hawara *Iliad*. The fibrous nature of the material is clearly visible.

II. Venice, Biblioteca Marciana, MS. gr. 454, fol. 41ʳ. 10th cent. This famous book from the collection of Cardinal Bessarion is generally known as Venetus A of the *Iliad*.

Plates I and II illustrate the relation between the Alexandrian critical signs and the commentary. They both show the same passage of the *Iliad* (ii. 856ff.); the papyrus has the critical signs in the margin but no scholia, the manuscript has both. It is not surprising to find that the signs are not quite identical. A *diplē* seems to be the correct sign at 856, but the papyrus apparently has the *diplē periestigmenē*; the scholia have simply a geographical note about the Alizones and add that there was another Hodios in the Greek camp, but there is no indication of a difference between Aristarchus and Zenodotus here. At 858 the papyrus has a *diplē*, and the manuscript a note that the name Chromis is elsewhere given as Chromios. 859–61 are obelized in the papyrus, 860–1 in the manuscript, and the ground given in the latter is that in the battle by the river the death of Chromis is not related, whereas Homer is careful to record the death of any commander of a contingent; this is a good example of an argument that does not satisfy the modern reader. At 863 both books have a *diplē*, and the manuscript gives a geographical note on the use of the name Phrygia.

III. Oxford, Bodleian Library, MS. E. D. Clarke 39, fol. 113ʳ. A.D. 895. Plato; the plate shows the opening of the *Sophist*. The text was written for Arethas by the scribe known as John the Calligrapher, who also prepared for Arethas a copy of Aelius Aristides (MSS. Laur. 60.3 and Paris gr. 2951). The marginal scholia are in Arethas' own hand; the first note begins: αὕτη ἡ ἐλαία οὐχ ὡς τινες ὑπέλαβον τῆς Ἰωνίας ἐστιν ἀλλὰ τῆς Ἰταλίας, εἴ τι δεῖ Στράβωνι πείθεσθαι τῷ γεωγράφῳ.

IV. Oxford, Bodleian Library, MS. Auct. V. 1.51, fol. 94ʳ. Late 10th cent. Notes on the *Odyssey*. The plate shows the outline of the story of Book XI (the descent to the underworld), followed by the beginning of the vocabulary list for that book. Such aids were necessary for readers in the Middle Ages and their existence throws light on the school curriculum. This

MS. is from the collection of Giovanni Aurispa and later belonged to the monastery of San Marco in Florence. The opening clause reads: ἀπαγγέλλει πῶς κατὰ τῆς Κίρκης ἐντολὰς λαβὼν εἰς Ἅιδου κατῆλθεν.

V. Oxford, Bodleian Library, MS. Auct. T. 4.13, fol. 132ʳ. 11th cent. The archetype of the works of Epictetus. It is thought that Arethas possessed a manuscript of this text, of which the Oxford MS. is perhaps a direct copy. The script displays a certain number of abbreviations. The opening words read: ἐλεύθερος ἐστιν ὁ ζῶν ὡς βούλεται, ὃν οὔτ' ἀναγκάσαι ἔστιν οὔτε κωλῦσαι βιάσασθαι.

VI. Edinburgh, National Library of Scotland, MS. Advocates' 18.7.15, fol. 98ᵛ. c. A.D. 1290 (the date is inferred from a note recording a lunar eclipse, not from a colophon). This copy of Aratus' *Phaenomena* is one of several manuscripts which can be identified as autographs of Planudes. The plate shows his deletion of two passages, for which he substituted verses of his own. The text is lines 487–506. At the end of line 500 Planudes has written a mark which is picked up by a similar mark in the lower margin, indicating where his own version of the passage begins. Line 501 reads: ἄλλος δ' ἀντιόωντι νότῳ μέσον Αἰγοκερῆα. Planudes' version alters the penultimate word to νότον. Such drastic treatment of literary texts is not common, but practical handbooks were probably exposed to it quite often.

VII. Oxford, Bodleian Library, MS. Holkham gr. 88, fol. 207ʳ. 15th cent. Aristophanes. This copy shows the text and scholia in the recension prepared about a century earlier by Demetrius Triclinius; it is the only known manuscript source for his scholia to four of the plays. Note in this plate Triclinius' scholium on metre at the foot of the page (beginning ἡ εἴσθεσις τοῦ παρόντος δράματος) and his misleading title to the main body of scholia, 'old scholia by Aristophanes the grammarian'.

VIII. The *editio princeps* of Aristophanes, Venice 1498, at the Aldine press. Text and scholia were prepared by Musurus, who had among his manuscript materials at least two copies of the Triclinian recension. In the style of type-face and arrangements of text and scholia there is a close resemblance to contemporary manuscripts. The marginal scholia, after the lemma ὀρθὴν κελεύεις, begin with the metrical note of Triclinius shown in the previous plate.

IX. Florence, Biblioteca Medicea-Laurenziana, MS. Laur. 39.1, fol. 8ʳ. This is the codex Mediceus of Vergil, written in Italy in the 5th century. It was corrected at Rome by Asterius, consul in 494, and later found its way to

Bobbio. The script is rustic capital. The plate shows the end of the *Eclogues*
(10.61–77). Abbreviations are few, here restricted to *B* · (*bus*) and *Q* ·
(*que*). Among the corrections, apparently by Asterius himself, we may note
in line 62 the change from *DRUSUM* to *RURSUS* and *NABIS* to *NOBIS,*
and in line 70 *HAES* corrected to *HAEC.* In line 63 the reading *RURSUSM*
suggests a *duplex lectio* at an earlier stage in the tradition (*RURSUS/M*). In
the space left vacant at the end of the *Eclogues*, Asterius has added a subscription recording his work on the manuscript, rounded off with a poem in
elegiacs. The subscription is written in a small hand and is somewhat
defaced; the first part reads (the abbreviations are expanded and enclosed
within brackets): *Turcius Rufius Apronianus Asterius v(ir) c(larissimus) et
inl(ustris), ex comite domest(icorum) protect(orum), ex com(ite) priv(atarum)
largit(ionum), ex praef(ecto) urbi, patricius et consul ordin(arius) legi et distincxi
codicem fratris Macharii v(iri) c(larissimi) non mei fiducia set eius cui si et ad omnia
sum devotus arbitrio XI Kal Mai(as) Romae.*

X. Biblioteca Apostolica Vaticana, MS. Vat. lat. 5757, fol. 171ʳ. The
famous palimpsest of Cicero's *De republica.* Originally a *de luxe* edition of
Cicero, it was reused in the 7th century at Bobbio to copy a text of Au-
gustine on the Psalms. The primary script is a bold uncial of the late 4th or
early 5th century, the secondary script is a small uncial of the 7th century.
Here we have part of *De republica* 2.33. The lower text reads: *ENIM SERPIT/
SED VOLAT IN/OPTIMUM STA/TUM INSTITU/TO TUO SERMO/NE
REMP · POS/TUM NUMAE/POMPILI NEPOS/EX FILIA REX/A POPULO
EST/ANCUS MAR/CIUS CONSTITU/(TUS).*

XI. Paris, Bibliothèque Nationale, MS. lat. 5730, fol. 77ᵛ. This uncial manuscript of Livy's third decade was written in Italy in the first half of the 5th
century and is the parent of all the complete extant manuscripts of this
decade. A direct copy of it, written at Tours about the year 800, is shown on
Plate XIII. For the history of this manuscript in the Carolingian Renaissance
see pp. 96–7. The parchment is so fine and thin that in places, as here, the
writing shows through from the other side of the leaf. Both this plate and
Plate XIII show the beginning of Book XXIII; in line 11 a second hand has
'corrected' *MOPSIORUM* to *COMPSINORUM,* and this further change in
an already corrupt passage has established itself in the text of the copy
(Plate XIII).

XII. Leiden, Bibliotheek der Rijksuniversiteit, MS. Voss. Lat. F. 4, fol. 20ᵛ.
This beautiful manuscript of the Elder Pliny, written in Anglo-Saxon

majuscule, was produced in Northumbria in the first half of the 8th century. The plate shows the opening of Book IV of the *Naturalis Historia*, beginning: *tertius europe simus acrocerauniis incipit montibus finitur helisponto amplectitur praeter minores simus* (i.e. *sinus*) *XIX.XXV passuum*. The first three words are repeated in the margin in minuscule.

XIII. Biblioteca Apostolica Vaticana, MS. Vat. Reg. lat. 762, fol. 32ʳ. Caroline minuscule. This manuscript of Livy's third decade was written at Tours about the year 800 and copied directly from the 5th-century uncial manuscript shown on Plate XI. Both plates show approximately the same passage from the beginning of Book XXIII. The survival of both ancient exemplar and minuscule copy enable one to examine the mistakes which arise when a medieval scribe copies an ancient book, and the errors made in this transcription have been collected and studied (F. W. Shipley, *Certain sources of corruption in Latin manuscripts*, New York 1904). The words are divided for the most part, there is little punctuation, and abbreviations are few, e.g. *q;* (*que*), *b;* (*bus*), *p̄* (*prae*). Some cursive elements survive from earlier scripts, the open *a* which appears along with the other forms of the letter and the ligatures of *et*, *rt*, *st*. The open *a* disappeared in time, and the majuscule *N*, here used alongside the minuscule form, later had a more restricted use.

XIV. Florence, Biblioteca Medicea-Laurenziana, MS. Laur. 68.2, fol. 6ᵛ. This is the manuscript which has preserved for us *Annals* XI–XVI and the *Histories* of Tacitus. It was written at Montecassino during the latter half of the 11th century and provides an example of Beneventan script of the best period. The plate shows the last words of *Annals* XI and the beginning of XII. The end of Book XI is seriously corrupt and reads: *sed ex quis* (glossed with *quibus*) *deterrima orerentur tristitiis multis*.

XV. London, British Museum, MS. Harley 2493, fol. 101ᵛ. The history of this manuscript of Livy, written about the year 1200 and later in the possession of both Petrarch and Valla, is told on pp. 130–1. The plate shows one of the passages of Livy (21.46.3) used by Valla to discredit the scholarship of his rivals Panormita and Facio (see pp. 142–3). The manuscript offers the corrupt *ex quo propinquo*. Valla points out that, while his rivals had failed to see anything wrong with the transmitted text, Petrarch had long since altered *ex quo* to *ex loco*, and Petrarch's correction can still be seen in the text. In the margin Valla has written his own conjecture *exque*, an emendation accepted by modern editors. One may note in passing the increased use of abbreviation at this period.

XVI. Florence, Biblioteca Medicea-Laurenziana, MS. Laur. 48.22, fol. 121ʳ.
This manuscript contains Cicero's *Philippics* and *Catilinarians* and was
written by Poggio in 1425. Here we have the end of *In Catilinam* IV.

PLATE I

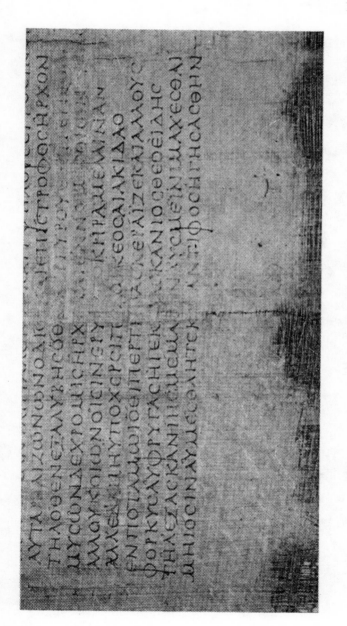

PLATE II

PLATE III

PLATE IV

PLATE V

PLATE VI

PLATE VII

PLATE VIII

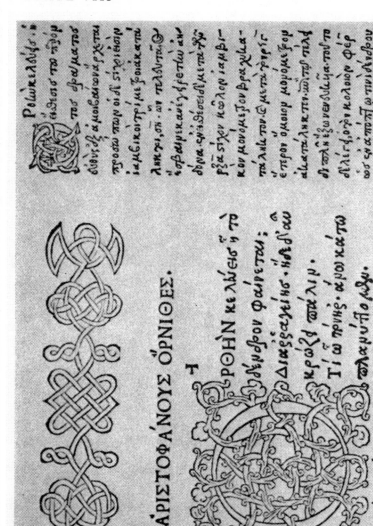

PLATE IX

PLATE X

PLATE XI

haecHANNIBALposteaN
Nensem_puenamcapta
xedireptaconfestim
exapuliinsamnium
moueratmacchusinhir
pinosasiatioponicen
tessecompsamtrasitu
pramcompsanoserat
trebiusmobitisinter
suosseiprenogneu
morsicilimperandux
militaeperlegatiamro
manumciuatponebatis
posiexpugnatoanie exo
sispugnaubotraderent
equetrebiserantomnib
aduenientumhaueiolba
ausscomcompsamuuf
bemexeesxisbenisi
neeirpaddenetrpon
tauirspoenioprado
diuimqacceptumnes
ebipraedaominimc
impeptmenueseuo
tisexeeretuparuuo
maconemuectonis

PLATE XII

PLATE XIII

INCIPIT LIBER VICESIMVS TERTIVS.

Haec hannibal post cannensem pugnam capta ac direpta con
festim ex apulia in samnium mouerat accitus in hirpinos ea sta
tio pollicentes se compositurum compsanus erat trebius nobilis inter
suos sed premebat eum compsinorum factio familiae pergratiae romano
rum potens post fusionem cannensis pugnae uolgata que trebi sermoni
bus aduentu hannibalis cum compsam urbem excessissent sine certamine
tradita urbs poeno praesidium que acceptaest ibi praedam omnis atque impedi
menta relicas exercitum pacto magone regionis eius urbes aut defia
entes ab romanis accipere aut detractantes cogere ad defactionem iubet
ipse per agrum campanum mare inferum petit oppugnaturus neapolim
urbem maritimam ut haberet ubi fines neapolitanorum intrauit tu
midas partim insidiis reples plerosque caius fundit ut us fines que occulta que
cum quae apte portae disposuit despoliat alios praedam agentis otiis

PLATE XIV

PLATE XV

PLATE XVI

FINIS . LIBRI . SCRIPSIT . POGGIVS .
ROMAE .

Printed in the United States
148683LV00001B/115/A